Just Past the Possible

AUTHORS

ELAINE MEI AOKI

VIRGINIA A. ARNOLD

JAMES FLOOD

JAMES V. HOFFMAN

DIANE LAPP

MIRIAM MARTINEZ

ANNEMARIE SULLIVAN PALINCSAR

MICHAEL PRIESTLEY

NANCY ROSER

CARL B. SMITH

WILLIAM H. TEALE

JOSEFINA VILLAMIL TINAJERO

ARNOLD W. WEBB

PEGGY E. WILLIAMS

KAREN D. WOOD

MACMILLAN/McGRAW-HILL SCHOOL PUBLISHING COMPANY

NEW YORK   CHICAGO   COLUMBUS

AUTHORS, CONSULTANTS, AND REVIEWERS

WRITE IDEA! Authors

Elaine Mei Aoki, James Flood, James V. Hoffman, Diane Lapp, Ana Huerta Macias, Miriam Martinez, Ann McCallum, Michael Priestley, Nancy Roser, Carl B. Smith, William Strong, William H. Teale, Charles Temple, Josefina Villamil Tinajero, Arnold W. Webb, Peggy E. Williams

The approach to writing in Macmillan/McGraw-Hill Reading/Language Arts is based on the strategies and approaches to composition and conventions of language in Macmillan/McGraw-Hill's writing-centered language arts program, WRITE IDEA!

Multicultural and Educational Consultants

Alma Flor Ada, Yvonne Beamer, Joyce Buckner, Helen Gillotte, Cheryl Hudson, Narcita Medina, Lorraine Monroe, James R. Murphy, Sylvia Peña, Joseph B. Rubin, Ramon Santiago, Cliff Trafzer, Hai Tran, Esther Lee Yao

Literature Consultants

Ashley Bryan, Joan I. Glazer, Paul Janeczko, Margaret H. Lippert

International Consultants

Edward B. Adams, Barbara Johnson, Raymond L. Marshall

Music and Audio Consultants

John Farrell, Marilyn C. Davidson, Vincent Lawrence, Sarah Pirtle, Susan R. Snyder, Rick and Deborah Witkowski

Teacher Reviewers

Terry Baker, Jane Bauer, James Bedi, Nora Bickel, Vernell Bowen, Donald Cason, Jean Chaney, Carolyn Clark, Alan Cox, Kathryn DesCarpentrie, Carol L. Ellis, Roberta Gale, Brenda Huffman, Erma Inscore, Sharon Kidwell, Elizabeth Love, Isabel Marcus, Elaine McCraney, Michelle Moraros, Earlene Parr, Dr. Richard Potts, Jeanette Pulliam, Michael Rubin, Henrietta Sakamaki, Kathleen Cultron Sanders, Belinda Snow, Dr. Jayne Steubing, Margaret Mary Sulentic, Barbara Tate, Seretta Vincent, Willard Waite, Barbara Wilson, Veronica York

ACKNOWLEDGMENTS

The publisher gratefully acknowledges permission to reprint the following copyrighted material:

Cover permission for ANNE OF AVONLEA by L. M. Montgomery. Copyright 1909 by L. C. Page and Company, Inc. Used by permission of Bantam Books, a division of Bantam Doubleday Dell Publishing Group, Inc.

Cover permission for ANNE OF INGLESIDE by L. M. Montgomery. Copyright 1939 by Frederick A. Stokes Company, Inc. Renewed © 1967 by E. S. MacDonald, as child of the author. Cover art © 1981 by Bantam Books, a division of Bantam Doubleday Dell Publishing Group, Inc.

Cover permission for ANNE OF THE ISLAND by L. M. Montgomery. Copyright 1915, 1943 by L. C. Page & Company, Inc. Used by permission of Bantam Books, a division of Bantam Doubleday Dell Publishing Group, Inc.

Cover permission for ANNE OF WINDY POPLARS by L. M. Montgomery. Copyright 1936, 1973 by McClelland and Stewart, Limited. Cover art © 1981 by Bantam Books, a division of Bantam Doubleday Dell Publishing Group, Inc. Used by permission of Bantam Books, a division of Bantam Doubleday Dell Publishing Group, Inc.

Cover permission for ANNE'S HOUSE OF DREAMS by L. M. Montgomery. Copyright 1922, 1972 by McClelland and Stewart Limited. Cover art © 1981 by Bantam Books, a division of Bantam Doubleday Dell Publishing Group, Inc. Used by permission of Bantam Books, a division of Bantam Doubleday Dell Publishing Group, Inc.

Cover illustration: From ASHANTI TO ZULU: AFRICAN TRADITIONS by Margaret Musgrove, pictures by Leo and Diane Dillon. Copyright © 1976 by Leo and Diane Dillon for pictures. Used by permission of Dial Books for Young Readers, a division of Penguin Books USA Inc.

"B Boy" from THE BREAK DANCE KIDS by Lillian Morrison. Copyright © 1985 by Lillian Morrison. Published by Lothrop, Lee & Shepard Books. Reprinted by permission of William Morrow and Company, Inc./Publishers, New York.

"Banner in the Sky" from BANNER IN THE SKY by James Ramsey Ullman. Copyright 1954 by James Ramsey Ullman (Lippincott). Reprinted by permission of HarperCollins Publishers.

"Bicycle Riding" by Sandra Liatsos appeared originally in *Cricket*. Copyright © 1984 by Sandra Liatsos. Reprinted by permission of the author.

"A Boat to Nowhere" is reprinted from A BOAT TO NOWHERE by Maureen Crane Wartski. Copyright © 1980 by Maureen Crane Wartski. Reprinted and used by permission of Westminster/John Knox Press.

"Brother to the Wind" from BROTHER TO THE WIND by Mildred Pitts Walter. Illustrated by Leo & Diane Dillon. Text copyright © 1985 by Mildred Pitts Walter. Illustrations copyright © 1985 by Leo & Diane Dillon. Published by Lothrop, Lee & Shepard Books and reprinted by permission of William Morrow and Company, Inc./Publishers, New York.

"Calendar Art" from CALENDAR ART by Leonard Everett Fisher. Copyright © 1987 by Leonard Everett Fisher. Reprinted with permission from Four Winds Press, an imprint of Macmillan Publishing Company.

"The Cay" from THE CAY by Theodore Taylor. Copyright © 1969 by Theodore Taylor. Used by permission of Doubleday, a division of Bantam Doubleday Dell Publishing Group, Inc.

Cover: from CHILDREN OF THE MAYA by Brent Ashabranner. Photograph by Paul Conklin. Photographs copyright © 1986 by Paul Conklin. Reprinted by permission of Paul Conklin.

"Cecilia Dowling" from CLASS DISMISSED II by Mel Glenn. Text copyright © 1986 by Mel Glenn. Reprinted by permission of Houghton Mifflin Company.

"Child of the Owl" from CHILD OF THE OWL by Laurence Yep. Copyright © 1977 by Laurence Yep. Reprinted by permission of HarperCollins Publishers.

"The Clock Ticks" from A SKY FULL OF POEMS by Eve Merriam. Copyright © 1964, 1970, 1973 by Eve Merriam. Used by permission of Marian Reiner for the author.

Copyright © 1993 Macmillan/McGraw-Hill School Publishing Company

Macmillan/McGraw-Hill School Division
10 Union Square East
New York, New York 10003

Printed in the United States of America
ISBN 0-02-178762-X / 6, L.12
4 5 6 7 8 9 RRW 99 98 97 96 95 94 93

To my daughters Stephanie and Rebecca Schaffer, and all the other wonderful young people who set their sights "just past the possible"—for it is the young whose dreams will shape the future.

DONNA SCHAFFER

To Dale and Mary Lou Felkins, parents who instilled a love of reading and nurtured the desire to know.

MARLA FELKINS

CLASS ACTS

FINDERS, SEEKERS

7

LEAVE IT TO ME

TIMELINES

250
Your Three Minutes Are Up

A humorous short story from the collection *If This Is Love, I'll Take Spaghetti*
by Ellen Conford, illustrated by Christoph Blumrich
California Young Reader's Medal and Pacific Northwest Young Reader's Choice Award–winning author

When Libby's monopoly on telephone time threatens to aggravate her family beyond endurance, she suddenly finds herself subject to some unpleasant new rules, with surprising results.

270
Calendar Art

An excerpt from the nonfiction social studies book
written and illustrated by Leonard Everett Fisher
Pulitzer Prize, Newbery Honor Award, Christopher Award, Parents' Choice Award, University of Southern Mississippi Medallion, and National Jewish Book Award–winning author

Examine the different systems that people have used to organize the days, months, and years, and consider the difficulties that took us thousands of years to overcome.

294
This Book Is About Time: The Inside Story on People Time

An excerpt from the nonfiction science book
by Marilyn Burns
Outstanding Science Books for Children Award–winning author

Your body has its own internal clocks. Learn some of the hows and whys behind these biological timekeepers in this fascinating article.

A Place in the Heart

PROFILES OF COURAGE

424
Number the Stars

Historical fiction from the novel
by Lois Lowry, illustrated by Larry Winborg
Newbery Medal, 1990; Notable Children's Book in the Field of Social Studies, 1989; School Library Journal Best Book of the Year, 1989

Annemarie and Ellen can scarcely imagine the frightening changes that Nazi occupation is bringing to their country, until their friendship becomes Ellen's only bridge to safety.

476
A Boat to Nowhere

Realistic fiction from the novel
by Maureen Crane Wartski, illustrated by Hui Han Liu
Child's Study Children's Book Committee at Bank Street College Award, 1980

Trapped in a desperate situation that only seems to get worse, Kien draws unexpected courage from the emotional bonds that have grown between him and his adopted family.

450
Danza!

Realistic fiction from the novel
by Lynn Hall
Boston Globe-Horn Book Award, Society of Midland Authors Children's Book Award, and Golden Kite Award–winning author

Paulo's love for his horse, Danza, gives him the strength to stand up against a system that values winning at any cost and the self-serving men who hold Danza's fate in their hands.

CONTENTS

CLASS ACTS

Who is wise?
One who learns from every person, as it is said,
From all my teachers have I gotten understanding.

BEN ZOMA

LAST SUMMER WITH MAIZON

BY JACQUELINE WOODSON

ILLUSTRATED BY CORNELIUS VAN WRIGHT

IT WAS THE SUMMER MARGARET TORY'S FATHER DIED. WHILE TRYING TO COME TO TERMS WITH THIS LOSS, MARGARET ALSO HAS TO FACE BEING SEPARATED FROM HER BEST FRIEND, MAIZON, WHO IS GOING AWAY TO BOARDING SCHOOL. AS MARGARET AND HER MOTHER ACCOMPANY MAIZON AND HER GRANDMOTHER TO THE TRAIN STATION IN NEW YORK CITY, BOTH GIRLS WONDER HOW THEY WILL GET ALONG WITHOUT EACH OTHER.

"Sure wish you weren't going away," Margaret said, choking back tears for what seemed like the millionth time. They were sitting on the M train, crossing the Williamsburg Bridge, and Margaret shivered as the train passed over the water. The L train would have made the trip easier but the L didn't go over the bridge and Maizon had wanted to ride over it once more before she left.

Maizon sat nervously drumming her fingers against the windowpane. "Me too," she said absently.

Margaret looked over at Mama and Grandma. Grandma stared out of her window. She looked old and out of place on the train.

"Maizon?" Margaret said, turning back toward her.

"Hmm?" Maizon frowned. She seemed to be concentrating on something in the water. It rippled and danced below them.

"Even though I wrote you those two letters, you only have to write me one back if you don't have a lot of time or something." Margaret looked down at her fingers. She had begun biting the cuticles, and now the skin surrounding her nails was red and ragged.

"I'll write you back," Maizon promised.

"Maizon . . ."

"What, Margaret!"

Margaret jumped and looked at Maizon. There was an uneasiness in her eyes she had never seen before.

"Forget it," she said.

Ms. Tory leaned over. "We'll be getting off in a few stops."

They rode the rest of the way in silence. At Delancey Street they changed for another train and a half hour later they were at Penn Station.

"I guess now we'll have to call each other to plan the same outfits," Maizon said as they waited for her train. Her voice sounded forced and fake, Margaret thought, like a grown-up trying to make a kid smile.

"I guess," Margaret said. The conductor called Maizon's train.

"I guess I gotta go," Maizon said softly, and Margaret felt a lump rise in her throat.

"I'll write you back, Margaret. Promise. Thanks for letting me keep the double-dutch trophy even if it is only second place." They hugged for a long time. Maizon sniffed loudly. "I'm scared, Margaret," she whispered.

Margaret didn't know what to say. "Don't be."

"Bye, Ms. Tory."

Margaret's mother bent down and hugged Maizon. "Be good," she said as Maizon and her grandmother made their way toward the train.

"Mama," Margaret said as they watched Maizon and her grandmother disappear into the tunnel.

"What, dear?"

"What's the difference between a best friend and an old friend?"

"I guess . . ." Her mother thought for a moment. "I guess an old friend is a friend you once had and a best friend is a friend you'll always have."

"Then maybe me and Maizon aren't best friends anymore."

"Don't be silly, Margaret. What else would you two be? Some people can barely tell you apart. I feel like I've lost a daughter."

"Maybe . . . I don't know . . . Maybe we're old friends now. Maybe this was our last summer as best friends. I feel like something's going to change now and I'm not going to be able to change it back."

Ms. Tory's heels made a clicking sound through the terminal. She stopped to buy tokens and turned to Margaret.

"Like when Daddy died?" she asked, looking worried.

Margaret swallowed. "No. I just feel empty instead of sad, Mama," she said.

Her mother squeezed her hand as they waited for the train. When it came, they took seats by the window.

Ms. Tory held on to Margaret's hand. "Sometimes it just takes a while for the pain of loss to set in."

"I feel like sometimes Maizon kept me from doing things, but now she's not here. Now I don't have any"—Margaret thought for a moment, but couldn't find the right words—"now I don't have any excuse not to do things."

When the train emerged from its tunnel, the late afternoon sun had turned a bright orange. Margaret watched it for a moment. She looked at her hands again and discovered a cuticle she had missed.

Margaret pressed her pencil to her lips and stared out the classroom window. The school yard was desolate and gray. But everything seemed that way since Maizon left. Especially since a whole week had passed now without even a letter from her. Margaret sighed and chewed her eraser.

"Margaret, are you working on this assignment?"

Margaret jumped and turned toward Ms. Peazle. Maizon had been right—Ms. Peazle was the crabbiest teacher in the school. Margaret wondered why she had been picked to teach the smartest class. If students were so smart, she thought, the least the school could do was reward them with a nice teacher.

"I'm trying to think about what to write, Ms. Peazle."

"Well, you won't find an essay on your summer vacation outside that window, I'm sure. Or is that where you spent it?"

The class snickered and Margaret looked down, embarrassed. "No, ma'am."

"I'm glad to hear that," Ms. Peazle continued, looking at Margaret over granny glasses. "And I'm sure in the next ten minutes you'll be able to read your essay to the class and prove to us all that you weren't just daydreaming. Am I right?"

"I hope so, ma'am," Margaret mumbled. She looked around the room. It seemed everyone in 6-1 knew each other from the previous year. On the first day, a lot of kids asked her about Maizon, but after that no one said much to her. Things had changed since Maizon left. Without her, a lot of the fun had gone out of sitting on the stoop with Ms. Dell, Hattie, and Li'l Jay. Maybe she could write about that. No, Margaret thought, looking down at the blank piece of paper in front of her. It was too much to tell. She'd never get finished and Ms. Peazle would scold her—making her feel too dumb to be in 6-1. Margaret chewed her eraser and stared out the window again. There had to be something she could write about quickly.

"Margaret Tory!" Ms. Peazle warned. "Am I going to have to change your seat?"

"Ma'am? I was just . . . "

"I think I'm going to have to move you away from that window unless you can prove to me that you can sit there without being distracted."

"I can, Ms. Peazle. It helps me write," she lied.

"Then I take it you should be ready to read your essay in"—Ms. Peazle looked at her watch—"the next seven minutes."

Margaret started writing frantically. When Ms. Peazle called her to the front of the room, her sheet of notebook paper shook in her hand. She pulled nervously at the hem of the maroon dress she and Maizon had picked out for school and tried not to look out at the twenty-six pairs of eyes she knew were on her.

"Last summer was the worst summer of my life. First my father died and then my best friend went away to a private boarding school. I didn't go anywhere except Manhattan. But that wasn't any fun because I was taking Maizon to the train. I hope next summer is a lot better."

She finished reading and walked silently back to her desk and tried to concentrate on not looking out the window. Instead, she rested her eyes on the half-written page. Margaret knew she could write better than that, but Ms. Peazle had rushed her. Anyway, she thought, that is what happened last summer.

"I'd like to see you after class, Margaret."

"Yes, ma'am," Margaret said softly. *This is the end,* she thought. One week in the smartest class and it's over. Maizon was smart enough to go to a better *school* and I can't even keep up in this class. Margaret sighed and tried not to stare out the window for the rest of the day.

When the three o'clock bell rang, she waited uneasily in her seat while Ms. Peazle led the rest of the class out to the school yard. Margaret heard the excited screams and laughter as everyone poured outside.

The empty classroom was quiet. She looked around at the desks. Many had words carved into them. They reminded her of the names she and Maizon had carved into the tar last summer. They were faded and illegible now.

Ms. Peazle came in and sat at the desk next to Margaret's. "Margaret," she said slowly, pausing for a moment to remove her glasses and rub her eyes tiredly. "I'm sorry to hear about your father . . ."

"That's okay." Margaret fidgeted.

"No, Margaret, it's not okay," Ms. Peazle continued, "not if it's going to affect your schoolwork."

"I can do better, Ms. Peazle, I really can!" Margaret looked up pleadingly. She was surprised at herself for wanting so badly to stay in Ms. Peazle's class.

"I know you can, Margaret. That's why I'm going to ask you to do this. For homework tonight . . ."

Margaret started to say that none of the other students had been assigned homework. She decided not to, though.

"I want you to write about your summer," Ms. Peazle continued. "I want it to express all of your feelings about your friend Maizon going away. Or it could be about your father's death and how you felt then. It doesn't matter what you write, a poem, an essay, a short story. Just so long as it expresses how you felt this summer. Is that understood?"

"Yes, ma'am." Margaret looked up at Ms. Peazle. "It's understood."

Ms. Peazle smiled. Without her glasses, Margaret thought, she wasn't that mean-looking.

"Good, then I'll see you bright and early tomorrow with something wonderful to read to the class."

Margaret slid out of the chair and walked toward the door.

"That's a very pretty dress, Margaret," Ms. Peazle said.

Margaret turned and started to tell her that Maizon was wearing the same one in Connecticut, but changed her mind. What did Ms. Peazle know about best friends who were almost cousins, anyway?

"Thanks, ma'am," she said instead, and ducked out of the classroom. All of a sudden, she had a wonderful idea!

The next morning Ms. Peazle tapped her ruler against the desk to quiet the class. "Margaret," she asked when the room was silent. "Do you have something you want to share with us today?"

Margaret nodded and Ms. Peazle beckoned her to the front of the room.

"This," Margaret said, handing Ms. Peazle the sheet of looseleaf paper. It had taken her most of the evening to finish the assignment.

Ms. Peazle looked it over and handed it back to her.

"We're ready to listen," she said, smiling.

Margaret looked out over the class and felt her stomach slide up to her throat. She swallowed and counted to ten. Though the day was cool, she found herself sweating. Margaret couldn't remember when she had been this afraid.

"My pen doesn't write anymore," she began reading.

"I can't hear," someone called out.

"My pen doesn't write anymore," Margaret repeated. In the back of the room, someone exaggerated a sigh. The class chuckled. Margaret ignored them and continued to read.

"It stumbles and trembles in my hand.
If my dad were here—he would understand.
Best of all—It'd be last summer again.

But they've turned off the fire hydrants
Locked green leaves away.
Sprinkled ashes on you
and sent you on your way.

I wouldn't mind the early autumn
if you came home today
I'd tell you how much I miss you
and know I'd be okay.

Mama isn't laughing now
She works hard and she cries
she wonders when true laughter
will relieve her of her sighs
And even when she's smiling
Her eyes don't smile along
her face is growing older
She doesn't seem as strong.
I worry cause I love her
Ms. Dell says, 'where there is love,
there is a way.'

It's funny how we never know
exactly how our life will go
It's funny how a dream can fade
With the break of day.

I'm not sure where you are now
though I see you in my dreams
Ms. Dell says the things we see
are not always as they seem.

So often I'm uncertain
if you have found a new home
and when I am uncertain
I usually write a poem.

Time can't erase the memory
and time can't bring you home
Last summer was a part of me
and now a part is gone."

It's funny how we never k
exactly how our life will
It's funny how a dream
with the break of day
not su
gh I t
Dall say
e n

The class stared at her blankly, silent. Margaret lowered her head and made her way back to her seat.

"Could you leave that assignment on my desk, Margaret?" Ms. Peazle asked. There was a small smile playing at the corners of her mouth.

"Yes, ma'am," Margaret said. Why didn't anyone say anything?

"Now, if everyone will open their history books to page two seventy-five, we'll continue with our lesson on the Civil War."

Margaret wondered what she had expected the class to do. Applaud? She missed Maizon more than she had in a long time. *She would know what I'm feeling,* Margaret thought. And if she didn't, she'd make believe she did.

Margaret snuck a look out the window. The day looked cold and still. *She'd tell me it's only a feeling poets get and that Nikki Giovanni feels this way all of the time.* When she turned back, there was a small piece of paper on her desk.

"I liked your poem, Margaret," the note read. There was no name.

Margaret looked around but no one looked as though they had slipped a note on her desk. She smiled to herself and tucked the piece of paper into her notebook.

The final bell rang. As the class rushed out, Margaret was bumped against Ms. Peazle's desk.

"Did you get my note?" Ms. Peazle whispered. Margaret nodded and floated home.

Ms. Dell, Hattie, and Li'l Jay were sitting on the stoop when she got home.

"If it weren't so cold," she said, squeezing in beside Hattie's spreading hips, "it would be like old times."

"Except for Maizon," Hattie said, cutting her eyes toward her mother.

"Hush, Hattie," Ms. Dell said. She shivered and pulled Li'l Jay closer to her. For a moment, Margaret thought she looked old.

"It's just this cold spell we're having," Ms. Dell said. "Ages a person. Makes them look older than they are."

Margaret smiled. "Reading minds is worse than eavesdropping, Ms. Dell."

"Try being her daughter for nineteen years," Hattie said.

"Hattie," Margaret said, moving closer to her for warmth. "How come you never liked Maizon?"

"No one said I never liked her."

"No one had to," Ms. Dell butted in.

"She was just too much ahead of everyone. At least she thought she was."

"But she was, Hattie. She was the smartest person at P.S. 102. Imagine being the smartest person."

"But she didn't have any common sense, Margaret. And when God gives a person that much brain, he's bound to leave out something else."

"Like what?"

Ms. Dell leaned over Li'l Jay's head and whispered loudly, "Like the truth."

She and Hattie laughed but Margaret couldn't see the humor. It wasn't like either of them to say something wrong about a person.

"She told the truth . . ." Margaret said weakly.

Ms. Dell and Hattie exchanged looks.

"How was school?" Hattie asked too brightly.

"Boring," Margaret said. She would tuck what they said away until she could figure it out.

"That's the only word you know since Maizon left. Seems there's gotta be somethin' else going on that's not so *boring* all the time," Ms. Dell said.

"Well, it's sure not school. I read a poem to that stupid class and no one but Ms. Peazle liked it." She sighed and rested her chin on her hand.

"That's the chance you gotta take with poetry," Ms. Dell said. "Either everybody likes it or everybody hates it, but you hardly ever know 'cause nobody says a word. Too afraid to

offend you or, worse yet, make you feel good."

Margaret looked from Ms. Dell to Hattie then back to Ms. Dell again.

"How come you know so much about poetry?"

"You're not the first li'l black girl who wanted to be a poet."

"And you can bet your dress you won't be the last," Hattie concluded.

"You wanted to be a poet, Hattie??!!"

"Still do. Still make up poems in my head. Never write them down, though. The paper just yellows and clutters useful places. So this is where I keep it all now," she said, pointing to her head.

"A poem can't exist inside your head. You forget it," Margaret said doubtfully.

"Poems don't exist, Miss Know-It-All. Poems live! In your head is where a poem is born, isn't it?"

Margaret nodded and Hattie continued. "Well, my poetry chooses to live there!"

"Then recite one for me, please." Margaret folded her arms across her chest the way she had seen Ms. Dell do so many times.

"Some poems aren't meant to be heard, smarty-pants."

"Aw, Hattie," Ms. Dell interrupted, "let Margaret be the judge of that."

"All right. All right." Hattie's voice

dropped to a whisper. "Brooklyn-bound robin redbreast followed me from down home / Brooklyn-bound robin, you're
a long way from your own / So fly among the pigeons and
circle the sky with your song."

They were quiet. Ms. Dell rocked Li'l Jay to sleep in
her arms. Hattie looked somberly over the block in silence
and Margaret thought of how much Hattie's poem made
her think of Maizon. What was she doing now that the sun
was almost down? she wondered. Had she found a new
best friend?

"Maybe," she said after a long time. "Maybe it wasn't that
the class didn't like my poem. Maybe it was like your poem,
Hattie. You just have to sit quietly and think about all the
things it makes you think about after you hear it. You have to
let . . . let it sink in!"

"You have to feel it, Margaret," Hattie said softly, draping
her arm over Margaret's shoulder.

"Yeah. Just like I felt when I wrote my poem, or you felt
when you found a place for that one in your head!"

"Margaret," Ms. Dell said, "you gettin' too smart for us
ol' ladies."

Margaret leaned against Hattie and listened to the fading
sounds of construction. Soon the building on Palmetto Street
would be finished. She closed her eyes and visions of last
summer came into her head. She saw herself running down
Madison Street arm in arm with Maizon. They were laughing.
Then the picture faded into a new one. She and Maizon were
sitting by the tree watching Li'l Jay take his first steps. He
stumbled and fell into Maizon's arms. Now it all seemed like
such a long time ago.

When she opened her eyes again, the moon was inching
out from behind a cloud. It was barely visible in the late
afternoon. The sky had turned a wintry blue and the street-
lights flickered on. Margaret yawned, her head heavy all of a
sudden from the long day.

"Looks like your mother's workin' late again. Bless that woman's heart. Seems she's workin' nonstop since your daddy passed."

"She's taking drawing classes. She wants to be an architect. Maybe she'll make a lot of money."

"Architects don't make a lot of money," Hattie said. "And anyway, you shouldn't be worrying your head over money."

"She has a gift," Ms. Dell said. "All of you Torys have gifts. You with your writing, your mama with her drawings, and remember the things your daddy did with wood. Oh, that man was something else!"

"What's Li'l Jay's going to be?"

Ms. Dell stood up and pressed Li'l Jay's face to her cheek.

"Time's gonna tell us, Margaret. Now, come inside and do your homework while I fix you something to eat. No use sitting out in the cold."

Margaret rose and followed them inside.

"You hear anything from Maizon yet?" Hattie asked.

Margaret shook her head. If only Maizon were running up the block!

"I wrote her two letters and she hasn't written me one. Maybe she knows we're not really best friends anymore." Margaret sighed. She had been right in thinking she and Maizon were only old friends now, not the friends they used to be. "Still, I wish I knew how she was doing," she said, turning away so Hattie wouldn't see the tears in her eyes.

"We all do, honey," Hattie said, taking Margaret's hand. "We all do."

MEET Jacqueline Woodson

A seven-year-old Jacqueline Woodson refused to give up her dream of becoming a writer—not even when her older sister told her that no one would publish her book of poems.

Years later, Woodson's determination to be a writer finally paid off. Her first published novel, *Last Summer with Maizon,* a book about friends and change, takes place on the Brooklyn street where Woodson once lived. It is based partly on her childhood friendship with a girl named Maria. "I wanted to write a book about friendship so that people could remember how important friends are." She explains further, "You can't write a book without putting a little bit of yourself into it. You mix that bit of yourself up with your imagination. That's how you create fiction. Well, that's how *I* create fiction."

BY NIKKI GIOVANNI

The World Is Not a Pleasant Place

the world is not a pleasant place
to be without
someone to hold and be held by

a river would stop
its flow if only
a stream were there
to receive it

an ocean would never laugh
if clouds weren't there
to kiss her tears

the world is not
a pleasant place to be without
someone

Place to Be

something WONDERFUL write away!

In "Last Summer with Maizon," Margaret's "wonderful idea" was to write a poem for her school assignment. That's inspiration! Inspiration is a powerful feeling you get from an experience, a thought, or an emotion. It makes you want to express that feeling creatively—perhaps by writing about it.

Maybe you have already been inspired to write about an adventure you have had. What would it take to see your work in print?

On these pages, you'll find a list of publications and contests for young writers. Look under the categories to find where to send your work. But before you send it, write a letter to the publication of your choice to request a copy of its guidelines.

Select your best work, and then write away!

When author Roald Dahl was twelve, he was given a box of assorted chocolates by a candy manufacturer and asked to rate the chocolates according to which he liked best. Dahl was struck by the idea that there were actually people whose job was to invent new kinds of candy. Thirty-five years later, he used that idea as the inspiration for his book *Charlie and the Chocolate Factory.*

Novelist and short story writer W. P. Kinsella's unique childhood inspired him to become a writer. He grew up in a log cabin in a remote section of Canada. With no playmates nearby, he invented imaginary friends and stories about them. Today, through his writing, he makes a living from his imagination.

When novelist Isaac Asimov was young, he liked to entertain his classmates by telling them stories. He would memorize the stories from borrowed books and magazines. But there was a problem—he never had enough stories. So Asimov was inspired to write tales of his own!

POETRY

Creative Kids Magazine
P.O. Box 6448
Mobile, AL 36660-0448

The Flying Pencil Press
P.O. Box 7667
Elgin, IL 60121

Highlights for Children
803 Church Street
Honesdale, PA 18431

Prism
1040 Bayview Drive
Suite 210
Ft. Lauderdale, FL 33304

Reflections
P.O. Box 368
Duncan Falls, OH 43743

Scholastic Scope
Student Writing
730 Broadway
New York, NY 10003

Stone Soup
The Magazine by Children
The Children's Art
Foundation
Box 83
Santa Cruz, CA 95063

CONTESTS

Byline Student Contests
P.O. Box 130596
Edmond, OK 73013

Contests & Contacts
P.O. Box 1028
Litchfield Park, AZ
85340-1028

National Written and
Illustrated By . . .
Awards Contests for Kids
by Landmark Editions, Inc.
1420 Kansas Avenue
Kansas City, MO 64127

NFSPS Student Award
National Federation of
State Poetry Societies, Inc.
Strophes Editor
Kay Kinnaman
1121 Major Avenue, N.W.
Albuquerque, NM 87107

Publish-a-Book Contest
Raintree Publishers, Inc.
310 West Wisconsin Avenue
Milwaukee, WI 53203

Teenage Fiction Contest
Teenage Magazine
217 Jackson Street
Box 948
Lowell, MA 01853

Young Writer's Contest
P.O. Box 6092
McLean, VA 22106

SHORT STORY PUBLICATIONS

Creative with Words
P.O. Box 223226
Carmel, CA 93922

The Flying Pencil Press
P.O. Box 7667
Elgin, IL 60121

Junior Editor
709 S.E. 52nd Avenue
Ocala, FL 32671

Prism
1040 Bayview Drive
Suite 210
Ft. Lauderdale, FL 33304

Reflections
P.O. Box 368
Duncan Falls, OH 43743

Scholastic Scope
Student Writing
730 Broadway
New York, NY 10003

Stone Soup
The Magazine by Children
The Children's Art Foundation
Box 83
Santa Cruz, CA 95063

MISCELLANEOUS

(nonfiction; prose; book
reviews; how-to articles;
plays; personal experiences;
fillers; artwork)

The Detroit Free Press
Kids Book Reviews
321 West Lafayette
Detroit, MI 48231
book reviews by kids

The Flying Pencil Press
P.O. Box 7667
Elgin, IL 60121
nonfiction; artwork

Jack & Jill
1100 Waterway Boulevard
P.O. Box 567
Indianapolis, IN 46206
letters; jokes and riddles

Scholastic Scope
Student Writing
730 Broadway
New York, NY 10003
plays; mini-mysteries

Stone Soup
The Magazine by Children
The Children's Art Foundation
Box 83
Santa Cruz, CA 95063
book reviews; artwork

ACH STUDENT AT SOUTH ORANGE RIVER MIDDLE SCHOOL IS REQUIRED TO PLAY ONE SPORT A YEAR. AFTER ALL, THE SCHOOL IS FAMOUS FOR ITS WINNING TEAMS. BUT ED SITROW AND HIS FRIENDS HAVE MANAGED TO SLIP THROUGH SIXTH GRADE WITHOUT PLAYING A SPORT, SO A SPECIAL SEVENTH GRADE SOCCER TEAM IS CREATED JUST FOR THEM. DESPITE ENCOURAGEMENT FROM EVERYONE, INCLUDING THE COACH, MR. LESTER, AND THE SCHOOL COUNSELOR, MR. TILLMAN, THE TEAM HAS LOST EVERY GAME SO FAR. THE PRESSURE IS ON FOR THEM TO WIN THEIR LAST GAME!

THE TENSION BUILDS...

I should have guessed what was going to happen next when this kid from the school newspaper interviewed me. It went this way.

NEWSPAPER: How does it feel to lose every game?

ME: I never played on a team that won, so I can't compare. But it's . . . interesting.

NEWSPAPER: How many teams have you been on?

ME: Just this one.

NEWSPAPER: Do you want to win?

ME: Wouldn't mind knowing what it feels like. For the novelty.

NEWSPAPER: Have you figured out why you lose all the time?

ME: They score more goals.

NEWSPAPER: Have you seen any improvement?

ME: I've been too busy.

NEWSPAPER: Busy with what?

ME: Trying to stop their goals. Ha-ha.

NEWSPAPER: From the scores, it doesn't seem like you've been too successful with that.

ME: You can imagine what the scores would have been if I wasn't there. Actually, I'm the tallest.

NEWSPAPER: What's that have to do with it?

ME: Ask Mr. Lester.

NEWSPAPER: No S.O.R. team has ever lost all its games in one season. How do you feel about that record?

ME: I read somewhere that records are made to be broken.

NEWSPAPER: But how will you feel?

ME: Same as I do now.

NEWSPAPER: How's that?

ME: Fine.

NEWSPAPER: Give us a prediction. Will you win or lose your last game?

ME: As captain, I can promise only one thing.

NEWSPAPER: What's that?

ME: I don't want to be there to see what happens.

Naturally, they printed all that. Next thing I knew some kids decided to hold a pep rally.

"What for?" asked Radosh.

"To fill us full of pep, I suppose."

"What's pep?"

Hays looked it up. "Dash," he read.

Saltz shook his head.

"What's dash?" asked Porter.

"Sounds like a deodorant soap," said Eliscue.

And then Ms. Appleton called me aside. "Ed," she said, sort of whispering (I guess she was embarrassed to be seen talking to any of us), "people are asking, 'Do they *want* to lose?'"

"Who's asking?"

"It came up at the last teachers' meeting. Mr. Tillman thinks you might be encouraging a defeatist attitude in the school. And Mr. Lester . . ."

"What about him?"

"He doesn't know."

It figured. "Ms. Appleton," I said, "why do people care so much if we win or lose?"

"It's your . . . attitude," she said. "It's so unusual. We're not used to . . . well . . . not winning sometimes. Or . . . or not caring if you lose."

"Think there's something the matter with us?" I wanted to know.

"No," she said, but when you say "no" the way she did, slowly, there's lots of

time to sneak in a good hint of "yes." "I don't think you _mean_ to lose."

"That's not what I asked."

"It's important to win," she said.

"Why? We're good at other things. Why can't we stick with that?"

But all she said was, "Try harder."

I went back to my seat. "I'm getting nervous," I mumbled.

"About time," said Saltz.

"Maybe we should defect."

"Where to?"

"There must be some country that doesn't have sports."

Then, of course, when my family sat down for dinner that night it went on.

"In two days you'll have your last game, won't you," my ma said. It was false cheerful, as if I had a terminal illness and she wanted to pretend it was only a head cold.

"Yeah," I said.

"You're going to win," my father announced.

"How do you know?" I snapped.

"I sense it."

"Didn't know you could tell the future."

"Don't be so smart," he returned. "I'm trying to be supportive."

"I'm sick of support!" I yelled and left the room.

Twenty minutes later I got a call. Saltz.

"Guess what?" he said.

"I give up."

"Two things. My father offered me a bribe."

"To lose the game?"

"No, to win it. A new bike."

"Wow. What did you say?"

"I told him I was too honest to win a game."

"What was the second thing?"

"I found out that at lunch tomorrow they are doing that pep rally, and worse. They're going to call up the whole team."

I sighed. "Why are they doing all this?" I asked.

"Nobody loves a loser," said Saltz.

"Why?" I asked him, just as I had asked everybody else.

"Beats me. Like everybody else does." He hung up.

I went into my room and flung myself on my bed and stared up at the ceiling. A short time later my father came into the room. "Come on, kid," he said. "I was just trying to be a pal."

"Why can't people let us lose in peace?"

"People think you feel bad."

"We feel *fine!*"

"Come on. We won't talk about it any more. Eat your dinner."

I went.

 ULL OF PEP...

Next day, when I walked into the school eating area for lunch there was the usual madhouse. But there was also a big banner across the front part of the room:

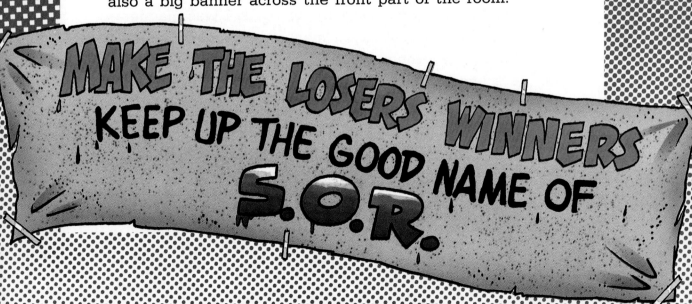

I wanted to start a food fight right then and there.

I'm not going through the whole bit. But halfway through the lunch period, the president of the School Council, of all people, went to a microphone and called for attention. Then she made a speech.

"We just want to say to the Special Seventh-Grade Soccer Team that we're all behind you."

"It's in front of us where we need people," whispered Saltz. "Blocking."

The president went on. "Would you come up and take a bow." One by one she called our names. Each time one of us went up, looking like cringing but grinning worms, there was some general craziness, hooting, foot stomping, and an occasional milk carton shooting through the air.

The president said: "I'd like the team captain, Ed Sitrow, to say a few words."

What could I do? Trapped, I cleared my throat. Four times. "Ah, well . . . we . . . ah . . . sure . . . hope to get there . . . and . . . you know . . . I suppose . . . play and . . . you know!"

The whole room stood up to cheer. They even began the school chant.

"Give me an S! Give me an O . . . "

After that we went back to our seats. I was madder than ever. And as I sat there, maybe two hundred and fifty kids filed by, thumping me hard on the back, shoulder, neck and head, yelling, "Good luck! Good luck!" They couldn't fool me. I knew what they were doing: beating me.

"Saltz," I said when they were gone and I was merely numb, "I'm calling an emergency meeting of the team."

SECRET MEETING...

Like thieves, we met behind the school, out of sight. I looked around. I could see everybody was feeling rotten.

"I'm sick and tired of people telling me we have to win," said Root.

"I think my folks are getting ready to disown me," said Hays. "My brother and sister too."

"Why can't they just let us lose?" asked Macht.

"Yeah," said Barish, "because we're not going to win."

"We might," Lifsom offered. "Parkville is supposed to be the pits too."

"Yeah," said Radosh, "but we're beneath the pits."

"Right," agreed Porter.

For a moment it looked like everyone was going to start to cry.

"I'd just like to do my math," said Macht. "I like that."

There it was. Something clicked. "Hays," I said, "you're good at music, right."

"Yeah, well, sure—rock 'n' roll."

"Okay. And Macht, what's the lowest score you've pulled in math so far?"

"A-plus."

"Last year?"

"Same."

"Lifsom," I went on, getting excited, "how's your painting coming?"

"I just finished something real neat and . . ."

"That's it," I cut in, because that kid can go on forever about his painting. "Every one of us is good at something. Right? Maybe more than one thing. The point is, *other* things."

"Sure," said Barish.

"Except," put in Saltz, "sports."

We were quiet for a moment. Then I saw what had been coming to me: "That's *their* problem. I mean, we are good, good at *lots* of things. Why can't we just plain stink in some places? That's got to be normal."

"Let's hear it for normal," chanted Dorman.

"Doesn't bother me to lose at sports," I said. "At least, it didn't bother me until I let other people make me bothered."

"What about the school record?" asked Porter. "You know, no team ever losing for a whole season. Want to be famous for that?"

"Listen," I said, "did we want to be on this team?"

"No!" they all shouted.

"I can see some of it," I said. "You know, doing something different. But I don't like sports. I'm not good at it. I don't enjoy it. So I say, so what? I mean if Saltz here writes a stinko poem—and he does all the time—do they yell at him? When was the last time Mr. Tillman came around and said, 'Saltz, I *believe* in your being a poet!'"

"Never," said Saltz.

"Yeah," said Radosh. "How come sports is so important?"

"You know," said Dorman, "maybe a loser makes people think of things *they* lost. Like Mr. Tillman not getting into pro football. Us losing makes him remember that."

"Us winning, he forgets," cut in Eliscue.

"Right," I agreed. "He needs us to win for *him,* not for us. Maybe it's the same for others."

"Yeah, but how are you going to convince them of that?" said Barish.

"By not caring if we lose," I said.

"Only one thing," put in Saltz. "They say this Parkville team is pretty bad too. What happens if we, you know, by mistake, win?"

That set us back for a moment.

"I think," suggested Hays after a moment, "that if we

just go on out there, relax, and do our best, and not worry so much, we'll lose."

There was general agreement on that point.

"Do you know what I heard?" said Eliscue.

"What?"

"I didn't want to say it before, but since the game's a home game, they're talking about letting the whole school out to cheer us on to a win."

"You're kidding."

He shook his head.

There was a long, deep silence.

"Probably think," said Saltz, "that we'd be ashamed to lose in front of everybody."

I took a quick count. "You afraid to lose?" I asked Saltz.

"No way."

"Hays?"

"No."

"Porter?"

"Nope."

And so on. I felt encouraged. It was a complete vote of no confidence.

"Well," I said, "they just might see us lose again. With Parkville so bad I'm not saying it's automatic. But I'm not going to care if we do."

"Right," said Radosh. "It's not like we're committing treason or something. People have a right to be losers."

We considered that for a moment. It was then I had my most brilliant idea. "Who has money?"

"What for?"

"I'm your tall captain, right? Trust me. And bring your soccer T-shirts to me in the morning, early."

WHO HAS MONEY?

I collected about four bucks and we split up. I held Saltz back.

"What's the money all about?" he wanted to know. "And the T-shirts."

"Come on," I told him. "Maybe we can show them we really mean it."

BACK WORDS...

When I woke the next morning, I have to admit, I was excited. It wasn't going to be an ordinary day. I looked outside and saw the sun was shining. I thought, "Good."

For the first time I *wanted* a game to happen.

I got to breakfast a little early, actually feeling happy.

"Today's the day," Dad announced.

"Right."

"Today you'll really win," chipped in my ma.

"Could be."

My father leaned across the table and gave me a tap. "Winning the last game is what matters. Go out with your head high, Ed."

"And my backside up if I lose?" I wanted to know.

"Ed," said my ma, "don't be so hard on yourself. Your father and I are coming to watch."

"Suit yourselves," I said, and beat it to the bus.

As soon as I got to class Saltz and I collected the T-shirts. "What are you going to do with them?" the others kept asking.

"You picked me as captain, didn't you?"

"Mr. Lester did."

"Well, this time, trust *me.*"

When we got all the shirts, Saltz and I sneaked into the home ec room and did what needed to be done. Putting them into a bag so no one would see, we went back to class.

"Just about over," I said.

"I'm almost sorry," confessed Saltz.

"Me too," I said. "And I can't figure out why."

"Maybe it's—the team that loses together, really stays together."

"Right. Not one fathead on the whole team. Do you think we should have gotten a farewell present for Mr. Lester?"

"Like what?"

"A begging cup."

It was hard getting through the day. And it's impossible to know how many people wished me luck. From all I got it was clear they considered me the un-luckiest guy in the whole world. I kept wishing I could have banked it for something important.

But the day got done.

It was down in the locker room, when we got ready, that I passed out the T-shirts.

Barish held his up. It was the regular shirt with "S.O.R." on the back. But under it Saltz and I had ironed on press letters. Now they all read:

Barish's reaction was just to stare. That was my only nervous moment. Then he cracked up, laughing like crazy. And the rest, once they saw, joined in. When Mr. Lester came down he brought Mr. Tillman. We all stood up and turned our backs to them.

"Oh, my goodness," moaned Mr. Lester.

"That's sick," said Mr. Tillman. "Sick!" His happy beads shook furiously.

"It's honest," I said.

"It's defeatist," he yelled.

"Mr. Tillman," I asked, "is that true, about your trying out for pro football?"

He started to say something, then stopped, his mouth open. "Yeah. I tried to make it with the pros, but couldn't."

"So you lost too, right?"

"Yeah," chimed in Radosh, "everyone loses sometime."

"Listen here, you guys," said Mr. Tillman, "it's no fun being rejected."

"Can't it be okay to lose sometimes? You did. Lots do. You're still alive. And we don't dislike you because of that."

"Right. We got other reasons," I heard a voice say. I think it was Saltz.

Mr. Tillman started to say something, but turned and fled.

Mr. Lester tried to give us a few final pointers, like don't touch the ball with our hands, only use feet, things that we didn't always remember to do.

"Well," he said finally, "I enjoyed this."

"You did?" said Porter, surprised.

"Well, not much," he admitted. "I never coached anything before. To tell the truth, I don't know anything about soccer."

"Now you tell us," said Eliscue. But he was kidding. We sort of guessed that before.

Just as we started out onto the field, Saltz whispered to me, "What if we win?"

"With our luck, we will," I said.

And on we went.

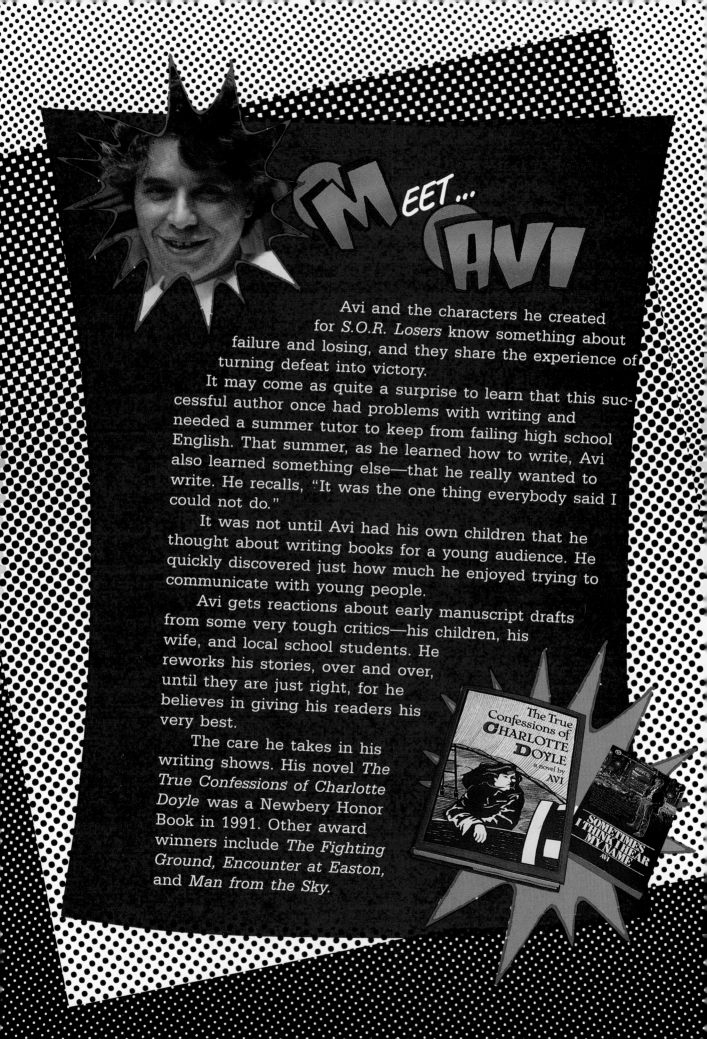

Meet... Avi

Avi and the characters he created for *S.O.R. Losers* know something about failure and losing, and they share the experience of turning defeat into victory.

It may come as quite a surprise to learn that this successful author once had problems with writing and needed a summer tutor to keep from failing high school English. That summer, as he learned how to write, Avi also learned something else—that he really wanted to write. He recalls, "It was the one thing everybody said I could not do."

It was not until Avi had his own children that he thought about writing books for a young audience. He quickly discovered just how much he enjoyed trying to communicate with young people.

Avi gets reactions about early manuscript drafts from some very tough critics—his children, his wife, and local school students. He reworks his stories, over and over, until they are just right, for he believes in giving his readers his very best.

The care he takes in his writing shows. His novel *The True Confessions of Charlotte Doyle* was a Newbery Honor Book in 1991. Other award winners include *The Fighting Ground, Encounter at Easton,* and *Man from the Sky.*

MAKING

THE GRADE

Mary McLeod Bethune: A Great American Educator
by Patricia C. McKissack
Childrens Press, 1985

Sydney, Herself
by Colby Rodowsky
Farrar, Straus & Giroux, 1989

Meet Gary Soto

Gary Soto's success as a writer may have surprised some people—perhaps even himself. Recalling his childhood in a poor Mexican-American family, Soto says, "I don't think I had any literary aspirations when I was a kid. . . . We didn't have books, and no one encouraged us to read."

Later, as a college student, Soto discovered a collection of poems and thought, "This is terrific; I'd like to do something like this." He felt that writing would be a way to communicate the problems and emotions of people like the Chicanos he knew.

"Seventh Grade" is from Soto's book of short stories *Baseball in April.* His other works include *Living up the Street,* a collection of autobiographical essays, and *A Fire in My Hands,* a book of poems.

Seventh grade

by Gary Soto

illustrated by John Ceballos

On the first day of school, Victor stood in line half an hour before he came to a wobbly card table. He was handed a packet of papers and a computer card on which he listed his one elective, French. He already spoke Spanish and English, but he thought some day he might travel to France, where it was cool; not like Fresno, where summer days reached 110 degrees in the shade. There were rivers in France, and huge churches, and fair-skinned people everywhere, the way there were brown people all around Victor.

Besides, Teresa, a girl he had liked since they were in catechism classes at Saint Theresa's, was taking French too. With any luck they would be in the same class. Teresa is going to be my girl this year, he promised himself as he left the gym full of students in their new fall clothes. She was cute. And good at math, too, Victor thought as he walked down the hall to his homeroom. He ran into his friend, Michael Torres, by the water fountain that never turned off.

They shook hands, *raza*-style, and jerked their heads at one another in a *saludo de vato*. "How come you're making a face?" asked Victor.

"I ain't making a face, *ese*. This *is* my face." Michael said his face had changed during the summer. He had read a *GQ* magazine that his older brother borrowed from the Book Mobile and noticed that the male models all had the same look on their faces. They would stand, one arm around a beautiful woman, and *scowl*. They would sit at a pool, their rippled stomachs dark with shadow, and *scowl*. They would sit at dinner tables, cool drinks in their hands, and *scowl*.

"I think it works," Michael said. He scowled and let his upper lip quiver. His teeth showed along with the ferocity of his soul. "Belinda Reyes walked by a while ago and looked at me," he said.

Victor didn't say anything, though he thought his friend looked pretty strange. They talked about recent movies, baseball, their parents, and the horrors of picking grapes in order

to buy their fall clothes. Picking grapes was like living in Siberia, except hot and more boring.

"What classes are you taking?" Michael said, scowling.

"French. How 'bout you?"

"Spanish. I ain't so good at it, even if I'm Mexican."

"I'm not either, but I'm better at it than math, that's for sure."

A tinny, three-beat bell propelled students to their homerooms. The two friends socked each other in the arm and went their ways, Victor thinking, man, that's weird. Michael thinks making a face makes him handsome.

On the way to his homeroom, Victor tried a scowl. He felt foolish, until out of the corner of his eye he saw a girl looking at him. Umm, he thought, maybe it does work. He scowled with greater conviction.

In homeroom, roll was taken, emergency cards were passed out, and they were given a bulletin to take home to their parents. The principal, Mr. Belton, spoke over the crackling loudspeaker, welcoming the students to a new year, new experiences, and new friendships. The students squirmed in their chairs and ignored him. They were anxious to go to first period. Victor sat calmly, thinking of Teresa, who sat two rows away, reading a paperback novel. This would be his lucky year. She was in his homeroom, and would probably be in his English and math classes. And, of course, French.

The bell rang for first period, and the students herded noisily through the door. Only Teresa lingered, talking with the homeroom teacher.

"So you think I should talk to Mrs. Gaines?" she asked the teacher. "She would know about ballet?"

"She would be a good bet," the teacher said. Then added, "Or the gym teacher, Mrs. Garza."

Victor lingered, keeping his head down and staring at his desk. He wanted to leave when she did so he could bump into her and say something clever.

He watched her on the sly. As she turned to leave, he stood up and hurried to the door, where he managed to catch her eye. She smiled and said, "Hi, Victor."

He smiled back and said, "Yeah, that's me." His brown face blushed. Why hadn't he said, "Hi, Teresa," or "How was your summer?" or something nice?

As Teresa walked down the hall, Victor walked the other way, looking back, admiring how gracefully she walked, one foot in front of the other. So much for being in the same class, he thought. As he trudged to English, he practiced scowling.

In English they reviewed the parts of speech. Mr. Lucas, a portly man, waddled down the aisle, asking, "What is a noun?"

"A person, place, or thing," said the class in unison.

"Yes, now somebody give me an example of a person— you, Victor Rodriguez."

"Teresa," Victor said automatically. Some of the girls giggled. They knew he had a crush on Teresa. He felt himself blushing again.

"Correct," Mr. Lucas said. "Now provide me with a place."

Mr. Lucas called on a freckled kid who answered, "Teresa's house with a kitchen full of big brothers."

After English, Victor had math, his weakest subject. He sat in the back by the window, hoping that he would not be called on. Victor understood most of the problems, but some of the stuff looked like the teacher made it up as she went along. It was confusing, like the inside of a watch.

After math he had a fifteen-minute break, then social studies, and, finally, lunch. He bought a tuna casserole with buttered rolls, some fruit cocktail, and milk. He sat with Michael, who practiced scowling between bites.

Girls walked by and looked at him.

"See what I mean, Vic?" Michael scowled. "They love it."

"Yeah, I guess so."

They ate slowly, Victor scanning the horizon for a glimpse of Teresa. He didn't see her. She must have brought lunch, he thought, and is eating outside. Victor scraped his plate and left Michael, who was busy scowling at a girl two tables away.

The small, triangle-shaped campus bustled with students talking about their new classes. Everyone was in a sunny mood. Victor hurried to the bag lunch area, where he sat down and opened his math book. He moved his lips as if he were reading, but his mind was somewhere else. He raised his eyes slowly and looked around. No Teresa.

He lowered his eyes, pretending to study, then looked slowly to the left. No Teresa. He turned a page in the book and stared at some math problems that scared him because he knew he would have to do them eventually. He looked to the right. Still no sign of her. He stretched out lazily in an attempt to disguise his snooping.

Then he saw her. She was sitting with a girlfriend under a plum tree. Victor moved to a table near her and daydreamed about taking her to a movie. When the bell sounded, Teresa looked up, and their eyes met. She smiled sweetly and gathered her books. Her next class was French, same as Victor's.

66

They were among the last students to arrive in class, so all the good desks in the back had already been taken. Victor was forced to sit near the front, a few desks away from Teresa, while Mr. Bueller wrote French words on the chalkboard. The bell rang, and Mr. Bueller wiped his hands, turned to the class, and said, *"Bonjour."*

"Bonjour," braved a few students.

"Bonjour," Victor whispered. He wondered if Teresa heard him.

Mr. Bueller said that if the students studied hard, at the end of the year they could go to France and be understood by the populace.

One kid raised his hand and asked, "What's 'populace'?"

"The people, the people of France."

Mr. Bueller asked if anyone knew French. Victor raised his hand, wanting to impress Teresa. The teacher beamed and said, *"Très bien. Parlez-vous français?"*

Victor didn't know what to say. The teacher wet his lips and asked something else in French. The room grew silent. Victor felt all eyes staring at him. He tried to bluff his way out by making noises that sounded French.

"La me vava me con le grandma," he said uncertainly.

Mr. Bueller, wrinkling his face in curiosity, asked him to speak up.

Great rosebushes of red bloomed on Victor's cheeks. A river of nervous sweat ran down his palms. He felt awful. Teresa sat a few desks away, no doubt thinking he was a fool. Without looking at Mr. Bueller, Victor mumbled, "Frenchie oh wewe gee in September."

Mr. Bueller asked Victor to repeat what he had said.

"Frenchie oh wewe gee in September," Victor repeated.

Mr. Bueller understood that the boy didn't know French and turned away. He walked to the blackboard and pointed to the words on the board with his steel-edged ruler.

"Le bateau," he sang.

"Le bateau," the students repeated.

"Le bateau est sur l'eau," he sang.

"Le bateau est sur l'eau."

Victor was too weak from failure to join the class. He stared at the board and wished he had taken Spanish, not French. Better yet, he wished he could start his life over. He had never been so embarrassed. He bit his thumb until he tore off a sliver of skin.

The bell sounded for fifth period, and Victor shot out of the room, avoiding the stares of the other kids, but had to return for his math book. He looked sheepishly at the teacher, who was erasing the board, then widened his eyes in terror at Teresa who stood in front of him. "I didn't know you knew French," she said. "That was good."

Mr. Bueller looked at Victor, and Victor looked back. Oh please, don't say anything, Victor pleaded with his eyes. I'll wash your car, mow your lawn, walk your dog—anything! I'll be your best student, and I'll clean your erasers after school.

Mr. Bueller shuffled through the papers on his desk. He smiled and hummed as he sat down to work. He remembered his college years when he dated a girlfriend in borrowed cars. She thought he was rich because each time he picked her up he had a different car. It was fun until he had spent all his money on her and had to write home to his parents because he was broke.

Victor couldn't stand to look at Teresa. He was sweaty with shame. "Yeah, well, I picked up a few things from movies and books and stuff like that." They left the class together. Teresa asked him if he would help her with her French.

"Sure, anytime," Victor said.

"I won't be bothering you, will I?"

"Oh no, I like being bothered."

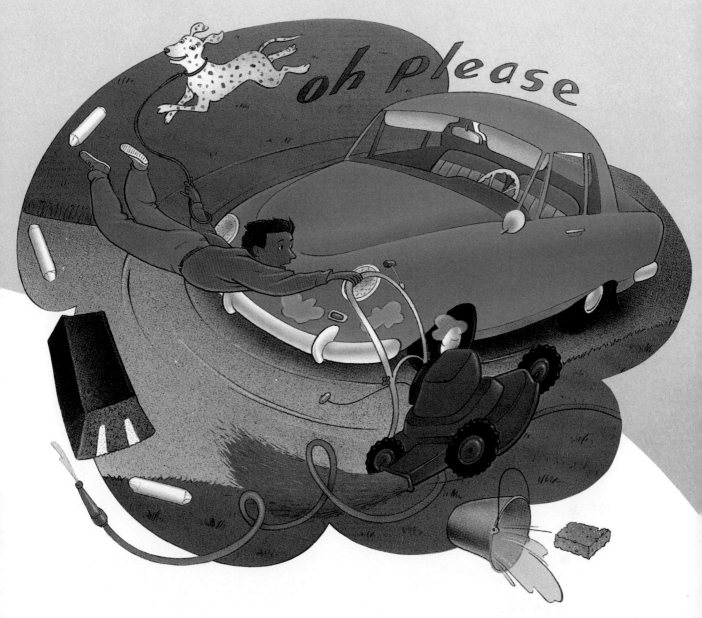

"*Bonjour,*" Teresa said, leaving him outside her next class. She smiled and pushed wisps of hair from her face.

"Yeah, right, *bonjour,*" Victor said. He turned and headed to his class. The rosebushes of shame on his face became bouquets of love. Teresa is a great girl, he thought. And Mr. Bueller is a good guy.

He raced to metal shop. After metal shop there was biology, and after biology a long sprint to the public library, where he checked out three French textbooks.

He was going to like seventh grade.

BEYOND WORDS

In "Seventh Grade," Victor's friend Michael *scowls*. He is trying to send an unspoken message—that he is as elegant as the magazine models that he is imitating.

People in all cultures communicate as much through gestures as through words. In fact, experts estimate that more than half of what a person communicates is through body language. However, researchers have discovered that there is no universal body language—there is no gesture that means the same thing to all people all over the world.

▲ In the United States, everyone knows that this gesture means "OK," or "everything is fine." But to the French, this gesture means "zero," or "worthless." And to the Japanese, the gesture seems to symbolize a coin, and thus means "money."

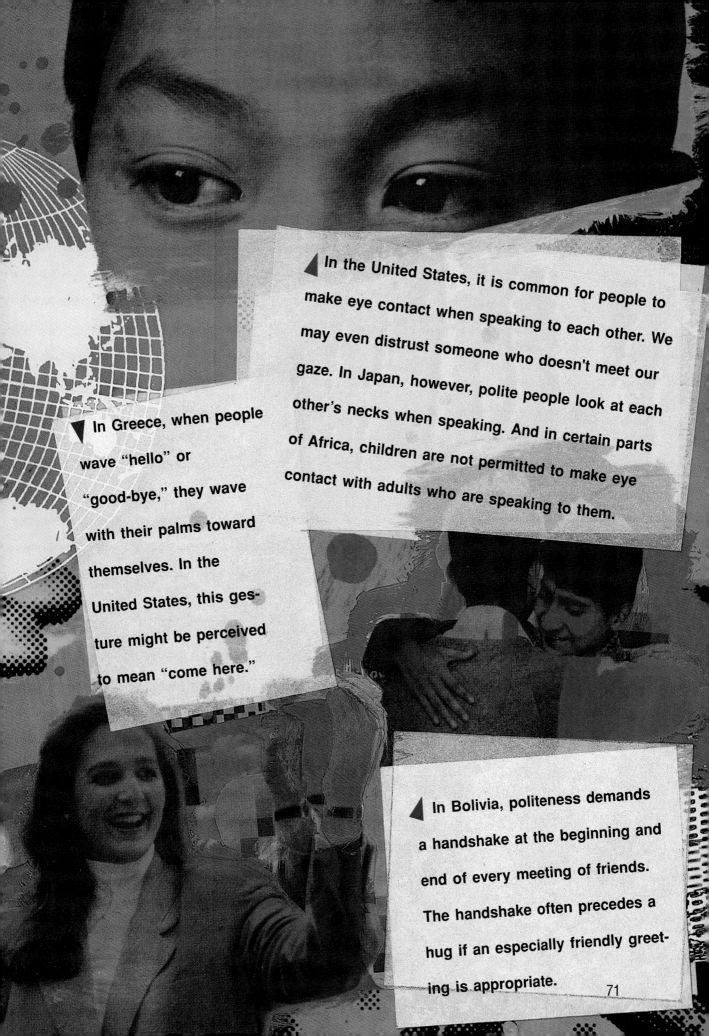

In the United States, it is common for people to make eye contact when speaking to each other. We may even distrust someone who doesn't meet our gaze. In Japan, however, polite people look at each other's necks when speaking. And in certain parts of Africa, children are not permitted to make eye contact with adults who are speaking to them.

In Greece, when people wave "hello" or "good-bye," they wave with their palms toward themselves. In the United States, this gesture might be perceived to mean "come here."

In Bolivia, politeness demands a handshake at the beginning and end of every meeting of friends. The handshake often precedes a hug if an especially friendly greeting is appropriate.

71

Cecilia Dowling

(One year later) By Mel Glenn

Dear Mr. Henderson,
I don't know exactly
Why I'm writing this letter.
You probably don't remember me,
But I remember everything you said,
Even though that was more than a year ago.
You were my favorite teacher.
You saw past my poor grades
And spotty attendance
And made me think I had value,
Substance even.
No, I didn't go to college.
I didn't even finish
The beauty school I went to.
I tried to learn makeup,
But all I learned was that no matter
What paint or brushes I used
I couldn't cover the blemishes
I saw in myself.
"It's not as bad as all that, Cecilia,"
You'd probably say.
No, it isn't.
I hear your words in my head
And in my heart, even now.
Why am I writing you this letter?
Because I want you to know
You mattered in my life — you still do.
            Love, C.

LYNN WAS BORN ON THE NAVAJO
RESERVATION IN ARIZONA. HER
RELATIVES HELPED HER FAMILY BY
PROVIDING THEM WITH PLACES TO
STAY. AS A RESULT, LYNN MOVED
AROUND THE RESERVATION
FREQUENTLY AS SHE GREW UP.

TO LIVE IN TWO WORLDS

By Brent Ashabranner
Photographs by Paul Conklin
Illustrated by Shonto Begay

Lynn was happiest when they stayed with her grandparents. They lived in a hogan, the traditional one-room Navajo dwelling made of logs and packed earth. It never seemed crowded despite extra people, and it was from her grandmother and grandfather that Lynn learned most about Navajo ways and beliefs.

She learned that the Navajo hogan is a home but also a holy place that must be built in the right way, just as the Holy People built the first hogans as examples for the Earth People. Before the hogan can be lived in, it must be blessed with songs from the blessing ceremony, and the door to every hogan must face east to catch the first light of the morning sun. In that way Changing Woman, the greatest of the Holy People, is honored. The sun was the father of Changing Woman's two sons, Monster Slayer and Born for the Water, and it was they who helped the Earth People in many ways.

On summer nights everyone slept outside the hogan, so that they could enjoy the soft breezes and the clean fresh air. Lynn would lie on her sheepskin and look up at the blanket of bright stars. Often as she drifted into sleep, she could hear the yipping bark of a coyote somewhere far off in the darkness, but she was not afraid.

Lynn went to school at four different places on the reservation, but moving around did not cause a learning problem for her. She had grown up speaking both Navajo and English, and her English improved quickly in school. She made top grades everyplace, and when she finished elementary school, she received a scholarship to go to a mission school in a large town off the reservation.

That was the beginning of a new life in a new world for Lynn. It was a world that kept opening up, expanding, showing her new things. The school had a library with more books than she could imagine. Even though she was only in the ninth grade, her teachers made it clear to her that she was at the mission school because they knew she could be a good student, and they expected her to be one.

The town was by far the biggest place she had ever been in. There were supermarkets, department stores, restaurants, motels, theaters,

THE NAVAJO COMMUNITY COLLEGE
IN TSAILE, ARIZONA, HAS USED
TRADITIONAL TRIBAL MOTIFS IN ITS
ARCHITECTURE. IN THE FOREGROUND
IS A HOGAN, TRADITIONAL HOME OF
THE SOUTHWESTERN DESERT. IN
THE BACKGROUND IS A MODERN NEW
ADMINISTRATION BUILDING IN WHICH
THE HOGAN SHAPE APPEARS IN GLASS.

NAVAJO WEAVER SPINNING HER WOOL

and even bookstores. Sometimes on Saturday afternoons she would walk down the main street, just looking in the shop windows and wandering through the supermarkets. She had no money to buy things, but that did not matter.

At first she was very homesick for her family and friends on the reservation. Before going to the mission school she had never spent a single night away from her family. But all of the students at the school were Navajos from the reservation and that helped a great deal.

TO HERSELF SHE SAID, "I KNOW I WON'T BE SELECTED, SO THERE IS NOTHING TO WORRY ABOUT."

Lynn thought that she would be at the mission school until she graduated from high school, and it was a complete surprise when, about midway in the second term of her sophomore year, a group of her teachers asked her to come in for a conference. They told her about a new government program for finding minority high school students—blacks, Hispanics, American Indians—who showed unusual

academic ability and sending them to some of the best college preparatory schools in America.

"We want you to try to win a place in the program," Lynn's teachers told her. "The competition will be very great, but we think you have a chance."

Lynn felt a small stab of fear. "If I am selected, where will I go?" she asked.

"We don't know," one of the teachers told her, "but most of the schools are in California and on the East Coast."

"That would be so far from the reservation," Lynn said.

Her teachers continued to talk to her over the following days, and they seemed so sure she should apply for the program that Lynn finally agreed to fill out the application papers and take the entrance examination. To herself she said, "I know I won't be selected, so there is nothing to worry about."

A short time later she took the entrance examination in which she had to compete with all of the other minority students across the country who wanted to get into the program. She had never taken a test like that before, and she was sure that she had done miserably on it. She put it out of her mind and returned to her classwork and school life. The term was nearly over, and the thought of going back to the reservation made her happy.

And then one day she was called to the principal's office. He smiled when she walked in and he held up a piece of paper. "Congratulations, Lynn," he said. "You've been chosen! You're going to Brandermill School in Vermont." (At Lynn's request, the name of the school has been changed.)

Lynn would never forget the numb feeling in the pit of her stomach. "But it's so far away," she said.

"Well," the principal said, "Brandermill is one of the best college preparatory schools in the country. You're very lucky to be going there."

Yes, Lynn thought, she was lucky. She knew that. And she did want a good education. But why did she have to go so far away to get it? "Will I go in September?" she asked.

"That is one thing you may not like so well," the principal replied. "There's a special summer program at the University of Texas. You'll get courses in speed reading, English, and math, so that you will be better prepared for the fall term at Brandermill."

The numb feeling grew in Lynn's stomach. "Do I have to go?" she asked. "To the summer school, I mean?"

The principal smiled again. "I'm afraid you do," he said. "And you really need that work to get ready for the fall."

Lynn could feel the hurting at the back of her eyes, but she fought back the tears. "But I need to go home," she said.

"You can go home," the principal told her, "but not for a long visit. The summer program starts in June."

And that was the way it was. Instead of three months at home she would have two weeks. Two weeks to be with her family! On the bus ride from the school back to the reservation she sat in a window seat, and when they crossed into the reservation, she stared out at the red earth, at the huge bare rocks sculpted over thousands of centuries by wind and water into fantastic shapes. She stared at the awesome bulk of Black Mesa in the background and at the little patches of spring desert wild flowers along the roadside, tiny spots of purple, red, yellow, and white.

Lynn went to her grandparents' hogan, and her mother and brother came there so that they were all together. The two weeks passed like the flashing of pictures on a screen, and yet like pictures, some scenes stood still, and Lynn knew that she could carry them with her anywhere.

HERE A NAVAJO LEARNS THE INTRICACIES OF ELECTRONIC ASSEMBLY AT A PLANT ON THE ARIZONA RESERVATION.

There were the times she would go with her grandfather for water. The hogan had no running water, and every few days he would drive his old pickup truck to a windmill down the road and fill two wooden barrels. Upon their return to the hogan, Lynn would help transfer the water from the barrels to containers inside and outside the house.

THE DAY CAME TOO QUICKLY WHEN LYNN TOOK A BUS TO PHOENIX AND BOARDED AN AIRPLANE FOR THE FLIGHT TO TEXAS.

Some mornings Lynn would sit with her grandmother and help her grind corn for bread or mush. One morning as they worked, her grandmother explained again why grinding stones are so important. They were first brought to Navajos by the Holy People, she said, and women who learn to use them properly will be happy and healthy and even live longer. And the greasewood stirring sticks, if they are kept clean, will mean that a family will never be hungry. Hunger, which is really an evil spirit, thinks that the sticks are arrows which will kill it, so it stays away.

These were not the kinds of things that a person learned in school, Lynn thought, but she was glad that she knew about them. They were the teachings that her grandmother and her Navajo ancestors had lived by, and Lynn felt truth and meaning in them. Perhaps hunger was not an evil spirit, but it was bad, and it had less chance of getting into homes where women were happy and busy and knew how to prepare clean and nutritious food.

The day came too quickly when Lynn took a bus to Phoenix and boarded an airplane for the flight to Texas. She had never flown before and she was excited. She had thought she would be frightened, but she was so nervous thinking about the summer program that first-time flying fears couldn't crowd their way into her mind.

I'll bet I won't even get through the summer program, she thought, as she stared out of the plane window at the blur of ground below. I'll never make it to Vermont.

But it was not that way at all. When she reached the university, she was plunged into such a whirlwind of activity that she had no time to be frightened, uncertain, or even homesick. The program instructors pushed her and the other students into all-day classroom and laboratory sessions in mathematics, reading improvement, and English.

The teaching staff used methods and equipment that Lynn had never heard of, but after only a week she knew that she was reading faster and understanding more of what she read than she ever had before. She was pleased and excited by what was happening to her, and she was sure that she was doing well in the math program. English was the only problem. All her life she had spoken both English and Navajo, but sometimes, especially when she was under stress, she thought in Navajo. It was a problem she would just have to work out, Lynn knew, and she was determined not to lose her Navajo language in solving it.

The other students in the program were a happy surprise for her. They were there because of their high test scores but also because they were from minority groups and poor families. They all wanted a good education.

These similarities made it easier for them to talk, to get to know each other, to relax together. After a hard day of classes, it was fun to get to-gether in someone's room and talk about how they got to this place and what was happening to them here. On weekends when a group of them would go out for pizza or to a movie, it seemed to Lynn that she had known them for a long time.

Almost before she knew it, the summer program was over. She said her good-byes, some of them sad ones. She packed her suitcase and caught the plane for the East Coast.

She would never forget her first impressions of Brandermill: the huge old ivy-covered buildings, the beautifully landscaped campus still green at summer's end, the hundreds of cool, confident white-skinned girls walking in pairs, sitting on building steps in small groups, laughing and talking. It seemed to Lynn that they all had long blonde hair.

She learned some things about Brandermill before arriving. She knew that it was a prep school for the children of rich people. The tuition for one year was several thousand dollars, which was more money than Lynn could imagine. The school could afford to hire the very best teachers and it did. Brandermill's academic standards were the highest. Everyone had told Lynn how lucky she was to get to go to such a school.

NAVAJO ON HORSEBACK HERDING
SHEEP DOWN SAND DUNES AT
MONUMENT VALLEY

NAVAJO HOLDING
HIS SAND PAINTING

NAVAJO WEAVERS
NEAR HOGAN

But two weeks into the school term she was miserable. She was desperately lonely and homesick for her family and Navajo friends. She longed to see the red earth of the reservation, the great rocks, the sheltering bulk of Black Mesa. In the muggy New England September, she could almost feel the crisp, clean Arizona air. The ache inside her was a physical thing.

And for the first time in her life Lynn knew what it meant to feel depressed. She sat silently in all her classes, afraid to speak up, feeling that she could not compete with her well-educated classmates. In literature class they talked about books and writers that she had never heard of but that everyone else seemed to know. Math had seemed easy; here at Brandermill it was suddenly hard. She was having problems with her written English. As the fall term wore on, Lynn was sure that she was failing.

And she made no friends. A few of the girls in her dorm talked briefly with her sometimes, usually about a class assignment, but no one made an effort to really get to know her. She did not make an effort either because she did not know how. She would have liked to know more about them, about how they lived, but they did not seem curious about her. Most of them had known each other from past years at Brandermill, and they were turned in on their friendships and little social groups. Lynn did not think that they were being deliberately unfriendly.

I'm not a part of their lives, so they just don't see me, Lynn thought. It's like I wasn't here.

By mid-October Lynn was sure that she should leave Brandermill and return to the reservation. She went to her counselor to tell him of her decision. He listened quietly as she explained that she was not making it in her classes and that she was unhappy with her life at the school.

"I'm a Navajo," she said, "and I should be back where I belong."

"You are a Navajo," her counselor replied, "and right now this is where you belong."

"But I'm failing," Lynn repeated.

"Only in your mind," the counselor said, "and we've got to change that. Have any of your teachers told you you're failing?"

"No," Lynn said. "I just know it."

The counselor smiled. "You just think you know it," he said. "I've been following your work. I've talked with all your teachers within the last week. You're doing okay in everything. You're doing well in history, in fact. Your written English needs work, but you're certainly not failing in English."

"But I'm not happy here," Lynn said.

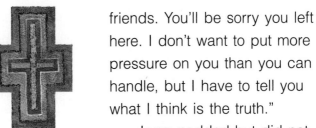

"YOU CAN DO IT," HE SAID. "WHEN YOU FIRST CAME HERE, I WASN'T SURE THAT YOU COULD, BUT NOW I AM."

"That's a different thing," the counselor said, "and that's why you think you're failing. What you are doing is about as hard to do as it can be. You have come out of a very special way of life into one that is entirely different. The people are different. The country is different. The school is different. There are very few people who could do what you're doing and succeed at it. That's why the selection board picked you. They believed you could do it."

"But I can't," Lynn said.

The counselor looked at her. "You can do it," he said. "When you first came here, I wasn't sure that you could, but now I am. If you leave school now and go back to the reservation, you won't feel good about yourself. You'll feel that you let down your tribe, your family, and your

friends. You'll be sorry you left here. I don't want to put more pressure on you than you can handle, but I have to tell you what I think is the truth."

Lynn nodded but did not say anything.

"Look," her counselor said, "you hang on until Christmas break. You'll get to go home then. Dig in now. Mark off the days on a calendar. Do anything you have to do to stick it out. When you get home, back to the reservation, you can decide whether you want to come back to Brandermill or whether you can come back. That's the place to make the decision."

Somehow it became a little easier after her talk with the counselor. Lynn did not mark off days on the calendar. What she did was throw herself into her studies with fierce energy. She spent more time at the library, more time going over her assignments a second and even a third time. The hard work made the days slide by more quickly.

She forced herself to speak up in her classes, even literature class, and it pleased and excited her that more than once the teachers praised her answers. She began to talk a little more to the other girls in the dorm, and now and then someone stopped by her room just to chat.

But on the last day before the Christmas break her excitement at the thought of going home was almost more than she could bear, and the feeling continued throughout the long flight to Phoenix. Just as in the summer, she again would have two weeks with her family in Navajoland. Then in so short a time she would have to go back to Vermont. But suppose she decided not to return. She could spend the rest of her life on the reservation. Was that what she wanted? The thought left Lynn confused and curbed some of the excitement inside her.

That night Lynn sat with her mother and grandparents in their hogan and ate mutton stew, corn, and fry bread for the first time in months. A cold winter wind howled around the hogan, but it was warm inside. They sat by the fire, and Lynn told them about Brandermill, her courses, her teachers, the big beautiful buildings, her fine dormitory room.

"I never thought I would be in a school as grand as that," Lynn said, "but I would rather be here, right where I am now."

"This is your home," her grandfather said.

During her visit Lynn talked to her mother and grandmother about something that was troubling her greatly. "What if I turn into a white person?" she asked. "If I learn white ways and how they think, if I learn their language and read their books, if I spend most of my time with them — won't I become a white person?"

Her grandmother answered in Navajo and used the Navajo word for their tribe, *Dine,* which means "The People." "You should learn the ways of the white people," she said. "But the ways of The People are deep inside you. I do not think you will forget who you are."

And her mother said, "Nothing can make you a white person unless you want to be one."

In that moment Lynn's decision was made. She would return to Brandermill. On the day she left the reservation and flew east to begin her second term, Lynn said her good-byes sadly, but she felt a confidence she had not known before.

When she arrived at Brandermill, the great campus, the fine buildings, the blonde students did not frighten her. She knew what was ahead for her, and she knew now that she could do the work. Most important, she was sure she could do it and still be what she was and wanted to be, a Navajo.

MEET
BRENT ASHABRANNER

When Brent Ashabranner was young, he roamed the world by reading about it. Books gave him a way to be in two places at once— the small Oklahoma town where he lived with his family and the far-away places he visited in stories.

Years later, an assignment with a foreign aid program took Ashabranner and his wife and children to Africa. After that, jobs took him to India, the Philippines, and Central America, among other places. Everywhere he traveled, Ashabranner listened to people. He began weaving what he heard into tales of his own. "No matter where I was or what I was doing," he says, "I have always had another life as a writer."

Ashabranner especially wants to help young readers understand people and cultures different from their own. Much of his writing is about cultural and ethnic groups in the United States. He feels that the years he spent abroad have helped him "understand better their hopes, desires, frustrations, and fears." In his award-winning book *To Live in Two Worlds,* Ashabranner explores the difficult choices Native Americans must make to find a place between two cultures: their own and that of white America. Two of his other award-winning books, *Morning Star, Black Sun* and *Children of the Maya,* also focus on issues of importance to Native Americans.

FROM Whitman

Consuelo Posloncec, 6th grade

When I go to school
I see
women & men running
to catch a bus.
I see
teachers
with their sunglasses
and long black raincoats,
their red nail polish
and gold jewelry.
I see
crossing guards with a
white banner helping
children.
I see
my building super
putting garbage bags in
garbage cans
with
his gray gloves
and blue jacket.

I see
other children going to school.
They have their lunchboxes
and bookbags.
I see
people with
briefcases and suits
talking to their
friends
with their red
skirts and high-heel shoes.
I see
people from all over the world
talking in different languages
with white scarves
around
their heads.
When I get to school
I see
things that become
a part of me.

Detail from *Looking Along Broadway Towards Grace Church*, by Red Grooms

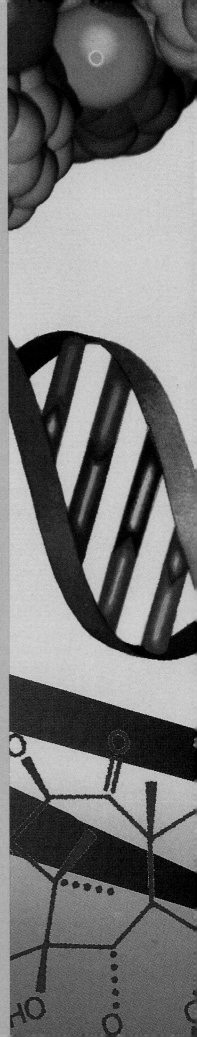

CONTENTS

Finders, Seekers

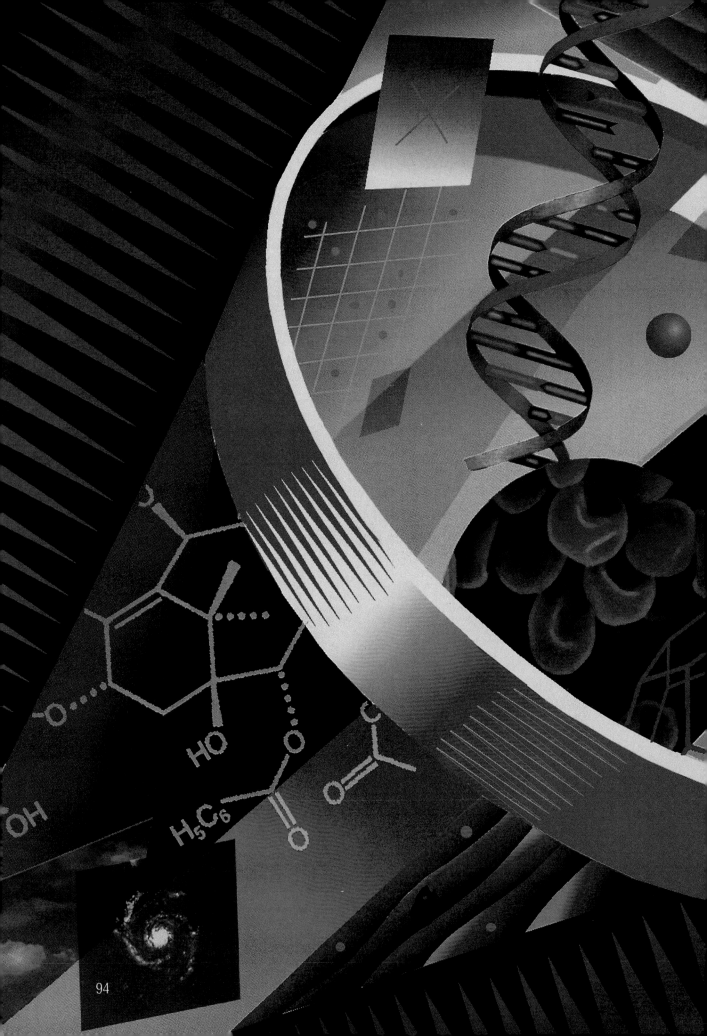

$$E_n = \frac{m_e e^4}{(4\pi\varepsilon_0)^2 2\hbar^2} \frac{1}{n^2}$$

No one can take from us
the joy of the first becoming
aware of something,
the so-called discovery.

GOETHE

EXPLORING THE TITANIC

By Robert D. Ballard

The ocean liner R.M.S. Titanic was built in 1911 and deemed "virtually unsinkable." However, on its maiden voyage in 1912, the ship struck an iceberg in the North Atlantic and sank, killing 1,500 of the 2,200 passengers aboard. In 1985, Robert D. Ballard and his team discovered the remains of the Titanic on the ocean floor. A year later, the team returned to explore the ship in their submarine *Alvin*, with the help of *Jason Jr.*, or *JJ*, their robot.

97

Rusticles hang from two large bollards.

As *Alvin*'s lights glow from above, *Jason Junior* explores the *Titanic*'s starboard anchor.

Our second view of the *Titanic* was breathtaking. As we glided soundlessly across the ocean bottom, the razor's edge of the bow loomed out of the darkness. The great ship towered above us. Suddenly it seemed to be coming right at us, about to run us over. My first reaction was that we had to get out of the way. But the *Titanic* wasn't going anywhere. As we gently brought our sub closer, we could see the bow more clearly. Both of her huge anchors were still in place. But the bow was buried more than sixty feet in mud, far too deep for anyone to pull her out of the ooze.

It looked as though the metal hull was slowly melting away. What seemed like frozen rivers of rust covered the ship's side and spread out over the ocean bottom. It was almost as if the blood of the great ship lay in pools on the ocean floor.

As *Alvin* rose in slow motion up the ghostly side of the ship, I could see our lights reflecting off the still-unbroken glass of the *Titanic*'s portholes. They made me think of cats' eyes gleaming in the dark. In places the rust formations over the portholes looked like eyelashes with tears, as though

This scale drawing shows the enormous distance between Ballard's search ship *Knorr* and the *Titanic* wreck.

437 ft/133 m
This is the deepest a scuba diver has ever gone.

1,500 ft/465 m
Naval submarines dive no deeper than this. There is no light below this level.

3,028 ft/940 m
Pioneer underwater explorers William Beebe and Otis Barton reached this depth in a ball-shaped bathysphere in 1930.

1 mile/1,609 m
Many sea creatures here are transparent or can glow in the dark.

2 miles/3,218 m
The water temperature at this depth stays a few degrees above the freezing point.

12,460 ft/3,965 m
The water pressure where the Titanic lies is approximately 6,000 lbs. per square inch.

Great Pyramid of Cheops El Gizeh, Egypt

Eiffel Tower Paris, France

Empire State Building New York, U.S.A.

Sears Tower Chicago, U.S.A.

Ostankino Tower Moscow U.S.S.R.

CN Tower Toronto, Canada

the *Titanic* were crying. I could also see a lot of reddish-brown stalactites of rust over the wreck, like long icicles. I decided to call them "rusticles." This rust turned out to be very fragile. If touched by our sub, it disappeared like a cloud of smoke.

As we rose further and began to move across the mighty forward deck, I was amazed at the sheer size of everything: giant bollards and shiny bronze capstans that were used for winding ropes and cables; the huge links of the anchor chains. When you were there on the spot, the ship was truly titanic.

The *Titanic*'s bridge in 1912

I strained to get a good look at the deck's wood planking, just four feet below us. Then my heart dropped to my stomach. "It's gone!" I muttered. Most of the *Titanic*'s wooden deck had been eaten away. Millions of little wood-eating worms had done more damage than the iceberg and the salt water. I began to wonder whether the metal deck below the destroyed wood planking would support our weight when *Alvin* landed.

We would soon find out. Slowly we moved into position to make our first landing test on the forward deck just next to the fallen mast. As we made our approach, our hearts beat quickly. We knew there was a real risk of crashing through the deck. The sub settled down, making a muffled crunching noise. If the deck gave way, we'd be trapped in collapsing wreckage. But it held, and we settled firmly. That meant there was a good chance that the *Titanic*'s decks would support us at other landing sites.

The *Titanic*'s bridge in 1986

We carefully lifted off and turned toward the stern. The dim outline of the ship's superstructure came into view: first B Deck, then A, finally the Boat Deck—the top deck where the bridge was located. It was here that

The bow section of the *Titanic*

the captain and his officers had guided the ship across the Atlantic. The wooden wheelhouse was gone, probably knocked away in the sinking. But the bronze telemotor control to which the ship's wheel had once been attached stood intact, polished to a shine by the current. We then safely tested this second landing site.

I had an eerie feeling as we glided along exploring the wreck. As I peered through my porthole, I could easily imagine people walking along the deck and looking out the windows of the ship that I was looking into. Here I was at the bottom of the ocean looking at a kind of time capsule from history.

Suddenly, as we rose up the port side of the ship, the sub shuddered and made a clanging noise. A waterfall of rust covered our portholes. "We've hit something!" I exclaimed. "What is it?"

"I don't know," our pilot replied. "I'm backing off." Unseen overhangs are the nightmare of the deep-sub pilot. Carefully, the pilot backed away from the hull and brought us slowly upward. Then, directly in front of our forward porthole, a big lifeboat davit slid by. We had hit one of the metal arms that held the lifeboats as they were lowered. This davit was one of the two that had held boat No. 8, the boat Mrs. Straus had refused to enter that night. She was the wife of the owner of Macy's department store in New York. When she had been offered a chance to save herself in one of the lifeboats, she had turned to her husband and said, "We have been living together for many years. Where you go, I go." Calmly, the two of them had sat down on a pile of deck chairs to wait for the end.

Now, as we peered out our portholes, it seemed as if the Boat Deck were crowded with passengers. I could almost hear the cry, "Women and children first!"

We knew from the previous year's pictures that the stern had broken off the ship, so we continued back to

The Grand Staircase in 1912

search for the severed end of the intact bow section. Just beyond the gaping hole where the second funnel had been, the deck began to plunge down at a dangerous angle. The graceful lines of the ship disappeared in a twisted mess of torn steel plating, upturned portholes, and jumbled wreckage. We saw enough to know that the decks of the ship had collapsed in on one another like a giant accordion. With an unexpectedly strong current pushing us toward this twisted wreckage, we veered away and headed for the surface.

The next day we landed on the deck next to the very edge of the Grand Staircase, which had once been covered by an elegant glass dome. The dome hadn't survived the plunge, but the staircase shaft had, and to me it still represented the fabulous luxury of the ship. *Alvin* now rested quietly on the top deck of the R.M.S. *Titanic* directly above the place where three elevators had carried first-class passengers who did not wish to use the splendid Grand Staircase.

We, however, would take the stairs with *JJ* the robot, our R2D2 of the deep. This would be the first deep-water test for our remote-controlled swimming eyeball, and we were very nervous about it. No one knew whether *JJ*'s motors could stand up to the enormous ocean pressure of more than 6,000 pounds per square inch.

Using a control box with a joystick that operated like a video game, the operator cautiously steered *JJ* out of his garage attached to the front of *Alvin*. Slowly *JJ* went inching down into the yawning blackness of the Grand Staircase. More and more cable was let out as he dropped deeper and deeper.

We could see what *JJ* was seeing on our video in the sub. But at first *JJ* could see nothing. Then, as he dropped deeper, a room appeared off the portside foyer on A Deck. *JJ* swung around and our co-pilot saw something in the distance. "Look at that," he said softly. "Look at that chandelier."

Now I could see it, too. "No, it can't be a chandelier," I said. "It couldn't possibly have survived."

I couldn't believe my eyes. The ship had fallen two and a half miles, hitting the bottom with the force of a train running into a mountain, and here was an almost perfectly preserved light fixture! *JJ* left the stairwell and

Jason Junior **illuminates a pillar still standing in the foyer of the Grand Staircase. *Alvin* has landed on the Boat Deck beside the collapsed roof that once held the glass dome over the staircase. From inside the submarine we guide *JJ* down the staircase shaft as far as B Deck. The illustration (*inset*) shows a cross-section of *JJ*'s descent with an outline of the original staircase.**

started to enter the room, managing to get within a foot of the fixture. To our astonishment, we saw a feathery piece of coral sprouting from it. We could even see the sockets where the light bulbs had been fitted! "This is fantastic," I exulted.

"Bob, we're running short of time. We have to return to the surface." Our pilot's words cut like a knife through my excitement. Here we were deep inside the *Titanic,* actually going down the Grand Staircase, but we had used up all the time that we had to stay safely on the bottom. I knew our pilot was just following orders, but I still wanted to shout in protest.

Captain Edward J. Smith

Our little robot soldier emerged from the black hole and shone his lights toward us, bathing the interior of the sub in an unearthly glow. For a moment it felt as if an alien spaceship were hovering nearby. But that feeling quickly gave way to one of victory, thanks to our little friend. *JJ* had been a complete success.

On our next day's dive, we crossed over what had once been Captain Smith's cabin. Its outer wall now lay collapsed on the deck, as though a giant had brought his fist down on it. We passed within inches of one of the cabin's windows. Was this, I wondered, a window that Captain Smith had cranked open to let a little fresh air into his cabin before going to bed?

Suddenly a large piece of broken railing loomed out of the darkness. It seemed to be heading right for my viewport. I immediately warned the pilot who quickly turned *Alvin*'s stern around, rotating us free of the obstacle.

Now we began to drop onto the starboard Boat Deck. As we glided along, I felt as though I were visiting a ghost town where suddenly one day everyone had closed up shop and left.

An empty lifeboat davit stood nearby. Ahead I could see where the *Titanic's* lifeboats had rested. It was on this very deck that the crowds of passengers had stood waiting to get into the boats. They had not known until the last moments that there were not

Wives saying goodbye to their husbands as lifeboats are loaded on the Boat Deck

enough lifeboats for everyone. It was also from this deck that you could have heard the *Titanic's* brave band playing cheerful music to boost the crowd's spirits as the slope of the deck grew steeper and steeper.

Jason Jr. now went for a stroll along the Boat Deck. As he slowly made his way along, he looked in the windows of several first-class cabins as well as into some passageways, including one that still bore the words, "First-Class Entrance." As *JJ* passed by the gymnasium windows, I could see bits and pieces of equipment amid the rubble, including some metal grill-work that had been part of the electric camel, an old-fashioned exercise machine. We could also see various wheel shapes and a control lever. Much of the gym's

Stern Section

■ A painted metal footboard from a bed (*top left*)

■ This sink from a second-class stateroom could be tipped to allow the water to drain out (*top middle*)

■ The white porcelain of this bathtub is almost hidden by rust in contrast (*top right inset*) to the way it appeared when new (*top right*).

■ The cast-iron frame of one of the benches from the *Titanic's* decks (*bottom right*)

ceiling was covered with rust. This was where the gym instructor, dressed in white flannel trousers, had urged passengers to try the gym machines. And, on the last night, passengers had gathered here for warmth as the lifeboats were being lowered.

I could see *JJ* far off down the deck, turning this way and that to get a better view inside doorways and various windows. It was almost as though our little robot had a mind of his own.

But now we had to bring him home. We had been on the *Titanic* for hours. Once again it was time to head back to the surface.

The morning of July 18 was lovely and warm, but I felt edgy about the day's mission. We had decided to visit the *Titanic's* debris field. Along the 1,970 feet that separated the broken-off bow and stern pieces of the wreck, there was a large scattering of all kinds of objects from

The Debris Field
**Between the separated sections of the *Titanic*
lie thousands of objects that spilled out of the
ship when she sank.**

Bow Section

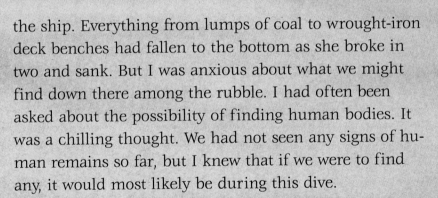

the ship. Everything from lumps of coal to wrought-iron
deck benches had fallen to the bottom as she broke in
two and sank. But I was anxious about what we might
find down there among the rubble. I had often been
asked about the possibility of finding human bodies. It
was a chilling thought. We had not seen any signs of human remains so far, but I knew that if we were to find
any, it would most likely be during this dive.

As the first fragments of wreckage began to appear
on the bottom, I felt like we were entering a bombed-
out museum. Thousands upon thousands of objects
littered the rolling fields of ocean bottom, many
of them perfectly preserved. The guts of the
Titanic lay spilled out across the ocean floor.
Cups and saucers, silver serving trays, pots and
pans, wine bottles, boots, chamber pots, space
heaters, bathtubs, suitcases, and more.

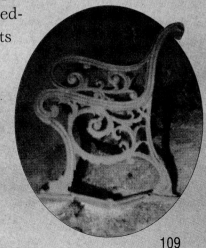

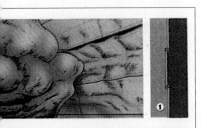

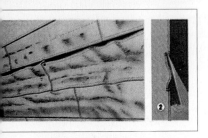

The iceberg scraping against the hull plates of the *Titanic* (*top*) popped many of the steel rivets that held them in place (*top right*). This allowed water to pour in through the seams (*above right*).

Then, without warning, I found myself looking into the ghostly eyes of a small, white smiling face. For a split second I thought it was a skull—and it really scared me. Then I realized I was looking at a doll's head, its hair and clothes gone.

My shock turned to sadness as I began to wonder who had owned this toy. Had the girl survived in one of the lifeboats? Or had she clutched the doll tightly as she sank in the icy waters?

We moved on through this amazing scenery. There were so many things scattered about that it became difficult to keep track of them. We came across one of the ship's boilers, and there on top of it sat an upright rusty metal cup like the ones the crew had used. It looked as though it had been placed there by a stoker moments before water had burst into the boiler room. It was astonishing to think that in fact this cup had just fluttered down that night to land right on top of a boiler.

Then in the light of *Alvin*'s headlights, we spotted a safe ahead of us. I had heard about the story of fabulous treasure, including a leather-bound book covered with jewels, being locked in the ship's safes when she sank. Here was the chance of a lifetime, and I wanted to get a good look at it.

The safe sat there with its door face up. The handle looked as though it was made of gold, although I knew it had to be brass. Next to it, I could see a small circular gold dial, and above both a nice shiny gold crest.

Why not try to open it? I watched as *Alvin*'s sample-gathering arm locked its metal fingers onto the handle. Its metal wrist began to rotate clockwise. To my surprise, the handle turned easily. Then it stopped. The door just wouldn't budge. It was rusted shut. I felt as if I'd been caught with my hand in the cookie jar.

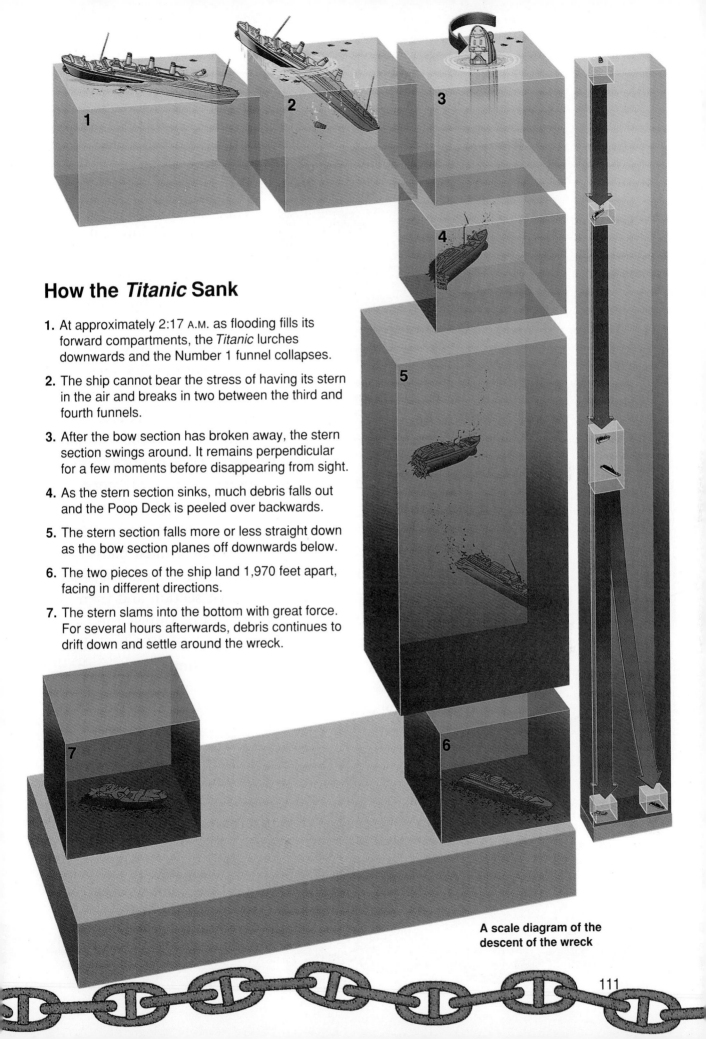

How the *Titanic* Sank

1. At approximately 2:17 A.M. as flooding fills its forward compartments, the *Titanic* lurches downwards and the Number 1 funnel collapses.

2. The ship cannot bear the stress of having its stern in the air and breaks in two between the third and fourth funnels.

3. After the bow section has broken away, the stern section swings around. It remains perpendicular for a few moments before disappearing from sight.

4. As the stern section sinks, much debris falls out and the Poop Deck is peeled over backwards.

5. The stern section falls more or less straight down as the bow section planes off downwards below.

6. The two pieces of the ship land 1,970 feet apart, facing in different directions.

7. The stern slams into the bottom with great force. For several hours afterwards, debris continues to drift down and settle around the wreck.

A scale diagram of the descent of the wreck

111

The dial and brass crest of this safe are still shiny. We turned the handle with *Alvin*'s mechanical arm.

Oh, well, I thought, it was probably empty, anyway. In fact, when we later looked at the video footage we had taken, we could see that the bottom of the safe had rusted out. Any treasure should have been spread around nearby, but there was none to be seen. Fortunately, my promise to myself not to bring back anything from the *Titanic* was not put to the test.

Two days passed before I went down to the *Titanic* again. After the rest, I was raring to go at it once more. This time we were going to explore the torn-off stern section that lay 1,970 feet away from the bow. It had been very badly damaged during the plunge to the bottom. Now it lay almost unrecognizable amidst badly twisted pieces of wreckage. We planned to land *Alvin* on the bottom directly behind the stern section and then send *JJ* in under the overhanging hull. Unless the *Titanic*'s three huge propellers had fallen off when she sank, I figured they still ought to be there, along with her enormous 101-ton rudder.

We made a soft landing on the bottom and discovered that one of *JJ*'s motors wouldn't work. Our dive looked like a washout. I sat glumly staring out of my viewport at the muddy bottom. Suddenly the mud started to move! Our pilot was slowly inching *Alvin* forward on its single ski right under the dangerous overhanging stern area. He was taking the sub itself to search for the huge propellers. Was he crazy? What if a piece of wreckage came crashing down? But our pilot was a professional, so I figured he must know exactly what he was doing.

I could see an area ahead covered with rusticles that had fallen from the rim of the stern above. Until now we had had ocean above us. Crossing this point was like taking a dangerous dare. Once on the other side, there was no sure way of escaping if disaster struck. None of us spoke. The only sound in the sub was our breathing.

Slowly a massive black surface of steel plating seemed to inch down toward us overhead. The hull seemed to be coming at us from all sides. As we looked closely, we could see that like the bow, the stern section was buried deep in the mud—forty-five feet or so. Both the middle and the starboard propellers were under the mud. Only about sixteen feet of the massive rudder could be seen rising out of the ooze.

In *Alvin* we explore under the overhanging deck of the *Titanic*'s severed stern section and photograph the buried rudder.

"Let's get out of here," I said. Ever so gently, *Alvin* retraced the path left by its ski. As we crossed over from the area covered with rusticles into the clear, we sighed with relief. We were out of danger. All of us were glad that this adventure was over.

Before we left the bottom this time, however, there was one mission that I wanted to complete. I wanted to place a memorial plaque on the twisted and tangled wreckage of the stern, in memory of all those lost on the *Titanic*. Those who had died had gathered on the stern as the ship had tilted bow first. This had been their final haven. So we rose up the wall of steel to the top of the stern. With great care, *Alvin*'s mechanical arm plucked the plaque from where it had been strapped outside the sub, and gently released it. We watched as it sank quietly to the deck of the stern.

As we lifted off and began our climb to the surface, our camera kept the plaque in view as long as possible. As we rose, it grew smaller and smaller, until finally it was swallowed in the gloom.

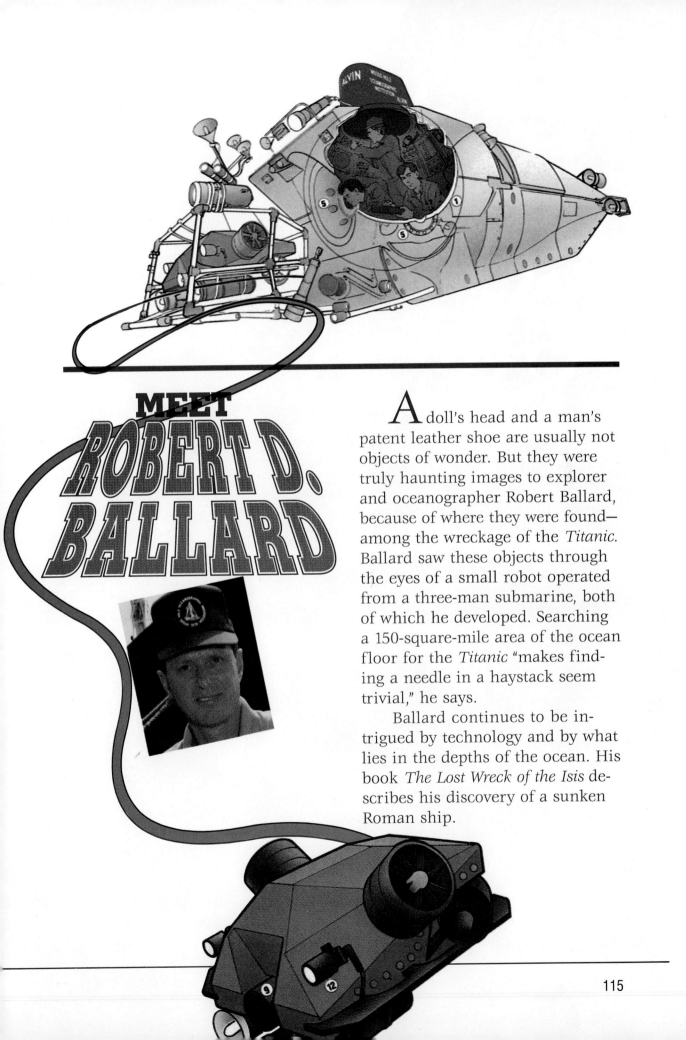

MEET ROBERT D. BALLARD

A doll's head and a man's patent leather shoe are usually not objects of wonder. But they were truly haunting images to explorer and oceanographer Robert Ballard, because of where they were found—among the wreckage of the *Titanic*. Ballard saw these objects through the eyes of a small robot operated from a three-man submarine, both of which he developed. Searching a 150-square-mile area of the ocean floor for the *Titanic* "makes finding a needle in a haystack seem trivial," he says.

Ballard continues to be intrigued by technology and by what lies in the depths of the ocean. His book *The Lost Wreck of the Isis* describes his discovery of a sunken Roman ship.

Ancient Secrets Run Deep

In 1982, a team of divers plunged into the Mediterranean Sea and traveled back thirty-four centuries! They found a shipwreck from the fourteenth century B.C. embedded in the ocean floor. Its vast cargo proved to be a remarkable discovery. The ship contained well-preserved items from seven different civilizations! It is believed that the ship sank along an ancient trade route after visiting some of the great cultural centers in the latter part of the Bronze Age.

1 The sunken ship may have looked like this Syrian trading ship, shown unloading its cargo in Egypt. Like other great Bronze Age civilizations, the Egyptians imported such goods as metals for weapons, oils for skin care, and cedar for shipbuilding from other cultures.

2 A gold chalice lies on the ocean floor. Although its exact origin is unknown, the chalice may be from Egypt. The Egyptians were chief exporters of gold during the Bronze Age.

3 Among the pottery that was recovered were jugs and cups from the island of Cyprus. This rustic pottery may have been a popular export item to neighboring cities.

4 Out of a large storage jar came the oldest book ever found. Known as a *diptych*, it was constructed of two pieces of wood hinged together. Inside, the inner surface was spread with beeswax. A pointed object was used to write in the wax.

5 Here a technician cleans and matches pieces of pottery.

6 A diver holds a sword believed to be from Canaan, the site of modern-day Israel, Lebanon, and Jordan. Besides metals, the Canaanites exported glass and ivory, from a time when elephants inhabited Syria.

Meet
Jean Craighead George

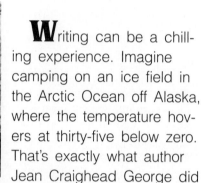

Writing can be a chilling experience. Imagine camping on an ice field in the Arctic Ocean off Alaska, where the temperature hovers at thirty-five below zero. That's exactly what author Jean Craighead George did for six weeks while writing a book about whales. She wanted her observations and discoveries to be not only accurate but also firsthand.

Much of George's fiction is about young people who learn from nature. When she was in elementary school, she ran away from home and planned to "live by a waterfall in the woods and catch fish on hooks made from the forks of tree limbs, as I had been taught by my father." She was gone that time for only forty minutes. But she later spent much more time in forests learning about plants and animals from her father, who was a scientist.

In *Julie of the Wolves,* which won a Newbery Medal, Julie survives the Arctic wilderness by observing the habits of a pack of wolves. *My Side of the Mountain* is the story of Sam Gribley, who runs away from his home in New York City to live in the Catskill Mountains. The book was made into a movie in 1969. ■

The Talking Earth

by Jean Craighead George

Illustrated by
Wayne Anthony Still

Billie Wind, along with her mother, Mamau Whispering Wind, her father, Iron Wind, her sister, Mary Wind, and her brother, lives with her Seminole tribe. Unlike her sister, who believes in the legends of the tribe, Billie follows the customs but feels that issues such as pollution of the earth are more real than the legends she is accused of doubting. When the medicine man, Charlie Wind, who is also her uncle and friend, confronts Billie Wind about her doubts, she sets out to find answers in the Florida Everglades, or the pa-hay-okee. She vows that she will not come back until she stops doubting the legends—that there are animal gods who talk, that there is a serpent who lives in the Everglades and punishes bad Seminoles, and that there are little people who live underground and play tricks on the Seminoles. Billie decides to spend the first night on an uninhabited island. There, she finds a large sinkhole—a pit—with a pool at the bottom and a cave at one side. When a raging fire threatens Billie, she takes refuge in the underground cave, and she begins to discover what truth the legends hold for her.

An hour before dawn, Billie Wind, who had not slept all night, lifted her head and looked up at the fire. It still raged. She pushed farther back in the cave. As she moved, her hand struck something hard and round. She brought it close to her face for inspection. It was a clay bowl.

"Burial ground," she said. "This is a burial ground of the Seminoles. I should not be here." Nervously she went to the entrance and held the bowl in the light of the fire shining down from above. Around its rim were feathery drawings. Her fingers ran lightly over the coils of clay that formed the dark bowl. It was gritty to her touch. The grittiness was typical of bowls fired in sand by the ancient Indians.

"Calusa," she said. "This is a Calusa pot." She glanced around the cave. "This place is very old; very, very old. The Calusas were killed off four hundred years ago.

"And it is not a burial ground. Burial pots are broken to let the spirits out.

"Someone lived here. Some ancient ancestor lived in this cave." The light flared up and she crawled around the room on hands and knees curious to see and learn. Near the far wall she found a conch shell. A hole had been drilled through it, and the tough, thick lip had been ground to a sharp edge.

"A pick," she said. "Hey, ghostly ancestor, you had a pick. Who were you and why were you down here in this cave?" She rocked back on her heels and saw that there was a long niche chipped into the wall.

"A bed." She climbed into it, stretched out and discovered that her head and feet touched the walls. "The ancestor was not much taller than I," she observed; then a thought occurred to her. She felt for human bones. To her relief she found none. "You did not die here," she said aloud. "You lived, and so will I."

As the sun came up the mood of the fire changed. The crackle and roar became a soft hum. The mist of morning was drifting across the island and seeping down into the pit. The air smelled of smoke and tree resin. Billie Wind coughed, took off her shirt and dipped it in the water. She held it over her nose and mouth to filter out the smoke. Lying on her belly, facedown, she breathed the heavy, cold air that still lay along the floor of the cave.

As the morning waned, the smoky mist vanished, leaving the air almost fresh. Billie Wind removed her filter, sat up and breathed deeply. A new sound was on the wind. It was a hiss, and beyond the hiss a splat.

"Rain!" she cried. "Mamau Whispering Wind, I hear rain. I'm all right. I'm all right."

Taking off her leggings and sneakers, clutching the bowl to her chest, she climbed into the bed of the ancient person and lay down. She closed her eyes and this time she did sleep.

Billie Wind awoke around noon but she did not get up. Instead she lay quietly on her back, staring at the limestone wall. Where was she? Why was she looking at a wall?

With a shiver she remembered. She was entombed by the fire serpent. She felt her legs. "I'm alive." Then she added, "I think." She moved her fingers and toes. "Yes, I am." Turning cautiously to her side, she peered out of the cave. The roaring fire of last night could not be heard. She sat up. The sun fell in pale patches on the log and the pool. The air was smoky but sunlit.

Sliding from her bed she walked out on the log and looked up. A few strands of smoke curled along the rim of the pit; an occasional flare marked the last gasp of a flame. The trees were black stalks, and the once lacy green canopy was gone. Although hot coals glowed along the rim of the pit, the worst of the fire seemed to be over. She was cheered. As her shoulders relaxed she became aware of a gnawing hunger and took out Mamau Whispering Wind's corn bread. She ate all but a small bite, then squatted on her heels and studied the sinkhole and sky. Where the walls had been festooned with ferns and mosses yesterday, they

were now bare. Without the plants as a cover, she could see that there were not just two ledges in the pit, but many. She studied them.

"Steps," she said. "I think they are steps. And steps are cut by persons." She crossed the log and measured them with her hand. "Yes, they are. Some person came and went on them." She pondered as to who it might have been. "Perhaps she was hiding from a fire . . . like me. No, fires did

not burn the moist islands in those days. Perhaps she hid from the conquistadores. Or maybe she was the leader of the little underground people, and this was the stairway to her council house." She smiled at her joke. "I wish it were so—then I could go home and tell Charlie Wind there *are* little underground people who build strange cities and save curious little Seminole Indian girls."

She pushed the little people out of her head and considered the stairs again. They were pocked and black with fire burn and oxidation; old but maybe not ancient. The Calusa built ramps. White men and Seminoles built steps. And yet, the Everglades and the south Florida west coast were dotted with the ruins of many

ingenious constructions; canals that led to fish-holding ponds, elevated village sites. One such structure lay just south of Big Cypress Reservation. Billie Wind and her mother had found shards of pottery there, black and rough like her pot.

"Where did the ancient people come from?" she had asked Whispering Wind as she turned a piece over in her hands.

"From Asia," she had answered. "They crossed the Bering land bridge to North America thousands and thousands of years ago with all the other American Indians. And they moved southward for thousands of years until they found the beautiful pa-hay-okee and lived in health and peace. The Great Spirit was good to them and to Florida."

Iron Wind told her this when she asked him:

"Some men say that the Calusa came across the Gulf of Mexico from Yucatan, because Calusa mounds resembled the Mayan mounds. I don't think so. But no one knows for sure, and unless we find new clues in the ruins, we'll never know."

She had pondered enough. She jumped down the steps to pack up her possessions and leave. She was eager to go home.

The bowl she packed carefully, wrapping it many times in the hammock. She would show it to Charlie Wind and he would send historical detectives to the island.

She pulled on her sneakers and leggings, checked her pocket to make sure her penknife was there, shouldered her pouch and ran across the log and up the steps. Near the top she was stopped by a blast of heat. She covered her face with her arm. The stones and soil were oven hot. She could not touch anything. Standing on her tiptoes, she peered over the rim of the pit. Flames leaped along fallen trees and red fires smouldered in the loam.

"I'm trapped," she said. "The earth is too hot to walk on." Biting her lips to keep them from trembling she turned and walked slowly back to the cave.

"I can't wait very long," she said. "I've got one piece of venison left." She sat down on the bed. "I'm going to die here.

It will take a long, long time for the earth to cool. I shall die in this pit." She dropped her head on her knees.

Presently a thought replaced her fear. She remembered that a tortoise had fallen into the water and that many, many snakes had slithered into the pit. All were good food. She unpacked her deerskin pouch, placed the pot on the ground and pondered.

In the light of the afternoon she saw that the bumps on the floor of the cave that she had thought to be rocks last night were piles of oysters, conches and cochinas. The sea must

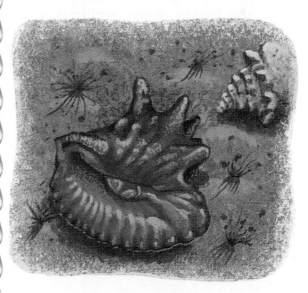

have been a short distance away when the ancient person lived here. Charlie Wind told old legends about the sea once covering all the pa-hay-okee. Maybe he was right.

Taking out her machete, she dug into a shell pile and uncovered a conch with its top cut off and the inside spiral removed.

"A cup," she exclaimed, recognizing the object from ones like it at Panther Paw. She put the cup aside and dug more carefully into the broken shells and dust. A few inches down she uncovered an oyster shell that had been chipped into a stirring spoon and near it, the heavy central column of an enormous fighting conch.

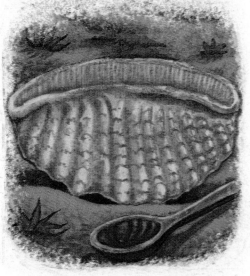

"A hammer." She brought it down sharply on the ground, and was surprised by how well it was balanced. She dug on, uncovering a wedge-shaped conch with a sharp edge. Two holes had been drilled in this instrument, which she recognized to be an adz.

"Like the steel one Charlie Wind uses to hew dugouts," she said and planned a new handle for it by running a rope from her hammock through the two holes and knotting it around a stick. The shell, though old, was still strong. She put it aside. After uncovering a few more cups and spoons, broken and unbroken, she noticed that the far wall was blackened.

"A cooking hearth," she said, wondering where the smoke vented. She glanced up and saw that the roof of the cave was riddled with holes typical of the Everglades limestone. The smoke, of course, went up through the porous rock.

A shrill whistle sounded. Billie Wind leaped to her feet and ran joyfully to the entrance of the cave.

"Charlie Wind!" she cried, recognizing his call to council.

"I'm here. I'm here." She crossed the log and climbed up the stairs.

"Hello, Charlie Wind!" She slowed as she neared the top. It couldn't be Charlie Wind. The earth was a red-hot inferno. Not even a medicine man could cross it. She peered at the smouldering forest floor.

No one was there.

Her hopes shattered, she sat down on a step and covered her face with her hands. She felt alone and frightened, even more so than that moment when she saw the fire coming toward her.

The whistle sounded again.

She lifted her head with renewed interest. "It's coming from inside the wall of the pit."

Someone grunted and coughed in a sooty hole at her feet. She leaned over and peered into a shadowy cavern.

"Who's there?" The human-like cough sounded again. Two bright eyes gleamed above a flat nose and upturned mouth. "I see a little person," she said, then added aloud: "Charlie Wind, forgive me." She thought again. This time more clearly. "Nonsense, there are no such things as little underground men."

The mouth in the hole moved as if to speak and she saw that the lips were rimmed with silvery whiskers.

"A petang, a petang," she cried joyfully. "Little otter, what are you doing here?" Holding out her hand she waited for him to smell her odor of friendship and come to her. Last year a black bear on Panther Paw had smelled her affection and had walked almost up to her before turning away.

But this little animal did not move. He huddled in the darkness. He was badly frightened. After a long wait Billie Wind

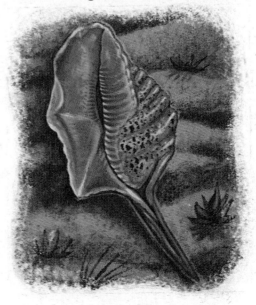

tiptoed down the steps and brought back the last piece of venison, which she chewed to soften. The petang twirled his whiskers and sniffed the food.

"Come, little friend," she said. "Come here to me. I shall take care of you whom the Indians of the north call petang.

"We are the only living things in this whole charred and black world."

Petang's nostrils flared. He backed up.

"Did you escape the fire by crawling into a pit like me? If so, we are fire spirits. We must console each other." Petang's eyes rolled from right to left and then up into Billie Wind's face. He seemed to sense something reassuring about her, for he poked his head out of the hole and whimpered. Then he grabbed the meat in his small teeth so vigorously that Billie Wind was forced to hold it with both hands.

"You are very strong," she said. "And very young," she added, for he stopped pulling and began sucking. "You are still nursing." She peered behind him into the hole to see if the mother otter was hiding there. She was not.

Hesitatingly, moving forward, back, forward, the little otter finally came all the way out of the hole and, placing one large, webbed foot on her hand, grunted wistfully. Then he sat up, propping himself erect like a little man with the support of his stout, tapering tail. Strong muscles rippled under his silver-brown fur. Billie Wind judged him to be about two months old, for she had once played with a young otter at the zoo on the Big Cypress Reservation. This little fellow was about the size of a marsh rabbit. He would grow to be about three feet long and nine or ten inches high at the shoulder.

Talking softly to this beautiful friend, she slipped one hand under him and drew him to her with the other. She held him against her body, stroking his head and body as do mother otters to encourage their little ones to eat. He sucked the meat. At the same time she peered into other holes searching for a mother or sister or brother. She saw nothing else alive, not even a snake, not even a mosquito. Then a frog piped from the bottom of the sinkhole.

"That makes three of us," she said. "You and me, Petang, and a frog."

Petang devoured most of the venison by simply sucking it down. When he was satisfied, he snuggled against her

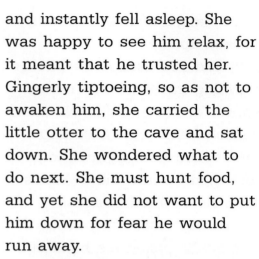

and instantly fell asleep. She
was happy to see him relax, for
it meant that he trusted her.
Gingerly tiptoeing, so as not to
awaken him, she carried the
little otter to the cave and sat
down. She wondered what to
do next. She must hunt food,
and yet she did not want to put
him down for fear he would
run away.

She stroked his head. He
snuggled closer making the

soft grunts and snorts little otters make to their mothers. Billie Wind was encouraged, for the noises said to her that the petang was accepting her as a substitute mother. He might stay with her. She had fed and stroked him, and that, she knew, spelled "mother" to all young mammals. Presently he folded his paws on his chest as if to say his world was all right again. Like the other members of his lively family, the mink, the weasel, the skunk and the wolverine, animals that run hard and sleep hard, Petang's sleep was deep. Even shifting him to her other arm did not awaken him.

As she sat holding the beautiful wild thing, she scanned the water in the bottom of the pit until at last her eyes came to rest on the frog. His head was protruding above the surface of the water near the log.

"How," she said to Petang, "how do I catch him? Even so small a bite will keep you and me alive for another day. And tomorrow it might rain again and we can leave." She looked at the remains of the venison.

"Half a meal for each of us. I'd better catch that frog."

A peal of thunder rumbled, and she looked up out of the pit. The sky was filled with rolling clouds; rain was indeed coming. She wouldn't have to catch the frog. The rumbling deluge would cool the soil, she hoped, and they could leave the pit today. She leaned back to wait for the thunderstorm to break, and then thought better of it. She had been fooled before. These were, after all, the years of the drought, and drought perpetuated drought. She eased Petang to the floor beside her deerskin pouch and carefully pulled out the hammock. He did not wake, and she smiled, cut off three feet of the hammock with her penknife and knotted the ragged ends so they would not unravel. She spread the net on the floor. Along one side she strung the heaviest of the shells and three long cords cut from the hammock ties. At the end of each cord she tied more shells. When she was done she had a fishnet, which she carried out on the log.

"Where are you, frog?" she asked. The wind trumpeted as it blew over the rim of the pit. Sparks exploded somewhere above her; but she did not heed them. Instead she concentrated on dropping the weighted end of the net across the deepest part of the pool. So that she could pull it up, she draped the cords over the log. The shells held them in place. Next she tied one corner of the un-weighted side to a fig root on the wall, the other to a sapling on the other side of the pit. The net was set. Squatting, she poised herself to grab the cords and yank. The frog would have to come to the sur-face to breathe pretty soon, for he had been under a long time, and he was an air breather. With a swish, the sapling thrashed. Billie Wind grabbed the cords and pulled. Flopping in the net was a big large-mouthed bass.

"Petang," she shouted ex-citedly. "We will live. A fish, a fish." With a quick jab she thrust her fingers into the gills to make sure the bass did not escape, set the net again and ran back to the cave.

"We can live a long time down here, Petang," she said. "We have a bed, a fireplace, a cooking bowl—and food." She slit the fish from anus to gills with her penknife, removed the entrails and saved them for bait to catch other fish.

"Petang," she said to the still-sleeping otter. "How do you suppose a fish got down in this pit? He can not crawl on land or fly. Did a bird drop him? Did an egg wash in on a flood? Did the little underground men bring him here?" She smiled. "Little underground men are very use-ful. They explain all nature's mysteries." Then a thought occurred to her and she glanced around the cave.

"Do you suppose this was a fish pond for the ancients? Perhaps they brought them here eons ago. Perhaps a fish keeper lived in this cave. The Calusa cultivated fish, you know."

Petang smelled the entrails in his sleep and came awake. He bounced to Billie Wind's side.

"Here," she said, cutting off a large chunk of the tail. "You must learn to eat, not suckle." The otter tossed the food in the air, caught it and dug in with

his teeth. Billie Wind put the remainder of the catch in the bowl with water from the pool.

"Now, how do I make a fire?" She glanced up at the top of the pit. "All that fire and no fire," she said, "but perhaps . . ."

Climbing to the last step of the sinkhole, she searched the embers until she found a flaming stick within reach. Licking her fingers she picked it up and backed down to the cave. To it she added chips from the

log, whacked off with her machete. The chips caught fire.

When the coals were red she placed the ancient bowl carefully among them, hoping the old clay could still withstand fire. Then she squatted on her heels. The water bubbled, but did not boil. It must boil. She dropped a hot stone into the pot and the water rolled, then boiled, the fish simmered and the smoke climbed through the porous holes in the limestone ceiling of the cave.

"Petang," she announced when the fish was tender. "Dinner is served. And you are going to have nice soft fish to suckle." She need not have been concerned about this problem. The little otter had chewed and swallowed the uncooked tail of the bass and was sitting on his haunches, short front legs crossed on his chest, begging for more, cooked or uncooked.

Billie Wind held out a warm bite and watched him eat it with gusto and pleasure. The sapling thrashed.

She put down her bowl and ran. Petang was close at her heels. What a mother otter does, a little otter does. Her next movements baffled him, however. She knelt down, reached out and pulled up a net. Then she lifted a fish above her head and cheered. Petang turned and scratched a flea.

"Fish," Billie Wind said addressing the bass. "Charlie Wind says that the animals talk. Tell me how you got here?"

The fish twisted in her hand. Its cold open mouth gave no answer.

Several days passed and the hot fires still burned. Each day Billie Wind would go to the surface hoping to be free, see that she was not, and climb down to play with Petang. They fished, slept and chased each other around the cave and up and down the log. Billie Wind laughed a lot at her

funny little friend and dreamed of rain. When he slept she dug into the floor, uncovering more and more treasures.

One morning she dug up the beak of a sawfish. It resembled a double-edged saw almost precisely, and she wondered if it was strong enough to cut wood.

"Three-Hands-on-the-Saddle once cut limbs with a sawfish beak," she said to herself. "Maybe I can, too." She walked out on the log and drew the strange beak across one of the limb stubs. The ancient bone crumbled.

"No more of that," she said, putting it back where she had found it. "I am going to come back here someday. I will bring an archeologist and Charlie Wind, and they will look at all these things and tell me who the ancient person was and how the fish got into this hole on this island.

"Maybe the cave will give up a secret that will solve the mystery of where the Calusa came from."

That night she lay awake for a long time thinking of her ancestors and the daily lives they lived. They had fire and tools and fish and they made beautiful pots. The ghosts of the distant past seemed to snuggle closely around her, and she felt safe. ■

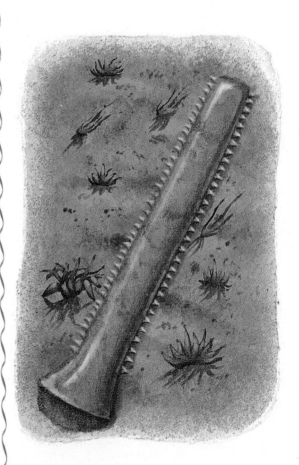

THE MOON AND THE YEAR

The moon and the year
travel and pass away:
also the day, also the wind.
Also the flesh passes away
to the place of its quietness.

a Mayan poem

Translated by John Bierhorst, based on the Spanish of Antonio Mediz Bolio

A stone bas-relief, depicting a warrior triumphing over his opponent, is located on the Tzompantli platform at Chichén Itzá, Mexico.

137

One-Eyed Cat
by Paula Fox
Dell, 1985

"Look!" he whispered.

A second cat, smaller than the first, followed it. The first cat stood straight up on its hind feet, and the second made a wreath around it. They leaped, they tumbled, they jumped and pounced, into patches of darkness then back into the light.

"They're dancing," Mama breathed.

**Almost the Real Thing:
Simulation in
Your High-Tech World**
by Gloria Skurzynski
Bradbury Press, 1991

Simulations are imitations of things that exist in the real world. Almost anything can be simulated—in images, in solid models you can touch, in sound, in motion, or in elements that you can feel, like the wind.

Mummies, Tombs, and Treasure

SECRETS OF ANCIENT EGYPT

by Lila Perl

A night view of the pyramid of King Khafre with the Sphinx in the foreground, lit by floodlights. Insets, clockwise from top: the coffin of a royal official of Thebes, a pendant from King Tutankhamen's tomb, and a statue of King Ramses II

*T*he ancient Egyptians believed that a dead person's spirit could live forever if the body was preserved as a mummy. They developed elaborate burial customs, building magnificent tombs to house the bodies of Egyptian royalty and upper-class citizens. A tomb contained everything the spirit would need for a comfortable life after death—favorite possessions, games, food, and water. Shabtis, miniature figures of humans, were placed in the tomb to act as servants to the dead. Containers called canopic jars held the deceased's preserved internal organs, which would magically rejoin the body in the afterlife. After the funeral, the tomb was sealed, supposedly forever. But often, robbers opened tombs in search of the riches buried within.

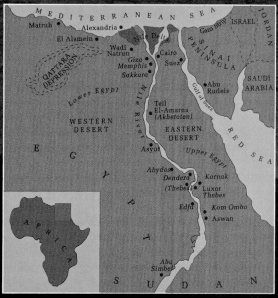

Map of Egypt today. Cities and sites of ancient Egypt are in italics.

141

A royal couple receiving offerings from their children

In the closing years of the New Kingdom, around 1100 B.C., robberies increased dramatically. Most likely this was simply because it was an age of great wealth for Egypt and there were so many rich tombs to rob. But some historians think there was another reason as well.

In the part of Asia that was closest to Egypt, the Iron Age had arrived. People learned to mine and work iron into sturdy tools and weapons. Egypt, however, did not have

The mummy of Ramses III in its tattered wrappings after its discovery in 1881 in an abandoned tomb, where it had been placed for safekeeping. The hieroglyphs at the border of this page, and the following pages, are taken from a list of ancient Egyptian rulers found at Abydos, in the Temple of Seti I.

large iron deposits. It was still making most of its tools out of bronze, a mixture of copper and tin. Egypt was forced to import iron. This caused such an increase in taxes and in the cost of living that many more people turned to thievery.

Whatever the reason, around 1000 B.C. a group of priests of the Twenty-first Dynasty took steps to rescue the tattered remains of some of the royal mummies whose graves had been looted. They found an abandoned tomb near the temple of Queen Hatshepsut and secretly transferred the mummies to the new hiding place. Many were re-bandaged and marked with their names taken from the old wrap-pings. Even the dates of rewrapping were inscribed on the cloth. Some of the mummies were given new coffins. Also reburied with them were those belongings the thieves had ignored as being of lesser value. Among them were papyrus scrolls, canopic jars, and *shabtis*.

For nearly three thousand years the mummies rested peace-fully in their new home. Then, in 1875, unusual objects began to ap-pear for sale in the shops, hotels, and bazaars of Luxor. This new city had sprung to life on the east bank of the Nile, on the site of ancient Thebes. Ever since the early 1800s, when Egypt's past had begun to be revealed through the discovery of the Rosetta Stone, the country had been swarming with foreign visitors. Among them were tourists, souvenir seekers, art col-lectors, and archaeologists who were studying the monuments and digging for the remains of Egypt's ancient civilization.

The mysterious objects that were coming on the market turned out to be scrolls, *shabtis*, and other articles belonging to various rulers of the New Kingdom and of the Twenty-first Dynasty, which followed it. Finally, in 1881, the Egyptian government tracked down the source of the articles. Sure enough, one of the old tomb-robbing fami-lies had been at work again. A pair of brothers had discovered the hid-ing place of the mummies near the temple of Queen Hatshepsut.

Aside from the items they had stolen, the modern tomb robbers had done little further damage to the mummies. Among them were such famed rulers of the New Kingdom as Ahmose, Amenhotep I, Thutmose I, II, and III, Seti I, and Ramses I, II, and III. With great care, the mummies were trans-ported to Cairo where many can be

seen today in the Mummy Room of the Cairo Museum.

In the case of Thutmose I, however, it was discovered that the priests of the Twenty-first Dynasty had made an error in rebandaging. The mummy labeled Thutmose I turned out to be that of an unknown youth of about eighteen. Thutmose I, who must have been about fifty when he died, has not so far been found.

In 1898, yet another tomb was found in the Valley of the Kings crammed with mummies hidden away for safekeeping by priests. In this group were found Amenhotep II, Thutmose IV, Amenhotep III, Ramses IV, and Ramses V, among others. They, too, were brought to the museum's Mummy Room to be displayed in glass cases.

Little by little the gaps in Egypt's royal history were being filled in. Mummies were being found, and so were the empty, echoing tombs of their onetime owners, magnificent with their painted walls and ceilings but bare of their contents. People wondered if anyone would ever uncover a royal tomb that looked just as it had on the day that the mourners departed and the entrance was sealed, presumably forever.

One such person was a British archaeologist named Howard Carter. He had come to Egypt in 1890 as a very young man and worked there for many years, dreaming constantly of finding an undisturbed tomb in the Valley of the Kings. Digging in the Valley was a costly undertaking, however. So Carter was lucky in having met up with a wealthy British nobleman, Lord Carnarvon, who shared Carter's goal and funded his work.

Because of his health, Lord Carnarvon spent winters in Egypt's warm, dry climate. The months from November to March were also the only time when digging in the Valley was possible. The summers were far too hot.

By 1922, Carter had spent six unsuccessful seasons fine-combing a particular part of the Valley in search of the burial place of a little-known pharaoh named Tutankhamen. Years earlier another archaeologist had discovered some puzzling remains both near and under a large tilted rock in the vicinity. They included a bit of gold leaf and a blue cup marked with Tutankhamen's name. There were also some dried floral collars and some animal bones left behind by the guests of a funeral banquet of long, long ago. Could they have

Two of the four seated sandstone colossi of the Great Temple of Ramses II, Abu Simbel, now located on the plateau above its original site

been the guests at the funeral banquet of Tutankhamen?

In the autumn of 1922 Carter arrived in the Valley for what was to be the very last season of the search for Tutankhamen. He brought with him a tiny companion, a canary, to keep him company in the small, domed house he had built for himself on the Valley road on the west bank of the Nile. The local Egyptians hired to work on the dig were amazed by the "golden bird." No songbirds had ever been seen or heard in the grim, treeless Valley.

Perhaps, as Carter's work team predicted, the little canary brought Carter luck. The site he had chosen for the last season's dig was directly under some ancient grave-workers' huts in front of the tomb of Ramses VI, a pharaoh who had lived about two hundred years later than Tutankhamen. In the past, Carter had hesitated to dig there because the empty tomb of Ramses VI was a heavily visited tourist attraction.

As it turned out, the innocent-appearing workers' huts stood atop none other than the long-forgotten tomb of Tutankhamen. On the very day that the foundations of the first hut were dug away, a step was discovered cut into the rock beneath it. Another step and then another revealed sixteen steps in all. These led down to a sealed passageway filled with broken rocks and then to a second sealed doorway leading into the tomb itself.

Carter sent a historic telegram to Lord Carnarvon who was still in England. It read: "At last have made wonderful discovery in Valley; a magnificent tomb with seals intact; re-covered same for your arrival; congratulations."

On November 26, 1922, with Lord Carnarvon beside him, Carter made an eye-level opening

Entrance **16 steps**

in the door to the tomb and put a candle through the hole. His own words record the thrill of that moment in which he glimpsed the inside of the tomb.

"At first I could see nothing, the hot air escaping from the chamber causing the candle to flicker, but presently, as my eyes grew accustomed to the light, details of the room within emerged slowly from the mist, strange animals, statues, and gold—everywhere the glint of gold. For the moment. . . . I was struck dumb with amazement, and when Lord Carnarvon, unable to stand the suspense any longer, inquired anxiously, 'Can you see anything?' it was all I could do to get out the words, 'Yes, wonderful things.'"

Carter was looking into the first of four rooms of a surprisingly small royal tomb. The Antechamber, as the first and largest room was called, was only about twelve by twenty-six feet, the measurements of a fair-sized living room. It was heaped with chairs, footstools, and chests of alabaster, ebony, and ivory, and strange couches of gilded wood in the form of animals, including a cow and a lion. Piled beneath the cow-bed were egg-shaped food containers made of clay.

Sealed doorways, one guarded by two gold-encrusted statues of Tutankhamen, led to the other three rooms of the tomb—an Annex that was even more jumbled than the Antechamber, the Burial Chamber in which the mummy lay, and a small room beyond that called the Treasury.

Carter was not surprised at the disarray that met his eyes, for he had already suspected that Tutankhamen's tomb had been broken into in ancient times. But the robbers had had to leave hastily, even dropping some gold rings and other small articles on their way out. Their lost loot had probably included the bit of gold leaf and the blue cup found outside the tomb in Carter's day. The cemetery officials of ancient times had apparently roughly tidied and resealed the tomb. Then, happily, its entrance had been completely covered over by the building of the Ramses VI workers' huts.

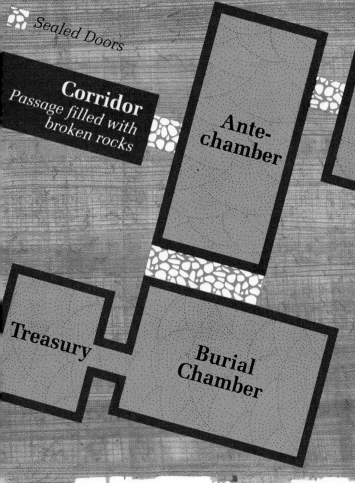

Sealed Doors

Corridor
Passage filled with broken rocks

Ante-chamber

Annex

Treasury

Burial Chamber

The floor plan of the tomb of Tutankhamen

Three anxious and tension-filled years were to pass before the great moment when Carter opened the coffin containing the mummy of Tutankhamen. During that time, while he was carefully cataloging and clearing the contents of the Antechamber, a number of strange events took place.

First, Carter's canary was eaten by a poisonous desert snake.

Those who were superstitious took it as a bad omen. Did the snake represent the pharaoh's anger at having had his tomb disturbed? On his death mask, it was later discovered, Tutankhamen wore the cobra and vulture, twin royal symbols of Lower and Upper Egypt.

Next, less than five months after the opening of the tomb, Lord

The jumbled treasure in the first room of Tutankhamen's tomb as first seen by Howard Carter

Carnarvon died of blood poisoning from a mysterious insect bite on his cheek that had become infected. He was never to see the great, carved stone coffin in the Burial Chamber that rested inside a series of four nested wooden cases covered with gold leaf. Nor was he ever to see the three richly gleaming mummy-shaped coffins nested inside the rectangular stone coffin or, of course, the mummy of Tutankhamen.

Lastly, soon after the discovery of the tomb, Carter himself ran up against numerous problems with the Egyptian government. One of the disputes had to do with which officials and their guests were to be permitted to visit the tomb while the delicate work of recording its contents was going on.

For a time the tomb was sealed up, and Carter actually left Egypt in anger and despair.

Did all of these unpleasant happenings have a hidden meaning? Was there such a thing as a "mummy's curse"? Were Carter and Carnarvon being punished for unearthing the resting place of the pharaoh who had slept longer in his treasure-filled tomb than any other yet known?

Many people thought so. They went to great trouble to try to prove that death was stalking and striking all who had worked with Carter, from the humblest laborer to the most distinguished archaeologist. But Carter himself never believed the wild stories that sprang from his discovery. And, in fact, he went on to live for many more years, dying in 1939 at the age of sixty-five.

The first viewing of Tutankhamen's mummy took place at last in the autumn of 1925. Of the three mummy-shaped coffins, the two outer ones were of wood covered with sheets of gold, while the innermost was of solid gold!

Inside the gold innermost coffin lay the bandaged mummy of Tutankhamen, its head and shoulders covered with a solid-gold mask

inlaid with blue lapis lazuli, other semi-precious stones, and colored glass. The mask, serene, youthful, and noble, shows the king wearing the ceremonial false beard and a striped headcloth called a *nemes* (NEM-eez) with the royal cobra and vulture at the brow.

The hasty thieves of ancient times who had invaded Tutankhamen's tomb had been looking only for small objects they could carry away quickly. They had entered the Burial Chamber but had never broken into any of its nested coffins.

On unwrapping the mummy, Carter discovered that there were thirteen layers of linen bandages containing one hundred and forty-three precious gold and bejeweled objects. Among them

The solid-gold mask found on the mummy of Tutankhamen (left)

The outermost gilded wood coffin in which the mummy of King Tutankhamen rests today in the Burial Chamber of his tomb (bottom)

were necklaces, collars, pendants, bracelets, rings, belts, gold-sheathed daggers, gold sandals, and slender golden tubes that encased the mummy's fingernails and toenails.

Beneath all this splendor, however, the mummy itself was a pitiful disappointment. Blackened and shrunken by the careless pouring on of oils and resins, it was one of the poorer examples of the New Kingdom art of mummification.

Who was Tutankhamen? Why was he buried in such a small tomb with such great riches? Why was his mummy so badly prepared?

To Carter's disappointment, no papyrus scrolls telling anything of Tutankhamen's reign or of his family history were found in the tomb. We know only that he is believed to have been either the brother or the illegitimate son of the previous king, Amenhotep IV, who had turned away from the many gods of Thebes to worship the sun as the one and only god. In so doing, Amenhotep IV changed his name to Akhenaten (Ahk-eh-NAH-ten), meaning "pleasing to Aten" (the sun). He also moved his capital from Thebes to a new site known as Akhetaten (Ahk-eh-TAH-ten), or "horizon of the Aten."

As Akhenaten's successor, Tutankhamen is thought to have come to the throne as a child of nine, to have reigned briefly, and to have died as a youth of eighteen. He married a princess who may have been his half-sister. He left no heirs. In the richly stocked Treasury, the room just off the Burial Chamber, Carter found two tiny coffins with the mummified remains of girl infants who had probably been dead at birth. Were they the children of Tutankhamen and his young wife?

As to Tutankhamen himself, we do not know how or why he died. Was his death caused by an accident, an illness, or could he have been murdered? There is a suspicious scar, possibly from an arrow tip, in front of the mummy's ear. Did the priests of Thebes who served the many gods want Tutankhamen dead because of his relationship with Akhenaten, who had turned his back on their religion?

Whatever the reason, Tutankhamen's sudden death may account for the small size of his tomb.

Perhaps it had been meant for someone else but was used for the young pharaoh because his own was not ready. On the other hand, Tutankhamen may simply have been an unimportant king who, through Howard Carter's discovery, became the most famous of all of Egypt's kings.

If Tutankhamen's treasure, however, was that of an "unimportant" king buried in a hastily prepared tomb, can we ever guess at the splendor of the contents of those much larger and grander tombs that the grave robbers of Egypt emptied thousands of years ago!

Gold collar from Tomb of Tutankhamen (left), c. 1342 B.C.; detail from Tomb of Amunherkhopshef, son of Ramses III (below), c. 1160 B.C.

Meet Lila Perl

Author Lila Perl says that when she was growing up, she "never thought of being a writer." But, as a child, she unknowingly laid the foundation for becoming one. As she says, "I read a lot. Every time I was told to 'go outside and play,' I went off somewhere with a book." She has written more than fifteen books, including cookbooks and fiction and nonfiction books for young adults.

Perl hopes that her joy in creating each story comes across to her readers. Letters from her readers are a source of great satisfaction to her, and she says that "every single letter is answered."

Perl's first book for young adults, *Red-Flannel Hash and Shoo-Fly Pie: American Regional Foods and Festivals,* was an ALA Notable Book.

From Top Hats to Baseball Caps, From Bustles to Blue Jeans
Why We Dress the Way We Do
by LILA PERL

UNDER WRAPS

*Did you ever wonder exactly
how the Egyptians were able to create mummies
that have lasted for thousands of years?*

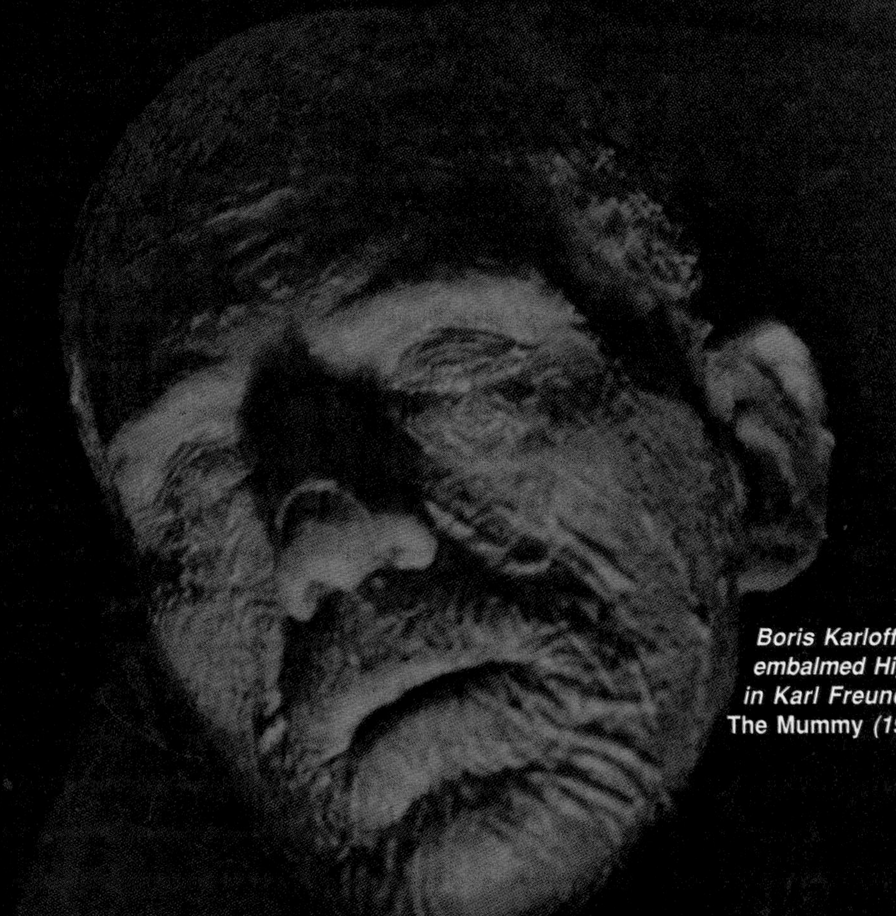

Boris Karloff as the
embalmed High Priest
in Karl Freund's
The Mummy *(1932)*

Egyptian mummification took about ten weeks to complete. First, the dead person's internal organs were removed, and the inside of the body was washed. Then, the body was covered with a drying powder called natron. The hot desert climate, aided by the powder, dried the body completely. Forty days later, the body was rubbed with oils, spices, and herbs. Resin, a varnishlike substance, was poured on the body to seal it. Finally, the body was wrapped in as much as 150 yards (135 meters) of linen. When the mummification was finished, priests placed the body in a coffin and buried it in a tomb.

Of course, the Egyptians were not the only ancient people to mummify their dead. Mummies have been unearthed all over the world. Some were made on purpose, while others were the result of natural conditions. All offer fascinating clues about the past.

The Incas mummified the bodies of everyone after death. A member of royalty who died, however, was given special treatment. The tomb was lavish, of course. In addition, workers served the mummy as if it were alive for about a year—even arranging for visitors that the dead ruler wished to see!

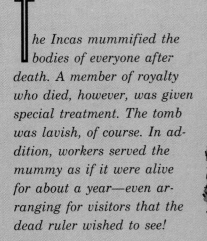

In this photo, a doctor X-rays a mummy that was discovered by construction workers in China in the 1970s. Inside the sealed burial mound, the workers found several coffins, one inside the other. The body of a woman lay in the innermost coffin. She was so well preserved that her joints could still be bent— 2,100 years after her burial!

Mummies are often created by natural conditions. A Native American found buried in a Wyoming cave had been preserved solely by the cave's dryness and stable temperature. The mummy's careful placement and ornamental collar showed that he had been an important person among his people. A mummy known today as the Tollund Man was found in the peat bogs of Denmark in 1950. Formed from dense layers of plants, the bogs contain few of the bacteria that normally break down dead matter. Although he was buried possibly two thousand years ago, the man appeared to have died only recently. Scientists even found traces of his last meal in his stomach!

Tollund Man, a two-thousand-year-old mummy, found in the peat bogs of Denmark, 1950.

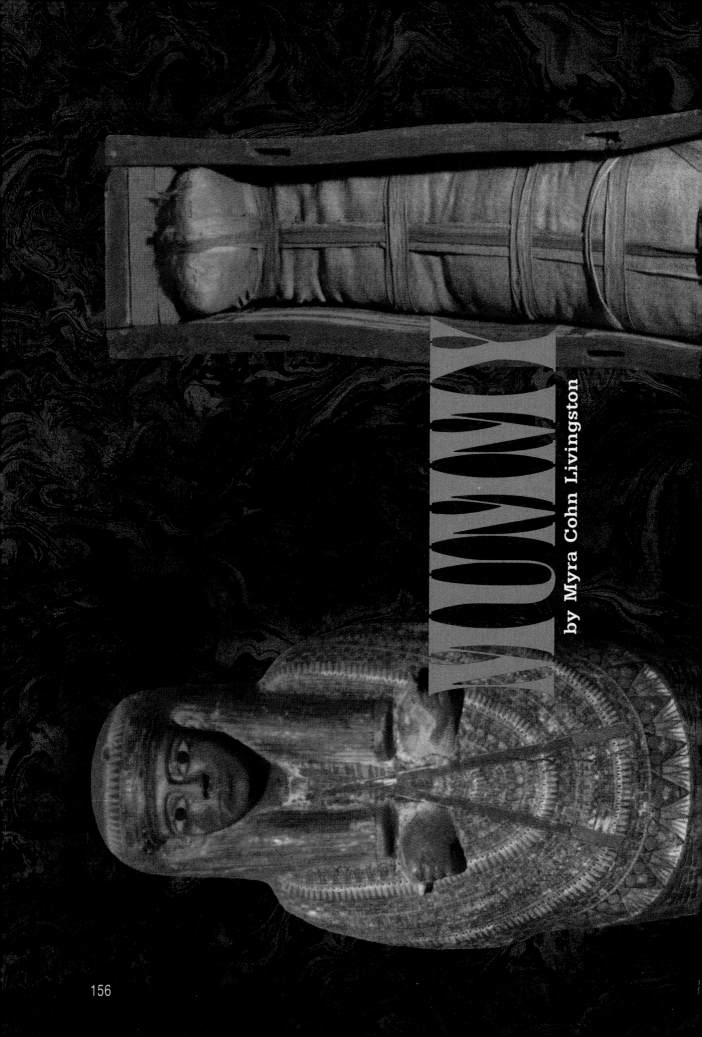

MUMMY

by Myra Cohn Livingston

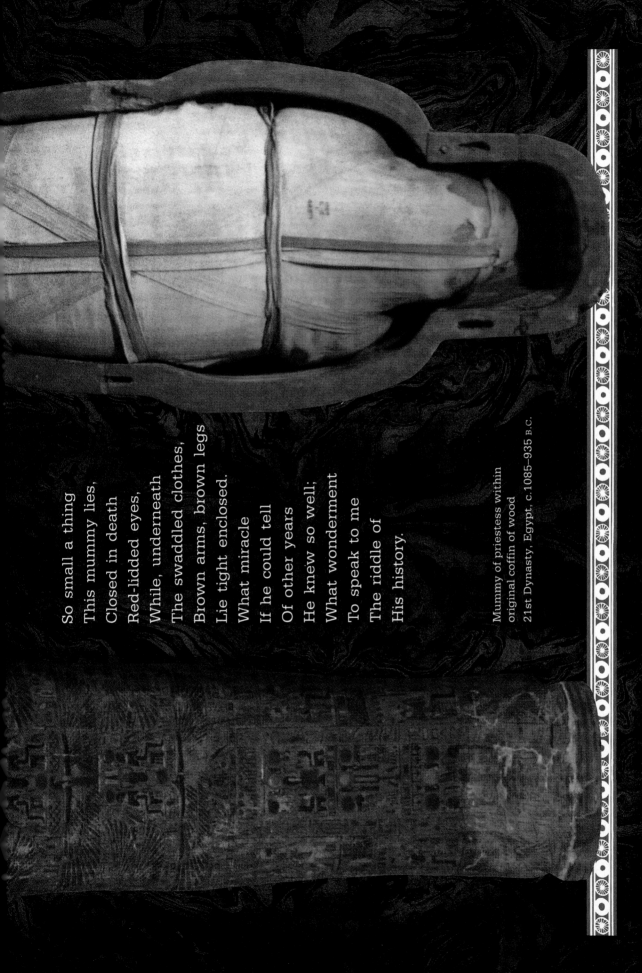

So small a thing
This mummy lies,
Closed in death
Red-lidded eyess,
While, underneath
The swaddled clothes,
Brown arms, brown legs
Lie tight enclosed.
What miracle
If he could tell
Of other years
He knew so well;
What wonderment
To speak to me
The riddle of
His history.

Mummy of priestess within
original coffin of wood
21st Dynasty, Egypt. c.1085–935 B.C.

157

Uranus Neptune Pluto

DARK WORLDS

by Patricia Lauber

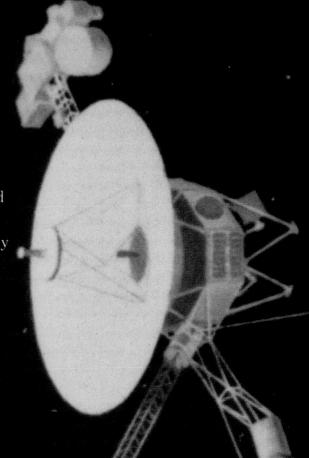

It takes very sharp eyes to see the dim gleam of Uranus in our night sky. The planet is one of the giants, but it is so far from the sun—1¾ billion miles—that it reflects little light. Through a telescope Uranus appears only as a ghostly blue-green globe.

Even so, astronomers had learned a surprising amount about Uranus before *Voyager 2* reached the planet in January 1986. They knew that the atmosphere held clouds of methane, which gave the planet its color. They knew that Uranus was oddly tilted on its axis. In effect, the planet lies on its side. For part of the year, the north pole faces the sun, then the equator does, then the south pole, then the equator.

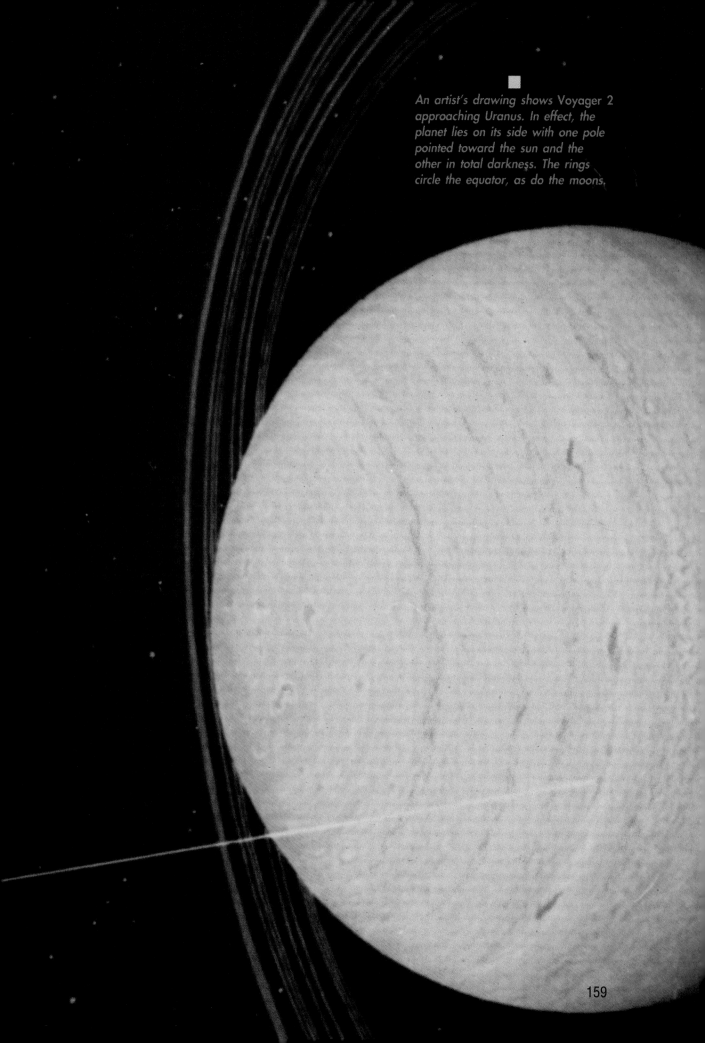

An artist's drawing shows Voyager 2 approaching Uranus. In effect, the planet lies on its side with one pole pointed toward the sun and the other in total darkness. The rings circle the equator, as do the moons.

Scientists think young Uranus may have collided with an Earth-sized object and been knocked onto its side. Uranus takes 84 years to complete one orbit of the sun.

Astronomers had also learned that Uranus had at least nine dark rings and five moons. *Voyager* gave them a good look at the rings and moons.

Unlike Saturn's broad rings of bright, icy particles, the Uranian ones are narrow bands made of chunks of black material that look like lumps of coal ranging in size from 3 to 3,000 feet across. They circle the planet at its equator and revolve around it once every eight hours. As well as the previously known rings, scientists saw two others. Among the rings they also discovered ten small moons. Two appear to be the kind of sheepdog moons found in the rings of Saturn.

The five known moons were surprising. Scientists had thought they might be balls of ice mixed with a little rock and pocked with craters. Instead, they found dingy surfaces, more rock than they had expected, and a number of strange features, perhaps caused by mammoth collisions with comets, perhaps by gravitational tugs from other moons and Uranus, perhaps

by the freezing of material inside the moons.

The two outermost moons, Oberon and Titania, are both about 1,000 miles in diameter and heavily cratered. Several craters on Oberon appear to have been flooded with some kind of dark material. The moon has a mountain that sticks up at least 12 miles above the horizon and a number of straight and curved cliffs. Titania has trenches and cliffs and a strange frostlike pattern that runs beside big cracks, suggesting that material sprayed out, froze, and fell to the surface.

The third moon is Umbriel. Its surface is dark, old, and covered

■

Titania (right) is marked by craters and fault valleys. What may be frost can be seen along the valley's right center. The icy face of Oberon (below), outermost of the moons, is scarred by impact craters with white rays. A crater with a peak can be seen at center. A mountain can be seen at the lower left edge of the moon.

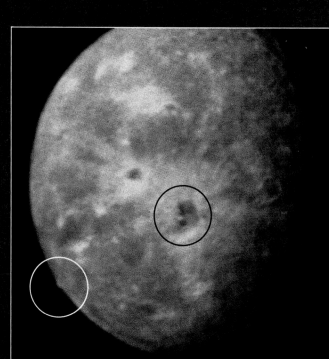

with big craters. No one knows why the surface is dark or why Umbriel does not show the signs of change that the other moons do.

Ariel, the next moon in, is about the same size as Umbriel—700 miles in diameter. It is crisscrossed with broad, curving valleys and has jagged canyons. Some of its features appear to have been smoothed over, perhaps by glaciers or flooding.

Strangest of all is Miranda, the innermost and smallest moon, only 300 miles in diameter. It looks like a patchwork of features from other moons and planets. Like Mars, Miranda has long, curving valleys. Like Jupiter's Ganymede, it has grooves; some come together in V-shaped patterns, while others form ovals within ovals, in a race-track pattern. Miranda has cratered highlands that look like those of Earth's moon and cliffs that are ten times higher than the walls of the Grand Canyon. Why Miranda looks as it does is a puzzle. One idea is that the small moon has been blasted apart in giant collisions and that its gravity plastered the pieces back together again.

Uranus itself also offered a number of surprises and puzzles. One puzzle has to do with the

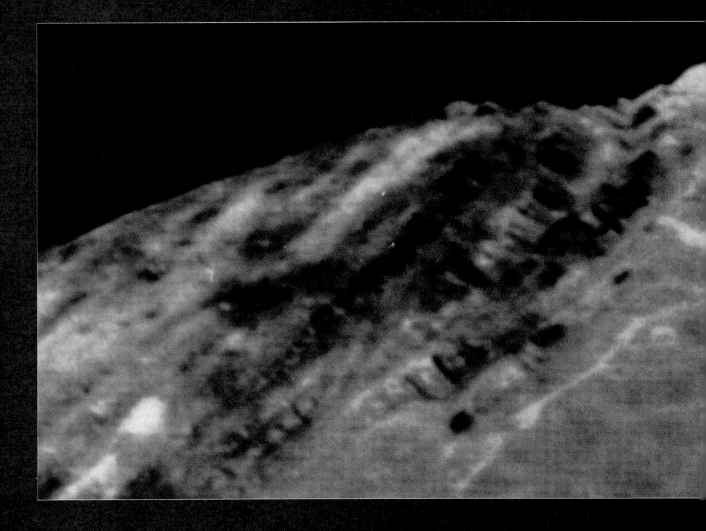

planet's magnetic poles. On other planets, such as Earth, the magnetic poles are close to the geographic poles. On Uranus they are not. If the earth's magnetic poles were like those of Uranus, one would be at Los Angeles and the other in the Indian Ocean. Another puzzle had to do with temperature, which was the same at the pole

Umbriel's cratered surface (left) is probably the oldest in the system of Uranian moons. Its strangest feature is the bright ring at top, which may be related to a crater.

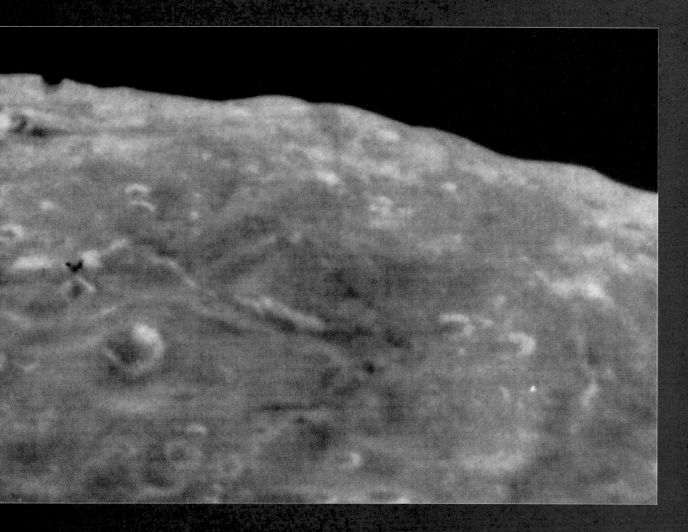

facing the sun as at the equator. The region between the two was colder. Scientists wondered whether these odd findings had to do with the fact that Uranus is tipped over on its side. Then, some three and a half years later, *Voyager* arrived at Neptune and made the same discoveries about tipped magnetic poles and temperatures. Because

■

Right, cliffs and winding valleys crisscross the crater-pocked face of Ariel. At the top left portion of the planet (above), stepped terraces jut up on Miranda. They mark the edge of one of the sets of ovals within ovals.

Neptune is not tipped over but sits upright, scientists knew they would have to start over in their search for an explanation.

At the time *Voyager* reached Neptune, in late summer of 1989, little was known about the planet. Outermost of the giants, it is so dim and distant that it cannot be seen from Earth without a telescope, and a telescope shows only a faint greenish planet with some markings in its atmosphere. Scientists knew that Neptune took 165 years to travel once around the sun, that it had at least two moons, a big one and a small one, and that it seemed to have pieces of rings. They expected to find a near-twin of Uranus. The two planets are about the same size. Each is a big ball of molten rock and water wrapped in an atmosphere of hydrogen, helium, and methane. They seem more closely related to comets than to Jupiter and Saturn—and may, indeed, have formed out of colliding comets.

But as *Voyager* neared Neptune, surprise followed surprise. Neptune turned out to be warmer than Uranus, even though it is a billion miles farther from the sun. The temperature in its upper atmosphere is 261 degrees below zero, as compared with –360 degrees on Uranus. Unlike Uranus, Neptune has its own heat, probably left over from the days of its formation. The heat disturbs the frigid gases of the atmosphere and sets them rolling, with winds of up to 1,500 miles an hour. And there is still more weather. Neptune has a giant storm system, the size of Earth, where winds blow at 700 miles an hour. Because it reminded them of Jupiter's Great Red Spot, scientists named it the Great Dark Spot. A smaller storm system lies farther south in the atmosphere.

Alone among the giant planets, Neptune has fleecy white clouds that look like cirrus clouds on Earth. Some stretch out for thousands of miles. The clouds may be pockets of frozen methane. Some seem attached to the Great Dark Spot and the smaller dark spot.

Before *Voyager* reached Neptune, the planet appeared to have pieces of rings—bright arcs— circling it. Pictures from the spacecraft show that Neptune's rings are complete and that there are at least five. One of them, however, has places where material clumps together and the ring thickens. From far, far away, these places looked like arcs.

The arcs turned out to be bright clumps of matter in Neptune's outer ring. This picture shows only the two brightest rings. Scientists cannot be sure exactly how many rings Neptune has.

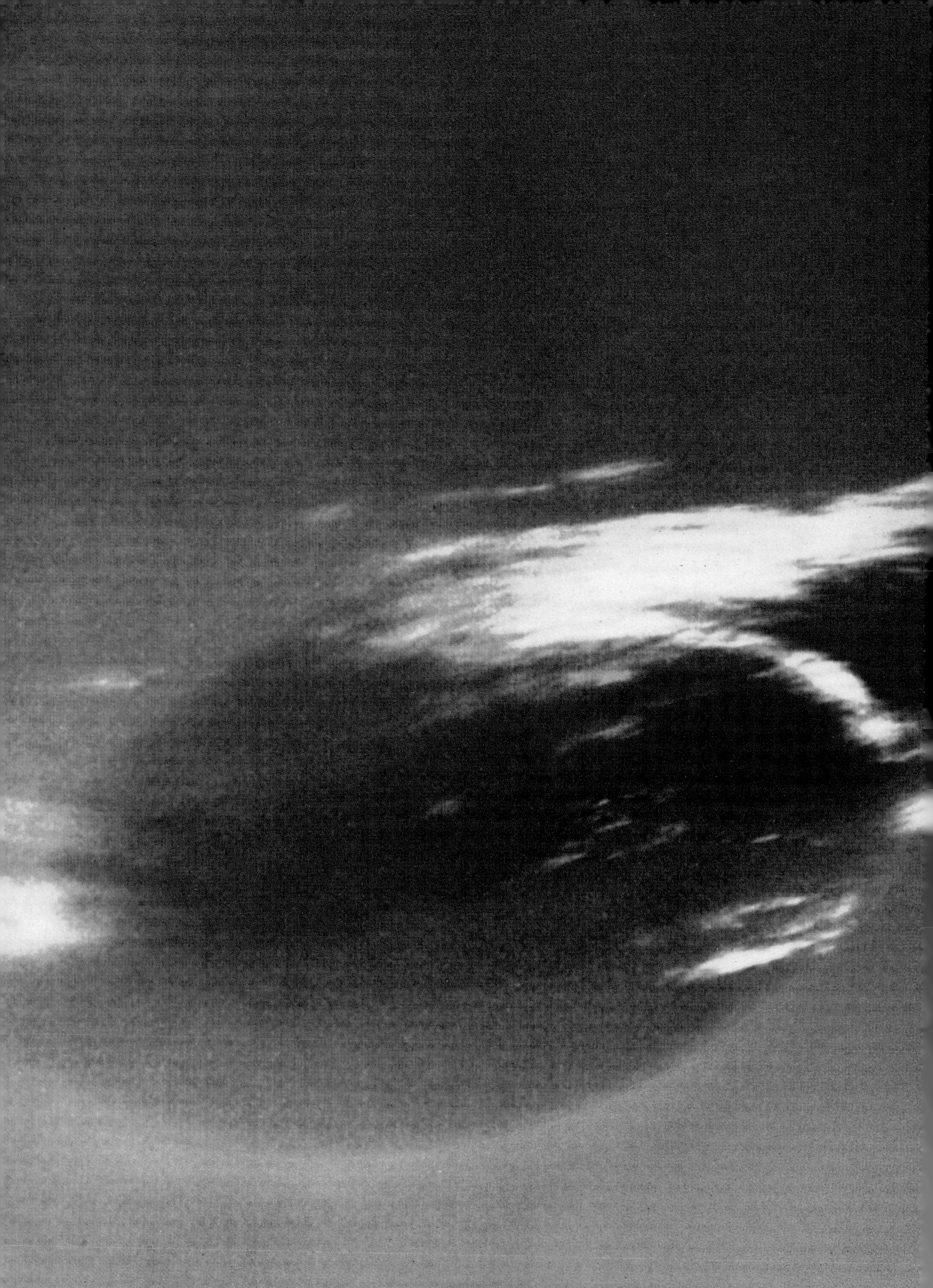

Scientists suspect that the clumping may be caused by the kind of sheepdog moons found in the rings of Saturn and Uranus, even though *Voyager* did not see any. But it did find six previously unknown moons, fewer than scientists had expected. All are dark and small—30 to 300 miles in diameter—with odd shapes and battered faces.

The two moons known earlier are Nereid and Triton. Nereid, which is the smaller, has an unusual orbit. It is both large and oval, unlike the circular orbits of most moons. Scientists think this moon may be an object, such as an asteroid, that was captured by Neptune's gravity.

Triton is "a world unlike any other," scientists say. Early pictures showed a ball glazed with methane and nitrogen ice blitzed pink by radiation. Closer up, the moon proved to have a large cap at its south pole, possibly made of nitrogen ice. The regions beyond the polar cap are crinkled landscapes of canyons and peaks that look like the skin of a cantaloupe. They are slashed by long cracks that meet in X's and Y's, like highway intersections. Surface temperatures are 400 degrees below zero, making Triton the coldest place known in the solar system.

Triton has a very thin atmosphere, made mostly of nitrogen. For reasons not yet understood, the top of the atmosphere is warmer than the surface of the moon.

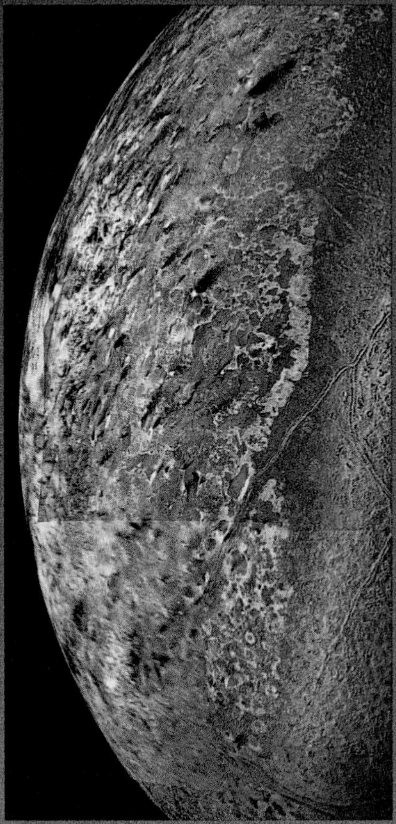

■

Voyager discovered two huge storm systems on Neptune, the Great Dark Spot and the smaller dark spot, with a bright center, farther south (shown opposite, far left). The small dark spot rotated at the same speed as the planet: once every 16 hours and three minutes. The Great Dark Spot took about 18 hours. Between the two storm systems is a bright feature nicknamed Scooter, because of the speed at which it moves. The white clouds are the only ones ever seen in the atmospheres of the outer planets. Triton's large south polar ice cap (above left) is to the left of a region that looks like the skin of a cantaloupe, marked by canyons and peaks and giant cracks that intersect one another. In this picture the cap is at the height of its 41-year-long summer and has evaporated away in places along its edge.

As scientists studied the surface of Triton, they were struck by the fact that the big moon had few craters, although like the planets and other moons, it too must have been bombarded. They think this is a sign of internal heat, that the moon must have been stretched and compressed, like Jupiter's Europa and Io. Slush forced its way up through the big cracks and resurfaced the moon, hiding the craters.

There is every reason to think that Triton still holds heat. The clue to this heat was the most surprising discovery of all: volcanoes. Careful study of pictures from *Voyager* showed violent plumes of gas erupting from the face of the moon and reaching several miles into space. The discovery made Triton the second moon known to have volcanoes.

Scientists had long known that Triton was a big moon. Close up, it proved to be 1,700 miles in diameter, a little smaller than anyone had thought and about 400 miles smaller than Earth's moon. They had also known that Triton orbited Neptune backward. Some small moons, which are probably captured asteroids, orbit their planets backward, but no other big moon does. Except for Triton, big moons all move in the same direction that their planets spin. This led scientists to wonder if Triton was originally a small planet that was captured by Neptune and became a big moon.

The new findings from *Voyager* support this idea. As Triton began to orbit Neptune, it would have swept up smaller moons, leaving only the few that *Voyager* saw. It would have been pumped by Neptune and heated up inside. And Pluto, which probably formed at the same time as Triton, would

Pluto's tiny size and great distance make it look like a faint star, even when photographed through a telescope. But Pluto is orbiting the sun and moving against the fixed stars.

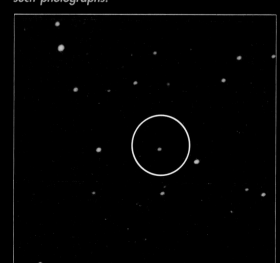

It can be identified in photographs taken only 24 hours apart, as these were. Pluto was discovered in 1930 by comparing such photographs.

have become the one small planet in the outer solar system, so far out that it takes 248 Earth years to orbit the sun.

Pluto's orbit is peculiar. It is more oval than that of any other planet, and it crosses Neptune's orbit. In 1979 Pluto's orbit brought the planet inside Neptune's, where it will stay until 1999. During that time Neptune will be the planet farthest from the sun.

Pluto is about the same size as Triton and probably also has a thin atmosphere. At least some of its surface is covered with ice. The small planet has a large moon named Charon, with a diameter nearly a third of its own. The moon orbits close to Pluto, and each always keeps the same face toward the other. They are more like a double planet than a planet and a moon.

Although *Voyager* could not visit Pluto, scientists feel, in a way, that they have already seen the planet—that when some spacecraft does reach Pluto, it will turn out to be much like Triton, but without volcanoes.

Meet Patricia Lauber

From the volcanoes of Earth to the farthest reaches of the solar system, Patricia Lauber's books span a wide variety of subjects. "My ideas come from everywhere—from things I read, from things people tell me about . . . from things I experience." Lauber believes that "sailing a boat or exploring a forest can often be described as 'doing research.'" It is important to Lauber that her subjects interest her very much, because then, she says, "I want to share them with other people and so I write about them."

Journey to the Planets, which includes the chapter "Uranus, Neptune, Pluto: Dark Worlds," received an American Book Award nomination. *Volcano: The Eruption and Healing of Mount St. Helens* was a Newbery Honor Book.

*The poem should be like a star
which is a world and looks like a diamond.*

—Juan Ramón Jiménez

Bicycle Riding

My feet rise
off the planet,
pedal wheels of steel
that sparkle as
they spin me through
the open space I feel
winging out
to galaxies
far beyond the sun,
where bicycles
are satellites,
their orbits never done.

—SANDRA LIATSOS

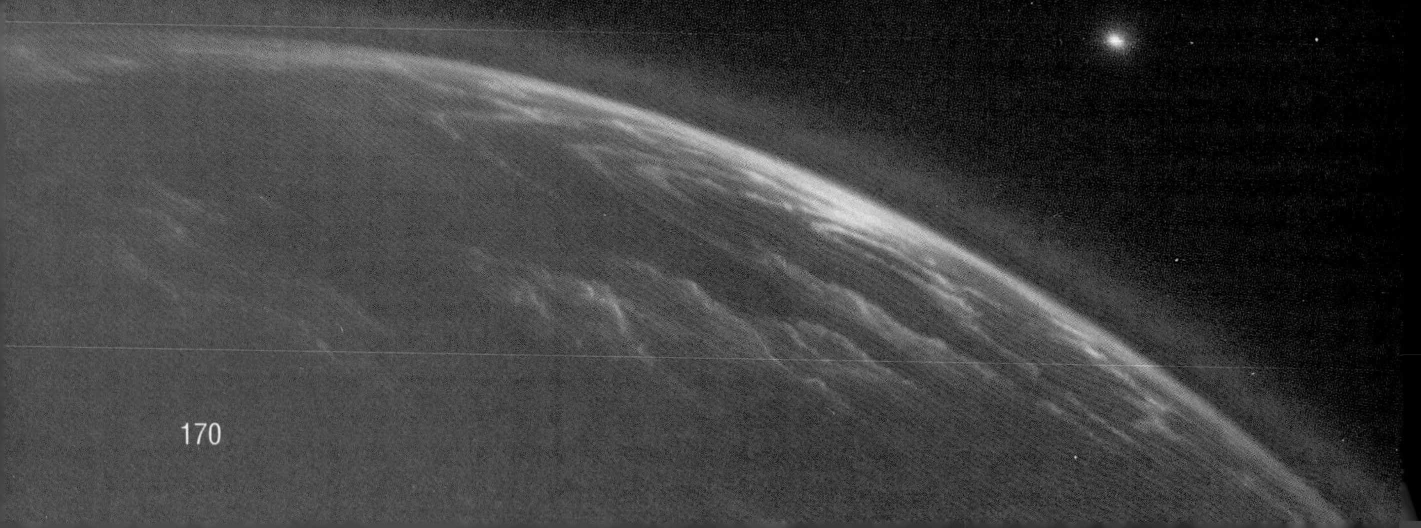

CONTENTS

AT THE TOP OF MY VOICE

When I stamp
The ground thunders,

When I shout
The world rings,

When I sing
The air wonders

How I do such things.

FELICE HOLMAN

Petronella

by Jay Williams

In the kingdom of Skyclear Mountain, three princes were always born to the king and queen. The oldest prince was always called Michael, the middle prince was always called George, and the youngest was always called Peter. When they were grown, they always went out to seek their fortunes. What happened to the oldest prince and the middle prince no one ever knew. But the youngest prince always rescued a princess, brought her home, and in time ruled over the kingdom. That was the way it had always been. And so far as anyone knew, that was the way it would always be.

illustrated by Joe Boddy

Until now?

Now was the time of King Peter the twenty-sixth and Queen Blossom. An oldest prince was born, and a middle prince. But the youngest prince turned out to be a girl.

"Well," said the king gloomily, "we can't call her Peter. We'll have to call her Petronella. And what's to be done about it, I'm sure I don't know."

There was nothing to be done. The years passed, and the time came for the princes to go out and seek their fortunes. Michael and George said good-bye to the king and queen and mounted their horses. Then out came Petronella. She was dressed in traveling clothes, with her bag packed and a sword by her side.

"If you think," she said, "that I'm going to sit at home, you are mistaken. I'm going to seek my fortune, too."

"Impossible!" said the king.

"What will people say?" cried the queen.

"Look," said Prince Michael, "be reasonable, Pet. Stay home. Sooner or later a prince will turn up here."

Petronella smiled. She was a tall, handsome girl with flaming red hair and when she smiled in that particular way it meant she was trying to keep her temper.

"I'm going with you," she said. "I'll find a prince if I have to rescue one from something myself. And that's that."

The grooms brought out her horse, she said good-bye to her parents, and away she went behind her two brothers.

They traveled into the flatlands below Skyclear Mountain. After many days, they entered a great dark forest. They came to a place where the road divided into three, and there at the fork sat a little, wrinkled old man covered with dust and spiderwebs.

Prince Michael said haughtily, "Where do these roads go, old man?"

"The road on the right goes to the city of Gratz," the man replied. "The road in the center goes to the castle of Blitz. The road on the left goes to the house of Albion the enchanter. And that's one."

"What do you mean by 'And that's one'?" asked Prince George.

"I mean," said the old man, "that I am forced to sit on this spot without stirring, and that I must answer one question from each person who passes by. And that's two."

Petronella's kind heart was touched. "Is there anything I can do to help you?" she asked.

The old man sprang to his feet. The dust fell from him in clouds.

"You have already done so," he said. "For that question is the one which releases me. I have sat here for sixty-two years waiting for someone to ask me that." He snapped his fingers with joy. "In return, I will tell you anything you wish to know."

"Where can I find a prince?" Petronella said promptly.

"There is one in the house of Albion the enchanter," the old man answered.

"Ah," said Petronella, "then that is where I am going."

"In that case I will leave you," said her oldest brother. "For I am going to the castle of Blitz to see if I can find my fortune there."

"Good luck," said Prince George. "For I am going to the city of Gratz. I have a feeling my fortune is there."

They embraced her and rode away.

Petronella looked thoughtfully at the old man, who was combing spiderwebs and dust out of his beard. "May I ask you something else?" she said.

"Of course. Anything."

"Suppose I wanted to rescue that prince from the enchanter. How would I go about it? I haven't any experience in such things, you see."

The old man chewed a piece of his beard. "I do not know everything," he said, after a moment. "I know that there are three magical secrets which, if you can get them from him, will help you."

"How can I get them?" asked Petronella.

"Offer to work for him. He will set you three tasks, and if you can do them you may demand a reward for each. You must ask him for a comb for your hair, a mirror to look into, and a ring for your finger."

"And then?"

"I do not know. I only know that when you rescue the prince, you can use these things to escape from the enchanter."

"It doesn't sound easy," sighed Petronella.

"Nothing we really want is easy," said the old man. "Look at me—I have wanted my freedom, and I've had to wait sixty-two years for it."

Petronella said good-bye to him. She mounted her horse and galloped along the third road.

It ended at a low, rambling house with a red roof. It was a comfortable-looking house, surrounded by gardens and stables and trees heavy with fruit.

On the lawn, in an armchair, sat a handsome young man with his eyes closed and his face turned to the sky.

Petronella tied her horse to the gate and walked across the lawn.

"Is this the house of Albion the enchanter?" she said.

The young man blinked up at her in surprise.

"I think so," he said. "Yes, I'm sure it is."

"And who are you?"

The young man yawned and stretched. "I am Prince Ferdinand of Firebright," he replied. "Would you mind stepping aside? I'm trying to get a suntan and you're standing in the way."

"I am Prince Ferdinand...."

Petronella snorted. "You don't sound like much of a prince," she said.

"That's funny," said the young man, closing his eyes. "That's what my father always says."

At that moment the door of the house opened. Out came a man dressed all in black and silver. He was tall and thin, and his eyes were as black as a cloud full of thunder. Petronella knew at once that he must be the enchanter.

He bowed to her politely. "What can I do for you?"

"I wish to work for you," said Petronella boldly.

Albion nodded. "I cannot refuse you," he said. "But I warn you, it will be dangerous. Tonight I will give you a task. If you do it, I will reward you. If you fail, you must die."

Petronella glanced at the prince and sighed. "If I must, I must," she said. "Very well."

That evening they all had dinner together in the enchanter's cozy kitchen. Then Albion took Petronella out to a stone building and unbolted its door. Inside were seven huge black dogs.

"You must watch my hounds all night," said he.

Petronella went in, and Albion closed and locked the door.

At once the hounds began to snarl and bark. They bared their teeth at her. But Petronella was a real princess. She plucked up her courage. Instead of backing away, she went toward the dogs. She began to speak to them in a quiet voice. They stopped snarling and sniffed at her. She patted their heads.

"I see what it is," she said. "You are lonely here. I will keep you company."

And so all night long, she sat on the floor and talked to the hounds and stroked them. They lay close to her, panting.

In the morning Albion came and let her out. "Ah," said he, "I see that you are brave. If you had run from the dogs, they would have torn you to pieces. Now you may ask for what you want."

"I want a comb for my hair," said Petronella.

The enchanter gave her a comb carved from a piece of black wood.

Prince Ferdinand was sunning himself and working at a crossword puzzle. Petronella said to him in a low voice, "I am doing this for you."

"That's nice," said the prince. "What's 'selfish' in nine letters?"

"You are," snapped Petronella. She went to the enchanter. "I will work for you once more," she said.

That night Albion led her to a stable. Inside were seven huge horses.

"Tonight," he said, "you must watch my steeds."

He went out and locked the door. At once the horses began to rear and neigh. They pawed at her with their iron hoofs.

But Petronella was a real princess. She looked closely at them and saw that their coats were rough and their manes and tails full of burrs.

"I see what it is," she said. "You are hungry and dirty."

She brought them as much hay as they could eat, and began to brush them. All night long she fed them and groomed them, and they stood quietly in their stalls.

In the morning Albion let her out. "You are as kind as you are brave," said he. "If you had run from them they would have trampled you under their hoofs. What will you have as a reward?"

"I want a mirror to look into," said Petronella.

The enchanter gave her a mirror made of silver.

She looked across the lawn at Prince Ferdinand. He was doing exercises leisurely. He was certainly handsome. She said to the enchanter, "I will work for you once more."

That night Albion led her to a loft above the stables. There, on perches, were seven great hawks.

"Tonight," said he, "you must watch my falcons."

As soon as Petronella was locked in, the hawks began to beat their wings and scream at her.

Petronella laughed. "That is not how birds sing," she said. "Listen."

She began to sing in a sweet voice. The hawks fell silent. All night long she sang to them, and they sat like feathered statues on their perches, listening.

In the morning Albion said, "You are as talented as you are kind and brave. If you had run from them, they would have pecked and clawed you without mercy. What do you want now?"

"I want a ring for my finger," said Petronella.

The enchanter gave her a ring made from a single diamond.

"I want a mirror..."

All that day and all that night Petronella slept, for she was very tired. But early the next morning, she crept into Prince Ferdinand's room. He was sound asleep, wearing purple pajamas.

"Wake up," whispered Petronella. "I am going to rescue you."

Ferdinand awoke and stared sleepily at her. "What time is it?"

"Never mind that," said Petronella. "Come on!"

"But I'm sleepy," Ferdinand objected. "And it's so pleasant here."

Petronella shook her head. "You're not much of a prince," she said grimly. "But you're the best I can do."

She grabbed him by the wrist and dragged him out of bed. She hauled him down the stairs. His horse and hers were in a separate stable, and she saddled them quickly. She gave the prince a shove, and he mounted. She jumped on her own horse, seized the prince's reins, and away they went like the wind.

They had not gone far when they heard a tremendous thumping. Petronella looked back. A dark cloud rose behind them, and beneath it she saw the enchanter. He was running with great strides, faster than the horses could go.

"What shall we do?" she cried.

"Don't ask me," said Prince Ferdinand grumpily. "I'm all shaken to bits by this fast riding."

Petronella desperately pulled out the comb. "The old man said this would help me!" she said. And because she didn't know what else to do with it, she threw the comb on the ground. At once a forest rose up. The trees were so thick that no one could get between them.

Away went Petronella and the prince. But the enchanter turned himself into an ax and began to chop. Right and left he chopped, slashing, and the trees fell before him.

Soon he was through the wood, and once again Petronella heard his footsteps thumping behind.

She reined in the horses. She took out the mirror and threw it on the ground. At once a wide lake spread out behind them, gray and glittering.

Off they went again. But the enchanter sprang into the water, turning himself into a salmon as he did so. He swam across the lake and leaped out of the water on to the other bank. Petronella heard him coming—*thump! thump!*—behind them again.

This time she threw down the ring. It didn't turn into anything, but lay shining on the ground.

The enchanter came running up. And as he jumped over the ring, it opened wide and then snapped up around him. It held his arms tight to his body, in a magical grip from which he could not escape.

"Well," said Prince Ferdinand, "that's the end of him."

Petronella looked at him in annoyance. Then she looked at the enchanter, held fast in the ring.

"Bother!" she said. "I can't just leave him here. He'll starve to death."

She got off her horse and went up to him. "If I release you," she said, "will you promise to let the prince go free?"

Albion stared at her in astonishment. "Let him go free?" he said. "What are you talking about? I'm glad to get rid of him."

It was Petronella's turn to look surprised. "I don't understand," she said. "Weren't you holding him prisoner?"

"Certainly not," said Albion. "He came to visit me for a weekend. At the end of it, he said, 'It's so pleasant here, do you mind if I stay on for another day or two?' I'm very polite and I said, 'Of course.' He stayed on, and on, and on. I didn't like to be rude to a guest and I couldn't just kick him out. I don't know what I'd have done if you hadn't dragged him away."

"But then—" said Petronella, "but then—why did you come running after him this way?"

"I wasn't chasing him," said the enchanter. "I was chasing *you*. You are just the girl I've been looking for. You are brave and kind and talented, and beautiful as well."

"Oh," said Petronella. "I see."

"Hmm," said she. "How do I get this ring off you?"

"Give me a kiss."

She did so. The ring vanished from around Albion and reappeared on Petronella's finger.

"I don't know what my parents will say when I come home with you instead of a prince," she said.

"Let's go and find out, shall we?" said the enchanter cheerfully.

He mounted one horse and Petronella the other. And off they trotted, side by side, leaving Prince Ferdinand of Firebright to walk home as best he could.

"Give me a kiss."

Meet

Jay Williams

Jay Williams believed that a good story should be "a web of surprises, tension, and wonderment." He loved to write about the way things *seem* to be and the way they really *are*.

Williams himself was not always who he seemed to be. Many people who enjoy the mystery books of a writer named Michael Delving do not realize that Delving was actually Williams.

Williams's most famous books are those in a humorous science fiction series about a young inventor named Danny Dunn. Two books in that series won the Young Reader's Choice Award. Another of his award-winning books is *The Practical Princess and Other Liberating Fairy Tales*, from which "Petronella" is taken.

WHAT'S SO FUNNY

The fairy tale "Petronella" is a parody, or kind of joke. It makes fun of the usual elements we expect in a fairy tale. Unlike most fairy tale princesses, Petronella does not wait to be rescued by a handsome prince.

Cartoons can be parodies, too. The cartoons on these pages are good examples. Take a look—or maybe two—and find out what's so funny.

"I think I'll wait for the next elevator."

Drawing by Chas. Addams; © 1988 The New Yorker Magazine, Inc.

"Someone's been sleeping in my bed, too, and there she is on Screen Nine!"

contains: glucose, dry skimmed milk, oil of peppermint . . .

OPERA, KARATE & BANDITS

from THE LAND I LOST

Adventures of a Boy in Vietnam

by Huynh Quang Nhuong
illustrated by Robert Roth

I was born on the central highlands of Vietnam in a small hamlet on a riverbank that had a deep jungle on one side and a chain of high mountains on the other. Across the river, rice fields stretched to the slopes of another chain of mountains.

There were fifty houses in our hamlet, scattered along the river or propped against the mountainsides.

The houses were made of bamboo and covered with coconut leaves, and each was surrounded by a deep trench to protect it from wild animals or thieves. The only way to enter a house was to walk across a "monkey bridge"—a single bamboo stick that spanned the trench. At night we pulled the bridges into our houses and were safe.

There were no shops or marketplaces in our hamlet. If we needed supplies—medicine, cloth, soaps, or candles —we had to cross over the mountains and travel to a town nearby. We used the river mainly for traveling to distant hamlets, but it also provided us with plenty of fish.

During the six-month rainy season, nearly all of us helped plant and cultivate fields of rice, sweet potatoes, Indian mustard, eggplant, tomatoes, hot peppers, and corn. But during the dry season, we became hunters and turned to the jungle.

Wild animals played a very large part in our lives. There were four animals we feared the most: the tiger, the lone wild hog, the crocodile, and the horse snake. Tigers were always trying to steal cattle. Sometimes, however, when a tiger became old and slow it became a maneater. But a lone wild hog was even more dangerous than a tiger. It attacked every creature in sight, even when it had no need for food. Or it did crazy things, such as charging into the hamlet in broad daylight, ready to kill or to be killed.

The river had different dangers: crocodiles. But of all the animals, the most hated and feared was the huge horse snake. It was sneaky and attacked people and cattle just for the joy of killing. It would either crush its victim to death or poison it with a bite.

Like all farmers' children in the hamlet, I started working at the age of six. My seven sisters helped by

working in the kitchen, weeding the garden, gathering eggs, or taking water to the cattle. I looked after the family herd of water buffaloes. Someone always had to be with the herd because no matter how carefully a water buffalo was trained, it always was ready to nibble young rice plants when no one was looking. Sometimes, too, I fished for the family while I guarded the herd, for there were plenty of fish in the flooded rice fields during the rainy season.

I was twelve years old when I made my first trip to the jungle with my father. I learned how to track game, how to recognize useful roots, how to distinguish edible mushrooms from poisonous ones. I learned that if birds, raccoons, squirrels, or monkeys had eaten the fruits of certain trees, then those fruits were not poisonous. Often they were not delicious, but they could calm a man's hunger and thirst.

My father, like most of the villagers, was a farmer and a hunter, depending upon the season. But he also had a college education, so in the evenings he helped to teach other children in our hamlet, for it was too small to afford a professional schoolteacher.

My mother managed the house, but during the harvest season she could be found in the fields, helping my father get the crops home; and as the wife of a hunter, she knew how to dress and nurse a wound and took good care of her husband and his hunting dogs.

I went to the lowlands to study for a while because I wanted to follow my father as a teacher when I grew up. I always planned to return to my hamlet to live the rest of my life there. But war disrupted my dreams. The land I love was lost to me forever.

These stories are my memories. . . .

—H.Q.N.

When she was eighty years old my grandmother was still quite strong. She could use her own teeth to eat corn on the cob or to chew on sugar plants to extract juice from them. Every two days she walked for more than an hour to reach the marketplace, carrying a heavy load of food with her, and then spent another hour walking back home. And even though she was quite old, traces of her beauty still lingered on: Her hands, her feet, her face revealed that she had been an attractive young woman. Nor did time do much damage to the youthful spirit of my grandmother.

One of her great passions was theater, and this passion never diminished with age. No matter how busy she was, she never missed a show when there was a group of actors in town. If no actors visited our hamlet for several months, she would organize her own show in which she was the manager, the producer, and the young leading lady, all at the same time.

My grandmother's own plays were always melodramas inspired by books she had read and by what she had seen on the stage. She always chose her favorite grandson to play the role of the hero, who would, without fail, marry the heroine at the end and live happily ever after. And when my sisters would tell her that she was getting too old to play the role of the young heroine anymore, my grandmother merely replied: "Anybody can play this role if she's young at heart."

When I was a little boy my grandmother often took me to see the opera. She knew Chinese mythology by heart, and the opera was often a dramatization of this mythology. On one special occasion, during the Lunar New Year celebrations—my favorite holiday, because children could do anything they wanted and by

tradition no one could scold them—I accompanied my grandmother to the opera.

When we reached the theater I wanted to go in immediately. But my grandmother wanted to linger at the entrance and talk to her friends. She chatted for more than an hour. Finally we entered the theater, and at that moment the "Faithful One" was onstage, singing sadly. The "Faithful One" is a common character in Chinese opera. He could be a good minister, or a valiant general, or someone who loved and served his king faithfully. But in the end he is unjustly persecuted by the king, whose opinion of him has been changed by the lies of the "Flatterer," another standard character.

When my grandmother saw the "Faithful One" onstage she looked upset and gave a great sigh. I was too interested in what was happening to ask her the reason, and we spent the next five hours watching the rest of the opera. Sometimes I cried because my grandmother cried at the pitiful situation of the "Faithful One." Sometimes I became as angry as my grandmother did at the wickedness of the "Flatterer."

When we went home that night my grandmother was quite sad. She told my mother that she would have bad luck in the following year because when we entered the theater, the "Faithful One" was onstage. I was puzzled. I told my grandmother that she was confused. It would be a good year for us because we saw the good guy first. But my mother said, "No, son. The 'Faithful One' always is in trouble and it takes him many years to vindicate himself. Our next year is going to be like one of his bad years."

So, according to my mother's and grandmother's logic, we would have been much better off in the new year if we had been lucky enough to see the villain first!

My grandmother had married a man whom she loved with all her heart, but who was totally different from her. My grandfather was very shy, never laughed loudly, and always spoke very softly. And physically he was not as strong as my grandmother. But he excused his lack of physical strength by saying that he was a "scholar."

About three months after their marriage, my grandparents were in a restaurant and a rascal began to insult my grandfather because he looked weak and had a pretty wife. At first he just made insulting remarks, such as, "Hey! Wet chicken! This is no place for a weakling!"

My grandfather wanted to leave the restaurant even though he and my grandmother had not yet finished their meal. But my grandmother pulled his shirt sleeve and signaled him to remain seated. She continued to eat and looked as if nothing had happened.

Tired of yelling insults without any result, the rascal got up from his table, moved over to my grandparents' table, and grabbed my grandfather's chopsticks. My grandmother immediately wrested the chopsticks from him and struck the rascal on his cheekbone with her elbow. The blow was so quick and powerful that he lost his balance and fell on the floor. Instead of finishing him off, as any street fighter would do, my grandmother let the rascal recover from the blow. But as soon as he got up again, he kicked over the table between him and my grandmother, making food and drink fly all over the place. Before he could do anything else, my grandmother kicked him on the chin. The kick was so swift that my grandfather didn't even see it. He only heard a heavy thud, and then saw the rascal tumble backward and collapse on the ground.

All the onlookers were surprised and delighted, especially the owner of the restaurant. Apparently the rascal, one of the best karate fighters of our area, came to his restaurant every day and left without paying for his food or drink, but the owner was too afraid to confront him.

While the rascal's friends tried to revive him, everyone else surrounded my grandmother and asked her who had taught her karate. She said, "Who else? My husband!"

After the fight at the restaurant people assumed that my grandfather knew karate very well but refused to use it for fear of killing someone. In reality, my grandmother had received special training in karate from my great-great uncle from the time she was eight years old.

Anyway, after that incident, my grandfather never had to worry again. Anytime he had some business downtown, people treated him very well. And whenever anyone happened to bump into him on the street, they bowed to my grandfather in a very respectful way.

When my father was about ten years old a group of bandits attacked our house. There had been a very poor harvest that year, and bandits had already attacked several homes in other hamlets. My grandmother had a premonition this would also happen to them, so she devised a plan. In case of danger, she would carry the children to safety, and my grandfather would carry the bow and arrows, a bottle of poison, and the box containing the family jewels.

It was night when the bandits came. My grandfather became scared to death and forgot his part of the plan, but my grandmother remained very calm. She led her husband and children to safety through a secret back door that opened into a double hedge of cactus

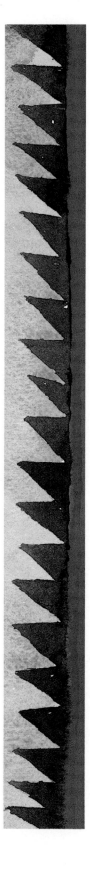

that allowed a person to walk inside, undetected, to the banana grove. When they were safely inside the banana grove, my grandfather realized that he had forgotten the bow and arrows and the bottle of poison. So my grandmother stole back into the house and retrieved the weapons.

The bandits were still trying to smash through our very solid front door when she sneaked out of the house for the second time. She dipped one arrow in poison and crawled around to the front of the house near the bandits. But, upon second thought, she put the poisoned arrow aside and took another arrow and carefully aimed at the leg of the bandit leader. When the arrow hit his thigh the bandit let out a loud cry and fell backward.

The night was so dark that none of the bandits knew where the arrow had come from. And moments later, friends started arriving and began to attack them from the road in front of our house. The bandits panicked and left in a hurry. But my grandmother spent the rest of the night with her family in the banana grove, just in case the bandits came back.

When my grandmother became older she felt sick once in a while. Before the arrival of the doctor, she would order everybody in the house to look sad. And during the consultation with the doctor she acted as if she were much sicker than she really was. My grandmother felt that she had to make herself look really sick so that the doctor would give her good medicine. She told the doctor that she had a pain in the head, in the shoulders, in the chest, in the back, in the limbs—pain everywhere. Finally the doctor would become confused and wouldn't know what could be wrong with her.

Whenever the doctor left, my mother would sneak out of the house, meet him at the other side of the garden, and tell him exactly where my grandmother hurt.

Two or three days later my grandmother usually felt much better. But before the doctor arrived for another visit she ordered us to look sad again—not as sad as the first time, but quite sad. She would tell the doctor that her situation had improved a little bit but that she still felt quite sick. My grandmother thought that if she told the doctor she had been feeling much better he would stop giving her good medicine. When the doctor left my mother sneaked out of the house again and informed him of the real condition of my grandmother.

I don't think my grandmother ever guessed it was my mother's reports to the doctor, and not her acting, that helped her get well.

One morning my grandmother wanted me to go outside with her. We climbed a little hill that looked over the whole area, and when we got to the top she looked at the rice field below, the mountain on the horizon, and especially at the river. As a young girl she had often brought her herd of water buffaloes to the river to drink while she swam with the other children of the village. Then we visited the graveyard where her husband and some of her children were buried. She touched her husband's tombstone and said, "Dear, I will join you soon." And then we walked back to the garden and she gazed at the fruit trees her husband had planted, a new one for each time she had given birth to a child. Finally, before we left the garden my sister joined us, and the two of them fed a few ducks swimming in the pond.

That evening my grandmother did not eat much of her dinner. After dinner she combed her hair and put on her best dress. We thought that she was going to go out again, but instead she went to her bedroom and told us that she didn't want to be disturbed.

The family dog seemed to sense something was amiss, for he kept looking anxiously at everybody and whined from time to time. At midnight my mother went to my grandmother's room and found that she had died, with her eyes shut, as if she were sleeping normally.

It took me a long time to get used to the reality that my grandmother had passed away. Wherever I was, in the house, in the garden, out on the fields, her face always appeared so clearly to me. And even now, many years later, I still have the feeling that my last conversation with her has happened only a few days before.

Meet
HUYNH QUANG NHUONG

Many people might have given up in despair if they had lost their homeland and had been disabled in a war. But not Huynh Quang Nhuong. After leaving Vietnam for medical treatment, he made a new home in the United States and went on to earn two college degrees as well as to become a prizewinning author and playwright.

Nhuong's first book, *The Land I Lost: Adventures of a Boy in Vietnam,* has won many awards. His plays have been produced in several cities, including his new hometown of Columbia, Missouri. In 1990, he received a grant from the National Endowment for the Arts to encourage his creative writing.

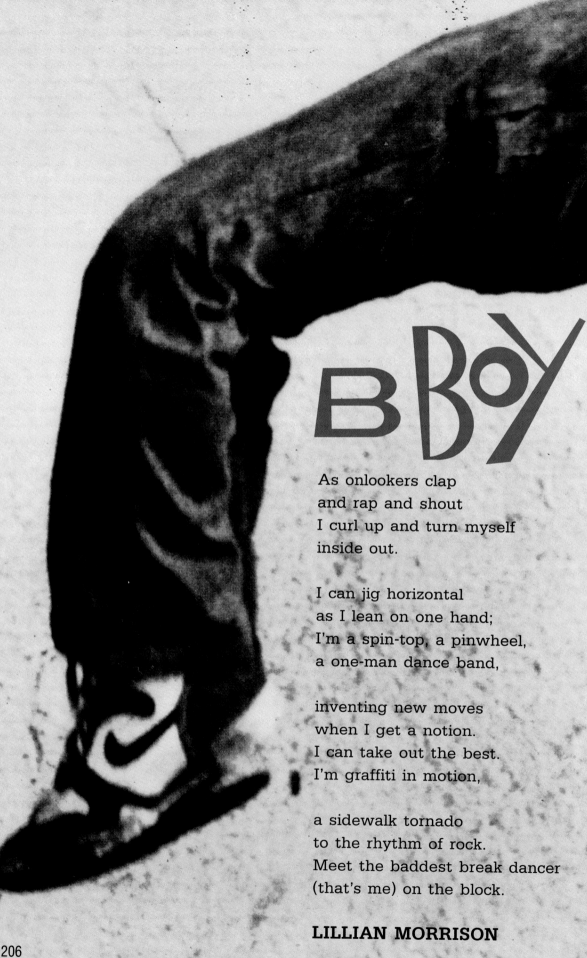

B BoY

As onlookers clap
and rap and shout
I curl up and turn myself
inside out.

I can jig horizontal
as I lean on one hand;
I'm a spin-top, a pinwheel,
a one-man dance band,

inventing new moves
when I get a notion.
I can take out the best.
I'm graffiti in motion,

a sidewalk tornado
to the rhythm of rock.
Meet the baddest break dancer
(that's me) on the block.

LILLIAN MORRISON

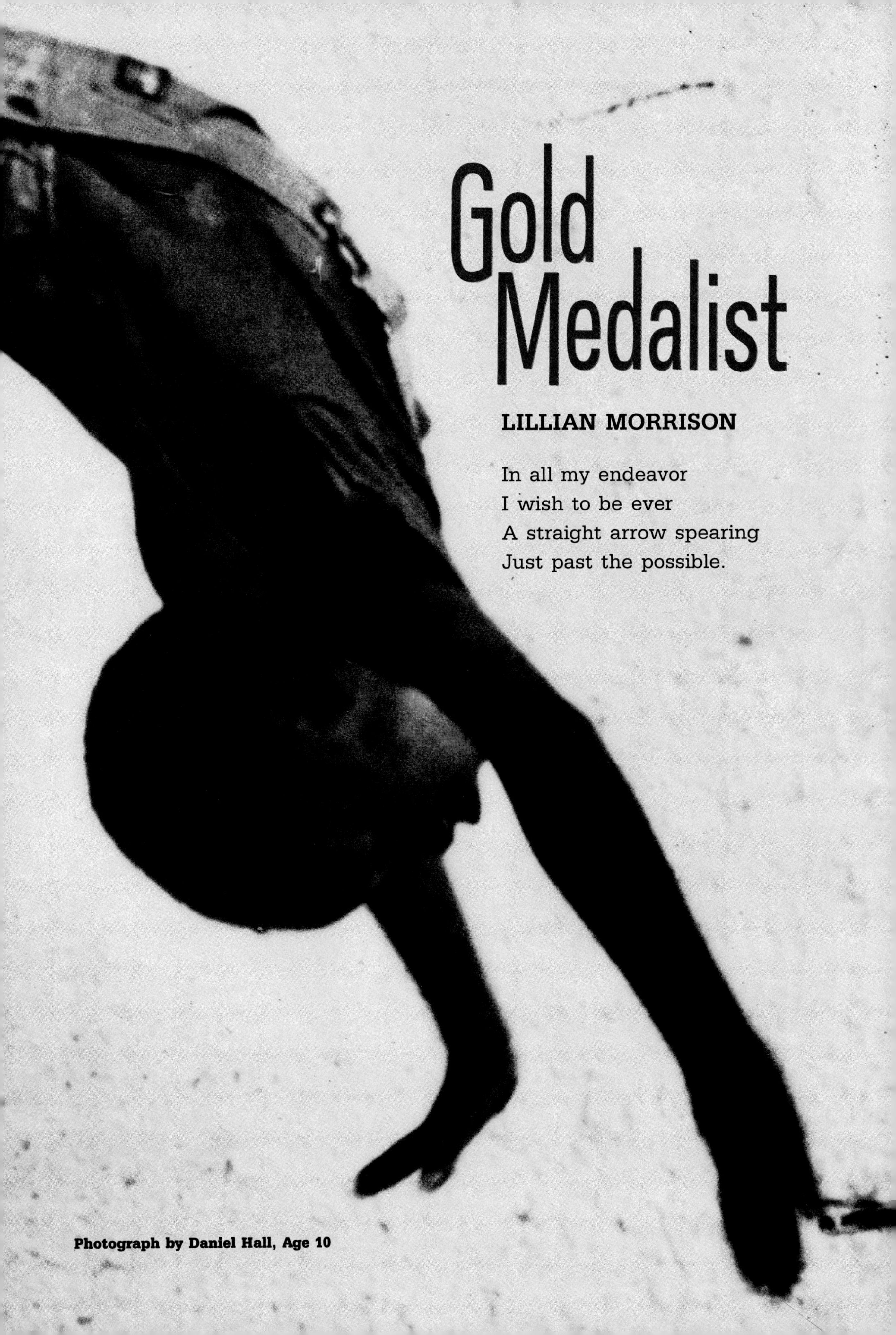

Gold Medalist

LILLIAN MORRISON

In all my endeavor
I wish to be ever
A straight arrow spearing
Just past the possible.

Photograph by Daniel Hall, Age 10

ODYSSEY

PRIDE OF PUERTO RICO

THE LIFE OF ROBERTO CLEMENTE

PAUL ROBERT WALKER

Pride of Puerto Rico:
The Life of
Roberto Clemente
by Paul Robert Walker
Harcourt Brace Jovanovich, 1988

As Willie Mays stepped to the plate in the top of the seventh inning, the Pirates were holding on to a 1-0 lead.

On the mound, the Pirate pitcher leaned back and delivered the pitch. Mays reached out and smashed a hard line drive down the right-field line. Roberto turned his back on the field and ran at full speed toward the right-field wall. I must catch it, he thought. I must catch it.

Yes I Can!

Journey Home
by Yoshiko Uchida
Aladdin, 1982

Was Papa saying they might never get to go home again? What would happen then to the thousands of Japanese who'd been uprooted from their homes and businesses and farms along the West Coast and were still in the concentration camps? Where would they all go if they couldn't go home to California after the war?

BANNER

IN THE SKY

SIXTEEN-YEAR-OLD RUDI MATT WAS

BORN IN THE SWISS VILLAGE OF

KURTAL, IN THE SHADOW OF THE

GREAT MOUNTAIN KNOWN AS THE

CITADEL. RUDI HAS STUDIED EVERY RIDGE

AND LEDGE OF THE CITADEL AND

SEVERAL TIMES HAS ASCENDED BOTH

THE DORNEL GLACIER AND THE BLUE

GLACIER, WHICH LIE AT THE BASE OF THE

MOUNTAIN. ONE SUNNY MIDSUMMER DAY,

RUDI CLIMBS BLUE GLACIER ONCE AGAIN.

BY JAMES RAMSEY ULLMAN

ILLUSTRATED BY STEVEN MADSON

Like all glaciers, the Blue was cut through by crevasses: deep splits and chasms caused by the pressures of the slow-moving ice. When hidden by snow these could be a great hazard to climbers; but on this midsummer day no snow had fallen in some time, the crevasses were plain to view, and there was no danger if one kept his eyes open and paid attention. Rudi zigzagged his way carefully upward. On the ice, of course, his smooth-soled shoes were even worse than on the boulders, but by skillful balancing and use of his stick he kept himself from slipping.

As he climbed, a black dot came into view on the high col ahead. This was an old hut, built many years before by the first explorers of the mountain, but now abandoned and all but forgotten by the people of the valleys. Rudi had twice spent nights there during his circuits of the Citadel, and he knew it well. But it was not there, specifically, that he was going now. He was not going anywhere, specifically, but only climbing, watching, studying. Every few paces now, he would stop and stare upward, motionless.

The east face of the Citadel rose above him like a battlement. Cliff upon cliff, it soared up from the glacier, its rock bulging and bristling, its walls veined with long streaks of ice. Far overhead, he could see a band of snow, which marked the mountain's first setback. Beyond it, the sloping walls disappeared for a space, only to bulge out again higher up—incredibly higher up—in a great gray thrust against the empty sky. So vast was it, so steep, so mighty, that it seemed more than a mere mass of rock and ice. More than a mere mountain. It seemed a new world rising up out of the old world that was its mother; a world with a life and a meaning of its own; beautiful and menacing, beckoning and unknown.

But it was not of beauty or terror that Rudi Matt was thinking as he gazed up at it now from the Blue Glacier. It was of a deep cleft, wide enough for a man's body, that slanted up the rock wall before him—and ended. Of a series of ledges, broad enough for a man's feet, that rose one above another toward the high belt of snow—and petered out. His eyes searched up and down, to the right and the left. He climbed on, stopped, and studied the next section of the face. Then he climbed on again.

He moved through absolute silence. Later in the day, when sun and melting snow had done their work, great rock-and-ice masses would break loose from the heights above and come roaring down the mountainside. But it was still too early for this. The Citadel rose up like a tower of iron. There was no movement anywhere. No stirring. No sound.

And then there was a sound. . . .

Rudi stood motionless. It was not the sound of the mountain, of falling rock and ice. It was a voice. He waited; he looked around him; every sense was straining. But he saw nothing. Nothing moved. It was his imagination, he thought: a trick of his mind, or of the stillness. Or was it—and now the cold finger of fear touched him again—was it the voice of a mountain demon?

He stood without breathing. And the sound came again. It seemed at the same time to come from nearby and far away. He waited. Once more it came. And then suddenly he knew where it came from. It was from beneath the ice. From a crevasse in the glacier.

He approached the nearest crevasse and called out. But there was no answer. He went on to a second. No answer. Again he waited and listened. Again the voice came, faintly. Straight ahead was a third chasm in the ice, and, advancing cautiously, he peered over the edge.

The crevasse was about six feet wide at the top and narrowed gradually as it went down. But how deep it was Rudi could not tell. After a few feet the blue walls of ice curved away at a sharp slant, and what was below the curve was hidden from sight.

"Hello!" Rudi called.

"Hello—" A voice answered from the depths.

"How far down are you?"

"I'm not sure. About twenty feet, I'd guess."

"On the bottom?"

"No. I can't even see the bottom. I was lucky and hit a ledge."

The voice spoke in German, but with a strange accent. Whoever was down there, Rudi knew, it was not one of the men of the valley.

"Are you hurt?" he called.

"Nothing broken—no," said the voice. "Just shaken up some. And cold."

"How long have you been there?"

"About three hours."

Rudi looked up and down the crevasse. He was thinking desperately of what he could do.

"Do you have a rope?" asked the voice.

"No."

"How many of you are there?"

"Only me."

There was a silence. When the voice spoke again, it was still quiet and under strict control. "Then you'll have to get help," it said.

Rudi didn't answer. To get down to Kurtal would take at least two hours, and for a party to climb back up would take three. By that time it would be night, and the man would have been in the crevasse for eight hours. He would be frozen to death.

"No," said Rudi, "it would take too long."

"What else is there to do?"

Rudi's eyes moved over the ice-walls: almost vertical, smooth as glass. "Have you an ax?" he asked.

"No. I lost it when I fell. It dropped to the bottom."

"Have you tried to climb?"

"Yes. But I can't get a hold."

There was another silence. Rudi's lips tightened, and when

he spoke again his voice was strained. "I'll think of something," he cried. "I'll think of *something!*"

"Don't lose your head," the voice said. "The only way is to go down for help."

"But you'll—"

"Maybe. And maybe not. That's a chance we'll have to take."

The voice was as quiet as ever. And, hearing it, Rudi was suddenly ashamed. Here was he, safe on the glacier's surface, showing fear and despair, while the one below, facing almost certain death, remained calm and controlled. Whoever it was down there, it was a real man. A brave man.

Rudi drew in a long, slow breath. With his climbing-staff he felt down along the smooth surface of the ice walls.

"Are you still there?" said the voice.

"Yes," he said.

"You had better go."

"Wait—"

Lying flat on the glacier, he leaned over the rim of the crevasse and lowered the staff as far as it would go. Its end came almost to the curve in the walls.

"Can you see it?" he asked.

"See what?" said the man.

Obviously he couldn't. Standing up, Rudi removed his jacket and tied it by one sleeve to the curved end of the staff. Then, holding the other end, he again lay prone and lowered his staff and jacket.

"Can you see it now?" he asked.

"Yes," said the man.

"How far above you is it?"

"About ten feet."

Again the staff came up. Rudi took off his shirt and tied one of its sleeves to the dangling sleeve of the jacket. This time, as he lay down, the ice bit, cold and rough, into his bare chest; but he scarcely noticed it. With his arms extended, all the shirt and half the jacket were out of sight beneath the curve in the crevasse.

"How near you now?" he called.

"Not far," said the voice.

"Can you reach it?"

"I'm trying."

There was the sound of scraping boot-nails; of labored breathing. But no pull on the shirtsleeve down below.

"I can't make it," said the voice. It was fainter than before.

"Wait," said Rudi.

For the third time he raised the staff. He took off his trousers. He tied the trouser-leg to the loose sleeve of the shirt. Then he pulled, one by one, at all the knots he had made: between staff and jacket, jacket and shirt, shirt and trousers. He pulled until the blood pounded in his head and the knots were as tight as his strength could make them. This done, he stepped back from the crevasse to the point where his toes had rested when he lay flat. With feet and hands he kicked and scraped the ice until he had made two holes. Then, lying down as before, he dug his toes deep into them. He was naked now, except for his shoes, stockings and underpants. The cold rose from the ice into his blood and bones. He lowered the staff and knotted clothes like a sort of crazy fishing line.

The trousers, the shirt and half of the jacket passed out of sight. He was leaning over as far as he could.

"Can you reach it now?" he called.

"Yes," the voice answered.

"All right. Come on."

"You won't be able to hold me. I'll pull you in."

"No you won't."

He braced himself. The pull came. His toes went taut in their ice-holds and his hands tightened on the staff until the knuckles showed white. Again he could hear a scraping sound below, and he knew that the man was clawing his boots against the ice-wall, trying both to lever himself up and to take as much weight as possible off the improvised lifeline. But the wall obviously offered little help. Almost all his weight was on

the lifeline. Suddenly there was a jerk, as one of the knots in the clothing slipped, and the staff was almost wrenched from Rudi's hands. But the knot held. And his hands held. He tried to call down, "All right?" but he had no breath for words. From below, the only sound was the scraping of boots on ice.

How long it went on Rudi could never have said. Perhaps only for a minute or so. But it seemed like hours. And then at last—at last—it happened. A hand came into view around the curve of the crevasse wall: a hand gripping the twisted fabric of his jacket, and then a second hand rising slowly above it. A head appeared. A pair of shoulders. A face was raised for an instant and then lowered. Again one hand moved slowly up past the other.

But Rudi no longer saw it, for now his eyes were shut tight with the strain. His teeth were clamped, the cords of his neck bulged, the muscles of his arm felt as if he were being drawn one by one from the bones that held them. He began to lose his toeholds. He was being dragged forward. Desperately, frantically, he dug in with his feet, pressed his whole body down, as if he could make it part of the glacier. Though all but naked on the ice, he was pouring with sweat. Somehow he stopped the slipping. Somehow he held on. But now suddenly the strain was even worse, for the man had reached the lower end of the staff. The slight "give" of the stretched clothing was gone, and in its place was rigid deadweight on a length of wood. The climber was close now. But heavy. Indescribably heavy. Rudi's hands ached and burned, as if it were a rod of hot lead that they clung to. It was not a mere man he was holding, but a giant; or a block of granite. The pull was unendurable. The pain unendurable. He could hold on no longer. His hands were opening. It was all over.

And then it was over. The weight was gone. There was a scraping sound close beneath him; a hand on the rim of ice; a figure pulling itself up onto the lip of the crevasse. The man was beside Rudi, turning to him, staring at him.

"Why—you're just a boy!" he said in astonishment.

Rudi was too numb to move or speak. Taking the staff from him, the man pulled up the line of clothes, untied the knots and shook them out.

"Come on now. Quickly!" he said.

Pulling the boy to his feet, he helped him dress. Then he rubbed and pummeled him until at last Rudi felt the warmth of returning circulation.

"Better?" the man asked, smiling.

Rudi nodded. And finally he was able to speak again. "And you, sir," he said, "you are all right?"

The man nodded. He was warming himself now: flapping his arms and kicking his feet together. "A few minutes of sun and I'll be as good as new."

Nearby, a black boulder lay embedded in the glacial ice, and, going over to it, they sat down. The sunlight poured over them like a warm bath. Rudi slowly flexed his aching fingers and saw that the man was doing the same. And then the man had raised his eyes and was looking at him.

"It's a miracle how you did it," he said. "A boy of your size. All alone."

"It was nothing," Rudi murmured.

"Nothing?"

"I—I only—"

"Only saved my life," said the man.

For the first time, now, Rudi was really seeing him. He was a man of perhaps thirty, very tall and thin, and his face, too, was thin, with a big hawklike nose and a strong jutting chin. His weather-browned cheeks were clean-shaven, his hair black, his eyes deep-set and gray. And when he spoke, his voice was still almost as quiet as when it had been muffled by the ice-walls of the crevasse. He is—what?—Rudi thought. Not Swiss, he knew. Not French or German. English, perhaps? Yes, English. . . . And then suddenly a deep excitement filled him, for he knew who the man was.

"You are Captain Winter?" he murmured.

"That's right."

"And I—I have saved—I mean—"

Rudi stopped in confusion, and the Englishman grinned. "You've saved," he said, smiling, "one of the worst imbeciles that ever walked on a glacier. An imbecile who was so busy looking up at a mountain that he couldn't even see what was at his feet."

Rudi was wordless—almost stunned. He looked at the man, and then away in embarrassment, and he could scarcely believe what had happened. The name of Captain John Winter was known through the length and breadth of the Alps. He was the foremost mountaineer of his day, and during the past ten years had made more first ascents of great peaks than any other man alive. Rudi had heard that he had come to Kurtal a few days before. He had hoped that at least he would see him in the hotel or walking by in the street. But actually to meet him—and in this way! To pull him from a crevasse—save him. . . . It was incredible!

MEET JAMES RAMSEY ULLMAN

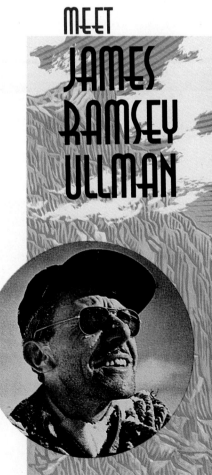

James Ramsey Ullman knew what it was like to face danger in the wilderness. In his lifetime, he climbed many of the world's highest mountains, including Mount Everest. He used his experiences to create exciting works of fiction, such as *The White Tower* and *River of the Sun*. In Ullman's novels, individuals must find the courage to make life-and-death decisions and to overcome great obstacles. *Banner in the Sky* was a Newbery Honor Book in 1955 and was made into a movie.

Ullman also understood the courage it takes to overcome obstacles in everyday life. In 1965, he took part in the Freedom March in Montgomery, Alabama, an important event in the struggle to secure civil rights for African Americans.

AiMiNG

When Sir George Mallory was asked why he wanted to climb Mount Everest, he answered, "Because it is there." For people like Mallory, there is nothing quite so irresistible as the challenge of a mountain just waiting to be climbed. If you're one of those people, read on for hints about how to aim high!

High

1 The most basic tools of mountain climbing are the hands and feet. You use your hands to grip and balance, and your feet to climb and support yourself.

2 Other basic tools are a rope, a piton, and a carabiner. A piton is a spike with a ring at one end that you drive into rock or ice. A carabiner is a metal ring that you snap into the ring of the piton. You thread your rope through the rings, creating your mountain-climbing lifeline.

3 Descending a mountain is even trickier than ascending it. The fastest way to get down is to *rappel*. You attach one end of a length of rope tightly to the mountain. You then wrap the coil of rope around your body and unwind it slowly to lower yourself.

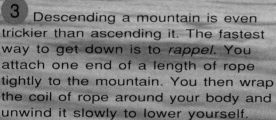

4 Climbing amid snow and ice requires additional equipment. The ice ax is used to probe dangerous crevasses, to help with balance, and to cut steps in ice.

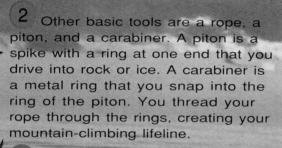

5 Crampons are another necessity for ice climbing. Strapped on your boot soles, these sets of spikes grip the ice and keep you from slipping.

YOUR WORLD

by Georgia Douglas Johnson

Your world is as big as you make it.
I know, for I used to abide
In the narrowest nest in a corner,
My wings pressing close to my side.

But I sighted the distant horizon
Where the skyline encircled the sea
And I throbbed with a burning desire
To travel this immensity.

I battered the cordons around me
And cradled my wings on the breeze
Then soared to the uttermost reaches
With rapture, with power, with ease!

225

Brother to the Wind

to the Wind

Mildred Pitts Walter

pictures by Diane and Leo Dillon

"Good Snake can make any wish come true," Emeke's grandmother often said. And every day in the village of Eronni, Emeke herded his family's goats and dreamed of finding Good Snake. He wanted to make a wish to fly.

Emeke rose early to herd the goats high up on the mountain. Dark clouds clung to the earth. Morning was almost like night. The rains would soon come.

"Say, Emeke," Ndumu shouted in the dim light, "still want to fly like a bird?" Other boys on the road laughed.

"Our friend thinks he can move like the wind," Mongo said.

"No, he really thinks he will find Good Snake and that Good Snake will help him fly." Nizam's words brought great bursts of laughter.

High up on the mountain, alone with his goats, Emeke looked out at the farms and his village below. Fires blazed and sent up smoke as the men cleared thick brush for new farmland. They worked hard to beat the rains. Their clothes, the colors of the rainbow, flowed with the wind.

Finally Emeke sat watching his goats eat greedily. Then, with his knees drawn to his chest and chin, he closed his eyes. He tried to imagine now what he had often felt in dreams. He wanted to feel the wind, to soar up, up, up, then wheel off like a bird. But his mind filled only with the laughter of his friends.

Then he remembered his grandmother's words: "If you find Good Snake, he will help you fly."

If only I could leave my goats for one day, he thought. I would go searching deep in the bush for Good Snake. But Father would never let me do that.

Maybe he should go into the bush at night when the village was asleep. No boy would go there after dark. Secrets of the bush unfold, and the silence of ghosts grows loud in the dark. No. No boy would do that. "But no boy in my village can fly," Emeke said aloud.

He would find Good Snake and make his wish.

Suddenly he heard a low rumbling noise. What could it be? Not thunder. Thunder came only with the rains. Emeke put his ear closer to the ground and heard the sound of many feet.

Then Emeke saw the strangest thing. A swarm of fire-flies moved in a circle in the distance. In their light Emeke saw animals moving toward a tree, not too far from where his goats were feeding.

Emeke jumped up. He saw Elephant, Rhinoceros, Giraffe, and Zebra. He moved closer and saw smaller animals: Turtle, Hyena, Wild Dog, and Hare. There were many birds too. How peacefully and quietly they all moved together. Emeke's goats were calm, still eating the short grass. They will be safe for a little while, Emeke thought.

Curious, he hurried.

Cautiously he fell in line with the animals.

When they reached the tree he saw an unusual thing.

A huge snake was wrapped around the biggest branch. His tail was hidden in the leaves, but his head hung down toward the ground. Emeke's heart beat wildly, his skin went hot, then cold, and his scalp tingled. This is Good Snake, he thought. Emeke wanted to run away, but his feet felt rooted to the spot.

Hyena, Elephant, Rhinoceros, and all the animals, one by one, made wishes. But Turtle stood off to the side, laughing. He did not believe in Good Snake.

As Emeke watched Turtle laughing, he thought of Ndumu, Nizam, and Mongo. Would he dare ask to fly like a bird?

Finally Good Snake nodded at him. Emeke knew it was now his turn. "Oh, Good Snake, I would like to fly."

Good Snake uncurled his tail and brought forth a rock. "Are you sure you want to fly?"

"Oh, yes, Good Snake," Emeke whispered, hardly able to speak.

Good Snake held out the rock. "This is what you must do: Before the rains come, find the bark of a baobab tree and three large bamboo poles. Then make a kite exactly like the one on the back of this rock."

Emeke took the rock and placed it in his pouch. But what did a rock and a kite have to do with flying, Emeke wondered. He wanted to say, Why make a kite? All I want to do is fly like a bird. Instead he listened as Good Snake went on: "Before the feast of the harvest, you must find the right wind for the kite."

"Good Snake, how will I know the right wind?" Emeke asked.

Good Snake curled up his tail again and looked at Emeke. "The right wind will whisper words that will let you know for sure. Then, on the day of the feast, meet me high on the mountaintop. If you have done all the things that I have asked, then on that day you will fly. One other thing: Keep that rock with you always. It will help you."

Emeke was so happy and excited he almost forgot to thank Good Snake as he hurried back to his goats.

Good Snake called after him. "Be sure you find the bark and bamboo before the rains come."

Turtle laughed. "He, he, he. Beware! Things without wings don't fly."

The dark heavy clouds threatened to overflow. Emeke hurried toward his goats, wondering how he would find bark and bamboo before it rained. He touched the rock and remembered: *The rock will help you.*

When he reached the place where his goats were feeding, he saw Hyena lurking nearby. Emeke hurriedly gathered his goats together to protect them. His goats did not seem at all alarmed. They kept right on eating greedily.

Hyena moved closer.

Emeke became more frightened, and touched the rock.

"Do not be scared," Hyena shouted. "I have come to herd your goats."

"*You?* Herd my goats?" Emeke asked in disbelief.

"Yes. I wished to have more patience and less greed. Be off to the bush to find your bamboo and bark. I'll care for your goats until you return."

Emeke did not trust Hyena.

He was still afraid.

Hyena sensed Emeke's fear and said, "Do you believe Good Snake can help you fly?"

Emeke realized he did not know whether he could trust Good Snake. But his grandmother believed in Good Snake. "Yes," he said. "I believe Good Snake can help me fly."

"Then believe that he can make me a goat herder."

Every few feet Emeke turned to look back, thinking his goats would be eaten. But Hyena was moving among the goats as a caring herder should. I must trust Hyena, he thought, and hurried on toward the bush.

The clouds made the bush almost as dark as night. Emeke stumbled along in the unfriendly quiet.

He must find the bark and bamboo before the rains came.

Suddenly he walked into something that felt like a wall. It moved. Emeke's heart beat wildly. Then he knew. It was not a wall at all. It was Elephant. Emeke was frightened; he squeezed the rock for comfort.

"I am here to help you find the baobab tree," Elephant said.

"How do you know I need bark from the baobab tree?"

"I made a wish too. I wished to be kind and helpful. My wish can come true, if I can help you." Elephant led the way into the bush.

Soon Emeke had enough bark for his kite. Emeke thanked Elephant. Now he must hurry to find the bamboo. His father would be furious if he found the goats left in Hyena's care.

At last Emeke found the watering hole where bamboo grew. To his surprise, Rhinoceros was waiting for him with three neatly cut poles.

"I knew you would come," Rhinoceros said. "I made a wish to be gentle and of service. My wish has come true."

It was night when Emeke returned to the pasture. His goats were gone! Emeke's heart skipped beats. He felt weak and his head seemed to swell. He ran here and there, everywhere, looking. Then, around a curve, he saw his goats. Hyena had gathered them all together.

The goats pushed and shoved around Emeke. Hyena was glad to see Emeke too. Emeke thanked Hyena and hurried down the mountain.

He had not gone far when he saw his father with men from the village. Emeke's friends were with them.

"Where were you?" his father demanded.

"On the mountain."

"No, you were not!" Ndumu shouted.

"We looked all over for you," Nizam said.

"And what is this burden you are carrying?" His father pointed to the bark and bamboo.

"I want to fly, Father, so—"

An explosion of laughter interrupted Emeke. Emeke looked at

his father and knew his father was humiliated. The men laughed because they thought Emeke was a lazy, careless boy who did not take his duties seriously.

"Why do you say foolish things, Emeke?" his father demanded. "Did you ever see humans fly?"

Emeke felt his father was more hurt than angry. He wanted to move closer to his father, but it was as though the laughter had turned him to stone.

Finally, with tears in his voice and with great respect, Emeke tried to explain again.

"Father, I did not leave the goats alone. Hyena cared for them. . . ."

There was another explosion of laughter. Over the laughter Emeke's father shouted, "Let me hear no more of this foolishness. Now, I want you to promise that you will never leave the goats unattended again."

Emeke remembered that he still had to find the right wind. He did not want to promise.

"Emeke," his father said, "if you leave the goats again, I will have to punish you. I want your word that you will not."

"I promise," Emeke said sadly.

Later that night, thunder rumbled and lightning lit up the village. Emeke heard the sound of drops like small pebbles pelting the roof. The rains had come. He had found the bark and bamboo just in time.

Rain fell in gray sheets, soaking the earth, filling the streams. Emeke could not herd his goats. While other children sat around the fire roasting maize and groundnuts, Emeke sat alone working on his kite.

With the rock close by, he worked every day. Soon word spread about the huge kite. Emeke's friends called him bird boy, wing-flapper. People in the village said Emeke was a foolish boy. His family was ashamed of him. Only his grandmother believed he might fly one day.

"Why such a heavy kite?" his mother asked.

"You will never fly that one on a string," his father said.

"It will fly me. I will soar in the wind, dive and wheel like a bird without falling," Emeke said proudly.

His grandmother beamed, but his father said, "Put the kite away. Forget this flying foolishness."

Finally the rain fell in drops as thin as needles against the sunlight. White clouds raced away, leaving the sky clean and blue. The sun shone bright and the wind blew cold. Emeke herded his goats at the foot of the mountain and wondered where he would ever find the right wind.

Days grew warmer. After many days and nights, the growing season ended and it was time for the harvest to begin.

The night before the harvest festival, the moon rose like a giant orange ball. The night slowly turned almost as bright as day.

Emeke lay listening to the wind. "Come out, come out, you don't have to break your promise," the wind sighed.

Emeke rushed outside. He hurried to the edge of his village. The grass grew tall, and the wind sang like the sound of the sea. The grass bowed left and right, moving like women's skirts in the dance. Emeke stood still, listening.

Then softly as the flutter of a bird's wing came a whisper: "My brother." Emeke trembled with the excitement that comes with dancing. Be still and listen, he told himself. Again the whisper: "My brother." That is the right wind! He felt light with happiness.

The rest of the night, Emeke slept without dreaming.

The morning of the festival came with the sound of many drums. The air was heavy with excitement. Today I will fly, Emeke thought when he awoke.

Emeke walked with his family to the center of the village. His friends gathered around him, excited about the games and races to be held at the festival.

"I will fly today," Emeke said matter-of-factly. "Look up and you will see me."

"Then look down," Ndumu said. "Oooh, no more Emeke! He is splattered like a bird's egg." Ndumu fell to the ground, arms and legs spread. All the boys bent with laughter.

"I will fly. You will see," Emeke said.

When the center of the village was overrun with people,
Emeke slipped away with his kite and rock. He hurried up the
mountain to meet Good Snake.

As he came near the top of the mountain, he heard a plodding sound. He looked around and saw Turtle struggling to join
him.

"Hey," Turtle shouted. "Beware! Boys were not made to fly."

"With the help of Good Snake, I can, and I will."

"What if you drift to the end of the earth or land on your feet in the mouth of Crocodile, or in Lion's lair?"

Emeke became frightened. He had thought only of flying. Then suddenly he heard the wind sighing softly. Emeke's confidence returned. "I am not afraid, Turtle." He hurried to find Good Snake.

High up on the mountain Good Snake was waiting.

"I made the kite and found the wind," Emeke said to Good Snake.

Good Snake turned the kite this way and that to make sure it was made well, safe for flying. Then he led Emeke to the edge of the mountain. "You will fly from here down into your village."

Emeke heard the drums from the distance. He looked down and saw the cloud of dust from dancing feet. He thought of Ndumu's words and of his friends' laughter. Turtle's words echoed: "Boys are not made to fly." Emeke hurriedly backed away from the edge. He looked at Good Snake and said, "I cannot fly."

"But everything is ready."

"With all those people in the center of the village, where will I land safely?" Emeke cried.

"You must think of nothing but flying. Trust me with the rest. Give me the rock. I leave you with the wind."

Emeke pointed the nose of his kite up slightly. Should he trust Good Snake? Would he really fly? He waited. He listened.

"My brother," the wind sighed.

Emeke felt the easy, steady wind. He forgot his fear. He balanced his kite and started running toward the edge of the mountain.

He kept his mind on running and keeping his kite's nose up.

Suddenly he was in the air. He flowed up, then floated down, gliding with the wind. His body seemed to disappear. There was only wind, sky, and the earth far below. He was flying! Soaring, turning, streaming down, then lightly, easily floating. "I am brother to the wind," he shouted.

He floated to his feet as lightly as a feather. His grandmother was the first to reach him. She hugged him, beaming with love. His mother and father smiled with pride. All of his friends rushed to examine the kite. "He did fly like a bird," Nizam said.

Drummers beat their drums, sending up sounds as great as all the thunder in the world. Dancing feet sent up clouds of dust. Emeke danced to the rhythms with his grandmother.

Meet
Mildred Pitts Walter

Being active in a variety of causes has been very much a part of Mildred Pitts Walter's life. Her concern for building a better understanding of the African-American experience has led her to write a number of books for young people that explore themes of going to school and growing up.

Walter is not afraid to make some tough decisions to support her beliefs. In fact, when she was awarded the Coretta Scott King Award for Literature *for* Justin and the Best Biscuits in the World, *she had to choose between appearing at the awards ceremony and participating in a peace walk in the Soviet Union. She says, "I struggled with the question: Which creates the best image for young people? To be in San Francisco to accept the award, or to walk for peace? . . . My answer came. I chose to walk."*

Meet
Diane and Leo Dillon

Since Leo and Diane Dillon met in art school in the 1950s, they have worked together illustrating books for both children and adults. The Dillons express their feelings about their craft when they say, "We believe in magic. To sit down with a blank piece of paper and see scenes and characters take form . . . it is magic."

Two of their books, Why Mosquitoes Buzz in People's Ears *and* Ashanti to Zulu: African Traditions, *won the American Library Association's Caldecott Medal for illustrated books. Another of their books is* Aïda, *which is based on an opera about an Ethiopian princess.*

243

I May,
I Might,
I Must

by Marianne Moore

If you will tell me why the fen
appears impassable, I then
will tell you why I think that I
can get across it if I try.

from POST-SCRIPT

by W. H. Auden

Since he weighs nothing,
Even the stoutest dreamer
Can fly without wings.

CONTENTS

Timelines

I have only just a minute,
Only sixty seconds in it,
Forced upon me—can't refuse it,
Didn't seek it, didn't choose it.
But it's up to me to use it.
I must suffer if I lose it.
Give account if I abuse it,
Just a tiny little minute—
But eternity is in it.

BENJAMIN E. MAYS

Minutes Are Up

by Ellen Conford

illustrated by Christoph Blumrich

And you're sure he was talking about me? You actually heard him say 'Libby Kalman'? I mean, maybe he was talking about Renee Kaplan. Our names sound alike. . . . Sure they do, if you say them fast—"

"Elizabeth, get off that phone!"

Libby held her hand over the mouthpiece and looked pleadingly at her mother. "Just two more minutes, Mom. Just two minutes."

"You've been talking for forty-five minutes already, and your father's expecting—"

"Mother, *please*. This call is really important. It could affect the entire course of my future."

"If you're not off that phone in two minutes you won't *have* a future."

Her mother strode out of the kitchen, her spine ramrod straight, like a soldier. Libby frowned. Whenever her mother squared her shoulders off like that, she meant business. But Libby couldn't worry about that now.

She gazed dreamily at the note pad next to the phone. She'd written the name Mark on it thirteen times. Some Marks were printed in capital letters, some all in small letters. Some she wrote out in her ordinary handwriting, and some she tried to do in elegant italic, like calligraphy.

She wrote the fourteenth Mark in block letters and began shading the *M*.

"But did he know you heard him? I mean, do you think he said it because he knew you were right there and would hear him? And then he'd know you'd tell me, because he knows we're friends? I mean, I think he knows we're friends, doesn't he? Actually, maybe he doesn't. How would he know? . . . You think so? . . . Well, I mean, did he want me to know he said it, or did you just sort of overhear it? . . . Well, because if he knows that I know he said it, he'd expect me to act entirely different than if he didn't know I knew he said it. . . . Sure. And see, if he *didn't* know I knew he said it, and I started acting different, he'd be suspicious, right? And then he'd think, she knows, and what if he really didn't *want* me to know? I mean, you have to deal with a whole other situation, right? Okay, so tell me again, right from the beginning, and don't leave anything out, because even the smallest detail might be—"

"Elizabeth!"

Her father and mother were suddenly looming over her, their faces purple and red—respectively—with rage.

"Get off that phone!" her father roared.

"Instantly!" her mother added.

Libby rolled her eyes toward the ceiling. "Look, Stace, I'll have to call you back—"

"You'll call no one back!" her father exploded. "You'll get off that phone and stay off!"

Her mother glared at her, arms folded, face red, shoulders squared. "In two seconds," she said dangerously, "I am going to rip that phone off the wall and *clobber you with it.*"

"Uh, Stace, listen, my mother is going berserk here, and my father's about to have a coronary, so I have to get off. Yeah, I know you heard. I'm sure the whole eastern seaboard heard."

Her mother reached for the phone cord.

"Bye, Stace!" Libby slammed the receiver down. "Okay, okay, I'm off."

"I have had it," her father said. "Your mother has had it. Your brother has had it. He'd be here telling you in person he's had it, but he's afraid to come near you because he might kill you, so he's up-stairs ripping apart a pillow with his bare hands."

"Fed up, Libby," her mother said. "Absolutely fed up to *here*. You don't own this phone. There are three other people in the house who need to use it and you haven't shown the slightest consideration for any of us."

"I get business calls, Elizabeth," her father went on. "Important calls. When people can't reach me for three hours, they stop trying. That's bad for business. Bad for my career. Bad for all of us. And I have to *make* calls. And I can't pick up that phone without you hanging over me asking when I'll get off, how long will I take, can I please hurry it up, because you're expecting another vitally important call."

"Well, if you'd just get me my own phone—"

"You can get your own phone when you're earning the money to pay your own phone bill!" her father shouted.

The phone rang. Libby lunged for it, but her father snatched up the receiver before she could get to it.

"No, Libby can't come to the phone now."

Libby's eyes opened wide in horror. "I'm *here,*" she whispered desperately. "I'm *right here.*"

"No, you'd better try her tomorrow. Sorry."

"How could you *do* that?" Libby cried. "Who was it? Was it a boy or a girl?"

"A boy, I suppose. And I did it because I had to. It's a matter of self-preservation. I'm expecting a very important call—"

"Mark!" Libby wailed. "It was Mark, I just know it. Do you realize what you've done? You've ruined my life, that's all. Just ruined my life. You've destroyed my one chance for happiness. I might as well just go upstairs and swallow everything in the medicine cabinet."

"Good luck with the shaving cream," her mother said drily.

"I can't believe it," Libby said. "I can't believe you did that to me."

"If you can't believe that," her mother said, "you're going to hate this next part."

"What next part?" What could be worse, Libby wondered bitterly, than what her father had already done?

"Look, Libby, I'm sorry, but this business with the phone has gotten completely out of hand." Her mother sat down next to her. "You no sooner get home from school than you're on the phone for three hours with people you've been talking to all day."

"You can't talk to people in *school!*"

"Why not?" her father demanded. "That's ridiculous."

"You just can't," Libby insisted. How could she explain it? It was hopeless to expect her parents to understand what would have been obvious to any teenager.

"Well, you're going to have to," he said, "because from now on you'll have a limit on your calls."

"What do you mean? Like no more than five a day?"

Her father laughed, but it was a short, humorless laugh.

"No, not just the number of calls you make, but the amount of time you spend on each one. Tomorrow I'm getting three egg timers, and I'm going to put one next to each extension. When you make a call, you turn over the egg timer. When the salt runs out of the top, you get off the phone. *Immediately.*"

"How long does it take," Libby asked, her voice weak with shock, "for the salt to run out?"

"Three minutes."

"*Three minutes!* That's impossible! That's crazy! How can you have a conversation in three minutes?"

Libby's father looked at her thoughtfully. "Look at it this way," he said. "Every time we ask you to get off the phone you say, 'Just two more minutes, just two more minutes.'"

Libby squirmed. He did a pretty good imitation of her.

"So we figure, when the pressure's on, you can wrap up these life-and-death matters in two minutes. When you really have to. We're giving you three minutes—an extra minute more than you always ask for. Anything vitally important that you have to say to anybody can be said in three minutes."

For a moment Libby was too stunned to speak. How could they do this to her? It was humiliating. It was barbaric. There are plenty of vitally important things that can't be said in three minutes. And even if *she* talked fast, what about the person on the other end of the phone? What if he was shy and hesitant and talked slowly, trying to work up his nerve, sort of build up to what he actually called about? Like, say, someone like Mark? Not that Mark would ever call her again, after tonight, but just as an example.

Of course, if they weren't going to limit the number of calls she made—Libby's eyes brightened for a moment. "Then what you're saying is, I have to hold each *individual* call down to three minutes, right?"

Her mother smiled. "Forget it, Libby. No more than three calls a day. You can't just hang up and call back, hang up and call back."

"But what about people who call me?"

"Incoming calls will be timed, too."

"Oh, no! You can't do that! It's not fair! I have *rights*. This is *America*."

"The Constitution," her father said, "does not give you the inalienable right to a telephone. And we've tried to be understanding and fair, but *you* haven't. We just can't think of any other way to solve this problem."

Dazed, Libby pulled herself out of the chair.

"I can't believe you're doing this to me." She shook her head. "I can't believe my own parents could be so . . . I've got to call Stacey. She'll never believe it either."

"Libby!" her father said. "You can tell Stacey tomorrow. The bad news will wait eight hours."

Libby turned to stare back at him, her face pale with the shock of betrayal. Then she trudged up to her room, shoulders slumping, to do her homework.

What else was there to do?

On the second day after the "Invasion of the Egg Timers," as Libby called it, she thought she'd found a loophole.

"My time is up," she said to Stacey loudly. She looked around furtively, then hunched over the phone. "Wait ten minutes," she whispered, "and call me back."

When the phone rang ten minutes later, Libby grabbed it. "Now look, when I have to get off, do the same thing again. Wait ten minutes and call me back."

"This is no way to hold a conversation."

"What can I do?" moaned Libby. "They've driven me to this."

The third time Stacey called, Libby's mother got to the phone first.

"Hello, Stacey. Yes, just a minute." She handed the phone to Libby with a knowing look. She held up three fingers.

"I know, I know," Libby grumbled. "Three minutes."

Her mother shook her head. "No. Three strikes and you're out."

"What?" Libby clamped her hand over the mouthpiece. "What do you mean?"

"That's the third time Stacey's called. No more. You may be sticking to the letter of the law, but you're violating the spirit of it."

"*What?*"

RRRING
RRRING

"In plain English: You can't get around it that way, but nice try."

"Why don't you just lock me in my room and throw away the key?" Libby wailed. "You're cutting off my lifeline to the outside world!"

Her brother came clumping down the stairs. "Are you still on that phone?"

"What do you mean, *still?*" Libby demanded. "I haven't even said hello yet."

"Then say hello," said her mother, and carefully turned over the egg timer.

What her parents did to her was bad enough, Libby felt, but what her friends did seemed even a worse betrayal. Within a week after the "Invasion of the Egg Timers," the grumbling started.

"Boy, Libby, you really loused things up for everybody," Renee Kaplan said, sitting down next to her in algebra.

"Me? What did I do?"

"You and those three-minute phone calls. My mother has me on egg timers now."

"But that's not my fault!" Libby said, outraged. "My parents did that, not me!"

"They're *your* parents," Renee said. "It all started with you."

"What all?"

"Suzanne's parents, Lauri's mother—you started an epidemic of egg timers."

"*I* didn't start anything!" Libby couldn't believe it. It was bad enough that her parents had turned on her, but now this? Her friends, too?

"Renee, I'm sorry, but really, it's not fair to blame me. What can I do?"

"Well, if you've got

any AT&T stock," Renee said coldly, "I suggest you sell."

Libby hadn't forgotten about Mark, though she was sure she might as well.

He was in only one of her classes, where he sat way in the back of the room next to his friend John Kelly, so she didn't even get to see him unless she got there early and watched him walk in or hung around after the bell and watched him walk out.

Libby began to think that Stacey had been mistaken—that day she thought she heard Mark talking about Libby, he was actually talking about Renee Kaplan. Either that or her father really *had* ruined everything the night he hung up on Mark, making her sound like a two year old who'd been banished to her room for throwing spinach at the cat.

Why Mark should like her she didn't know. Just because *she* liked him? Just because she thought he was cute? But she did. And he was. And there was no hope for it now, if there ever had been. If, by some remote chance, Mark finally called her one night, he'd barely have enough time to say who it was before she had to hang up. And a shy person like Mark might need a good ten minutes to relax enough to sort of casually work whatever it was he *really* wanted to say into the conversation.

So between rounds of nursing her bruised feelings and snapping at her family, Libby sighed a lot and thought about what was never to be but might have been.

And wrote *Mark* a few hundred times on the memo pad on top of her desk.

Monday night when the phone rang, Libby didn't even run for it. She was too disheartened. Her spirit had been broken. And it probably wasn't for her, anyhow. Half of her friends had had their phone lines cut off, and most of them blamed it on Libby. Those people who were still speaking to her—mostly the ones who *hadn't* been invaded by egg timers—didn't call her because what kind of a satisfying talk could you have in three minutes?

"It's for you," her brother said, pounding on the door. "Don't forget to turn your timer."

"I won't forget to turn my timer," Libby mimicked. "I probably won't even have to. It's just someone who wants to know what the homework is. That's all we have time to say anymore."

Libby went into her parents' bedroom and picked up the phone.

"Hello," she said dully.

"Uh, hi, Libby?" It was a boy's voice. A boy's shy, hesitant voice.

Libby exhaled so hard she was sure he must have heard her.

The egg timer slipped out of her fingers and rolled under the bed.

"Yes, this is me," she said softly. Wow, did that sound dumb. Well, what could you expect? She wasn't getting much practice in the art of telephone conversation lately.

"It's Mark Welch. Uh"—he cleared his throat—"I know you can't stay on the phone very long. . . ."

The whole world knows my problems, Libby thought bitterly. This is humiliating.

"So I'll—uh—get right to the point."

He probably wants to know what the homework is in earth science, Libby thought.

"You know they're having this—uh—Sixties Dance in school next Saturday, and I was wondering if you'd—I mean, I don't dance really well or anything, but—well, you know, if you want to—"

I don't believe it! Libby thought. I'm going to faint. Faint later! she told herself. Your three minutes are almost up. She felt for her heart; it was still beating. Very rapidly.

"I mean, what I thought was maybe we could go, you know, together, if you want."

"That would be really nice," Libby said. How calm she sounded! Just as if Mark called her every day! Just as if she hadn't been waiting and hoping for weeks for this moment. "I'd really like that."

"You would?" Mark sounded like he couldn't believe it. Like he'd expected her to say no. "Oh, good. Great. I'll pick you up about eight, okay?"

"Eight is fine."

"Well. Well, okay. I guess you have to get off now."

"Right, right," Libby said, dazed. "I guess I'd better. Bye."

"Bye. Take care."

Libby dropped the receiver back on the hook and threw herself across her parents' bed. *Now* she was going to faint. She was going to faint from shock and then die of happiness.

No. Not yet.

First she had to call Stacey.

"Stace? Stace, you're not going to believe this—"

"He called?" Stacey asked excitedly. "Did he call yet?"

"What? How did you know—"

"He did call! Did he ask you?"

"Stacey, how do you know all this?" Libby demanded.

"John sort of hinted around at it—I wormed most of it out of him."

"Why didn't you tell me?"

"Because John said he was so nervous about it he might chicken out at the last minute, and I didn't want to get your hopes up for nothing. But he really called?"

"Yes," sighed Libby. "Yesss. . . ."

"Well, it's really bizarre, Lib. Listen, you're not going to believe this. He tried to call you for two weeks."

"What?"

"But your line was always busy." Stacey giggled. "Isn't that ironic?"

"What?"

"And he was too shy to talk to you in school, with people all around. And when he finally did reach you, your father said you couldn't come to the phone. So he gave up. He figured you were so popular you'd never go out with him. All those phone calls and all."

"What?"

"You're repeating yourself, Libby. So anyhow, when

265

this thing with the time limit came up, he figured he'd be able to get you now, but he was still sure you wouldn't be interested in him. It took a whole week for John to help him work up the nerve to try."

In a haze, Libby slid off the bed and down to the floor. Still holding onto the receiver, she groped around under the bed till she found the egg timer. She put it down carefully on the night table.

"Libby? You still there?"

"Yeah, I'm still here. My time's almost up, though. I don't believe this."

"I told you you wouldn't. Oh, Lib, did you die? Were you surprised? I would have died."

"No, no, I'm saving that for later," Libby said distractedly.

Her mother walked into the room. She looked at the egg timer, which had never been turned over, and saw that all the salt was on the bottom, as if it had run out. She stared pointedly at Libby.

"I have to go, Stace. Talk to you later. I mean, tomorrow."

"Okay. Take care."

Libby hung up the phone and walked dreamily toward the door.

She paused just before leaving the bedroom and looked at her mother almost fondly.

"You know," she murmured, "you might be right."

"About what?" her mother asked, startled.

Libby trailed her fingers gently around the doorknob.

"Maybe you *can* say anything you have to say in three minutes . . . if it's important enough."

Meet Ellen Conford

Ellen Conford wants to entertain her readers. She explains, "I don't write to pound home a message, or to teach a lesson. . . . I want to write books that are fun to read."

One of the things that makes Conford's books entertaining is her use of humor. She believes that we laugh when we read about people like ourselves or about situations that we have been in.

Conford often writes about problems and situations that her readers might face—how to get someone you like to notice you, how to adjust to a new school, what to do when you get the worst part in a school play. "I write books about things that could or do happen to 75 percent of the kids I know who face the normal problems of growing up," she says.

Conford's first book was *Impossible, Possum*, a children's book about a possum who can't seem to hang by his tail like every other possum. Another of her popular books is *Dreams of Victory*, in which Victory Benneker's imagination helps her cope with everyday disappointments. Both *Impossible, Possum* and *Dreams of Victory* were Junior Literary Guild selections.

CALLING ALL PHONE FANS

On March 10, 1876, Alexander Graham Bell was preparing to test a new transmitter for an invention he was working on. He accidentally spilled some acid and shouted to his assistant, "Mr. Watson, come here. I want you!" Watson, in the next room, heard Bell's cry over the transmitter. Bell had invented the first telephone.

Today, it's difficult to imagine life without a telephone. The average American household has about three telephones; that's more than 200 million nationwide. In addition, modern telephones and telephone technology can perform some amazing tasks—tasks that Bell himself probably never dreamed of!

There are amazing features that can be added to the phones already in your home.

Messages recorded for each family member in separate "mailboxes"—each family member has a secret code to get the messages from the "mailbox."

Three separate numbers and three different rings on one phone—you can tell if a call is for you by listening for your special ring.

This voice-controlled phone dials the correct number when verbally commanded to do so.

Automatic redial of a busy number—as soon as the call goes through, your phone will ring to let you know.

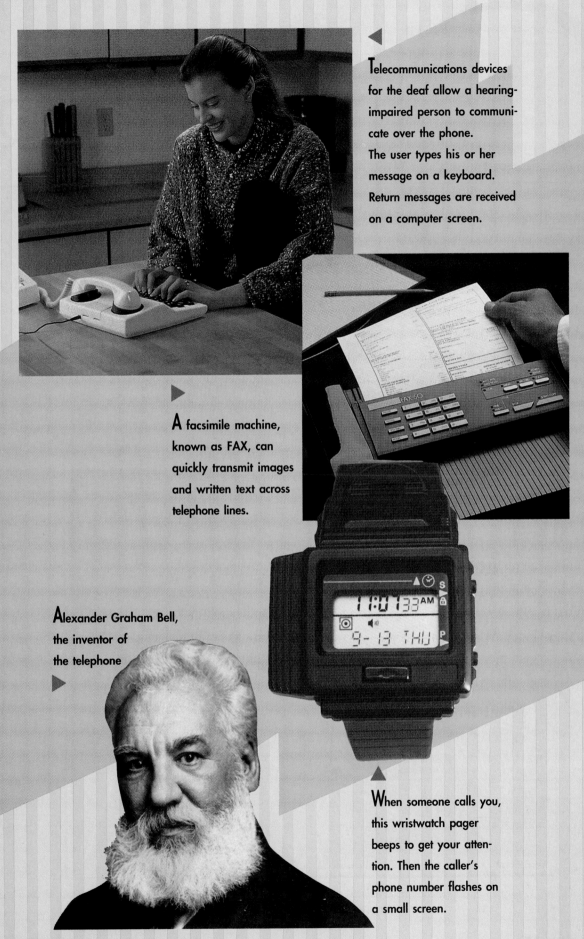

Telecommunications devices for the deaf allow a hearing-impaired person to communicate over the phone. The user types his or her message on a keyboard. Return messages are received on a computer screen.

A facsimile machine, known as FAX, can quickly transmit images and written text across telephone lines.

Alexander Graham Bell, the inventor of the telephone

When someone calls you, this wristwatch pager beeps to get your attention. Then the caller's phone number flashes on a small screen.

CALENDAR

Gregorian sun and moon (upper left); Mayan month (upper right); Babylonian sun (lower left);
Egyptian solar disc (lower right)

by
Leonard
Everett
Fisher

Days, Weeks, Months, and Years

Throughout the existence of humankind, people have been aware of the special rhythms of the sun and the moon. Primitive humans saw that the sun rose in one place, turning night into day, and that it set in another place, turning day into night. To them the moon, too, seemed to emerge from one position, move across the star-strewn sky, and disappear with the night at another position. They believed, then, that each day and each night the sun and the moon traveled an endless, repetitive course.

In other words, early people thought that the earth stood still as heavenly objects circled around it. Their knowledge was limited in this way from the dawn of the human epoch, about 500 thousand years ago, until about 440 years ago. It was then that the astronomer Nicolaus Copernicus

(1473–1543) offered a startling idea: that the sun stood still, that the earth was one of a group of heavenly bodies moving around it, and that as the earth moved in a measurable orbit around the sun, the moon traveled around the earth in its own measurable path.

Whatever the limits of early people's knowledge of the heavens, they knew there was a passage of time—from sunrise to sunset. And they knew that aging, growing from young to old, was a process of time. While they did not measure a day in seconds, minutes, and hours, they knew when it began and ended, and that it took 365¼ days for the sun to appear and disappear at identical positions—a solar year. Early people knew, too, that in some mysterious way the position of the sun determined the seasons.

The moon also provided a broad measure of timekeeping for these people. In the darkness they watched the moon change from no shape at all—the invisible new moon—to a slim crescent, a half-moon, an oval, or *gibbous,* a full moon, then back to a gibbous, half-moon, and crescent, before it became the shadowy new moon again. These phases of the moon always spanned 29½ days.

WINTER

This was the length of time it took the moon to orbit the earth once—the lunar month.

Our word *month* derives from *moon.* Early people knew that 12 lunar months nearly equaled one solar year, falling short by about 11 days. And as civilization evolved, people realized that they had to try to compensate for those days. A rough estimate of nature's timing was no longer good enough. People needed a chart to tell them with certainty when to plant and harvest their crops, when to work, and when to pray. They needed a time-measuring system—a calendar.

The Greek and Roman civilizations gave us the word *calendar.* Its roots are in the Greek *kalend,* "I shout," and in the Roman *calends,* the first day of a Roman month. The ancient Greek who shouted *kalend* was a public timetable who informed the people when to pay their taxes, when the magistrates would try criminals, and when marketing days and religious and athletic events would take place.

SPRING

Other cultures—Aztec, Chinese, Jewish, Moslem—used varying systems to calculate days, weeks, months, and years. There was no standard calendar in use anywhere in the ancient world. And most of these systems, if not all, were based on either the lunar month or the solar year.

The ancient Sumerians devised the first lunar calendar

SUMMER

about 5,000 years ago. Later, Babylonians divided months into weeks and a week into 7 days. The Jews, once captive in Babylonia, used the Babylonian 7-day week, as did the sun-worshiping Egyptians, who developed a 52-week solar calendar based on the 7-day week.

The schemes were too complicated, however, and calendar dates and seasons became mismatched. The problem worsened each year. Farmers could not rely on these calendars to plant crops. Religious celebrants never knew the right day for a particular festival. Fall weeks of one year would become winter weeks the next year.

Julius Caesar (circa 100–44 B.C.) tried to adjust the calen-dar so that it would repeat itself the same way every year. Progress was made, but not enough. Then early Christians modified Caesar's "Julian" calendar so that all years following year 1, when Jesus Christ was born, would be known as A.D., or *anno domini,* "in the year of the Lord," and those that came before as B.C., before Christ, or B.C.E., before the common era. Still, calendar errors continued to multiply.

Finally, Pope Gregory XIII (1502–1585) corrected the calendar. Now its dates would conform year after year to the proper seasons with almost no error. The "Gregorian" calendar continues to be the calendar of our modern world.

FALL

On the following pages, you will read about the calendars of various cultures. The examples represent ancient as well as modern attempts to keep track of time.

273

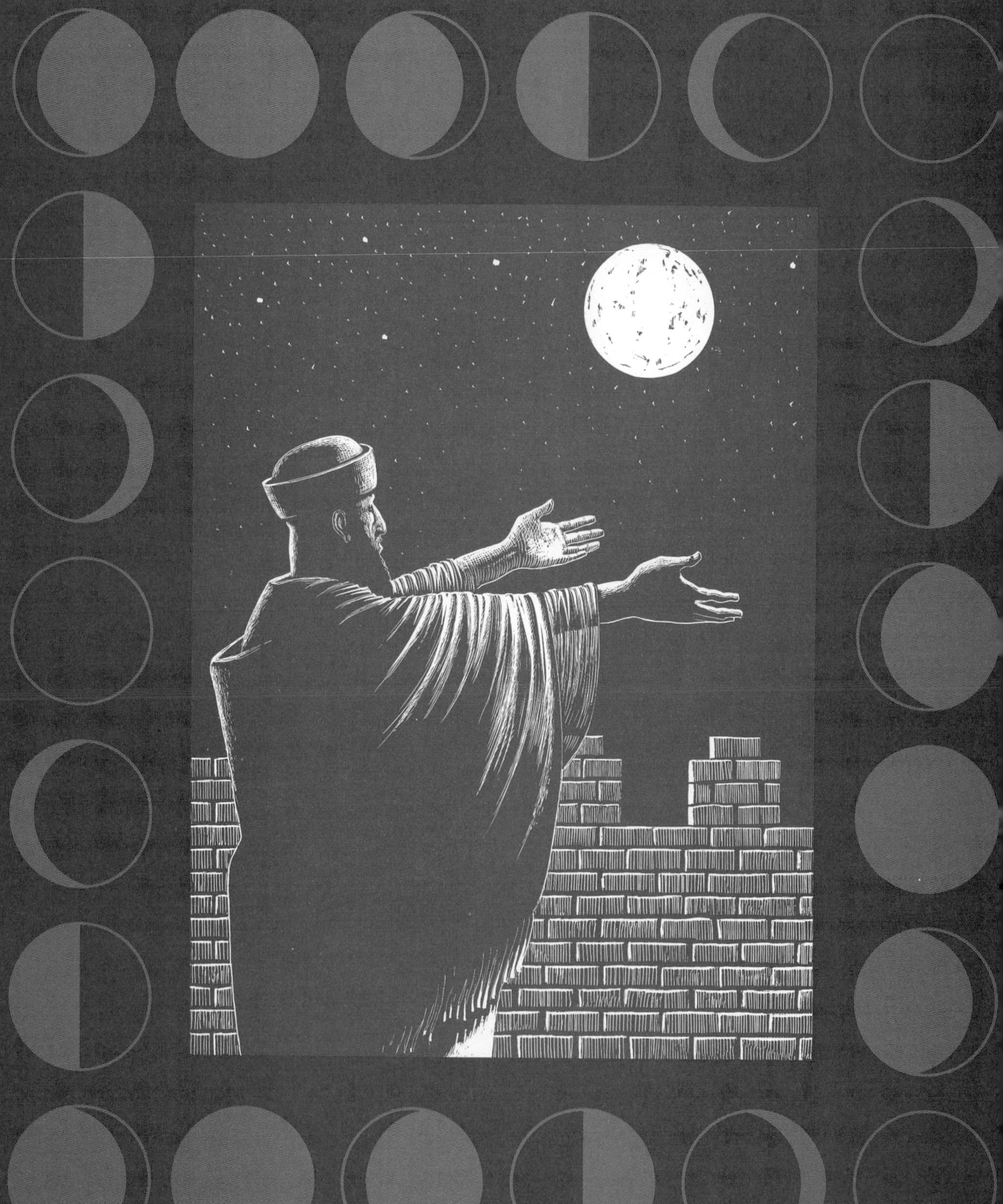

BABYLONIAN

STAR

About 3000 B.C., long before the Greeks named the hot desert region between the Tigris and Euphrates rivers Mesopotamia, "the land between rivers," nomadic tribes quit wandering and formed farming towns. Chief among these towns was Ur, located on the banks of the Euphrates River at the northern rim of the Persian Gulf. The area was called Sumer. To help them deal with the dry land, the Sumerian farmers relied on their priest-astronomers to interpret the movement of the stars. They developed a 30-day lunar calendar and used it to plan their farming. These same Sumerians invented the first writing system, *cuneiform*. With it came the beginning of history: the written record.

Ur and the Sumerians faded after a 700-year presence. Babylon—the biblical Babel—and Babylonians arose in their place. However, during the kingdom of Hammurabi, circa 1750 B.C., a revised Sumerian calendar emerged as a Babylonian calendar.

The Babylonians devised a 354-day lunar calendar with 12 alternating months of 29 and 30 days. But it fell 11¼ days short of the 365¼-day solar year. To correct the calendar so that the seasons matched their dates somewhat each year, they *intercalated,* or "inserted," two extra months seven times within every 19-year period.

MOON

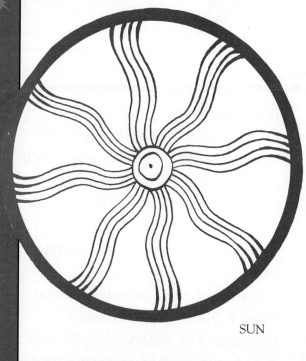

SUN

Also, the Babylonians were among the first civilizations to divide their year into 7-day weeks. The Babylonian week was based solely on the worship of the sun, moon, and five planets: Shamash (Sun/Sunday), Sin (Moon/Monday), Nebo (Mercury/Tuesday), Ishtar (Venus/Wednesday), Nergal (Mars/Thursday), Marduk (Jupiter/Friday), and Ninurta (Saturn/Saturday).

BABYLONIAN MONTHS

￹Y￺ 1. **NISANU**	￹YY￺ 2. **AIARU**	￹YYY￺ 3. **SIMANU**
￹YYY / Y￺ 4. **DUZU**	￹YYY / YY￺ 5. **ABU**	￹YYY / YYY￺ 6. **ULULU**
￹YYY / YYY / Y￺ 7. **TASHRITU**	￹YYY / YYY / YY￺ 8. **ARAHSAMNU**	￹YYY / YYY / YYY￺ 9. **KISLIMU**
￹<￺ 10. **TEBETU**	￹<Y￺ 11. **SHABATU**	￹<YY￺ 12. **ADDARU**

Intercalated months: ULULU II (29 days) ADDARU II (30 days)

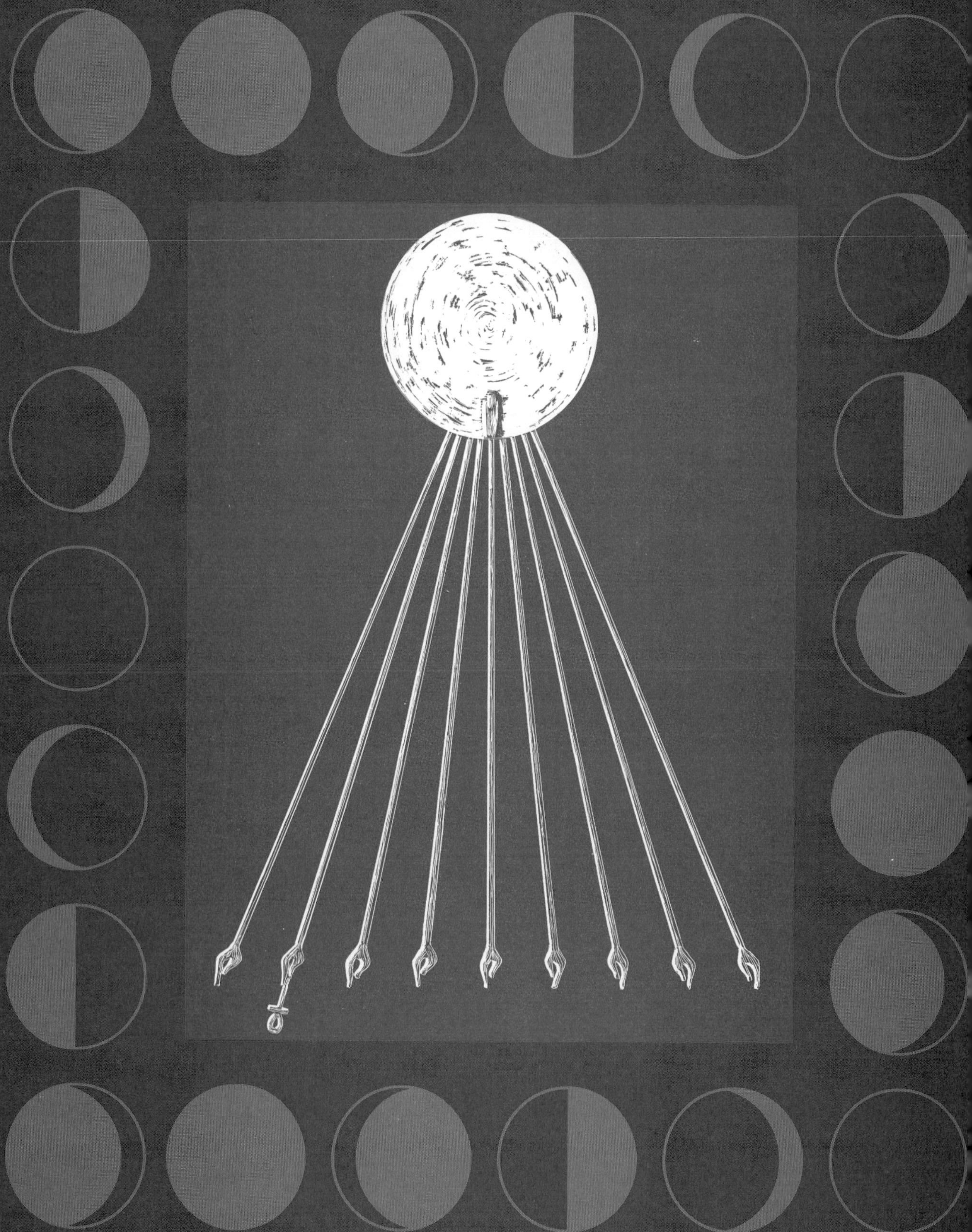

EGYPTIAN

| FIRST MONTH OF SUMMER | FIRST MONTH OF WINTER | FIRST MONTH OF SPRING |

An object of ancient worship, the Nile River is the spirit and lifeblood of Egypt. For without that great wash of water flowing from Ethiopia to the Mediterranean Sea, Egypt would be a desert. Once each year for the past 5,000 years of Egyptian recorded time, the Nile has flooded the 600-mile-long valley to create a green and fertile tract for planting.

Early Nile Valley farmers had to know when the river would flood in order to save their crops, their property, and even their lives. They knew that the flooding would begin whenever the brightest fixed star, Sirius (Sothis to the Egyptians), rose on the eastern horizon. This took place about once every 365 days, just before sunrise. So they developed a lunar calendar in which a year began with the first new moon following the appearance of Sirius. The lunar calendar year, containing 12 months with 29½ days each, covered 354 days, 11 short of 365. To make sure the flooding of the Nile and the calendar date always matched, they added an extra month every so often.

In time the Egyptians created a more accurate 360-day solar calendar with 12 months of 30 days each, along with the 7-day week favored by Jews and Babylonians. Since this, too, fell short, they added 5 days to the last month of the year. Of course, Egyptian

ANCIENT EGYPTIAN MONTHS (named after Egyptian gods)

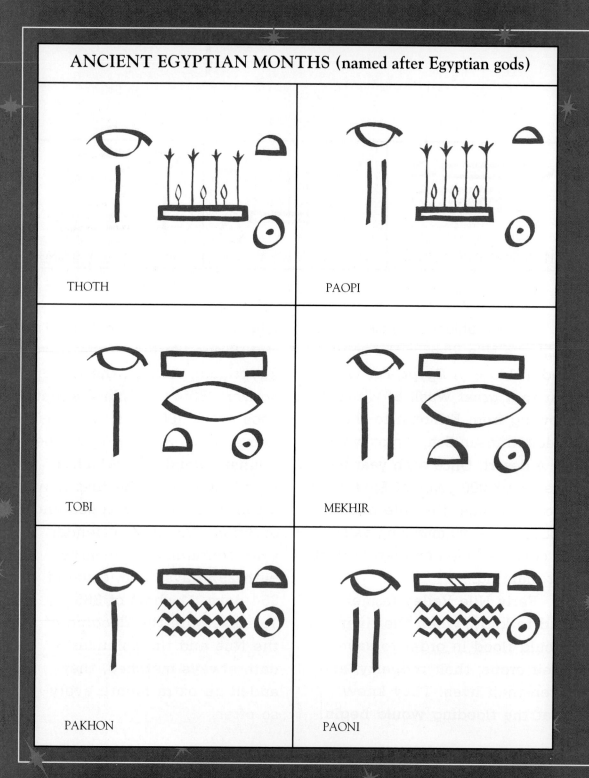

THOTH

PAOPI

TOBI

MEKHIR

PAKHON

PAONI

astronomers knew that a year was 365¼ days long. But their priests, guardians of centuries of tradition, forbade them to correct the calendar by adding an extra day every four years—a leap year. Eventually the calendar fell out of line with the seasonal flooding.

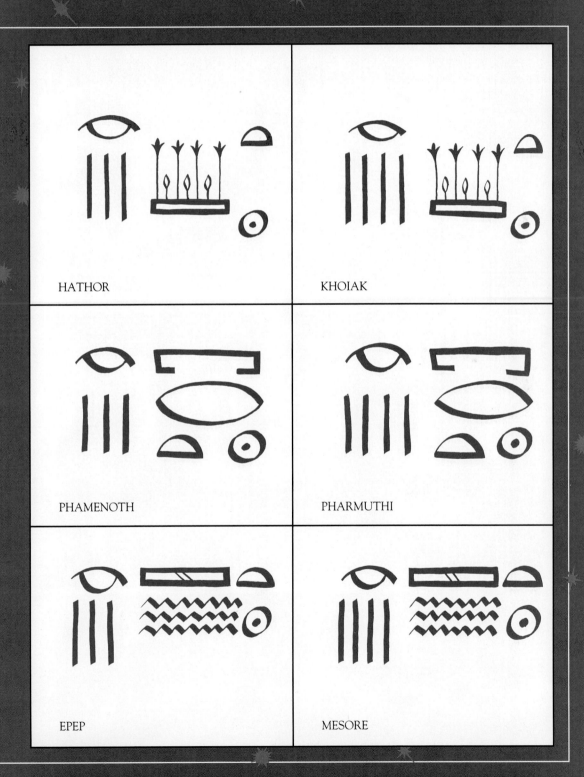

HATHOR

KHOIAK

PHAMENOTH

PHARMUTHI

EPEP

MESORE

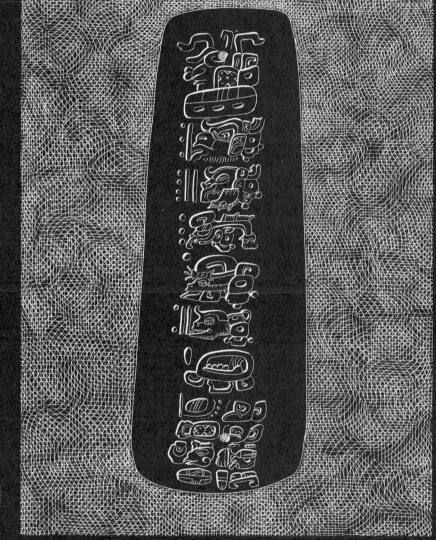

MAYAN

ZOTZ (Bat)

Mexico's Yucatan Peninsula and present-day Honduras and Guatemala were once the lands of the Maya. Long before Europeans arrived in the Western Hemisphere during the 1500s, the Mayan Indians had achieved a distinctive civilization. Their large cities —Copan, Chichen Itza, Tikal, and others—were administered by priests whose writings and astronomical observations, carved in stone or set down on tree-bark paper, provided a record of history, science, medicine, and religion, including human sacrifice. The priest-astronomers had developed a precise numbering system to manage Mayan lives at least 300 years before the birth of Christ, some 2,300 years ago. It enabled them precisely to measure planetary movements, time, and eclipses, and to develop a calendar for religious and civil affairs.

Mayan dating indicates that an accurate solar calendar was in use by them early in the common era in Europe, about the year 300. The Maya relied on two calendars working together in 52-year cycles called the *xiuhmolpilli*. One was the *haab*, a 365-day civil calendar having 18 months of 20 days each, plus a nineteenth month of 5 days. An extra day was added every fourth year. The 18-month period was called a *tun*.

MAYAN MONTH GLYPHS

Question marks indicate that researchers have been unable to translate glyphs.

Tun

Katun

1. Pop (mat)
2. Uo (frog)
3. Zip (goddess)
4. Zotz (bat)
4. Zotz (bat)
5. Tzec (?)
6. Xul (?)
7. Yaxkin (summer)
8. Mol (?)
9. Chen (?)
9. Chen (?)
10. Yax (green)
11. Zac (white)
12. Ceh (deer)
13. Mac (?)
14. Kankin (ribs)
14. Kankin (ribs)
15. Muan (falcon)
16. Pax (?)
17. Kayab (turtle)
17. Kayab (turtle)
18. Cumku (?)
19. Uayeb (?)

Twenty tuns were a *katun*. The other was a religious calendar, or *tzolkin*, having 260 sacred days.

The Maya did not have a written language that expressed sound. Instead, like the Egyptians, they used symbols called *hieroglyphs*, or *glyphs*, to express an idea. And they used a variety of number, word, and name glyphs to work out their calendar and convey its meaning.

		Tzolkin	Haab	Kin (day)
MAYAN DAY GLYPHS				
1. Imix (water)		2. Ik (air)	3. Akbal (night)	
4. Kan (corn)	5. Chicchan (serpent)	6. Cimi (death)		7. Manik (deer)
8. Lamat (rabbit)		9. Muluc (rain)		10. Oc (dog)
10. Oc (dog)		11. Chuen (monkey)	12. Eb (broom)	
12. Eb (broom)	13. Ben (reed)	14. Ix (jaguar)		15. Men (eagle)
16. Cib (owl)	17. Caban (earth)		18. Eznab (knife)	19. Cauac (storm)
20. Ahau (lord)				

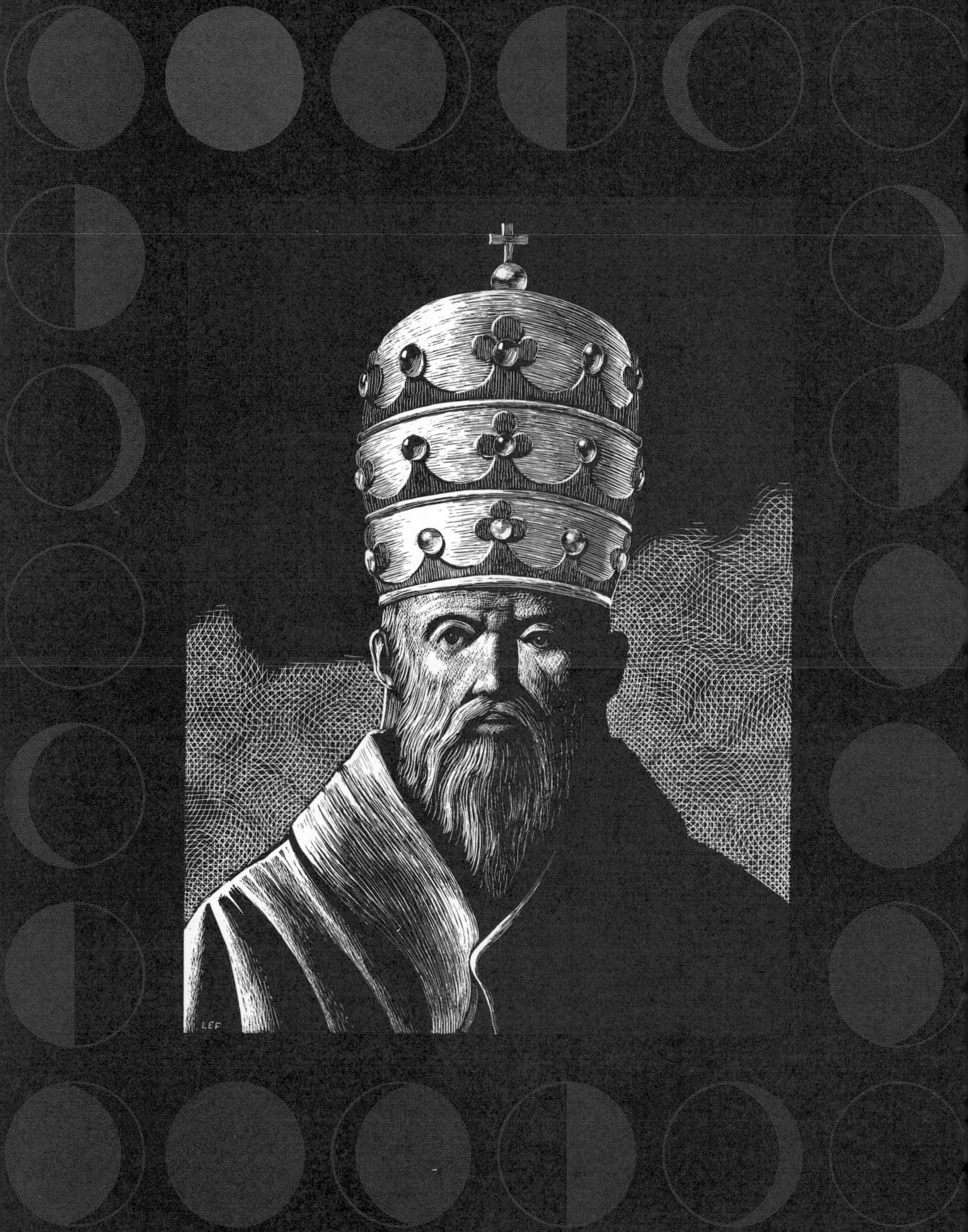
LEF

GREGORIAN

SUN AND MOON

By the sixteenth century, errors in the Julian calendar had become a problem for the Catholic Church. Easter was supposed to be celebrated on the vernal equinox, the day the sun crosses the equator, turning winter into spring in the Northern Hemisphere, summer to fall in the Southern Hemisphere. And the vernal equinox was supposed to occur on the first Sunday after the first full moon after March 21. But March 21 had moved 10 days ahead of the equinox. While the vernal equinox would occur every 365¼

days, as usual, March 21 would soon be in midsummer.

Pope Gregory XIII ordered the calendar changed to correct the errors. After ten years of study, the Pope decreed that October 5, 1582, would become October 15, 1582, to bring the dates into line with the sun's position. Ten days were dropped from the calendar. Also, though January 1 would continue to be New Year's Day, leap year would no longer be any year divisible by four. While a leap year still would occur every four years by adding one day to February, the last year of a century could not be a leap year unless it was divisible by 400. The year 1900, for example, could not be a leap year. The year 2000 would be a leap year. Now it would be 30,000 years before the calendar would become 10 days out of line.

It took two hundred years for Protestant Europe, namely, England and Germany, to accept the Gregorian calendar. The Russians did not adopt it until 1918. Moslems, Jews, and Greek Orthodox people continue to use their own ancient calendars for religious events. But the business of nearly the entire modern world is conducted by the Gregorian calendar.

DAYS OF THE WEEK AROUND THE MODERN WORLD

ENGLISH	LATIN	FRENCH	SPANISH	ITALIAN	DANISH	DUTCH
Sunday	Dies Dominica Lord's Day	Dimanche	Domingo	Domenica	Soendag	Zondag
Monday	Dies Lunae Moon's Day	Lundi	Lunes	Lunedì	Mandag	Maandag
Tuesday	Dies Martis Mars's Day	Mardi	Martes	Martedì	Tirsdag	Dinsdag meeting day
Wednesday	Dies Mercurii Mercury's Day	Mercredi	Miércoles	Mercoledì	Onsdag	Woensdag Woden's day
Thursday	Dies Jovis Jupiter's Day	Jeudi	Jueves	Giovedì	Torsdag	Donderdag thunder day
Friday	Dies Veneris Venus's Day	Vendredi	Viernes	Venerdì	Fredag	Vrijdag
Saturday	Dies Saturni Saturn's Day	Samedi	Sábado sabbath	Sabato sabbath	Loerdag bath day	Zaterdag

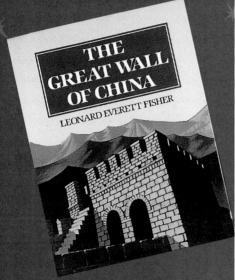

Meet
Leonard Everett Fisher

Painting and illustration are central to the books Leonard Everett Fisher creates. "I want to present art in nonfiction—to have people look at the power and dynamics of art. . . ."

Winner of a Pulitzer Prize for his painting, Fisher uses a variety of techniques and color schemes in his books. The illustrations in *Calendar Art* were created using the scratchboard technique. White board was covered with blue ink that was then scratched away to reveal the white underneath. In other books, such as *The Blacksmith*, Fisher used black ink.

Full-color paintings illustrate the book *Celebrations* by Myra Cohn Livingston, a poet Fisher has collaborated with for several collections. In *The Great Wall of China*, Fisher used black, white, and gray to create dramatic effects. He also used red blocks called "chops" to sign his work, just as Chinese artists have done since ancient times.

As Fisher says, "I design according to the idea."

THE
Y
e
a
r

goes
skidding
down
to
the
bottom
of the
cal-
en-
dar
slip-
ping
out
the
end.
Then
ZOOM............... Up

HAPPY NEW YEAR!
top
the
to
Up

by Felice Holman

A Chinese New Year parade, featuring a dancing dragon, winds through the streets of Singapore.

TIME &

Tuck Everlasting
by Natalie Babbitt
Farrar, Straus & Giroux,
1975

She knew very well what
she would see in it;
her reflection had long
since ceased to
interest her.
For Mae Tuck, and
her husband, and Miles
and Jesse, too, had all looked
exactly the same for eighty-seven years.

AGAIN

**The Secret Clocks:
Time Senses
of Living Things**

by Seymour Simon
Viking, 1979

Cockroaches have
been found to have
a true time sense.
They begin to run
around just as
darkness falls. For a
few hours they are very active, and
then they become quiet.

THE SECRET CLOCKS
Time Senses of Living Things
SEYMOUR SIMON · Illustrated by Jan Brett

This Book Is About Time

The Inside Story on People Time

by Marilyn Burns

You have your own inner clocks. They do the inside job of timing what goes on in your body. They're not like the clocks that help you time your activities during the day. Those clocks are out where you can easily see them—on walls, on wrists, sitting on table tops. Those timekeepers sometimes need your attention for winding or resetting.

But your inner clocks aren't visible to you. They don't need to be wound. You don't have to check them to see how time is moving. They do their job, day in and day out, automatically, with no help needed from you.

Inner clocks are what keep your biological rhythms well timed. They keep the inside parts of your body working together and

295

timed with the outside world too. Do you know what some of your biological rhythms are?

Scientists have the same questions about human biological rhythms that they've had about the inner clocks of plants and animals. Even though your rhythms aren't as noticeable as plant and animal rhythms, they're there. And you can learn a great deal about them.

This article has information on what people have found out about human cycles. There are also activities and experiments, so you can try out some of what scientists have learned firsthand. Here's a chance for you to take a look at your own inner timing.

The Clock in You

How is your own sense of time? Take a quick check. Try guessing what time you think it is right now. Don't look at a clock yet. First make your guess as accurate as you think you can. Now go and check the clock. How close were you?

Investigate the time sense of some other people in your family. Try asking them what time they think it is. Do this on and off during the next several days. See how close their guesses are.

Some people set an alarm clock at night to be sure they'll get up in the morning by a certain time. Do you? Lots of people have reported that they always seem to wake up just before the alarm goes off. Has this ever happened to you? Has it happened to people you know? Ask your parents. Check with other people who use alarm clocks; see if this is generally true or untrue for them. If it's true for them, ask how come they still keep on setting the alarm at night?

Do you have a dog or a cat? If you do, try to observe their time sense. Some people notice that their pets seem to ask to be fed just about the same time every day. If you have a pet, check the times it shows up around the kitchen sniffing for some supper.

Not everyone's inner timing works with the same accuracy. Maybe you could improve your time sense. Try guessing the time on and off during the day whenever you remember. See if you can get more accurate. Do you think it's possible to sharpen your inner timekeeping?

The Man Who Was as Regular as Clockwork

A newspaper in England in the late 1880s reported that a man in a small village used to count out the chimes to tell the time when the village clock struck each hour. When the clock broke, he could still call out the hours at the right time. Do you know anyone who is as regular as clockwork?

People's Pacemakers

Some scientists feel that there is a pacemaker in everyone's brain that gives people some sense of time. Scientists don't know too much about this pacemaker. They do know that it's not a very trustworthy or accurate timekeeper for most people. They also know that humans don't do nearly as well as plants and animals do in keeping track of time. Maybe that's why people have spent so much of their energy inventing clocks to keep the time for them.

Scientists know that people's timing abilities are easily thrown off by changes. Heat is one of those changes. Have you ever had the feeling on a hot, hot day that time seems to be moving very slowly? Heat speeds up your pacemaker so your own sense of time is moving faster than time really is. Then things seem to take longer, as if they're happening in slow motion.

When you've got the flu or some nasty sickness that gives you a fever, the fever will have the same effect. Being sick in bed for a day with a fever often makes a day feel very long and slow.

When Frank Brown investigated the fiddler crab, heat changes had no effect whatsoever on the crab's daily color changes. When Henri-Louis Duhamel experimented with the plants that opened and closed their leaves on a daily cycle, temperature changes didn't change the plants' cycles at all. Your inner clocks just aren't that reliable.

Are You an On-Time Person?

Are you a punctual person? Are you usually an early arriver, or are you a latecomer? Most people fit clearly into one of those three timely groups. What about you?

easily, or do you depend on someone else to keep you moving? Are you the one who always has to wait for someone else to finish getting ready?

What about the other people you live with or your friends? Predict whether you think they are on-timers, early arrivers, or latecomers. Then ask them what they think, and see if your opinions agree.

Here are some questions to ask yourself if you're not sure which you are. When your mom or dad tells you to be home at 5:00 P.M., do you get home on time? Is it a struggle to do so, racing at the last minute to get there, or is it something you just plan for, so it's no big hassle?

Do you get ready to leave for school on time in the morning

How Late Is Late?

Some people think that arriving five minutes after an agreed-on time isn't really being late. Some people think that maybe ten minutes off would be late. Others think twenty minutes or half an hour can pass before someone would be too late. What do you think?

299

The Human Rhythms

One thing scientists have learned from their experiments to investigate human biological cycles is this: Many of your body rhythms operate on a twenty-four-hour cycle. These are daily rhythms. They operate automatically, without any effort from you.

These daily body rhythms are called circadian rhythms. The word *circadian* comes from two Latin words. *Circa* means "about" and *dies* means "day." Here's a listing of some of the circadian rhythms that are part of your everyday life.

1. *Your sleep-awake cycle.* This is an easy cycle for you to notice. Your brain controls your sleep-awake rhythm, and some of your other circadian rhythms are keyed to this one.

2. *Your body-temperature cycle.* Your temperature is regulated by the part of your brain called the hypothalamus. During a twenty-four-hour period, your temperature rises and falls about 1½ to 2 degrees Fahrenheit. It's lowest when you're asleep. And for most people, it's highest in the late afternoon.

Do you ever notice that when you're up watching a late movie on TV, you get really cold and need to huddle under a blanket? That's because your temperature is dropping for the night.

3. *Your oxygen-use rhythm.* Your cells need oxygen. How much oxygen they require varies in a daily cycle. When you run or exercise a lot, you breathe harder because your cells need more oxygen then. During the time of day that you're usually most active, your body's oxygen consumption is higher. When is this time of day for you? What's interesting is that even when you're not so active on some days, your rhythm of oxygen increase continues.

4. *The rhythm of your heartbeats.* The rate of your heartbeats changes on a daily cycle. When you're asleep, your heart beats slowest. Scientists have measured people's pulses and have found that they're usually lowest between 10 P.M. and 7 A.M. During the day, your pulse will vary according to how active you are. But even when you're resting or napping in the daytime, it won't be as low as it is at night.

5. *Your kidney-excretion cycle.* Your kidneys filter out the waste products from your blood. It expels these waste products in your urine. Your kidneys do most of this work during the day and less of it at night, when you're asleep. That's convenient, so you usually don't have to get up during the night to urinate.

6. *Your taste, smell, and hearing rhythms.* For most people, the sense of taste and smell and hearing are sharpest in late afternoon or evening. That's when people seem to be more aware of how good the dinner that's cooking smells, and how good it is to sit down and eat a yummy meal, and how sounds seem so much clearer or louder. Have you ever noticed any of these for yourself?

There are other body rhythms that scientists have discovered too. The ones listed are the ones you can observe most easily in yourself and in the people around you. Later in this article some experiments will help you take a closer look at your own cycles.

A Reminder About Rhythms

It's important to remember that people's individual cycles aren't all exactly the same. Living in a family where people's rhythms aren't all tuned in together makes for differences. Talk about these human rhythms with the other people in your family. Maybe you can get them interested in trying some of the activities that follow. That may give all of you another way to understand your differences and similarities.

Your Sleeping-Awake Cycle

Everyone needs to sleep. That's a biological law. When you sleep, your body gets a chance to restore the energy you've used up. When you don't have enough sleep, you act tired, you can't keep your attention on things well, you can't react as fast as you normally can, and you get generally grumpy.

How many hours do you sleep daily? Figure this out. If you're not sure, keep a record for a week. You can do that by making a chart like this and writing down the time you go to bed every night and when you get up every morning. Do you get up a different time on days that you don't have to go to school? Does that change how much sleep you get?

	Went to Bed	Got Up	Hours
Monday			
Tuesday			
Wednesday			
Thursday			
Friday			
Saturday			
Sunday			

Kings Need to Sleep Too

Not everyone has believed that sleep is necessary. Napoleon I, emperor of France, and Frederick the Great, king of Prussia, were two of these people. Even though they were leaders of their different countries at different times, they had one thing in common. They both thought sleep was just a bad habit that wasted time, and they both tried to prove it. They didn't do this together, but they both had the same method—staying up. But neither one lasted more than two nights, and they both needed several days to recover from their experiment.

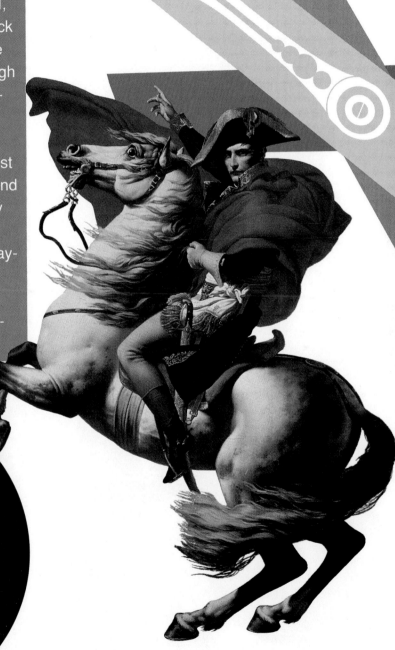

Frederick the Great, king of Prussia (left), and Napoleon I, emperor of France (above)

Sleeping Ages with Time

The amount of sleep people need varies for individuals, but experiments have shown that age makes a big difference too. When you were a newborn baby, you slept on and off all during the day and night. You were asleep twice as much as you were awake, which meant you were sleeping about sixteen hours a day.

As you grow older, you need less and less sleep. Up until the time you are a teenager, you may sleep an average of about ten hours every night.

Grownups don't all need the same amount of sleep, but on an average, adults are awake twice as long as they are asleep. That means they sleep about eight hours out of every day. When grownups get older, they need even less sleep than that. People who are over sixty years old usually need only five to six hours.

Check these sleep times with people you know—friends, parents, grandparents, other relatives. See if the information you find agrees with what the experts have learned.

Sleepy Statistics

People spend about 33 percent of their lives asleep. Cows spend only 3 percent of their lives sleeping. Maybe that's because they have four stomachs, and they've got to spend a lot more time chewing than humans do.

Horses sleep just a little less of their lives than humans do, about 29 percent. But gorillas are asleep 70 percent of the time.

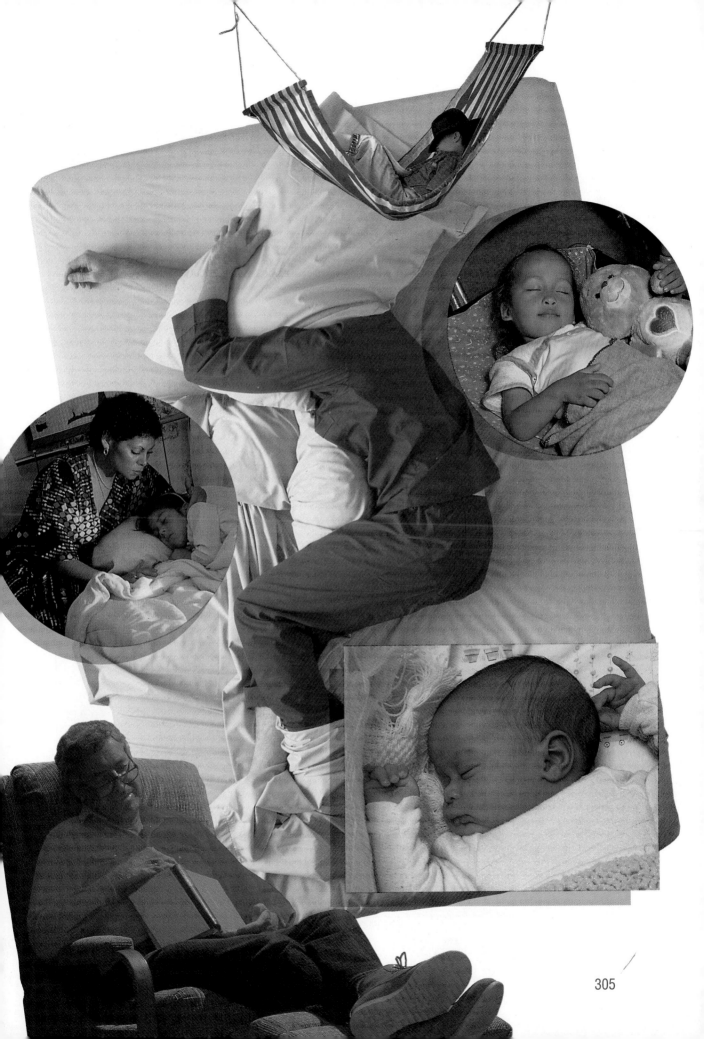

Scientists have also discovered that there are cycles you go through as you sleep. You plunge down into deep sleep, up to lighter sleep, and down again to deep sleep. This happens all the time you're sleeping, in cycles that last about an hour and a half each. Scientists have learned this from studying people's brain waves while they're asleep. Here's the difference in how brain waves look when you're awake and when you're asleep, including different stages. Scientists have also learned that you do your dreaming when you're in the light-sleep stage.

Brain Wave Patterns

Awake	
Dozing	
Light Sleep	
Deep Sleep	
Very Deep Sleep	

Here's a way to take a look at two of your daily cycles— your temperature cycle and your heartbeat cycle. The best time to do this experiment is on a day when you're not in school, so you can keep a record all through the day at regular times.

Get ready the night before you'll be doing the experiment. First make a recording chart, like the one shown. A piece of notebook-size paper will do fine. Notice that the chart is marked off every two hours. You'll start recording on your chart at the time listed that is closest to when you get up. Then take

Date _____			
Time	Temperature	Pulse	Follow-up Questions
6 AM			1.
8 AM			2.
10 AM			3.
12 Noon			4.
2 PM			5.
4 PM			6.
6 PM			7.
8 PM			8.
10 PM			9.
			10.

measurements at the other times listed during the day, stopping when you go to bed at night. Notice the space for answering the ten follow-up questions. You'll do that after you've taken all your statistics for the day.

The next thing to do is collect the equipment you'll need. You'll need a thermometer for taking your temperature, a thumbtack, a short piece of a straw—an inch or less—for taking your pulse. You'll also need a clock or watch with a second hand to time both your temperature taking and your pulse.

It's a good idea to practice taking both of these measurements once just to make sure you know how to do it. Here's how.

Taking Your Pulse

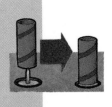

1. Put the piece of straw on the point of the thumbtack.

2. Place one hand, palm up, on a table top.

3. Put the straw-thumbtack apparatus on your wrist, on the outside edge. Move it about until you find the spot where your pulse is the strongest. You can tell because the straw moves more.

4. Count each time the straw moves up. Do this for fifteen seconds.

5. Multiply the number you counted by four. This will give you the number of times your heart beats in one minute.

Check with your parents for a quickie lesson about how to take your temperature and read the thermometer, if you're not sure. The average human body temperature is 98.6 degrees Fahrenheit, but not everyone has exactly that temperature normally. Don't be concerned if yours is a degree or two above or below this figure.

Taking Your Temperature

1. Clean the thermometer. Use soapy water or alcohol. Rinse well.

2. Shake the thermometer down until it reads less than 96 degrees.

3. Put the bulb under your tongue. It needs to stay there for a good three minutes, so time that with the clock or watch. (Notice how long three minutes seems like too.)

4. Read your temperature.

5. Clean the thermometer before putting it away.

If you know another way to take your pulse, that's fine too. When you do the experiment, take your temperature readings and pulse counts carefully all through the day. When you've got your chart completed, see how your information measures up to these follow-up questions.

According to scientists, your temperature should have been highest late in the afternoon or in the evening, and lowest in the early morning. Does your cycle agree with this? Also scientists say that most people have a 1½ to 2 degree variation all day. Was this true for you? Your pulse should have been lowest when you first got up, according to scientists. It should be highest at your usual time of greatest activity.

What Does Your Chart Show?

1. What's the lowest temperature you recorded all day?

2. What's the highest temperature?

3. How big a difference is there between these two readings?

4. At what time was the highest reading?

5. When was your temperature the lowest?

6. What was the slowest pulse reading you took?

7. What was the fastest pulse measurement?

8. When was your pulse the fastest?

9. When was it the slowest?

10. Can you see any relationship between when your pulse was fastest and when your temperature was highest?

A Statistical Caution

Remember, scientists did many, many tests before they came up with their conclusions. What you've done is just one sample of your daily cycle of temperature and pulse changes. Not only can your cycles differ somewhat from what the reported averages are, your own rhythms can change a bit from day to day. You've got a lifetime to spend with your body rhythms. Trying the experiment on another day will give you a chance to take another look.

Meet Marilyn Burns

Time flies when you're having fun and drags miserably when you've got the flu. Marilyn Burns explains why in "The Inside Story on People Time," from *This Book Is About Time.*

Burns's lighthearted humor and chatty writing style are evident throughout the book, which is dedicated to "the tortoise, the hare, and anyone else who has ever had a run-in with time." Burns is one of a group of writers who works with educators and artists to create the Brown Paper School book series. The group believes that "learning happens only when it is wanted, that it can happen anywhere and doesn't require fancy tools." One book in this series, *The I Hate Mathematics! Book,* was named an Outstanding Science Book for Children.

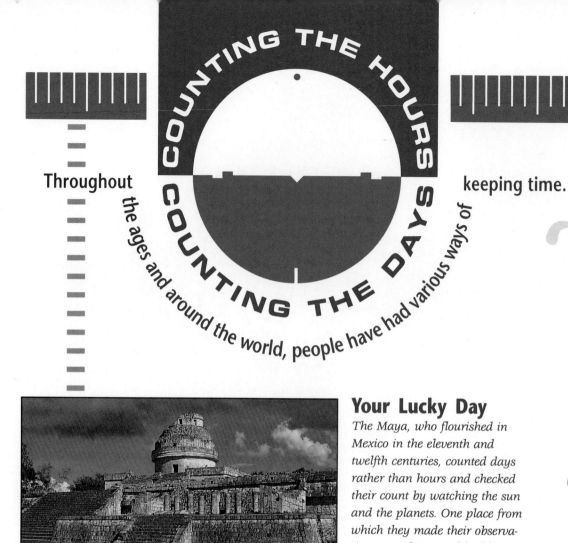

COUNTING THE HOURS
COUNTING THE DAYS

Throughout *the ages and around the world, people have had various ways of* keeping time.

Your Lucky Day

The Maya, who flourished in Mexico in the eleventh and twelfth centuries, counted days rather than hours and checked their count by watching the sun and the planets. One place from which they made their observations was this round building in the city of Chichén Itzá.

Follow the Sun

An upright pointer in the center of a sundial casts a shadow that moves around the dial as the sun moves.

Su Sung's Heavenly Clock

Chinese rulers of long ago believed in lucky days for conducting government business. The Heavenly Clock that Su Sung built for the emperor in A.D. 1090 was designed to determine those days.

The Nose Knows

The Chinese invented a clock that used the sense of smell to tell time! A trail of several kinds of incense was laid down in a mazelike path. As each kind of incense along the path began to burn, a different, wonderful aroma was given off. Since each variety of incense burned for a set length of time, one could judge what time it was by the odor.

Drip, Drop, Drip

The water clock, called a clepsydra, *was a simple stone pot with a hole in the bottom. The pot was filled with water that leaked slowly out. As time passed, the water level could be checked against marks on the pot, and the marks indicated how much time had elapsed.*

THE CLOCK TICKS

by Eve Merriam

get up get up
clatter a cup

spoon stir
toaster pop

stoke up
down the drain

door knob
click lock

clip clop
walk the block

books to school   read spell
wheels to work   file write

rush clack   window blind
lurch slack   lights on

hup stop   open shut
out all out   button press

clip clop   going up
walk the block   to the top

into the building
into the box

lights off
button press
back inside   going down
sun set   ground floor

out to lunch   out of the box
sandwich bag   clip clop

number please   books from school
hurry wait   wheels from work

stamp type   rush clack
carbon call   lurch slack

                                    hup stop
                                    out all out

                                 walk the block
                                 lock unlock

                              glass drain
                              plate scrape

                           teevee box
                           head to bed

                    tick tock
                    get up get up

Meet Norton Juster

An architect who writes in his spare time, Norton Juster says about the book *The Phantom Tollbooth*, "I began to write what I thought was a short story—for my own relaxation. Before I knew it, it had created its own life and I was hooked. *The Phantom Tollbooth* was the result."

Juster says, "I am always a little embarrassed to call myself a writer." For, as he puts it, "The way I see things and think about things is as an architect." However, Juster has written a number of other books in addition to *The Phantom Tollbooth*.

The New York Times listed *The Phantom Tollbooth* as a best-selling children's book in 1962, as well as one of the fifty best books of 1960–1965. The book was made into a movie in 1970.

THE PHANTOM TOLLBOOTH

by Norton Juster
illustrated by David Goldin

Milo comes home from school one day to find a mysterious package waiting for him. In it he finds a ready-to-assemble phantom tollbooth, complete with a rule book and a map to strange lands that Milo has never heard of before. Milo chooses Dictionopolis as his destination, drives his toy car up to the tollbooth, deposits a coin, and takes off on his fantastic voyage. As Milo drives along, the unfamiliar landscape gets grayer and grayer, Milo gets sleepier and sleepier, and the car moves slower and slower until it finally stops.

"I wonder where I am," said Milo in a very worried tone.

"You're . . . in . . . the . . . Dol . . . drums," wailed a voice that sounded far away.

He looked around quickly to see who had spoken. No one was there, and it was as quiet and still as one could imagine.

"Yes . . . the . . . Dol . . . drums," yawned another voice, but still he saw no one.

"WHAT ARE THE DOLDRUMS?" he cried loudly, and tried very hard to see who would answer this time.

"The Doldrums, my young friend, are where nothing ever happens and nothing ever changes."

This time the voice came from so close that Milo jumped with surprise, for, sitting on his right shoulder, so lightly that he hardly noticed, was a small creature exactly the color of his shirt.

"Allow me to introduce all of us," the creature went on. "We are the Lethargarians, at your service."

Milo looked around and, for the first time, noticed dozens of them—sitting on the car, standing in the road, and lying all over the trees and bushes. They were very difficult to see, because whatever they happened to be sitting on or near was exactly the color they happened to be. Each one looked very much like the other (except for the color, of course) and some looked even more like each other than they did like themselves.

"I'm very pleased to meet you," said Milo, not sure whether or not he was pleased at all. "I think I'm lost. Can you help me please?"

"Don't say 'think,'" said one sitting on his

shoe, for the one on his shoulder had fallen asleep. "It's against the law." And he yawned and fell off to sleep, too.

"No one's allowed to think in the Doldrums," continued a third, beginning to doze off. And as each one spoke, he fell off to sleep and another picked up the conversation with hardly any interruption.

"Don't you have a rule book? It's local ordinance 175389-J."

Milo quickly pulled the rule book from his pocket, opened to the page, and read, "Ordinance 175389-J: It shall be unlawful, illegal, and unethical to think, think of thinking, surmise, presume, reason, meditate, or speculate while in the Doldrums. Anyone breaking this law shall be severely punished!"

"That's a ridiculous law," said Milo, quite indignantly. "Everybody thinks."

"We don't," shouted the Lethargarians all at once.

"And most of the time *you* don't," said a yellow one sitting in a daffodil. "That's why you're here. You weren't thinking, and you weren't paying attention either. People who don't pay attention often get stuck in the Doldrums." And with that he toppled out of the flower and fell snoring into the grass.

Milo couldn't help laughing at the little creature's strange behavior, even though he knew it might be rude.

"Stop that at once," ordered the plaid one clinging to his stocking. "Laughing is against the law. Don't you have a rule book? It's local ordinance 574381-W."

Opening the book again, Milo found Ordinance 574381-W: "In the Doldrums, laughter is frowned upon and smiling is permitted only on alternate Thursdays. Violators shall be dealt with most harshly."

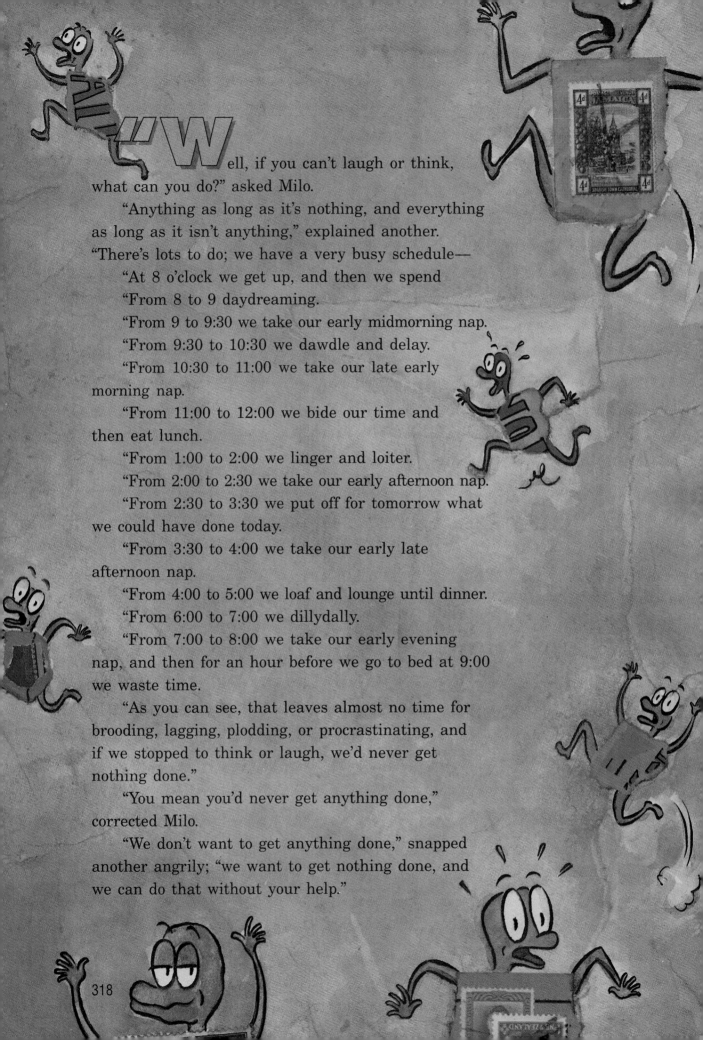

"**W**ell, if you can't laugh or think, what can you do?" asked Milo.

"Anything as long as it's nothing, and everything as long as it isn't anything," explained another. "There's lots to do; we have a very busy schedule—

"At 8 o'clock we get up, and then we spend

"From 8 to 9 daydreaming.

"From 9 to 9:30 we take our early midmorning nap.

"From 9:30 to 10:30 we dawdle and delay.

"From 10:30 to 11:00 we take our late early morning nap.

"From 11:00 to 12:00 we bide our time and then eat lunch.

"From 1:00 to 2:00 we linger and loiter.

"From 2:00 to 2:30 we take our early afternoon nap.

"From 2:30 to 3:30 we put off for tomorrow what we could have done today.

"From 3:30 to 4:00 we take our early late afternoon nap.

"From 4:00 to 5:00 we loaf and lounge until dinner.

"From 6:00 to 7:00 we dillydally.

"From 7:00 to 8:00 we take our early evening nap, and then for an hour before we go to bed at 9:00 we waste time.

"As you can see, that leaves almost no time for brooding, lagging, plodding, or procrastinating, and if we stopped to think or laugh, we'd never get nothing done."

"You mean you'd never get anything done," corrected Milo.

"We don't want to get anything done," snapped another angrily; "we want to get nothing done, and we can do that without your help."

"You see," continued another in a more conciliatory tone, "it's really quite strenuous doing nothing all day, so once a week we take a holiday and go nowhere, which was just where we were going when you came along. Would you care to join us?"

"I might as well," thought Milo; "that's where I seem to be going anyway."

"Tell me," he yawned, for he felt ready for a nap now himself, "does everyone here do nothing?"

"Everyone but the terrible watchdog," said two of them, shuddering in chorus. "He's always sniffing around to see that nobody wastes time. A most unpleasant character."

"The watchdog?" said Milo quizzically.

"THE WATCHDOG," shouted another, fainting from fright, for racing down the road barking furiously and kicking up a great cloud of dust was the very dog of whom they had been speaking.

"RUN!"

"WAKE UP!"

"RUN!"

"HERE HE COMES!"

"THE WATCHDOG!"

Great shouts filled the air as the Lethargarians scattered in all directions and soon disappeared entirely.

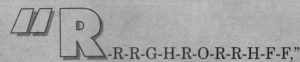"R-R-R-G-H-R-O-R-R-H-F-F,"
exclaimed the watchdog as he dashed up to the car,
loudly puffing and panting.

Milo's eyes opened wide, for there in front of him
was a large dog with a perfectly normal head, four
feet, and a tail—and the body of a loudly ticking
alarm clock.

"What are you doing here?" growled the watchdog.

"Just killing time," replied Milo apologetically.
"You see—"

"KILLING TIME!" roared the dog—so furiously
that his alarm went off. "It's bad enough wasting time
without killing it." And he shuddered at the thought.
"Why are you in the Doldrums anyway—don't you have
anywhere to go?"

"I was on my way to Dictionopolis when I got
stuck here," explained Milo. "Can you help me?"

"Help you! You must help yourself," the dog
replied, carefully winding himself with his left hind
leg. "I suppose you know why you got stuck."

"I guess I just wasn't thinking," said Milo.

"PRECISELY," shouted the dog as his alarm went
off again. "Now you know what you must do."

"I'm afraid I don't," admitted Milo, feeling
quite stupid.

"Well," continued the watchdog impatiently, "since
you got here by not thinking, it seems reasonable to
expect that, in order to get out, you must start thinking." And with that he hopped into the car.

"Do you mind if I get in? I love automobile rides."

Milo began to think as hard as he could (which
was very difficult, since he wasn't used to it). He
thought of birds that swim and fish that fly. He
thought of yesterday's lunch and tomorrow's dinner.

He thought of words that began with J and numbers that end in 3. And, as he thought, the wheels began to turn.

"We're moving, we're moving," he shouted happily.

"Keep thinking," scolded the watchdog.

The little car started to go faster and faster as Milo's brain whirled with activity, and down the road they went. In a few moments they were out of the Doldrums and back on the main highway. All the colors had returned to their original brightness, and as they raced along the road Milo continued to think of all sorts of things; of the many detours and wrong turns that were so easy to take, of how fine it was to be moving along, and, most of all, of how much could be accomplished with just a little thought. And the dog, his nose in the wind, just sat back, watchfully ticking.

"You must excuse my gruff conduct," the watchdog said, after they'd been driving for some time, "but you see it's traditional for watchdogs to be ferocious . . ."

Milo was so relieved at having escaped the Doldrums that he assured the dog that he bore him no ill will and, in fact, was very grateful for the assistance.

"Splendid," shouted the watchdog. "I'm very pleased—I'm sure we'll be great friends for the rest of the trip. You may call me Tock."

"That is a strange name for a dog who goes tick-ticktickticktick all day," said Milo. "Why didn't they call you—"

"**D**on't say it," gasped the dog, and Milo could see a tear well up in his eye.

"I didn't mean to hurt your feelings," said Milo, not meaning to hurt his feelings.

"That's all right," said the dog, getting hold of himself. "It's an old story and a sad one, but I can tell it to you now.

"When my brother was born, the first pup in the family, my parents were overjoyed and immediately named him Tick in expectation of the sound they were sure he'd make. On first winding him, they discovered to their horror that, instead of going tickticktickticktick, he went tocktocktocktocktocktock. They rushed to the Hall of Records to change the name, but too late. It had already been officially inscribed, and nothing could be done. When I arrived, they were determined not to make the same mistake twice and, since it seemed logical that all their children would make the same sound, they named me Tock. Of course, you know the rest—my brother is called Tick because he goes tocktocktocktocktocktocktock and I am called Tock because I go tickticktickticktickticktick and both of us are forever burdened with the wrong names. My parents were so overwrought that they gave up having any more children and devoted their lives to doing good work among the poor and hungry."

"But how did you become a watchdog?" interjected Milo, hoping to change the subject, as Tock was sobbing quite loudly now.

"That," he said, rubbing a paw in his eye, "is also traditional. My family have always been watchdogs— from father to son, almost since time began.

"You see," he continued, beginning to feel better, "once there was no time at all, and people found it

very inconvenient. They never knew whether they were eating lunch or dinner, and they were always missing trains. So time was invented to help them keep track of the day and get places when they should. When they began to count all the time that was available, what with 60 seconds in a minute and 60 minutes in an hour and 24 hours in a day and 365 days in a year, it seemed as if there was much more than could ever be used. 'If there's so much of it, it couldn't be very valuable,' was the general opinion, and it soon fell into disrepute. People wasted it and even gave it away. Then we were given the job of seeing that no one wasted time again," he said, sitting up proudly. "It's hard work but a noble calling. For you see"—and now he was standing on the seat, one foot on the windshield, shouting with his arms outstretched—"it is our most valuable possession, more precious than diamonds. It marches on, it and tide wait for no man, and—"

At that point in the speech the car hit a bump in the road and the watchdog collapsed in a heap on the front seat with his alarm again ringing furiously.

"Are you all right?" shouted Milo.

"Umphh," grunted Tock. "Sorry to get carried away, but I think you get the point."

TODAY I'M GOING

by Jack Prelutsky

Today I'm going yesterday
as quickly as I can,
I'm confident I'll do it,
I've devised a clever plan,
it involves my running backward
at a constant rate of speed,
if I'm mindful of my timing,
I'll undoubtedly succeed.

Today I'm going yesterday,
I'm moving very fast
as I'm putting off the future
for the rather recent past,
I can feel the present fading
as I hastily depart,
and look forward to arriving
on the day before I start.

Today I'm going yesterday,
I'm slipping out of sight
and anticipate I'll vanish
just a bit before tonight,
when I reach my destination,
I'll compose a note to say
that I'll see you all tomorrow,
which of course will be today.

CONTENTS

A Place in the Heart

It just takes wood
    to build a house.
Fill it with people
    and you have a home.
Fill it with love
    and people take root.
It's just like a tree
    where each branch
    becomes a family.

HAL DAVID

MANIAC

BY JERRY SPINELLI

Jeffrey Magee is orphaned at three and runs away from his aunt and uncle at eleven. A year later, he shows up in the town of Two Mills, where he immediately begins to become a legend. He runs everywhere instead of walking; he hits six home runs off Giant John McNab, who had struck out thirty-five Little League players. His first friend is Amanda Beale, who so loves books that she carries hers in a suitcase to and from school every day in order to protect them. He convinces her to lend him a book, promising to return it to her house at 728 Sycamore Street.

Illustrated by Oscar Hernandez

The town was buzzing. The schools were buzzing. Hallways. Lunchrooms. Streets. Playgrounds. West End. East End.

Buzzing about the new kid in town. The stranger kid. Scraggly. Carrying a book. Flap-soled sneakers.

The kid who intercepted Brian Denehy's pass to Hands Down and punted it back longer than Denehy himself ever threw it.

The kid who rescued Arnold Jones from Finsterwald's backyard.

The kid who tattooed Giant John McNab's fastball for half a dozen home runs, then circled the sacks on a bunted frog.

Nobody knows who said it first, but somebody must have: "Kid's gotta be a maniac."

And somebody else must have said: "Yeah, reg'lar maniac."

And somebody else: "Yeah."

And that was it. Nobody (except Amanda Beale) had any other name for him, so pretty soon, when they wanted to talk about the new kid, that's what they called him: Maniac.

The legend had a name.

But not an address. At least, not an official one, with numbers.

What he did have was the deer shed at the Elmwood Park Zoo, which is where he slept his first few nights in town. What the deer ate, especially the carrots, apples, and day-old hamburger buns, he ate.

He started reading Amanda Beale's book his second day in town and finished it that afternoon. Ordinarily, he would have returned it immediately, but he was so fascinated by the story of the Children's Crusade that he kept it and read it the next day. And the next.

When he wasn't reading, he was wandering. When most people wander, they walk. Maniac Magee ran. Around town, around the nearby townships, always carrying the book, keeping it in perfect condition.

This is what he was doing when his life, as it often seemed to do, took an unexpected turn.

John McNab had never in his life met a kid he couldn't strike out. Until the runt. Now, as he thought about it, he came to two conclusions:

1. He couldn't stand having this blemish on his record.
2. If you beat a kid up, it's the same as striking him out.

So McNab and his pals went looking for the kid. They called themselves the Cobras. Nobody messed with them. At least, nobody in the West End.

The Cobras had heard that the kid hung around the park and the tracks, and that's where they spotted him one Saturday afternoon, on the tracks by the path that ran from the Oriole Street dead end to the park. He was down by Red Hill and heading away from them, book in hand, as usual.

But the Cobras just stood there, stunned.

"I don't believe it," one Cobra said.

"Must be a trick," said another.

"I heard about it," said another, "but I didn't believe it."

It wasn't a trick. It was true. The kid was *running* on the rail.

McNab scooped up a handful of track stones. He launched one. He snarled, "He's dead. Let's get 'im!"

By the time Maniac looked back, they were almost on him. He wobbled once, leaped from the rail to the ground, and took off. He was at the Oriole Street dead end, but his instincts said no, not the street, too much open space. He

stuck with the tracks. Coming into view above him was the house on Rako Hill, where he had eaten spaghetti. He could go there, to the whistling mother, the other kids, be safe. They wouldn't follow him in there. Would they?

Stones clanked off the steel rails. He darted left, skirted the dump, wove through the miniature mountain range of stone piles and into the trees . . . skiing on his heels down the steep bank and into the creek, frogs plopping, no time to look for stepping rocks . . . yells behind him now, war whoops, stones pelting the water, stinging his back . . . ah, the other side, through the trees and picker bushes, past the armory jeeps and out to the park boulevard, past the Italian restaurant on the corner, the bakery, screeching tires, row houses, streets, alleys, cars, porches, windows, faces staring, faces, faces . . . the town whizzing past Maniac, a blur of faces, each face staring from its own window, each face in its own personal frame, its own house, its own address, someplace to be when there was no other place to be, how lucky to be a face staring out from a window . . .

And then—could it be?—the voices behind him were growing faint. He slowed, turned, stopped. They were lined up at a street a block back. They were still yelling and shaking their fists, but they weren't moving off the curb. And now they were laughing. Why were they laughing?

The Cobras were standing at Hector Street. Hector Street was the boundary between the East and West Ends. Or, to put it another way, between the blacks and whites. Not that you never saw a white in the East End or a black in the West End. People did cross the line now and then, especially if they were adults, and it was daylight.

But nighttime, forget it. And if you were a kid, day *or* night, forget it. Unless you had business on the other side, such as a sports team or school. But don't be just *strolling* along, as if you *belonged* there, as if you weren't *afraid,* as if you didn't even *notice* you were a different color from everybody around you.

The Cobras were laughing because they figured the dumb, scraggly runt would get out of the East End in about as good shape as a bare big toe in a convention of snapping turtles.

Of course, Maniac didn't know any of that. He was simply glad the chase was over. He turned and started walking, catching his breath.

East Chestnut. East Marshall. Green Street. Arch Street. He had been around here before. That first day with the girl named Amanda, other days jogging through. But this was Saturday, not a school day, and there was something different about the streets—kids. All over.

One of them jumped down from a front step and planted himself right in front of Maniac. Maniac had to jerk to a stop to keep from plowing into the kid. Even so, their noses were practically touching.

Maniac blinked and stepped back. The kid stepped forward. Each time Maniac stepped back, the kid stepped forward. They traveled practically half a block that way. Finally Maniac turned and started walking. The kid jumped around and plunked himself in front again. He bit off a chunk of the candy bar he was holding. "Where *you* goin'?" he said. Candy bar flakes flew from his mouth.

"I'm looking for Sycamore Street," said Maniac. "Do you know where it is?"

"Yeah, I know where it is."

Maniac waited, but the kid said nothing more. "Well, uh, do you think you could tell me where it is?"

Stone was softer than the kid's glare. "No."

Maniac looked around. Other kids had stopped playing, were staring.

Someone called: "Do 'im, Mars!"

Someone else: "Waste 'im!"

The kid, as you probably guessed by now, was none other then Mars Bar Thompson. Mars Bar heard the calls, and the stone got harder. Then suddenly he stopped glaring, suddenly he was smiling. He held up the candy bar, an inch from Maniac's lips. "Wanna bite?"

Maniac couldn't figure. "You sure?"

"Yeah, go ahead. Take a bite."

Maniac shrugged, took the Mars Bar, bit off a chunk, and handed it back. "Thanks."

Dead silence along the street. The kid had done the unthinkable, he had chomped on one of Mars's own bars. Not only that, but white kids just didn't put their mouths where black kids had had theirs, be it soda bottles, spoons, or candy bars. And the kid hadn't even gone for the unused end; he had chomped right over Mars Bar's own bite marks.

Mars Bar was confused. Who *was* this kid? *What* was this kid?

As usual, when Mars Bar got confused, he got mad. He thumped Maniac in the chest. "You think you bad or somethin'?"

Maniac, who was now twice as confused as Mars Bar, blinked. "Huh?"

"You think you come down here and be bad? That what you think?" Mars Bar was practically shouting now.

"No," said Maniac, "I don't think I'm bad. I'm not saying I'm an angel, either. Not even real good. Somewhere in between, I guess."

Mars Bar jammed his arms downward, stuck out his chin, sneered. "Am I bad?"

Maniac was befuddled. "*I* don't know. One minute you're yelling at me, the next minute you're giving me a bite of your candy bar."

The chin jutted out more. "Tell me I'm bad."

Maniac didn't answer. Flies stopped buzzing.

"I said, tell me I'm bad."

Maniac blinked, shrugged, sighed. "It's none of my business. If you're bad, let your mother or father tell you."

Now it was Mars Bar doing the blinking, stepping back, trying to sort things out. After a while he looked down. "What's that?"

Before Maniac answered, "A book," Mars Bar had snatched it from his hand. "This ain't yours," he said. He flipped through some pages. "Looks like mine."

"It's somebody else's."

"It's mine. I'm keepin' it."

With rattlesnake speed, Maniac snatched the book back—except for one page, which stayed, ripped, in Mars Bar's hand.

"Give me the page," said Maniac.

Mars Bar grinned. "Take it, fishbelly."

Silence. Eyes. The flies were waiting. East End vultures.

Suddenly neither kid could see the other, because a broom came down like a straw curtain between their faces, and a voice said, "*I'll* take it."

It was the lady from the nearest house, out to sweep her steps. She lowered the broom but kept it between them. "Better yet," she said to Mars Bar, "just give it back to him."

Mars Bar glared up at her. There wasn't an eleven-year-old in the East End who could stand up to Mars Bar's glare. In the West End, even high-schoolers were known to crumble under the glare. To old ladies on both sides of Hector Street,

it was all but fatal. And when Mars Bar stepped off a curb and combined the glare with his super-slow dip-stride slumpshuffle, well, it was said he could back up traffic all the way to Bridgeport while he took ten minutes to cross the street.

But not this time. This time Mars Bar was up against an East End lady in her prime, and she was matching him eyeball for eyeball. And when it was over, only one glare was left standing, and it wasn't Mars Bar's.

Mars Bar handed back the torn page, but not before he crumpled it into a ball. The broom pushed him away, turned him around, and swept him up the street.

The lady looked down at Maniac. A little of the glare lingered in her eyes. "You better get on, boy, where you belong. I can't be following you around. I got things to do."

Maniac just stood there a minute. There was something he felt like doing, and maybe he would have, but the lady turned and went back inside her house and shut the door. So he walked away.

Now what?

Maniac uncrumpled the page, flattened it out as best he could. How could he return the book to Amanda in this condition? He couldn't. But he had to. It was hers. Judging from that morning, she was pretty finicky about her books. What would make her madder—to not get the book back at all, or to get it back with a page ripped out? Maniac cringed at both prospects.

He wandered around the East End, jogging slowly, in no hurry now to find 728 Sycamore Street. He was passing a vacant lot when he heard an all-too-familiar voice: "Hey, fish-belly!" He stopped, turned. This time Mars Bar wasn't alone. A handful of other kids trailed him down the sidewalk.

Maniac waited.

Coming up to him, Mars Bar said, "Where you runnin', boy?"

"Nowhere."

"You runnin' from us. You afraid."

"No, I just like to run."

"You wanna run?" Mars Bar grinned. "Go ahead. We'll give you a head start."

Maniac grinned back. "No thanks."

Mars Bar held out his hand. "Gimme my book."

Maniac shook his head.

Mars Bar glared. "Gimme it."

Maniac shook his head.

Mars Bar reached for it. Maniac pulled it away.

They moved in on him now. They backed him up. Some high-schoolers were playing basketball up the street, but they weren't noticing. And there wasn't a broom-swinging lady in sight. Maniac felt a hard flatness against his back. Suddenly his world was very small and very simple: a brick wall behind him, a row of scowling faces in front of him. He clutched the book with both hands. The faces were closing in. A voice called: "That you, Jeffrey?"

The faces parted. At the curb was a girl on a bike— Amanda! She hoisted the bike to the sidewalk and walked it over. She looked at the book, at the torn page. "Who ripped my book?"

Mars Bar pointed at Maniac. "He did."

Amanda knew better. "*You* ripped my book."

Mars Bar's eyes went big as headlights. "I did *not!*"

"You *did*. You lie."

"I *didn't!*"

"You *did!*" She let the bike fall to Maniac. She grabbed the book and started kicking Mars Bar in his beloved sneakers. "I got a little brother and a little sister that crayon all over my books, and I got a dog that eats them and poops on them and that's just inside my own family, and I'm *not*—gonna have *nobody*—else *messin'*—with my *books!* You under-*stand?*"

By then Mars Bar was hauling on up the street past the basketball players, who were rolling on the asphalt with laughter.

Amanda took the torn page from Maniac. To her, it was the broken wing of a bird, a pet out in the rain. She turned misty eyes to Maniac. "It's one of my favorite pages."

Maniac smiled. "We can fix it."

The way he said it, she believed. "Want to come to my house?" she said.

"Sure," he said.

When they walked in, Amanda's mother was busy with her usual tools: a yellow plastic bucket and a sponge. She was scrubbing purple crayon off the TV screen.

"Mom," said Amanda, "this is Jeffrey—" She whispered, "What's your last name?"

He whispered, "Magee."

She said, "Magee."

Mrs. Beale held up a hand, said, "Hold it," and went on scrubbing. When she finally finished, she straightened up, turned, and said, "Now, what?"

"Mom, this is Jeffrey Magee. You know."

Amanda was hardly finished when Maniac zipped across the room and stuck out his hand. "Nice to meet you, Mrs. . . . Mrs. . . ."

"Beale."

"Mrs. Beale."

They shook hands. Mrs. Beale smiled. "So you're the book boy." She started nodding. "Manda came home one day— 'Mom, there's a boy I loaned one of my books out to!' 'Loaned a *book? You?*' 'Mom, he practically *made* me. He really likes books. I met him on—'"

"Mo-om!" Amanda screeched. "I never said all *that!*"

343

Mrs. Beale nodded solemnly—"No, of course you didn't"—and gave Maniac a huge wink, which made Amanda screech louder, until something crashed in the kitchen. Mrs. Beale ran. Amanda and Maniac ran.

The scene in the kitchen stopped them cold: one little girl, eyes wide, standing on a countertop; one little boy, eyes wide, standing just below her on a chair; one shattered glass jar and some stringy pale-colored glop on the floor; one growing cloud of sauerkraut fumes.

The girl was Hester, age four; the boy was Lester, age three. In less than five minutes, while Mrs. Beale and Amanda cleaned up the floor, Hester and Lester and their dog Bow Wow were in the backyard wrestling and tickling and jumping and just generally going wild with their new buddy—and victim—Maniac Magee.

Maniac was still there when Mr. Beale came home from his Saturday shift at the tire factory.

He was there for dinner, when Hester and Lester pushed their chairs alongside his.

He was there to help Amanda mend her torn book.

He was there watching TV afterward, with Hester riding one knee, Lester the other.

He was there when Hester and Lester came screaming down the stairs with a book, Amanda screaming even louder after them, the kids shoving the book and themselves onto Maniac's lap, Amanda finally calming down because they didn't want to crayon the book, they only wanted Maniac to read. And so he read *Lyle, Lyle, Crocodile* to Hester and Lester and, even though they pretended not to listen, to Amanda and Mr. and Mrs. Beale.

And he was there when Hester and Lester were herded upstairs to bed, and Mrs. Beale said, "Don't you think it's about time you're heading home, Jeffrey? Your parents'll be wondering."

So Maniac, wanting to say something but not knowing how, got into the car for Mr. Beale to drive him home. And then he made his mistake. He waited for only two or three blocks to go by before saying to Mr. Beale, "This is it."

Mr. Beale stopped, but he didn't let Maniac out of the car. He looked at him funny. Mr. Beale knew what his passenger apparently didn't: East End was East End and West End was West End, and the house this white lad was pointing to was filled with black people, just like every other house on up to Hector Street.

Mr. Beale pointed this out to Maniac. Maniac's lip started to quiver, and right there, with the car idling in the middle of the street, Maniac told him that he didn't really have a home, unless you counted the deer shed at the zoo.

Mr. Beale made a U-turn right there and headed back. Only Mrs. Beale was still downstairs when they walked into the house. She listened to no more than ten seconds' worth of Mr. Beale's explanation before saying to Maniac, "You're stay-ing here."

Not long after, Maniac was lying in Amanda's bed, Amanda having been carried over to Hester and Lester's room, where she often slept anyway.

Before Maniac could go to sleep, however, there was something he had to do. He flipped off the covers and went downstairs. Before the puzzled faces of Mr. and Mrs.

Beale, he opened the front door and looked at the three cast-iron digits nailed to the door frame: seven two eight. He kept staring at them, smiling. Then he closed the door, said a cheerful "Goodnight," and went back to bed.

Maniac Magee finally had an address.

meet JERRY SPINELLI

As unlikely as it may seem, some fried chicken played a part in launching Jerry Spinelli's career as a writer of books for young people. His plan to eat the leftover fowl for lunch was foiled when one of his children beat him to it. Spinelli chose to write about the experience. From that piece of writing grew *Space Station Seventh Grade*, Spinelli's first published book.

It was not the first time that Spinelli had been prompted to write about events in his own life. At sixteen, he celebrated his high school football team's victory by composing a poem. Spinelli remembers, "The poem was published in the local newspaper, and I've been a writer ever since."

Spinelli's attempts at writing for adults proved unsuccessful. However, with the publication of his first book for young adults, he realized that his memories of growing up in Norristown, Pennsylvania, were rich sources of material. Inspired by those memories and by the experiences of his children, he has been writing successfully for young people since 1982. His novels are often funny but also deal honestly with the concerns, feelings, and problems that go with being young.

Maniac Magee won the 1991 Newbery Medal. Spinelli's other books include *Who Put That Hair in My Toothbrush?* and *Dump Days*.

Are you a running maniac like Jeffrey Magee? Or are you crazy about some other sport? Either way, a little know-how can help your game. Using the right technique can help you run faster, and choosing the right shoes can improve your performance, no matter what sport you play.

ON THE

ANATOMY OF A SPORTS SHOE

LAST The last is the over-all shape of the shoe. A curved last will tend to tip your feet inward. The last of your shoe should help your feet work better.

UPPER The upper part of the shoe should be leather or nylon.

LACES Laces are an important source of stability for your foot. Be sure to keep them firmly tied.

TOE BREAK The toe break, where your shoe folds when you stand on your toes, should bend easily.

HEEL COUNTER The heel counter provides stability by preventing your foot from rolling from side to side.

TOE BOX The toe box should fit snugly around your toes without rubbing them.

MIDSOLE The midsole supports your foot during impact. It should flatten slightly and then return to its original shape.

SOLE The sole contacts the ground and should be firm.

RUN

THE RIGHT SHOE FOR THE RIGHT SPORT

Basketball Look for a shoe with strong side supports to hold your foot upright when you pivot, turn, or stop. High tops can protect your heel and ankle. **Tennis** Strong side supports are important because of pivots, turns, and sudden stops. **Gymnastics** A cross-training shoe—one designed to be worn for more than one sport—is best. Because shoes are not usually allowed during competition, use tape on your feet for support. **Aerobics** The denser midsole of a cross-training shoe may be a better choice than an aerobics shoe. **Baseball/Softball/Soccer** Spiked shoes can cause heel pain. Look for a good solid insole. Adding felt lifts or a heel counter may help prevent pain.

Child of the Owl

of the

OWL

BY LAURENCE YEP

Casey was just a small child when her mother, Jeanie, died. Since then, Casey has been brought up by her father, Barney. When Barney is hospitalized, Casey goes to stay with her uncle Phil and his family. Used to a free-spirited life with her father, Casey is uncomfortable in Phil's strict household. In turn, Phil's family is unwilling to accept Casey's attitudes, ideas, and behavior. The situation is tense for everyone, so Phil decides to take Casey to San Francisco's Chinatown to live with Paw-Paw, her grandmother. On the way, Casey is nervous. She has never met Paw-Paw, and she feels alone and out of place in the unfamiliar setting.

ILLUSTRATED BY WINSON TRANG

351

Phil headed up Sacramento Street—a steep, slanting street that just zoomed on and on to the top of Nob Hill, where the rich people lived and where they had the swanky hotels. Phil turned suddenly into a little dead-end alley wide enough for only one car. On one side was a one-story Chinese school of brick so old or so dirty that the bricks were practically a purple color. On the other side as we drove by was a small parking lot with only six spaces for cars. Phil stopped the car in the middle of the alley and I could see the rest of it was filled with apartment houses. Somewhere someone had a window open and the radio was blaring out "I Want to Hold Your Hand" by that new group, the Beatles. I couldn't find the place where it was coming from but I did see someone's diapers and shirts hung in the windows and on the fire escape of one apartment.

"Why do they hang their laundry in the windows?" I asked Phil.

"That's what people from Hong Kong use for curtains," Phil grumbled.

The sidewalk in front of Paw-Paw's house was cracked like

someone had taken a sledgehammer to it, and there were iron grates over the lower windows. The steps up to the doorway were old, worn concrete painted red. To the left were the mailboxes, which had Chinese words for the names or had no labels at all. To the right were the doorbells to all the nine apartments. Phil picked out the last and rang. He jabbed his thumb down rhythmically. Three short. Three long. Three short.

"Why are you doing that?" I asked.

"Signaling your Paw-Paw," he grumbled. "She never answers just one buzz like any normal person, or even just three bursts. It's got to be nine buzzes in that way or she doesn't open the door. She says her friends know what she means."

So did I. It was Morse code for SOS. The buzzer on the door sounded like an angry bee. Phil the Pill opened the door, putting his back against it and fighting against the heavy spring that tried to swing it shut. "Go on. Up three flights. Number nine."

I walked into an old, dim hallway and climbed up the wooden steps. As I turned an angle on the stairs, I saw light burning fierce and bright from a window. When I came to it, I looked out at the roof of the Chinese school next door. Someone had thrown some old 45's and a pair of sneakers down there. If I were some kind of kid that felt sorry for herself, I would almost have said that was the way I felt: like some piece of old, ugly junk that was being kicked around on the discard pile while Barney was getting better.

I didn't stay by the window long, though, because Phil was coming up the stairs and I didn't want to act like his kids' stories about Paw-Paw had scared me. Anybody could be better than Phil the Pill and his family. . . I hoped. I stopped by the number-nine room,

afraid to knock. It could not be the right place because I could hear "I Want to Hold Your Hand" coming through the doorway. I scratched my head and checked the numbers on the other doors on the landing. Phil the Pill was still a flight down, huffing and puffing up the steps with my duffel bag—it wasn't that heavy; Phil was just that much out of shape. "Go on. Go on. Knock, you little idiot," he called up the stairwell.

I shrugged. It wasn't any of my business. I knocked at the door. I heard about six bolts and locks being turned. Finally the door swung open and I saw a tiny, pleasant, round-faced woman smiling at me. Her cheeks were a bright red. Her gray hair was all curly and frizzy around her head and a pair of rimless, thick eyeglasses perched on her nose. She was round and plump, wearing a sweater even on a hot day like this, a pair of cotton black slacks, and a pair of open-heeled, flat slippers.

"Paw-Paw?" I asked.

"Hello. Hello." She opened up her arms and gave me a big hug, almost crushing me. It was funny, but even though it was like I said—Barney and me never went in much for that sentimental stuff like hugging and kissing—I suddenly found myself holding on to her. Underneath all the soft layers of clothing I could feel how hard and tough she was. She patted me on the back three times and then left me for a moment to turn down her radio. It really was her old, white, beat-up radio playing rock music.

"Hey, how about a hand?" Phil puffed as he finally got to the landing.

Paw-Paw shuffled out to the landing in her slippered feet and made shooing motions. "You can go home now. We can do all right by ourselves."

Phil heaved his shoulders up and down in a great sigh and set the bag down. "Now, Momma—"

"Go on home," she said firmly. "We need time by ourselves."

I saw that Phil must have had some fine speech all prepared, probably warning Paw-Paw about me and warning me about ingratitude. He was not about to give up such an opportunity to make a speech.

"Now, Momma—"

"Go on. You're still not too old for a swat across the backside."

Phil ran his hand back and forth along the railing. "Really, Momma. You oughtn't—"

"Go on." Paw-Paw raised her hand.

Phil gulped. The thought of having a former district president of the lawyers spanked by his own mother must have been too much for him. He turned around and started down the steps. He still had to get in the last word though. "You mind your Paw-Paw, young lady. You hear me?" he shouted over his shoulder.

waited till I heard the door slam. "Do you know what those buzzes stand for?"

"Do you?" Her eyes crinkled up.

"It stands for SOS. But where did you learn it?"

"When I worked for the American lady, her boy had a toy... what do you call it?" She made a tapping motion with her finger.

"Telegraph?"

"Yes. It's a good joke on such a learned man, no?" Her round red face split into a wide grin and then she began to giggle and when she put her hand over her mouth, the giggle turned into a laugh.

I don't think that I had laughed in all that time since Barney's accident a month ago. It was like all the laughter I hadn't been able to use came bubbling up out of some hidden well—burst out of the locks and just came up. Both of us found ourselves slumping on the landing, leaning our heads against the banister, and laughing.

Finally Paw-Paw tilted up her glasses and wiped her eyes. "Philip always did have too much dignity for one person. Ah." She leaned back against the railing on the landing before the stairwell, twisting her head to look at me. "You'll go far," she nodded. "Yes, you will. Your eyebrows are beautifully curved, like silkworms. That means you'll be clever. And your ears are small and close to your head and shaped a certain way. That means you're adventurous and win much honor."

"Really?"

She nodded solemnly. "Didn't you know? The face is the map of the soul." Then she leaned forward and raised her glasses and pointed to the corners of her eyes where there were two small hollows, just shadows, really. "You see those marks under my eyes?"

"Yes." I added after a moment, "Paw-Paw."

"Those marks, they mean I have a temper."

"Oh." I wondered what was to happen next.

She set her glasses back on her nose. "But I will make a deal with you. I can keep my temper under control if you can do the same with your love of adventure and intelligence. You see, people, including me, don't always understand a love of adventure and intelligence. Sometimes we mistake them for troublemaking."

"I'll try," I grinned.

I went and got my bag then and brought it inside Paw-Paw's place and looked around, trying to figure out where I'd put it. Her place wasn't more than ten by fifteen feet and it was crowded with her stuff. Her bed was pushed lengthwise against the wall next to the doorway leading out to the landing. To the right of the door was another doorway, leading to the small little cubicle of a kitchen, and next to that door was her bureau. The wall opposite the bed had her one window leading out to the fire escape and giving a view of the alley, which was so narrow that it looked like we could have shaken hands with the people in the apartment house across from us. Beneath the window was a stack of newspapers for wrapping up the garbage. Next to the window was a table with a bright red-and-orange-flower tablecloth. Paw-Paw pulled aside her chair and her three-legged stool and told me to put my bag under the table. A metal cabinet and stacks of boxes covered the rest of the wall and the next one had hooks from which coats and other stuff in plastic bags hung.

In the right corner of the old bureau were some statues and an old teacup with some dirt in it and a half-burnt incense stick stuck into it. The rest of the top, though, was covered with old photos in little cardboard covers. They filled the bureau top and the mirror too, being stuck into corners of the mirror or actually taped onto the surface.

Next to the photos were the statues. One was about eight inches high in white porcelain of a pretty lady holding a flower and with the most patient, peaceful expression on her face. To her left was a statue of a man with a giant-sized, bald head. And then there were eight little statues, each only about two inches high. "Who are they?" I asked.

"Statues of some holy people," Paw-Paw said reluctantly.

There was something familiar about the last statue on Paw-Paw's bureau. It was of a fat, balding god with large ears, who had little children crawling over his lap and climbing up his shoulders. "Hey," I said. "Is that the happy god?"

Paw-Paw looked puzzled. "He's not the god of happiness."

"But they call him the happy god. See?" I pulled Barney's little plastic charm out of my pocket and pointed to the letters on the back.

Paw-Paw didn't even try to read the lettering. Maybe Barney had already shown it to her long ago. "He's not the god of happiness. He just looks happy. He's the Buddha—the Buddha who will come in the future. He's smiling because everyone will be saved by that time and he can take a vacation. The children are holy people who become like children again."

"What about the others, Paw-Paw?"

"I don't have the words to explain," Paw-Paw said curtly, like the whole thing was embarrassing her.

I sat down by the table on the stool, which was painted white with red flowers. "Sure you do. I think your English is better than mine."

"You don't want to know any of that stuff." With her index finger Paw-Paw rubbed hard against some spot on the tablecloth. "That stuff's only for old people. If I tell you any more, you'll laugh at it like all other young people do." There was bitter hurt and anger in her voice.

I should have left her alone, I guess; but we had been getting close to one another and suddenly I'd found this door between us—a door that wouldn't open. I wasn't so much curious now as I was desperate: I didn't want Paw-Paw shutting me out like that. "I won't laugh, Paw-Paw. Honest."

"That stuff's only for old people who are too stupid to learn American ways," she insisted stubbornly.

"Well, maybe I'm stupid too."

"No." Paw-Paw pressed her lips together tightly; and I saw that no matter how much I pestered her, I wasn't going to get her to tell me any more about the statues on her bureau. We'd been getting along so great before that I was sorry I'd ever started asking questions.

We both sat, each in our own thoughts, until almost apologetically Paw-Paw picked up a deck of cards from the table. "Do you play cards?"

"Some," I said. "Draw poker. Five-card stud. Things like that."

Paw-Paw shuffled the cards expertly. "Poker is for old men who like to sit and think too much. Now I know a game that's for the young and quick."

"What's that?"

"Slapjack." She explained that each of us took half

of a deck and stacked it in front
without looking at it. Then we
would take turns taking the top
card off and putting it down in
the middle. Whenever a jack appeared, the first one to put her
hand over the pile of cards got it.
She then mixed the new cards
with all the cards she still had in
front of her. The first one to get
all the cards won the game. It
would sound like the advantage
was with the person who was
putting out the card at that time,
but she was supposed to turn
up the card away from her so
she couldn't see it before the
other player.

Paw-Paw had played a lot
of card games, since she lived by
herself, so she seemed to know
when the jacks were going to come
up. For a while all you could hear
was the *slap-slap-slap*ping of cards
and sometimes our hands smack-
ing one another trying to get the
pile. And sometimes I'd have
more cards and sometimes Paw-
Paw would. Eventually, though,
she beat me. She shuffled the
deck again. "You're a pretty good
player," she grudged.

"Not as good as you, though."

Paw-Paw shuffled the cards, tapping them against the table so the cards in the pack were all even. "We used to play all the time. Your mother, Phil, everyone. We'd hold big contests and make plenty of noise. Only when Phil got older, he only wanted to play the games fancy Americans played like—what's that word for a road that goes over water?"

"A bridge? Phil wanted to play bridge."

"Yes." Paw-Paw put the deck on the table. I wandered over to the bed.

The radio was in a little cabinet built into the head-board of the bed. I lay down on the bed and looked at the radio dial. "Do you like rock music, Paw-Paw?"

"It's fun to listen to," Paw-Paw said, "and besides, *Chinese Hour* is on that station every night."

"Chinese Hour?"

"An hour of news and songs all in Chinese." Paw-Paw slipped the cards back carefully into their box. "They used to have some better shows on that station like mystery shows."

"I bet I could find some." I started to reach for the dial.

"Don't lose that station." Paw-Paw seemed afraid suddenly.

"Don't worry, Paw-Paw, I'll be able to get your station back for you." It was playing "Monster Mash" right then. I twisted the dial to the right and the voices and snatches of song slid past and then I turned the dial back to her station, where "Monster Mash" was still playing. "See?"

"As long as you could get it back," Paw-Paw said reluctantly.

I fiddled with the dial some more until I got hold of *Gunsmoke*. It'd gone off the air three years ago but

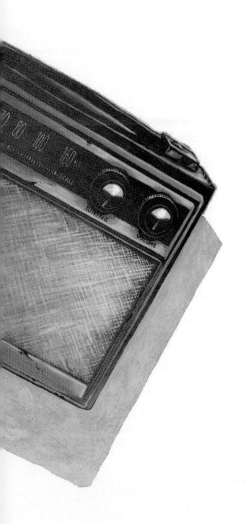

some station was playing reruns. Paw-Paw liked that, especially the deep voice of the marshal. It was good to sit there in the darkening little room, listening to Marshal Dillon inside your head and picturing him as big and tall and striding down the dusty streets of Dodge City. And I got us some other programs too, shows that Paw-Paw had never been able to listen to before.

Don't get the idea that Paw-Paw was stupid. She just didn't understand American machines that well. She lived with them in a kind of truce where she never asked much of them if they wouldn't ask much of her.

"It's getting near eight," Paw-Paw said anxiously. It was only when I got the station back for her that she began to relax. "I was always so worried that I would not be able to get back the station, I never tried to listen to others. Look what I missed."

"But you have me now, Paw-Paw," I said.

"Yes," Paw-Paw smiled briefly, straightening in her chair. "I guess I do."

MEET
Laurence Yep

For much of his early life, Laurence Yep knew what it was like to feel that he did not belong. He lived in a neighborhood where he was the only Chinese-American boy, and, despite his Chinese heritage, he was one of the few Chinese-American students at his school who could not speak Chinese.

Yep's feeling of being an outsider led him to read science fiction. There, he found characters and situations that seemed familiar, he says, "because in those books children were taken to other lands and other worlds where they had to learn strange customs and languages—and that was something I did every time I got on and off the bus."

Yep sold his first story when he was eighteen and was paid a penny per word. Not surprisingly, that piece was science fiction, as are many of Yep's later works. He also writes realistic novels, often drawing upon his Chinese-American background. One of these is *Dragonwings*, which was a Newbery Honor Book. Another is *Child of the Owl*, which won the Boston Globe–Horn Book Award in 1979.

My
Grandmother
Would ROCK
and Quietly
Hum

in her house
she would rock quietly and hum
until her swelled hands
calmed

in summer
she wore thick stockings
sweaters
and gray braids

(when *el cheque* came
we went to Payless
and I laughed greedily
when given a quarter)

mornings,
sunlight barely lit
the kitchen
and where
there were shadows
it was not cold

she quietly rolled
flour tortillas—
the *papas*
crackling in hot lard
would wake me

she had lost her teeth
and when we ate
she had bread
soaked in *café*

always her eyes
were clear
and she could see
as I cannot yet see—
through her eyes
she gave me herself

she would sit
and talk
of her girlhood—
of things strange to me:
    México
    epidemics
    relatives shot
    her father's hopes
    of this country—
how they sank
with cement dust
to his insides

now
when I go
to the old house
the worn spots
by the stove
echo of her shuffling
and México
still hangs in her fading
calendar pictures

—LEONARD ADAMÉ

THE GREAT
ANCESTOR HUNT
BY LILA PERL
CLARION, 1989

Coming Home

A FAMILY APART
BY JOAN LOWERY NIXON
BANTAM, 1988

Maxine B. Rosenberg

"A handicapped child, an adopted one, a twin, a child emigrating from another country or a child born of two races, all have joys and pains they want to share. By putting their feelings in books," Maxine Rosenberg says, "I offer children in special situations the comfort of knowing there are others like them." Many people have told Rosenberg that her books have helped them feel better about themselves.

Rosenberg's desire to be a writer began when she adopted a Korean child and recorded the experience in a journal. Now the author of several books, she declares, "I'm so happy with what I do that often I have to remind myself that this is my job."

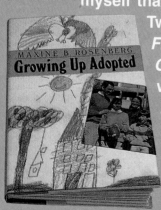

Two of her books, *My Friend, Leslie* and *Growing Up Adopted*, were named American Library Association Notable Books.

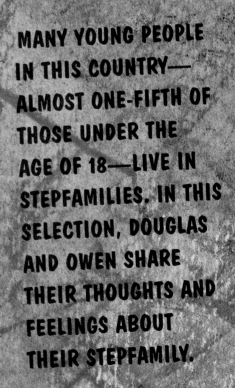

MANY YOUNG PEOPLE IN THIS COUNTRY— ALMOST ONE-FIFTH OF THOSE UNDER THE AGE OF 18—LIVE IN STEPFAMILIES. IN THIS SELECTION, DOUGLAS AND OWEN SHARE THEIR THOUGHTS AND FEELINGS ABOUT THEIR STEPFAMILY.

TALKING About STEPFAMILIES

by Maxine B. Rosenberg

DOUGLAS

"A house should be peaceful."

"About five years ago, my parents got divorced. When they decided to break up, I felt miserable most of the time. Suddenly, after doing so well in school, I lost interest in my work, and my grades began to slip. Mostly I dreaded hearing my parents argue with each other. They just couldn't get along, and that's why their marriage fell apart.

"It was also hard not knowing any other children in the same situation. My friends acted as if I was weird. They couldn't understand what was going on in my life, but neither could I. A year and a half later, when Dad told me he was marrying Pat, I was relieved to be back in a family. I thought he and Pat could make things work. In my mind, marriage was supposed to last. It was my parents who were strange for divorcing."

Since his parents' separation and divorce, Douglas and his older brother, Daniel, have alternated homes each week. "When their marriage broke up, Mom moved into her own apartment, while Dad kept the house. Because they lived so close to each other, joint custody worked out.

"In my opinion, switching homes every week is rotten. Of all the things that happened because of the divorce, that's been the hardest for me. I'm better adjusted to it than I was, but it's still confusing.

"At Dad's I live with three rowdy brothers—Daniel plus my stepbrothers, Owen and Eric—and our dog, Rudy. There, my bedtime is eleven o'clock. When I go to Mom's, I'm in a totally different atmosphere. Her house is so quiet with just the two of us, since Daniel's usually off with his friends. Bedtime at Mom's is ten o'clock. After having been at Dad's, I'm not tired then, so for the first night or two, I have trouble falling asleep. When I finally get settled in, I have to move again."

To make his life easier, Douglas keeps clothing at both places. But each week he has to bring some extras, depending upon the weather or school activities. "It never fails that I forget one small thing and have to go back to the other house to get it. That can be a real pain, especially for the person who has to drive me.

"Having two different homes can be embarrassing, too. Sometimes in school I'm asked to write on forms that don't have enough lines for my two different addresses. It's annoying having to explain why I need another sheet of paper."

Once his father married Pat, Douglas had another adjustment to make: living with two stepbrothers. In the beginning there were many awkward situations. "Although I feel close to Owen and Eric today, it didn't happen overnight. During those early months, I had no idea what to talk about with them or how we should play together. Gradually, we worked things out.

"One thing in particular helped us get along better—our dog, Rudy. From the moment he arrived, we shared responsibilities: feeding and walking him, and cleaning up his mess. Rudy was the one subject we didn't fight about. We even played with him together without arguing."

When Douglas and Daniel's father remarried, Owen and Eric began attending their stepbrothers' school. "Owen and I were both in fourth grade, but in different classes. On the first day of school, I introduced him to my friends as my stepbrother, not knowing how they would react.

"One thing in particular helped us get along better— our dog, Rudy."

"We're good athletes. The only time we compete is when we're playing on opposite teams."

Fortunately, Owen gets along well with everybody and was quickly accepted. Since he's also good in sports, it made it easier for him to join in. Pretty soon I started thinking of him as my school friend, rather than my stepbrother.

"Now Owen and I are in seventh grade, and we do well. We both have lots of friends; some we share, and some we don't. And we're good athletes. The only time we compete is when we're playing on opposite teams.

"The best thing about having Owen for a stepbrother is that we're the same age. That means we can help each other in math or go to parties together. Although we're not biologically related, Owen's definitely part of my family.

"Having lived with him and Eric for four years, I'm glad they're my stepbrothers. Even though we have different last names I consider them my brothers.

"Still, the stepfamily arrangement is not always easy. For one thing, being the youngest and smallest of the kids, I get all the hand-me-downs. Of course, if I *really* need something, Mom or Dad will get it for me, but first I have to explain why it has to be something new.

"Also, because Owen is seven months older than I, he thinks of himself as my big brother and sometimes acts a little cocky. And because he's older, things happen to him first. Although I started Hebrew school before he moved here, he had his Bar Mitzvah and got all the attention and gifts ahead of me. While I'm looking forward to my celebration, I wish it had come before his."

As for his relationship with Pat, Douglas liked her from the start—even before she married his father. "I'd see Pat when I was staying at Dad's house and she'd come to visit. One weekend, after Pat and Dad had been dating for a while, her family and ours got together and played baseball. While I can't remember anything about the wedding day, I'll never forget that baseball game. It was great.

"Of all the adults in my family now, I have the most fun with Pat. She's home more than the others because she doesn't work, so I get to do a lot of things with her. Since we're the only two who like eating Thai food, we go to those restaurants together. More than that, Pat gives me a lot of attention. Besides being a nice person and a great cook, she's a good listener."

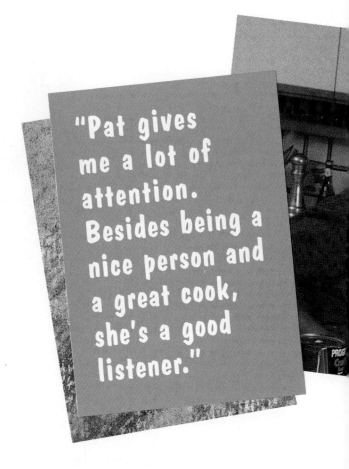

"Pat gives me a lot of attention. Besides being a nice person and a great cook, she's a good listener."

The only time Douglas becomes uncomfortable with his stepmother is when the subject of his parents' divorce comes up. "Pat takes my father's side and sees things from his point of view. But I remember *both* of my parents arguing all the time, so I can't say who's most at fault.

"Anyhow, my mother will always be my parent, and that will never change. I guess that's why I don't like anyone talking badly about her. Sometimes Mom does things that upset me, but other times she's there when I need her. While I realize that she and Dad couldn't make it together, at least I know they both love me.

"When Dad married Pat, I thought I'd finally be in a normal family. In my head, a divorced family was peculiar. Thinking about my life today, I see that I've landed in a more unusual setup than I expected. But fortunately, things have turned out all right.

"Still, I have some questions about my future. After all I've been through, marriage might be a problem for me. I wouldn't want to get divorced and go through the kind of arguing I heard between Mom and Dad. I'll never forget how upset Mom was at that time."

Arguing—especially between his parents—continues to make Douglas anxious. "Once in a while Mom and Dad have a fight on the phone. Usually they disagree about small things. Even so, I don't like to hear them raise their voices. It reminds me of what went on during the divorce years. Thank goodness they're much better than they used to be, and I can count on them getting along in public.

"Pat and Dad have fights, too, but just little ones. Still, that makes me nervous. I think, What if *they* don't make it?"

In Douglas's fantasies, the ideal family would include a dog like Rudy, a cute baby girl like his new cousin, two nice brothers who have the same ability in sports and can have fun together, and, to make life easier, the original parents. "Most important, everyone has to get along. I realize families have to have an occasional fight, but a house should be peaceful.

"As for being in a stepfamily, I've pretty much gone with the flow. Now I can't imagine what I'd be like if Pat, Owen, and Eric hadn't come into my life. Surely I'd be a different person than I am today, and I'm happy to be me. That alone makes me believe that everything will work out in my future."

Owen's father died when he was six months old. "I have a lot of pain when I think about my dad. And for a long time I was angry that he died. Mom took me to a therapist when I was in second grade, and after going for three years, I felt much better."

While Owen was in therapy, his mother started dating Ron. "Mom had gone out with lots of guys, but she liked Ron the best. Still, I had no idea how serious she was with him or what the man was really like. The few times I spoke to him were when he came to our apartment to pick Mom up. He seemed nice.

"Then one day Mom told me that Ron had invited the three of us to his house. I suspected something was up because my older brother, Eric, agreed to come along. That Sunday visit made an impression on me. Even though Eric and I had never met Daniel and Douglas—Ron's two boys—before, we all had a lot of fun playing baseball."

After that weekend the two families went on ski trips together, visited museums, and even shared holidays. When Owen's mother had known Ron for a year, she told Owen and Eric that she would be getting married the following September. "Mom also announced that, three weeks before the wedding, we would be moving into a new house in the suburbs. That way Eric and I could begin the school year with everyone else. Although Eric was upset about leaving the city, it didn't bother me. In a way, I was ready for the change. In fact, I had no objections to anything she told us. Having never been in a stepfamily, I couldn't imagine what it would be like—good or bad—and decided to wait and see.

"But moving before the wedding scared me to death. What if Mom suddenly decided not to go through with the marriage, after giving up our apartment and her job, and switching our schools? Thank goodness everything turned out well, but those were three long weeks.

"After that, my life changed. Until Mom's marriage, there were just three people in my house. Within minutes, our family doubled in size."

Before Owen's mother married Ron, the two families met a few times so everybody could talk about their concerns. While

OWEN

"There's no way to predict how things will work out."

Owen doesn't remember what was discussed at these meetings, he says they at least helped him feel more comfortable with his future stepfather. "There's no way to predict how things will work out. You have to live with people to understand what they're about. For me, the biggest issue became getting used to a second adult in the house. For almost my entire life, I only had to listen to my mother. Now suddenly Ron was in charge, too, and he did things differently from the way I had been brought up.

"From the start, Ron was stricter than Mom. While he wasn't real harsh, he grounded me or sent me to my room when I misbehaved. Even today, he punishes me that way.

"Mom, on the other hand, was always lenient with Eric and me. As soon as she remarried, though, *she* started disciplining us more, too. It took me a while to get used to this, and I'm still not thrilled with how she's changed.

"What makes it harder is that my stepfather relaxes the rule when it comes to disciplining Douglas. I admit that

Douglas doesn't talk back to his father as much as I do, but it's still not fair."

Despite these feelings, Owen has no fantasies about living with his biological father instead. "Maybe if I had known my dad better, I would feel differently. But there's no sense wishing for the kind of person who may never have existed. I was so young when Dad died that I have no memories of him. Whatever I create in my mind about him is just make-believe.

"At least with all the people in my family today, I don't get bored around here. But at times it's hard living with so many different personalities. I never realized how much energy it takes learning how to behave with each individual. It can be years before some things are worked out. Truthfully, if I had to do it over, I would have been less cautious with my stepbrothers. It's easy to say that now, because I trust them and like them a lot. When I first met them, though, I kept my distance."

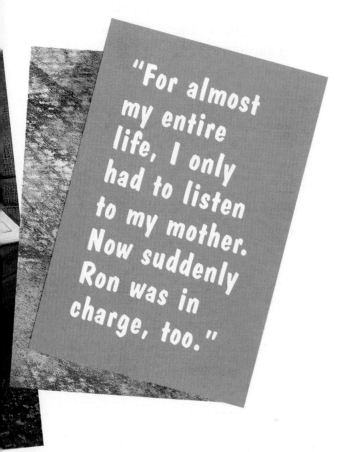

"For almost my entire life, I only had to listen to my mother. Now suddenly Ron was in charge, too."

Owen's acceptance of his stepbrothers was complicated by the fact that he and Douglas were in the same grade (as were Eric and Daniel). And Owen's stepbrothers live alternate weeks with their mother. "Even though it's hectic with the four of us together, in some ways it's easier for me. The weeks Douglas and Daniel are away, Eric and I fight. But when Eric has Daniel to hang out with, my brother and I get along pretty well.

"I've discovered other advantages to having a big family, too. For one, there's a variety of people around, and always someone to do something with. If I want to shoot baskets, I ask Eric and Daniel, who are stronger and more challenging. If I want to walk around the village, I choose Douglas, since we're in the same grade and have a lot in common. When I need to talk to somebody, I go to Daniel, who's interested in what I have to say. I have fun with my brother, Eric, too, but unfortunately he insists on treating me like a kid."

Owen noticed a big change in his feelings about his family after they spent a summer

"We all agree about what's good for our dog. Nobody complains when it's his turn to take Rudy out."

vacation together. "Two years ago, the six of us went to the beach. With everyone away from the house, school, and work, we were all much calmer. By the end of the holiday I started thinking about Douglas and Daniel as my real family.

"Other changes—some big, some little—helped me enjoy being with the family more, too. For one, I disliked family meals because they were so noisy. Then, a few months ago, Mom started serving in the dining room. Somehow the formal setting quieted everyone down. Although we haven't turned into

saints, we have fewer arguments than before. Now when Mom calls us to eat, I think of the event as a special occasion.

"Getting a dog—Mom's idea—helped cement the combined families. When Rudy came to our house, everyone was immediately attached to him. Even Eric, who's not the most gentle, laid-back person, acted mellow around Rudy. While we're a family that can argue over silly things, we all agree about what's good for our dog. Nobody complains when it's his turn to take Rudy out.

"Another thing that helped my family become closer was my interest in Judaism, and my Bar Mitzvah. I owe that to Ron and his sister's strong religious feelings. Mom was never all that religious and she hadn't bothered to enroll Eric or me in Hebrew school. But Ron took Douglas and Daniel to Sunday school. I watched them go each week and, having nothing to do, asked Mom if I could join, too. From the start I enjoyed the whole experience. While a lot of the kids in the class griped that Hebrew school was a drag, I didn't mind it at all. In fact, I'm still going, even though I already had my Bar Mitzvah."

At Owen's Bar Mitzvah, all of Ron's relatives and Owen's, too, were together in one place for the first time. "It meant so much to me that I decided to make that the subject of my speech. And now that I know a lot about the holidays, celebrating them is more special. Sometimes Ron's parents, Grandpa Lou and Grandma Belle, come up from Florida, which is even better.

"Because all of us have worked so hard, my stepfamily situation has improved. Years back, I never would have dreamed that I could feel the way I do about everyone I live with today. Now that I'm getting older I understand that, although my stepfamily and I are not related by birth, it's still possible to feel very close to each person."

"I never would have dreamed that I could feel the way I do about everyone I live with today".

ONE BIG HAP

Television families have changed through the years. In the early days, they were, well, a little too good to be true. Dad worked, mom kept house, and the kids faced problems that were no more serious than accidentally breaking a window with a thrown baseball. Difficulties were usually solved easily, and everyone was healthy and happy.

Trouble was, no real family was like that. Viewers wanted to see families and problems like their own, and eventually television programs became more realistic. Today, television families—and their problems—are as varied as those in real life.

1950s

"Leave It to Beaver" stars Jerry Mathers as Theodore "Beaver" Cleaver. His parents, played by Hugh Beaumont and Barbara Billingsley, and his brother, played by Tony Dow, find Beaver's adventures a constant source of amusement.

50's

60's

ANYTHING LIKE ANY FAMILY YOU KNOW IN REAL LIFE?

PY FAMILY

TWENTIETH TELEVISION, a division of Twentieth Century Fox Film Corporation.

70'S

Photo courtesy of the National Broadcasting Company, Inc. and Carsey-Werner.

80'S

1960s

In "Lassie," June Lockhart and Hugh Reilly play Ruth and Paul Martin, who run a large farm. Their family also includes an orphan named Timmy, played by Jon Provost, and the real star of the show, an intelligent collie named Lassie. Through the years, Lassie was played by many collies. Today, Lassie has a new family and many new adventures.

1970s

"Julia" is Julia Baker, a professional nurse. Her husband having died in Vietnam, she and her son, Corey, have moved to Los Angeles. This comedy centers on the family's struggle to get ahead. Julia is played by Diahann Carroll, and Corey is played by Marc Copage.

1980s

"The Cosby Show" is about an upper-middle-class family that lives in Brooklyn. The mother, played by Phylicia Rashad, is a lawyer, and the father, played by Bill Cosby, is a doctor.

1990s

"Life Goes On" tells the story of a family in which one of the children was born with Down syndrome. Chris Burke, an actor who has Down syndrome in real life, plays the part of the son. His mother is played by Patti LuPone, and his father by Bill Smitrovich.

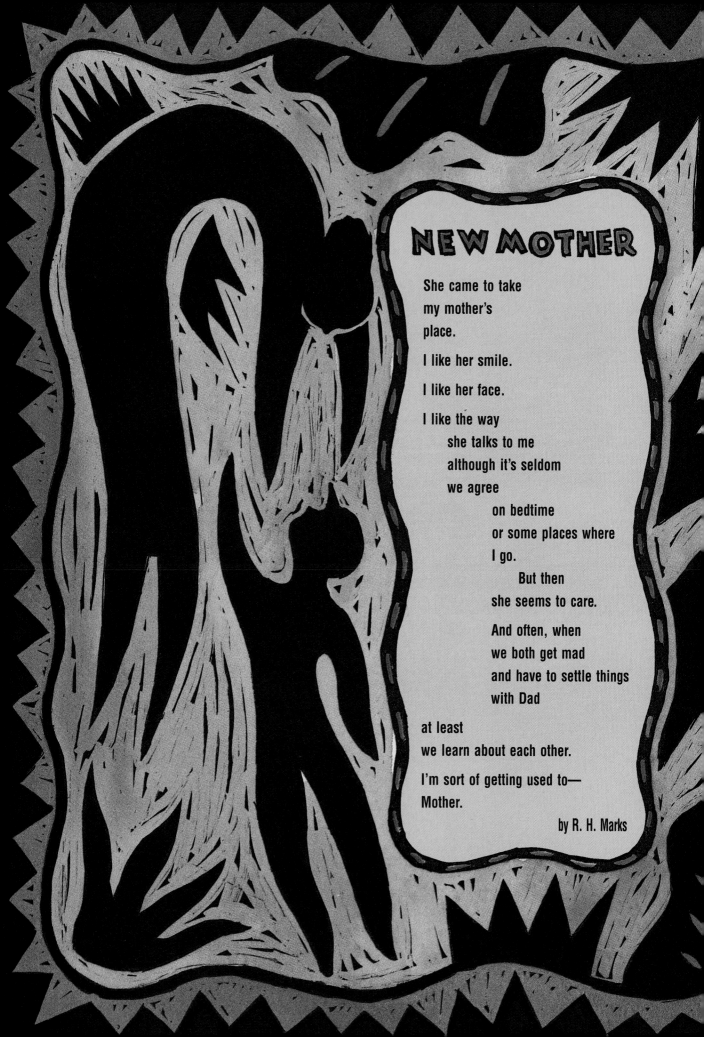

NEW MOTHER

She came to take
my mother's
place.

I like her smile.

I like her face.

I like the way
    she talks to me
    although it's seldom
    we agree
            on bedtime
            or some places where
            I go.
                But then
            she seems to care.

    And often, when
    we both get mad
    and have to settle things
    with Dad
at least
we learn about each other.

I'm sort of getting used to—
Mother.

by R. H. Marks

MY JOSÉ

When he sees friends come home with me
he always says hello,
and if they're new friends
I'm supposed to tell their names and his name.
The problem is I don't know what to call him.

Stepfather is strange.

He's not my dad.

Mister is an uptight word.

I try to get outdoors to play
before he notices,
but if I can't I finally just say,

Hey guys, this is my José.

by Martha Robinson

Anne of Green Gables

BY L. M. MONTGOMERY

ILLUSTRATED BY MONA CONNER

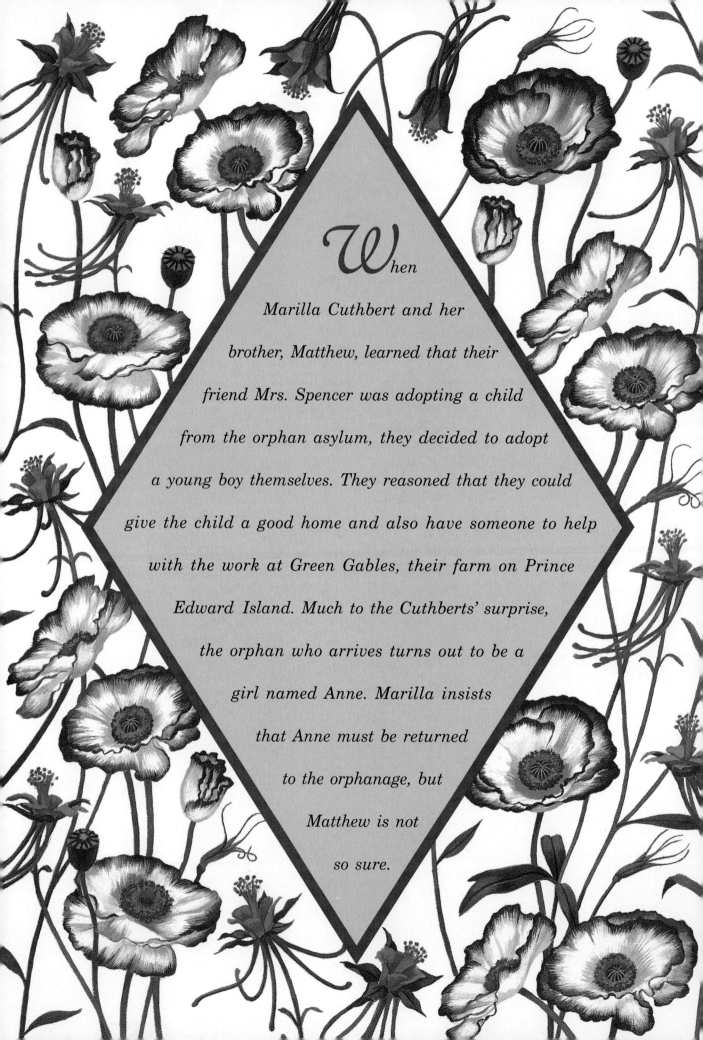

*W*hen Marilla Cuthbert and her brother, Matthew, learned that their friend Mrs. Spencer was adopting a child from the orphan asylum, they decided to adopt a young boy themselves. They reasoned that they could give the child a good home and also have someone to help with the work at Green Gables, their farm on Prince Edward Island. Much to the Cuthberts' surprise, the orphan who arrives turns out to be a girl named Anne. Marilla insists that Anne must be returned to the orphanage, but Matthew is not so sure.

It was broad daylight when Anne awoke and sat up in bed, staring confusedly at the window through which a flood of cheery sunshine was pouring and outside of which something white and feathery waved across glimpses of blue sky.

For a moment she could not remember where she was. First came a delightful thrill, as of something very pleasant; then a horrible remembrance. This was Green Gables and they didn't want her because she wasn't a boy!

But it was morning and, yes, it was a cherry-tree in full bloom outside of her window. With a bound she was out of bed and across the floor. She pushed up the sash—it went up stiffly and creakily, as if it hadn't been opened for a long time, which was the case; and it stuck so tight that nothing was needed to hold it up.

Anne dropped on her knees and gazed out into the June morning, her eyes glistening with delight. Oh, wasn't it beautiful? Wasn't it a lovely place? Suppose she wasn't really going to stay here! She would imagine she was. There was scope for imagination here.

A huge cherry-tree grew outside, so close that its boughs tapped against the house, and it was so thick-set with blossoms that hardly a leaf was to be seen. On both sides of the house was a big orchard, one of apple trees and one of cherry trees, also showered over with blossoms; and their grass was all sprinkled with dandelions. In the garden below were lilac trees purple with flowers, and their dizzily sweet fragrance drifted up to the window on the morning wind.

Below the garden a green field lush with clover sloped down to the hollow where the brook ran and where scores of white birches grew, upspringing airily out of an undergrowth suggestive of delightful possibilities in ferns and mosses and woodsy things generally. Beyond it was a hill, green and feathery with spruce and fir; there was a gap in it where the gray gable end of the little house she had seen from the other side of the Lake of Shining Waters was visible.

Off to the left were the big barns and beyond them, away down over green, low-sloping fields, was a sparkling blue glimpse of sea.

Anne's beauty-loving eyes lingered on it all, taking everything greedily in; she had looked on so many unlovely places in her life, poor child; but this was as lovely as anything she had ever dreamed.

She knelt there, lost to everything but the loveliness around her, until she was startled by a hand on her shoulder. Marilla had come in unheard by the small dreamer.

"It's time you were dressed," she said curtly.

Marilla really did not know how to talk to the child, and her uncomfortable ignorance made her crisp and curt when she did not mean to be.

Anne stood up and drew a long breath.

"Oh, isn't it wonderful?" she said, waving her hand comprehensively at the good world outside.

"It's a big tree," said Marilla, "and it blooms great, but the fruit don't amount to much never—small and wormy."

"Oh, I don't mean just the tree; of course it's lovely—yes, it's *radiantly* lovely—it blooms as if it meant it—but I meant everything, the garden and the orchard and the brook and the woods, the whole big dear world. Don't you feel as if you just loved the world on a morning like this? And I can hear the brook laughing all the way up here. Have you ever noticed what cheerful things brooks are? They're always laughing. Even in wintertime I've heard them under the ice. I'm so glad there's a brook near Green Gables. Perhaps you think it doesn't make any difference to me when you're not going to keep me, but it does. I shall always like to remember that there is a brook at Green Gables even if I never see it again. If there wasn't a brook I'd be *haunted* by the uncomfortable feeling that there ought to be one. I'm not in the depths of despair this morning. I never can be in the morning. Isn't it a splendid thing that there are mornings? But I feel very sad. I've just been imagining that it was really me you wanted after all and that I was to stay here for ever and ever. It was a great comfort while it lasted. But the worst of imagining things is that the time comes when you have to stop and that hurts."

"You'd better get dressed and come downstairs and never mind your imaginings," said Marilla as soon as she could get a word in edgewise. "Breakfast is waiting. Wash your face and comb your hair. Leave the window up and turn your bedclothes back over the foot of the bed. Be as smart as you can."

Anne could evidently be smart to some purpose for she was downstairs in ten minutes' time, with her clothes neatly on, her hair brushed and braided, her face washed, and a comfortable consciousness pervading her soul that she had

fulfilled all Marilla's requirements. As a matter of fact, however, she had forgotten to turn back the bedclothes.

"I'm pretty hungry this morning," she announced, as she slipped into the chair Marilla placed for her. "The world doesn't seem such a howling wilderness as it did last night. I'm so glad it's a sunshiny morning. But I like rainy mornings real well, too. All sorts of mornings are interesting, don't you think? You don't know what's going to happen through the day, and there's so much scope for imagination. But I'm glad it's not rainy today because it's easier to be cheerful and bear up under affliction on a sunshiny day. I feel that I have a good deal to bear up under. It's all very well to read about sorrows and imagine yourself living through them heroically, but it's not so nice when you really come to have them, is it?"

"For pity's sake hold your tongue," said Marilla. "You talk entirely too much for a little girl."

Thereupon Anne held her tongue so obediently and thoroughly that her continued silence made Marilla rather nervous, as if in the presence of something not exactly natural. Matthew also held his tongue—but this at least was natural—so that the meal was a very silent one.

As it progressed Anne became more and more abstracted, eating mechanically, with her big eyes fixed unswervingly and unseeingly on the sky outside the window. This made Marilla more nervous than ever; she had an uncomfortable feeling that while this odd child's body might be there at the table her spirit was far away in some remote airy cloudland, borne aloft on the wings of imagination. Who would want such a child about the place?

Yet Matthew wished to keep her, of all unaccountable things! Marilla felt that he wanted it just as much this morning as he had the night before, and that he would go on wanting it. That was Matthew's way—take a whim into his head and cling to it with the most amazing silent persistency—a persistency ten times more potent and effectual in its very silence than if he had talked it out.

When the meal was ended Anne came out of her reverie and offered to wash the dishes.

"Can you wash dishes right?" asked Marilla distrustfully.

"Pretty well. I'm better at looking after children though. I've had so much experience at that. It's such a pity you haven't any here for me to look after."

"I don't feel as if I wanted any more children to look after than I've got at present. *You're* problem enough in all conscience. What's to be done with you I don't know. Matthew is a most ridiculous man."

"I think he's lovely," said Anne reproachfully. "He is so very sympathetic. He didn't mind how much I talked—he seemed to like it. I felt that he was a kindred spirit as soon as ever I saw him."

"You're both queer enough, if that's what you mean by kindred spirits," said Marilla with a sniff. "Yes, you may wash the dishes. Take plenty of hot water, and be sure you dry them well. I've got enough to attend to this morning for I'll have to drive over to White Sands in the afternoon and see Mrs. Spencer. You'll come with me and we'll settle what's to be done with you. After you've finished the dishes go upstairs and make your bed."

Anne washed the dishes deftly enough, as Marilla, who kept a sharp eye on the process, discerned. Later on she made her bed less successfully, for she had never learned the art of wrestling with a feather tick. But it was done somehow and smoothed down; and then Marilla, to get rid of her, told her she might go out-of-doors and amuse herself until dinner time.

Anne flew to the door, face alight, eyes glowing. On the very threshold she stopped short, wheeled about, came back and sat down by the table, light and glow as effectually blotted out as if some one had clapped an extinguisher on her.

"What's the matter now?" demanded Marilla.

"I don't dare go out," said Anne, in the tone of a martyr relinquishing all earthly joys. "If I can't stay here there is no use in my loving Green Gables. And if I go out there and get acquainted with all those trees and flowers and the orchard and the brook I'll not be able to help loving it. It's hard enough now, so I won't make it any harder. I want to go out so much—everything seems to be calling to me, 'Anne, Anne, come out to us. Anne, Anne, we want a playmate'—but it's better not. There is no use in loving things if you have to be torn from them, is there? And it's *so* hard to keep from loving things, isn't it? That was why I was so glad when I thought I was going to live here. I thought I'd have so many things to love and nothing to hinder me. But that brief dream is over. I am resigned to my fate now, so I don't think I'll go out for fear I'll get unresigned again. What is the name of that geranium on the windowsill, please?"

"That's the apple-scented geranium."

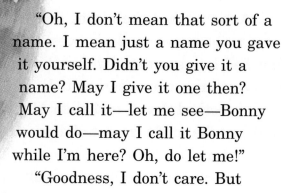

"Oh, I don't mean that sort of a name. I mean just a name you gave it yourself. Didn't you give it a name? May I give it one then? May I call it—let me see—Bonny would do—may I call it Bonny while I'm here? Oh, do let me!"

"Goodness, I don't care. But where on earth is the sense of naming a geranium?"

"Oh, I like things to have handles even if they are only geraniums. It makes them seem more like people. How do you know but that it hurts a geranium's feelings just to be called a geranium and nothing else? You wouldn't like to be called nothing but a woman all the time. Yes, I shall call it Bonny. I named that cherry tree outside my bedroom window this morning. I called it Snow Queen because it was so white. Of course, it won't always be in blossom, but one can imagine that it is, can't one?"

"I never in all my life saw or heard anything to equal her," muttered Marilla, beating a retreat down cellar after potatoes. "She *is* kind of interesting, as Matthew says. I can feel already that I'm wondering what on earth she'll say next. She'll be casting a spell over me, too. She's cast it over Matthew. That look he gave me when he went out said everything he said or hinted last night over again. I wish he was like other men and would talk things out. A body could answer back then and argue him into reason. But what's to be done with a man who just *looks?*"

Anne had relapsed into reverie, with her chin in her hands and her eyes on the sky, when Marilla returned from her cellar pilgrimage. There Marilla left her until the early dinner was on the table.

"I suppose I can have the mare and buggy this afternoon, Matthew?" said Marilla.

Matthew nodded and looked wistfully at Anne. Marilla intercepted the look and said grimly:

"I'm going to drive over to White Sands and settle this thing. I'll take Anne with me and Mrs. Spencer will probably make arrangements to send her back to Nova Scotia at once. I'll set your tea out for you and I'll be home in time to milk the cows."

Still Matthew said nothing and Marilla had a sense of having wasted words and breath. There is nothing more aggravating than a man who won't talk back—unless it is a woman who won't.

Matthew hitched the sorrel into the buggy in due time and Marilla and Anne set off. Matthew opened the yard gate for them, and as they drove slowly through, he said, to nobody in particular as it seemed:

"Little Jerry Buote from the Creek was here this morning, and I told him I guessed I'd hire him for the summer."

Marilla made no reply, but she hit the unlucky sorrel such a vicious clip with the whip that the fat mare, unused to such treatment, whizzed indignantly down the lane at an alarming pace. Marilla looked back once as the buggy bounced along and saw that aggravating Matthew leaning over the gate, looking wistfully after them.

"Do you know," said Anne confidentially, "I've made up my mind to enjoy this drive. It's been my experience that you can nearly always enjoy things if you make up your mind firmly that you will. Of course, you must make it up *firmly*. I am not going to think about going back to the asylum while we're having our drive. I'm just going to think about the drive. Oh, look, there's one little early wild rose out! Isn't it lovely? Don't you think it must be glad to be a rose? Wouldn't it be nice if roses could talk? I'm sure they could tell us such lovely things. And isn't pink the most bewitching color in the world? I love it, but I can't wear it. Redheaded people can't wear pink, not even in imagination. Did you ever know of anybody whose hair was red when she was young, but got to be another color when she grew up?"

"No, I don't know as I ever did," said Marilla mercilessly, "and I shouldn't think it likely to happen in your case, either."

Anne sighed.

"Well, that is another hope gone. My life is a perfect graveyard of buried hopes. That's a sentence I read in a book once, and I say it over to comfort myself whenever I'm disappointed in anything."

"I don't see where the comforting comes in myself," said Marilla.

"Why, because it sounds so nice and romantic, just as if I were a heroine in a book, you know. I am so fond of romantic things, and a graveyard full of buried hopes is about as romantic a thing as one can imagine, isn't it? I'm rather glad I have one. Are we going across the Lake of Shining Waters today?"

"We're not going over Barry's pond, if that's what you mean by your Lake of Shining Waters. We're going by the shore road."

"Shore road sounds nice," said Anne dreamily. "Is it as nice as it sounds? Just when you said 'shore road' I saw it in a picture in my mind, as quick as that! And White Sands is a pretty name, too; but I don't like it as well as Avonlea. Avonlea is a lovely name. It just sounds like music. How far is it to White Sands?"

"It's five miles; and as you're evidently bent on talking you might as well talk to some purpose by telling me what you know about yourself."

"Oh, what I *know* about myself isn't really worth telling," said Anne eagerly. "If you'll only let me tell you what I *imagine* about myself you'll think it ever so much more interesting."

"No, I don't want any of your imaginings. Just you stick to bald facts. Begin at the beginning. Where were you born and how old are you?"

"I was eleven last March," said Anne, resigning herself to bald facts with a little sigh. "And I was born in Bolingbroke, Nova Scotia. My father's name was Walter Shirley, and he was a teacher in the Bolingbroke High School. My mother's name was Bertha Shirley. Aren't Walter and Bertha lovely names? I'm so glad my parents had nice names. It would be a real disgrace to have a father named—well, say Jedediah, wouldn't it?"

"I guess it doesn't matter what a person's name is as long as he behaves himself," said Marilla, feeling herself called upon to inculcate a good and useful moral.

"Well, I don't know." Anne looked thoughtful. "I read in a book once that a rose by any other name would smell as sweet, but I've never been able to believe it. I don't believe a rose *would* be as nice if it was called a thistle or a skunk cabbage. I suppose my father could have been a good man even if he had been called Jedediah; but I'm sure it would have been a cross. Well, my mother was a teacher in the High School, too, but when she married father she gave up teaching, of course. A husband was enough responsibility. Mrs. Thomas said that they were a pair of babies and as poor as church mice. They went to live in a weeny-teeny little yellow house in Bolingbroke. I've never seen that house, but I've imagined it thousands of times. I think it must have had honeysuckle over the parlor window and lilacs in the front yard and lilies of the valley just inside the gate. Yes, and muslin curtains in all the windows. Muslin curtains give a house such an air. I was born in that house. Mrs. Thomas said I was the homeliest baby she ever saw, I was so scrawny and tiny and nothing but eyes, but that mother thought I was perfectly beautiful. I should think a mother would be a better judge than a poor woman who came in to scrub, wouldn't you? I'm glad she was satisfied with me anyhow; I would feel so sad if I thought I was a disappointment to her— because she didn't live very long after that, you see. She died of fever when I was just three

months old. I do wish she'd lived long enough for me to remember calling her mother. I think it would be so sweet to say 'mother,' don't you? And father died four days afterwards from fever, too. That left me an orphan and folks were at their wits' end, so Mrs. Thomas said, what to do with me. You see, nobody wanted me even then. It seems to be my fate. Father and mother had both come from places far away and it was well known they hadn't any relatives living. Finally Mrs. Thomas said she'd take me, though she was poor and had a drunken husband. She brought me up by hand. Do you know if there is anything in being brought up by hand that ought to make people who are brought up that way better than other people? Because whenever I was naughty Mrs. Thomas would ask me how I could be such a bad girl when she had brought me up by hand—reproachful-like.

"Mr. and Mrs. Thomas moved away from Bolingbroke to Marysville, and I lived with them until I was eight years old. I helped look after the Thomas children—there were four of them younger than me—and I can tell you they took a lot of looking after. Then Mr. Thomas was killed falling under a train and his mother offered to take Mrs. Thomas and the children, but she didn't want me. Mrs. Thomas was at *her* wits' end, so she said, what to do with me. Then Mrs. Hammond from up the river came down and said she'd take me, seeing I was handy with children, and I went up the river to live with her in a little clearing among the stumps. It was a very lonesome place. I'm sure I could never have lived there if I hadn't had an imagination. Mr. Hammond worked a little sawmill up there, and Mrs. Hammond had eight children. She had twins three times. I like babies in moderation, but twins three times in succession is *too much.* I told Mrs. Hammond so firmly, when the last pair came. I used to get so dreadfully tired carrying them about.

"I lived up river with Mrs. Hammond over two years, and then Mr. Hammond died and Mrs. Hammond broke up housekeeping. She divided her children among her relatives and went to the States. I had to go to the asylum at Hopeton, because nobody would take me. They didn't want me at the asylum, either; they said they were overcrowded as it was. But they had to take me and I was there four months until Mrs. Spencer came."

Anne finished up with another sigh, of relief this time. Evidently she did not like talking about her experiences in a world that had not wanted her.

"Did you ever go to school?" demanded Marilla, turning the sorrel mare down the shore road.

"Not a great deal. I went a little the last year I stayed with Mrs. Thomas. When I went up river we were so far from a school that I couldn't walk it in winter and there was vacation in summer, so I could only go in the spring and fall. But of course I went while I was at the asylum. I can read pretty well and I know ever so many pieces of poetry off by heart— 'The Battle of Hohenlinden' and 'Edinburgh after Flodden,' and 'Bingen on the Rhine,' and lots of the 'Lady of the Lake' and most of 'The Seasons,' by James Thompson. Don't you just love poetry that gives you a crinkly feeling up and down your back? There is a piece in the Fifth Reader—'The Downfall of Poland'—that is just full of thrills. Of course, I wasn't in the Fifth Reader—I was only in the Fourth—but the big girls used to lend me theirs to read."

"Were those women—Mrs. Thomas and Mrs. Hammond—good to you?" asked Marilla, looking at Anne out of the corner of her eye.

"O-o-o-h," faltered Anne. Her sensitive little face suddenly flushed scarlet and embarrassment sat on her brow. "Oh, they *meant* to be—I know they meant to be just as good and kind as possible. And when people mean to be good to you, you don't mind very much when they're not quite—always. They had a good deal to worry them, you know. It's very trying to have a drunken husband, you see; and it must be very trying to have twins three times in succession, don't you think? But I feel sure they meant to be good to me."

Marilla asked no more questions. Anne gave herself up to a silent rapture over the shore road and Marilla guided the sorrel abstractedly while she pondered deeply. Pity was suddenly stirring in her heart for the child. What a starved, unloved life she had had—a life of drudgery and poverty and neglect; for Marilla was shrewd enough to read between the lines of Anne's history and divine the truth. No wonder she had been so delighted at the prospect of a real home. It was a pity she had to be sent back. What if she, Marilla, should indulge Matthew's unaccountable whim and let her stay? He was set on it; and the child seemed a nice, teachable little thing.

"She's got too much to say," thought Marilla, "but she might be trained out of that. And there's nothing rude or slangy in what she does say. She's ladylike. It's likely her people were nice folks."

The shore road was "woodsy and wild and lonesome." On the right hand, scrub firs, their spirits quite unbroken by

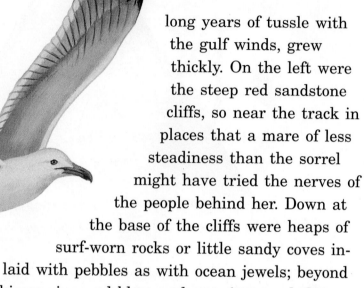

long years of tussle with the gulf winds, grew thickly. On the left were the steep red sandstone cliffs, so near the track in places that a mare of less steadiness than the sorrel might have tried the nerves of the people behind her. Down at the base of the cliffs were heaps of surf-worn rocks or little sandy coves inlaid with pebbles as with ocean jewels; beyond lay the sea, shimmering and blue, and over it soared the gulls, their pinions flashing silvery in the sunlight.

"Isn't the sea wonderful?" said Anne, rousing from a long, wide-eyed silence. "Once, when I lived in Marysville, Mr. Thomas hired an express wagon and took us all to spend the day at the shore ten miles away. I enjoyed every moment of that day, even if I had to look after the children all the time. I lived it over in happy dreams for years. But this shore is nicer than the Marysville shore. Aren't those gulls splendid? Would you like to be a gull? I think I would—that is, if I couldn't be a human girl. Don't you think it would be nice to wake up at sunrise and swoop down over the water and away out over that lovely blue all day; and then at night to fly back to one's nest? Oh, I can just imagine myself doing it. What big house is that just ahead, please?"

"That's the White Sands Hotel. Mr. Kirke runs it, but the season hasn't begun yet. There are heaps of Americans come there for the summer. They think this shore is just about right."

"I was afraid it might be Mrs. Spencer's place," said Anne mournfully. "I don't want to get there. Somehow, it will seem like the end of everything."

Get there they did, however, in due season. Mrs. Spencer lived in a big yellow house at White Sands Cove, and she came to the door with surprise and welcome mingled on her benevolent face.

"Dear, dear," she exclaimed, "you're the last folks I was looking for today, but I'm real glad to see you. You'll put your horse in? And how are you, Anne?"

"I'm as well as can be expected, thank you," said Anne smilelessly. A blight seemed to have descended on her.

"I suppose we'll stay a little while to rest the mare," said Marilla, "but I promised Matthew I'd be home early. The fact is, Mrs. Spencer, there's been a queer mistake somewhere, and I've come over to see where it is. We sent word, Matthew and I, for you to bring us a boy from the asylum. We told your brother Robert to tell you we wanted a boy ten or eleven years old."

"Marilla Cuthbert, you don't say so!" said Mrs. Spencer in distress. "Why, Robert sent the word down by his daughter Nancy and she said you wanted a girl—didn't she, Flora Jane?" appealing to her daughter who had come out to the steps.

"She certainly did, Miss Cuthbert," corroborated Flora Jane earnestly.

"I'm dreadful sorry," said Mrs. Spencer. "It is too bad; but it certainly wasn't my fault, you see, Miss Cuthbert. I did the best I could and I thought I was following your instructions.

Nancy is a terrible flighty thing. I've often had to scold her well for her heedlessness."

"It was our own fault," said Marilla resignedly. "We should have come to you ourselves and not left an important message to be passed along by word of mouth in that fashion. Anyhow, the mistake has been made and the only thing to do now is to set it right. Can we send the child back to the asylum? I suppose they'll take her back, won't they?"

"I suppose so," said Mrs. Spencer thoughtfully, "but I don't think it will be necessary to send her back. Mrs. Peter Blewett was up here yesterday, and she was saying to me how much she wished she'd sent by me for a little girl to help her. Mrs. Peter has a large family, you know, and she finds it hard to get help. Anne will be the very girl for her. I call it positively providential."

Marilla did not look as if she thought Providence had much to do with the matter. Here was an unexpectedly good chance to get this unwelcome orphan off her hands, and she did not even feel grateful for it.

She knew Mrs. Peter Blewett only by sight as a small, shrewish-faced woman without an ounce of superfluous flesh on her bones. But she had heard of her. "A terrible worker and driver," Mrs. Peter was said to be; and discharged servant girls told fearsome tales of her temper and stinginess, and her family of pert, quarrelsome children. Marilla felt a qualm of conscience at the thought of handing Anne over to her tender mercies.

"Well, I'll go in and we'll talk the matter over," she said.

"And if there isn't Mrs. Peter coming up the lane this

blessed minute!" exclaimed Mrs. Spencer, bustling her guests through the hall into the parlor, where a deadly chill struck on them as if the air had been strained so long through dark green, closely drawn blinds that it had lost every particle of warmth it had ever possessed. "That is real lucky, for we can settle the matter right away. Take the armchair, Miss Cuthbert. Anne, you sit here on the ottoman and don't wriggle. Let me take your hats. Flora Jane, go out to put the kettle on. Good afternoon, Mrs. Blewett. We were just saying how fortunate it was you happened along. Let me introduce you two ladies. Mrs. Blewett, Miss Cuthbert. Please excuse me for just a moment. I forgot to tell Flora Jane to take the buns out of the oven."

Mrs. Spencer whisked away, after pulling up the blinds. Anne, sitting mutely on the ottoman, with her hands clasped tightly in her lap, stared at Mrs. Blewett as one fascinated. Was she to be given into the keeping of this sharp-faced, sharp-eyed woman? She felt a lump coming up in her throat and her eyes smarted painfully. She was beginning to be afraid she couldn't keep the tears back when Mrs. Spencer returned, flushed and beaming, quite capable of taking any and every difficulty, physical, mental or spiritual, into consideration and settling it out of hand.

"It seems there's been a mistake about this little girl, Mrs. Blewett," she said. "I was under the impression that Mr. and Miss Cuthbert wanted a little girl to adopt. I was certainly told so. But it seems it was a boy they wanted. So if you're still of the same mind you were yesterday, I think she'll be just the thing for you."

Mrs. Blewett darted her eyes over Anne from head to foot.

"How old are you and what's your name?" she demanded.

"Anne Shirley," faltered the shrinking child, not daring to make any stipulations regarding the spelling thereof, "and I'm eleven years old."

"Humph! You don't look as if there was much to you. But you're wiry. I don't know but the wiry ones are the best after all. Well, if I take you you'll have to be a good girl, you know—good and smart and respectful. I'll expect you to earn your keep, and no mistake about that. Yes, I suppose I might as well take her off your hands, Miss Cuthbert. The baby's awful fractious, and I'm clean worn out attending to him. If you like I can take her right home now."

Marilla looked at Anne and softened at sight of the child's pale face with its look of mute misery—the misery of a helpless little creature who finds itself once more caught in the trap from which it had escaped. Marilla felt an uncomfortable conviction that, if she denied the appeal of that look, it would haunt her to her dying day. Moreover, she did not fancy Mrs. Blewett. To hand a sensitive, "highstrung" child over to such a woman! No, she could not take the responsibility of doing that!

"Well, I don't know," she said slowly. "I didn't say that Matthew and I had absolutely decided that we wouldn't keep her. In fact, I may say that Matthew is disposed to keep her. I just came over to find out how the mistake had occurred. I think I'd better take her home again and talk it over with Matthew. I feel that I oughtn't to decide on anything without consulting him. If we make up our mind not to keep her we'll

bring or send her over to you tomorrow night. If we don't you may know that she is going to stay with us. Will that suit you, Mrs. Blewett?"

"I suppose it'll have to," said Mrs. Blewett ungraciously.

During Marilla's speech a sunrise had been dawning on Anne's face. First the look of despair faded out; then came a faint flush of hope; her eyes grew deep and bright as morning stars. The child was quite transfigured; and, a moment later, when Mrs. Spencer and Mrs. Blewett went out in quest of a recipe the latter had come to borrow she sprang up and flew across the room to Marilla.

"Oh, Miss Cuthbert, did you really say that perhaps you would let me stay at Green Gables?" she said, in a breathless whisper, as if speaking aloud might shatter the glorious possibility. "Did you really say it? Or did I only imagine that you did?"

"I think you'd better learn to control that imagination of yours, Anne, if you can't distinguish between what is real and what isn't," said Marilla crossly. "Yes, you did hear me say just that and no more. It isn't decided yet and perhaps we will conclude to let Mrs. Blewett take you after all. She certainly needs you much more than I do."

"I'd rather go back to the asylum than go to live with her," said Anne passionately. "She looks exactly like a—like a gimlet."

Marilla smothered a smile under the conviction that Anne must be reproved for such a speech.

"A little girl like you should be ashamed of talking so about a lady and a stranger," she said severely. "Go back and sit down quietly and hold your tongue and behave as a good girl should."

"I'll try to do and be anything you want me, if you'll only keep me," said Anne, returning meekly to her ottoman.

When they arrived back at Green Gables that evening Matthew met them in the lane. Marilla from afar had noted him prowling along it and guessed his motive. She was prepared for the relief she read in his face when he saw that she had at least brought Anne back with her. But she said nothing to him, relative to the affair, until they were both out in the yard behind the barn milking the cows. Then she briefly told him Anne's history and the result of the interview with Mrs. Spencer.

"I wouldn't give a dog I liked to that Blewett woman," said Matthew with unusual vim.

"I don't fancy her style myself," admitted Marilla, "but it's that or keeping her ourselves, Matthew. And, since you seem to want her, I suppose I'm willing—or have to be. I've been thinking over the idea until I've got kind of used to it. It seems a sort of duty. I've never brought up a child, especially a girl, and I dare say I'll make a terrible mess of it. But I'll do my best. So far as I'm concerned, Matthew, she may stay."

Matthew's shy face was a glow of delight.

"Well now, I reckoned you'd come to see it in that light, Marilla," he said. "She's such an interesting little thing."

"It'd be more to the point if you could say she was a useful little thing," retorted Marilla, "but I'll make it my business to see she's trained to be that. And mind, Matthew, you're not to go interfering with my methods. Perhaps an old

maid doesn't know much about bringing up a child, but I guess she knows more than an old bachelor. So you just leave me to manage her. When I fail it'll be time enough to put your oar in."

"There, there, Marilla, you can have your own way," said Matthew reassuringly. "Only be as good and kind to her as you can be without spoiling her. I kind of think she's one of the sort you can do anything with if you only get her to love you."

Marilla sniffed, to express her contempt for Matthew's opinions concerning anything feminine, and walked off to the dairy with the pails.

"I won't tell her tonight that she can stay," she reflected, as she strained the milk into the creamers. "She'd be so excited that she wouldn't sleep a wink. Marilla Cuthbert, you're fairly in for it. Did you ever suppose you'd see the day when you'd be adopting an orphan girl? It's surprising enough; but not so surprising as that Matthew should be at the bottom of it, him that always seemed to have such a mortal dread of little girls. Anyhow, we've decided on the experiment and goodness only knows what will come of it."

Meet L. M. Montgomery

Growing up on her grandparents' farm on Prince Edward Island, Lucy Maud Montgomery used her imagination as a "passport to fairyland." Montgomery wrote, "I had no companionship except that of books and solitary rambles in wood and fields. This drove me in on myself and early forced me to construct for myself a world of fantasy and imagination very different indeed from the world in which I lived." Although she had a family, her childhood and early youth were lonely.

Montgomery drew on memories of those childhood feelings and experiences to write stories for children. The success of her book Anne of Green Gables led to five sequels and two more books about its heroine, Anne Shirley. Years after their publication, several of the books were made into movies.

O n warm summer nights

the porch becomes our living room

where Mama takes her reading

and Dad and I play games

in the patch of brightness

the lamp scatters on the floor.

From the darkness, others come—

small round bodies

clinging to the screens

which separate us

from the yard beyond.

Drawn to our light,

the June bugs watch our games

and listen to our talk till bedtime

when Mama darkens the porch

and breaks the spell

that holds them close to us.

ANTMENT

By
Joanne
Ryder

419

CONTENTS

PROFILES OF COURAGE

You gain strength, courage and
confidence by every experience
in which you really stop to
look fear in the face. . . .
You must do the thing you
cannot do.

ELEANOR ROOSEVELT

423

Number the Stars

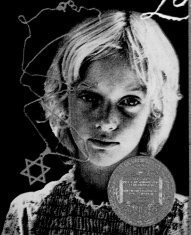

by Lois Lowry

It is 1943 and the Nazis have occupied Denmark. As the German soldiers begin their campaign to "relocate" all the Jews in Denmark, the Johansen family takes in Annemarie Johansen's best friend, Ellen Rosen.

Illustrations by Larry Winborg

Alone in the apartment while Mama was out shopping with Kirsti, Annemarie and Ellen were sprawled on the living room floor playing with paper dolls. They had cut the dolls from Mama's magazines, old ones she had saved from past years. The paper ladies had old-fashioned hair styles and clothes, and the girls had given them names from Mama's very favorite book. Mama had told Annemarie and Ellen the entire story of *Gone With the Wind,* and the girls thought it much more interesting and romantic than the king-and-queen tales that Kirsti loved.

"Come, Melanie," Annemarie said, walking her doll across the edge of the rug. "Let's dress for the ball."

"All right, Scarlett, I'm coming," Ellen replied in a sophisticated voice. She was a talented performer; she often played the leading roles in school dramatics. Games of the imagination were always fun when Ellen played.

The door opened and Kirsti stomped in, her face tear-stained and glowering. Mama followed her with an exasperated look and set a package down on the table.

"I won't!" Kirsti sputtered. "I won't ever, *ever* wear them! Not if you chain me in a prison and beat me with sticks!"

Annemarie giggled and looked questioningly at her mother. Mrs. Johansen sighed. "I bought Kirsti some new shoes," she explained. "She's outgrown her old ones."

"Goodness, Kirsti," Ellen said, "I wish my mother would get *me* some new shoes. I love new things, and it's so hard to find them in the stores."

"Not if you go to a *fish* store!" Kirsti bellowed. "But most mothers wouldn't make their daughters wear ugly *fish* shoes!"

"Kirsten," Mama said soothingly, "you know it wasn't a fish store. And we were lucky to find shoes at all."

Kirsti sniffed. "Show them," she commanded. "Show Annemarie and Ellen how ugly they are."

Mama opened the package and took out a pair of little girl's shoes. She held them up, and Kirsti looked away in disgust.

"You know there's no leather anymore," Mama explained. "But they've found a way to make shoes out of fish skin. I don't think these are too ugly."

Annemarie and Ellen looked at the fish skin shoes. Annemarie took one in her hand and examined it. It was odd-looking; the fish scales were visible. But it was a shoe, and her sister needed shoes.

"It's not so bad, Kirsti," she said, lying a little.

Ellen turned the other one over in her hand. "You know," she said, "it's only the color that's ugly."

"Green!" Kirsti wailed. "I will never, *ever* wear green shoes!"

"In our apartment," Ellen told her, "my father has a jar of black, black ink. Would you like these shoes better if they were black?"

Kirsti frowned. "Maybe I would," she said, finally.

"Well, then," Ellen told her, "tonight, if your mama doesn't mind, I'll take the shoes home and ask my father to make them black for you, with his ink."

Mama laughed. "I think that would be a fine improvement. What do you think, Kirsti?"

Kirsti pondered. "Could he make them shiny?" she asked. "I want them shiny."

Ellen nodded. "I think he could. I think they'll be quite pretty, black and shiny."

Kirsti nodded. "All right, then," she said. "But you mustn't tell anyone that they're *fish.* I don't want anyone to know." She took her new shoes, holding them disdainfully, and put them on a chair. Then she looked with interest at the paper dolls.

"Can I play, too?" Kirsti asked. "Can I have a doll?" She squatted beside Annemarie and Ellen on the floor.

Sometimes, Annemarie thought, Kirsti was such a pest, always butting in. But the apartment was small. There was no other place for Kirsti to play. And if they told her to go away, Mama would scold.

"Here," Annemarie said, and handed her sister a cut-out little girl doll. "We're playing *Gone With the Wind.* Melanie and Scarlett are going to a ball. You can be Bonnie. She's Scarlett's daughter."

Kirsti danced her doll up and down happily. "I'm going to the ball!" she announced in a high, pretend voice.

Ellen giggled. "A little girl wouldn't go to a ball. Let's make them go someplace else. Let's make them go to Tivoli!"

"Tivoli!" Annemarie began to laugh. "That's in Copenhagen! *Gone With the Wind* is in America!"

"Tivoli, Tivoli, Tivoli," little Kirsti sang, twirling her doll in a circle.

"It doesn't matter, because it's only a game anyway," Ellen pointed out. "Tivoli can be over there, by that chair. 'Come, Scarlett,'" she said, using her doll voice, "'we shall go to Tivoli to dance and watch the fireworks, and maybe there will be some handsome men there! Bring your silly daughter Bonnie, and she can ride on the carousel.'"

Annemarie grinned and walked her Scarlett toward the chair that Ellen had designated as Tivoli. She loved Tivoli Gardens, in the heart of Copenhagen; her parents had taken her there, often, when she was a little girl. She remembered the music and the brightly colored lights, the carousel and ice cream and especially the magnificent fireworks in the evenings: the huge colored splashes and bursts of lights in the evening sky.

"I remember the fireworks best of all," she commented to Ellen.

"Me too," Kirsti said. "I remember the fireworks."

"Silly," Annemarie scoffed. "You never saw the fireworks." Tivoli Gardens was closed now. The German occupation forces had burned part of it, perhaps as a way of punishing the fun-loving Danes for their lighthearted pleasures.

Kirsti drew herself up, her small shoulders stiff. "I did too," she said belligerently. "It was my birthday. I woke up in the night and I could hear the booms. And there were lights in the sky. Mama said it was fireworks for my birthday!"

Then Annemarie remembered. Kirsti's birthday was late in August. And that night, only a month before, she, too, had been awakened and frightened by the sound of explosions. Kirsti was right—the sky in the southeast had been ablaze, and Mama had comforted her by calling it a birthday celebration. "Imagine, such fireworks for a little girl five years old!" Mama had said, sitting on their bed, holding the dark curtain aside to look through the window at the lighted sky.

The next evening's newspaper had told the sad truth. The Danes had destroyed their own naval fleet, blowing up the vessels one by one, as the Germans approached to take over the ships for their own use.

"How sad the king must be," Annemarie had heard Mama say to Papa when they read the news.

"How proud," Papa had replied.

It had made Annemarie feel sad and proud, too, to picture the tall, aging king, perhaps with tears in his blue eyes, as he looked at the remains of his small navy, which now lay submerged and broken in the harbor.

"I don't want to play anymore, Ellen," she said suddenly, and put her paper doll on the table.

"I have to go home, anyway," Ellen said. "I have to help Mama with the housecleaning. Thursday is our New Year. Did you know that?"

"Why is it yours?" asked Kirsti. "Isn't it our New Year, too?"

"No. It's the Jewish New Year. That's just for us. But if you want, Kirsti, you can come that night and watch Mama light the candles."

Annemarie and Kirsti had often been invited to watch

Mrs. Rosen light the Sabbath candles on Friday evenings. She covered her head with a cloth and said a special prayer in Hebrew as she did so. Annemarie always stood very quietly, awed, to watch; even Kirsti, usually such a chatterbox, was always still at that time. They didn't understand the words or the meaning, but they could feel what a special time it was for the Rosens.

"Yes," Kirsti agreed happily. "I'll come and watch your mama light the candles, and I'll wear my new black shoes."

*B*ut this time was to be different. Leaving for school on Thursday with her sister, Annemarie saw the Rosens walking to the synagogue early in the morning, dressed in their best clothes. She waved to Ellen, who waved happily back.

"Lucky Ellen," Annemarie said to Kirsti. "She doesn't have to go to school today."

"But she probably has to sit very, very still, like we do in church," Kirsti pointed out. "*That's* no fun."

That afternoon, Mrs. Rosen knocked at their door but didn't come inside. Instead, she spoke for a long time in a hurried, tense voice to Annemarie's mother in the hall. When Mama returned, her face was worried, but her voice was cheerful.

"Girls," she said, "we have a nice surprise. Tonight Ellen will be coming to stay overnight and to be our guest for a few days! It isn't often we have a visitor."

Kirsti clapped her hands in delight.

"But, Mama," Annemarie said, in dismay, "it's their New Year. They were going to have a celebration at home! Ellen told me that her mother managed to get a chicken some-place, and she was going to roast it—their first roast chicken in a year or more!"

"Their plans have changed," Mama said briskly. "Mr. and Mrs. Rosen have been called away to visit some relatives. So Ellen will stay with us. Now, let's get busy and put clean sheets on your bed. Kirsti, you may sleep with Mama and Papa tonight, and we'll let the big girls giggle together by themselves."

Kirsti pouted, and it was clear that she was about to argue. "Mama will tell you a special story tonight," her mother said. "One just for you."

"About a king?" Kirsti asked dubiously.

"About a king, if you wish," Mama replied.

"All right, then. But there must be a queen, too," Kirsti said.

Though Mrs. Rosen had sent her chicken to the Johansens, and Mama made a lovely dinner large enough for second helpings all around, it was not an evening of laughter and talk. Ellen was silent at dinner. She looked frightened. Mama and Papa tried to speak of cheerful things, but it was clear that they were worried, and it made Annemarie worry, too. Only Kirsti was unaware of the quiet tension in the room. Swinging her feet in their newly blackened and shiny shoes, she chattered and giggled during dinner.

"Early bedtime tonight, little one," Mama announced after the dishes were washed. "We need extra time for the long story I promised, about the king and queen." She disappeared with Kirsti into the bedroom.

"What's happening?" Annemarie asked when she and Ellen were alone with Papa in the living room. "Something's wrong. What is it?"

Papa's face was troubled. "I wish that I could protect you children from this knowledge," he said quietly. "Ellen, you already know. Now we must tell Annemarie."

He turned to her and stroked her hair with his gentle hand. "This morning, at the synagogue, the rabbi told his congregation that the Nazis have taken the synagogue lists of all the Jews. Where they live, what their names are. Of course the Rosens were on that list, along with many others."

"Why? Why did they want those names?"

"They plan to arrest all the Danish Jews. They plan to take them away. And we have been told that they may come tonight."

"I don't understand! Take them where?"

Her father shook his head. "We don't know where, and we don't really know why. They call it 'relocation.' We don't even know what that means. We only know that it is wrong, and it is dangerous, and we must help."

Annemarie was stunned. She looked at Ellen and saw that her best friend was crying silently.

"Where are Ellen's parents? We must help them, too!"

"We couldn't take all three of them. If the Germans came to search our apartment, it would be clear that the Rosens were here. One person we can hide. Not three. So Peter has helped Ellen's parents to go elsewhere. We don't know where. Ellen doesn't know either. But they are safe."

Ellen sobbed aloud, and put her face in her hands. Papa put his arm around her. "They are safe, Ellen. I promise you that. You will see them again quite soon. Can you try hard to believe my promise?"

Ellen hesitated, nodded, and wiped her eyes with her hand.

"But, Papa," Annemarie said, looking around the small apartment, with its few pieces of furniture: the fat stuffed sofa, the table and chairs, the small bookcase against the wall. "You said that we would hide her. How can we do that? Where can she hide?"

Papa smiled. "That part is easy. It will be as your mama said: you two will sleep together in your bed, and you may giggle and talk and tell secrets to each other. And if anyone comes—"

Ellen interrupted him. "Who might come? Will it be soldiers? Like the ones on the corners?" Annemarie remembered how terrified Ellen had looked the day when the soldier had questioned them on the corner.

"I really don't think anyone will. But it never hurts to be prepared. If anyone should come, even soldiers, you two will be sisters. You are together so much, it will be easy for you to pretend that you are sisters."

He rose and walked to the window. He pulled the lace curtain aside and looked down into the street. Outside, it was beginning to grow dark. Soon they would have to draw the black curtains that all Danes had on their windows; the entire city had to be completely darkened at night. In a nearby tree, a bird was singing; otherwise it was quiet. It was the last night of September.

"Go, now, and get into your nightgowns. It will be a long night."

Annemarie and Ellen got to their feet. Papa suddenly crossed the room and put his arms around them both. He kissed the top of each head: Annemarie's blond one, which reached to his shoulder, and Ellen's dark hair, the thick curls braided as always into pigtails.

"Don't be frightened," he said to them softly. "Once I had three daughters. Tonight I am proud to have three daughters again."

o you really think anyone will come?" Ellen asked nervously, turning to Annemarie in the bedroom. "Your father doesn't think so."

"Of course not. They're always threatening stuff. They just like to scare people." Annemarie took her nightgown from a hook in the closet.

"Anyway, if they did, it would give me a chance to practice acting. I'd just pretend to be Lise. I wish I were taller, though." Ellen stood on tiptoe, trying to make herself tall. She laughed at herself, and her voice was more relaxed.

"You were great as the Dark Queen in the school play last year," Annemarie told her. "You should be an actress when you grow up."

"My father wants me to be a teacher. He wants *everyone* to be a teacher, like him. But maybe I could convince him that I should go to acting school." Ellen stood on tiptoe again, and made an imperious gesture with her arm. "I am the Dark Queen," she intoned dramatically. "I have come to command the night!"

"You should try saying, 'I am Lise Johansen!'" Annemarie said, grinning. "If you told the Nazis that you were the Dark Queen, they'd haul you off to a mental institution."

Ellen dropped her actress pose and sat down, with her legs curled under her, on the bed. "They won't really come here, do you think?" she asked again.

Annemarie shook her head. "Not in a million years." She picked up her hairbrush.

The girls found themselves whispering as they got ready for bed. There was no need, really, to whisper; they were, after all, supposed to be normal sisters, and Papa had said they could giggle and talk. The bedroom door was closed.

But the night did seem, somehow, different from a normal night. And so they whispered.

"How did your sister die, Annemarie?" Ellen asked suddenly. "I remember when it happened. And I remember the funeral—it was the only time I have ever been in a Lutheran church. But I never knew just what happened."

"I don't know *exactly*," Annemarie confessed. "She and Peter were out somewhere together, and then there was a telephone call, that there had been an accident. Mama and Papa rushed to the hospital—remember, your mother came and stayed with me and Kirsti? Kirsti was already asleep and she slept right through everything, she was so little then. But I stayed up, and I was with your mother in the living room when my parents came home in the middle of the night. And they told me Lise had died."

"I remember it was raining," Ellen said sadly. "It was still raining the next morning when Mama told me. Mama was crying, and the rain made it seem as if the whole *world* was crying."

Annemarie finished brushing her long hair and handed her hairbrush to her best friend. Ellen undid her braids, lifted her dark hair away from the thin gold chain she wore around her neck—the chain that held the Star of David—and began to brush her thick curls.

"I think it was partly because of the rain. They said she was hit by a car. I suppose the streets were slippery, and it was getting dark, and maybe the driver just couldn't see," Annemarie went on, remembering. "Papa looked so angry. He made one hand into a fist, and he kept pounding it into the other hand. I remember the noise of it: slam, slam, slam."

Together they got into the wide bed and pulled up the covers. Annemarie blew out the candle and drew the dark curtains aside so that the open window near the bed let in some air. "See that blue trunk in the corner?" she said, pointing through the darkness. "Lots of Lise's things are in there. Even her wedding dress. Mama and Papa have never looked at those things, not since the day they packed them away."

Ellen sighed. "She would have looked so beautiful in her wedding dress. She had such a pretty smile. I used to pretend that she was *my* sister, too."

"She would have liked that," Annemarie told her. "She loved you."

"That's the worst thing in the world," Ellen whispered. "To be dead so young. I wouldn't want the Germans to take my family away— to make us live someplace else. But still, it wouldn't be as bad as being dead."

Annemarie leaned over and hugged her. "They won't take you away," she said. "Not your parents, either. Papa promised that they were safe, and he always keeps his promises. And you are quite safe, here with us."

For a while they continued to murmur in the dark, but the murmurs were interrupted by yawns. Then Ellen's voice stopped, she turned over, and in a minute her breathing was quiet and slow.

Annemarie stared at the window where the sky was outlined and a tree branch moved slightly in the breeze. Everything seemed very familiar, very comforting. Dangers were no more than odd imaginings, like ghost stories that children made up to frighten one another: things that couldn't possibly happen. Annemarie felt completely safe here in her own home, with her parents in the next room and her best friend asleep beside her. She yawned contentedly and closed her eyes.

It was hours later, but still dark, when she was awakened abruptly by the pounding on the apartment door.

Annemarie eased the bedroom door open quietly, only a crack, and peeked out. Behind her, Ellen was sitting up, her eyes wide.

She could see Mama and Papa in their nightclothes, moving about. Mama held a lighted candle, but as Annemarie watched, she went to a lamp and switched it on. It was so long a time since they had dared to use the strictly rationed electricity after dark that the light in the room seemed startling to Annemarie, watching through the slightly opened bedroom door. She saw her mother look automatically to the blackout curtains, making certain that they were tightly drawn.

Papa opened the front door to the soldiers.

"This is the Johansen apartment?" A deep voice asked the question loudly, in the terribly accented Danish.

"Our name is on the door, and I see you have a flashlight," Papa answered. "What do you want? Is something wrong?"

"I understand you are a friend of your neighbors the Rosens, Mrs. Johansen," the soldier said angrily.

"Sophy Rosen is my friend, that is true," Mama said quietly. "Please, could you speak more softly? My children are asleep."

"Then you will be so kind as to tell me where the Rosens are." He made no effort to lower his voice.

"I assume they are at home, sleeping. It is four in the morning, after all," Mama said.

Annemarie heard the soldier stalk across the living room toward the kitchen. From her hiding place in the narrow sliver of open doorway, she could see the heavy uniformed man, a holstered pistol at his waist, in the entrance to the kitchen, peering in toward the sink.

Another German voice said, "The Rosens' apartment is empty. We are wondering if they might be visiting their good friends the Johansens."

"Well," said Papa, moving slightly so that he was standing in front of Annemarie's bedroom door, and she could see nothing except the dark blur of his back, "as you see, you are mistaken. There is no one here but my family."

"You will not object if we look around." The voice was harsh, and it was not a question.

"It seems we have no choice," Papa replied.

"Please don't wake my children," Mama requested again. "There is no need to frighten little ones."

The heavy, booted feet moved across the floor again and into the other bedroom. A closet door opened and closed with a bang.

Annemarie eased her bedroom door closed silently. She stumbled through the darkness to the bed.

"Ellen," she whispered urgently, "take your necklace off!"

Ellen's hands flew to her neck. Desperately she began trying to unhook the tiny clasp. Outside the bedroom door, the harsh voices and heavy footsteps continued.

"I can't get it open!" Ellen said frantically. "I never take it off—I can't even remember how to open it!"

Annemarie heard a voice just outside the door. "What is here?"

"Shhh," her mother replied. "My daughters' bedroom. They are sound asleep."

"Hold still," Annemarie commanded. "This will hurt." She grabbed the little gold chain, yanked with all her strength, and broke it. As the door opened and light flooded into the bedroom, she crumpled it into her hand and closed her fingers tightly.

Terrified, both girls looked up at the three Nazi officers who entered the room.

One of the men aimed a flashlight around the bedroom. He went to the closet and looked inside. Then with a sweep of his gloved hand he pushed to the floor several coats and a bathrobe that hung from pegs on the wall.

There was nothing else in the room except a chest of drawers, the blue decorated trunk in the corner, and a heap of Kirsti's dolls piled in a small rocking chair. The flashlight beam touched each thing in turn. Angrily the officer turned toward the bed.

"Get up!" he ordered. "Come out here!"

Trembling, the two girls rose from the bed and followed him, brushing past the two remaining officers in the doorway, to the living room.

Annemarie looked around. These three uniformed men were different from the ones on the street corners. The street soldiers were often young, sometimes ill at ease, and Annemarie remembered how the Giraffe had, for a moment, let his harsh pose slip and had smiled at Kirsti.

But these men were older and their faces were set with anger.

Her parents were standing beside each other, their faces tense, but Kirsti was nowhere in sight. Thank goodness that Kirsti slept through almost everything. If they had wakened her, she would be wailing—or worse, she would be angry, and her fists would fly.

"Your names?" the officer barked.

"Annemarie Johansen. And this is my sister—"

"Quiet! Let her speak for herself. Your name?" He was glaring at Ellen.

Ellen swallowed. "Lise," she said, and cleared her throat. "Lise Johansen."

The officer stared at them grimly.

"Now," Mama said in a strong voice, "you have seen that we are not hiding anything. May my children go back to bed?"

The officer ignored her. Suddenly he grabbed a handful of Ellen's hair. Ellen winced.

He laughed scornfully. "You have a blond child sleeping in the other room. And you have this blond daughter—" He gestured toward Annemarie with his head. "Where did you get the dark-haired one?" He twisted the lock of Ellen's hair. "From a different father? From the milkman?"

Papa stepped forward. "Don't speak to my wife in such a way. Let go of my daughter or I will report you for such treatment."

"Or maybe you got her someplace else?" the officer continued with a sneer. "From the Rosens?"

For a moment no one spoke. Then Annemarie, watching in panic, saw her father move swiftly to the small bookcase and take out a book. She saw that he was holding the family photograph album. Very quickly he searched through its pages, found what he was looking for, and tore out three pictures from three separate pages.

He handed them to the German officer, who released Ellen's hair.

"You will see each of my daughters, each with her name written on the photograph," Papa said.

442

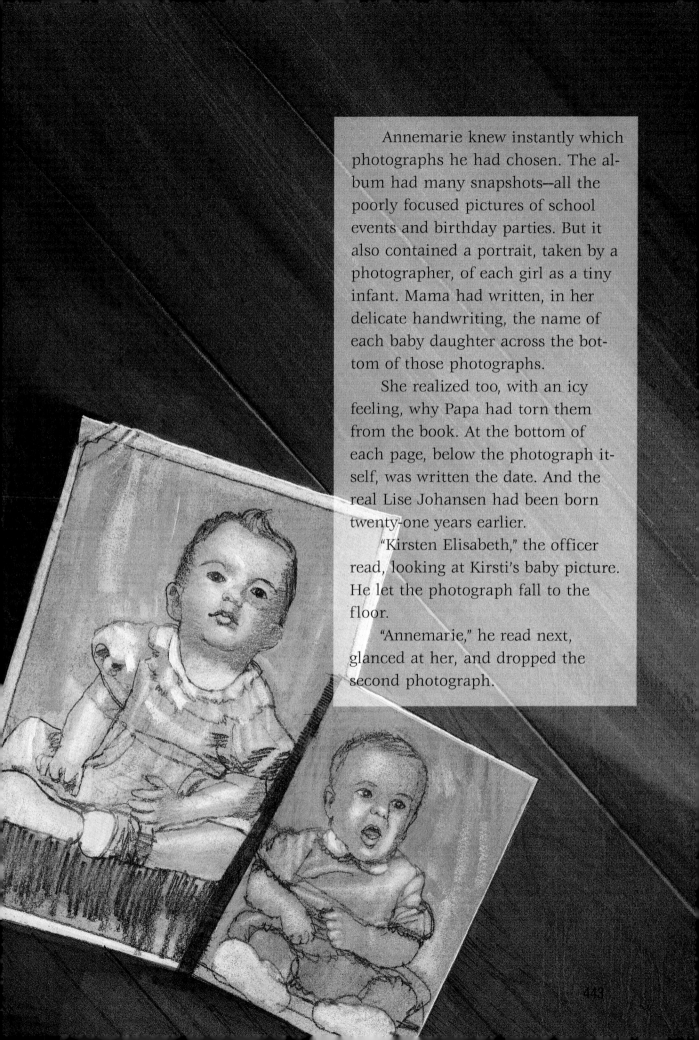

Annemarie knew instantly which photographs he had chosen. The album had many snapshots—all the poorly focused pictures of school events and birthday parties. But it also contained a portrait, taken by a photographer, of each girl as a tiny infant. Mama had written, in her delicate handwriting, the name of each baby daughter across the bottom of those photographs.

She realized too, with an icy feeling, why Papa had torn them from the book. At the bottom of each page, below the photograph itself, was written the date. And the real Lise Johansen had been born twenty-one years earlier.

"Kirsten Elisabeth," the officer read, looking at Kirsti's baby picture. He let the photograph fall to the floor.

"Annemarie," he read next, glanced at her, and dropped the second photograph.

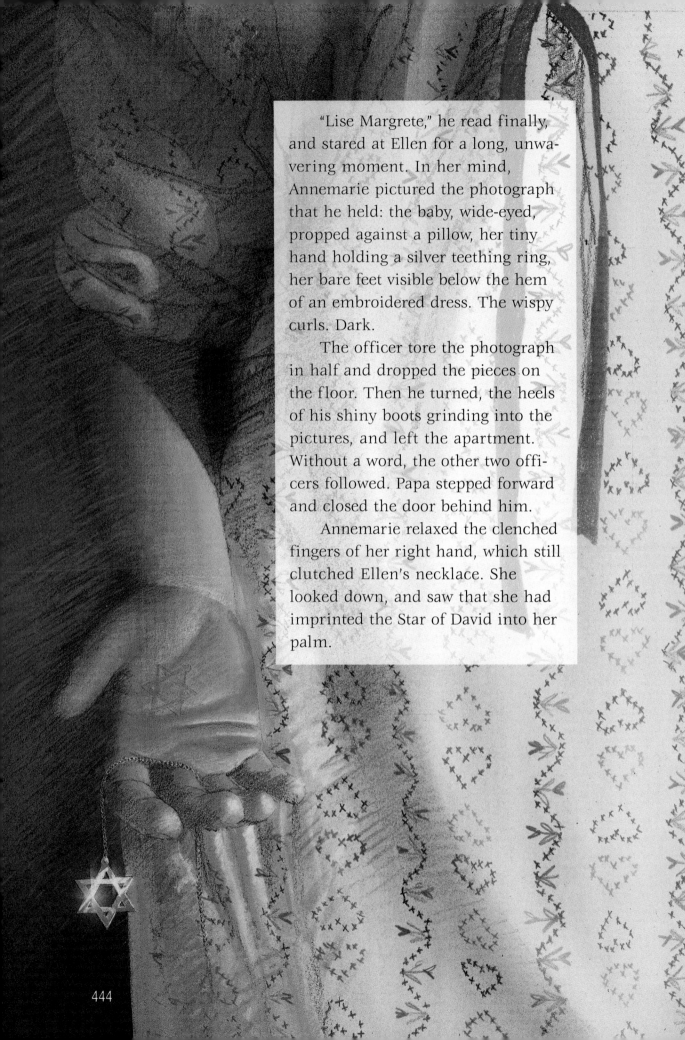

"Lise Margrete," he read finally, and stared at Ellen for a long, unwavering moment. In her mind, Annemarie pictured the photograph that he held: the baby, wide-eyed, propped against a pillow, her tiny hand holding a silver teething ring, her bare feet visible below the hem of an embroidered dress. The wispy curls. Dark.

The officer tore the photograph in half and dropped the pieces on the floor. Then he turned, the heels of his shiny boots grinding into the pictures, and left the apartment. Without a word, the other two officers followed. Papa stepped forward and closed the door behind him.

Annemarie relaxed the clenched fingers of her right hand, which still clutched Ellen's necklace. She looked down, and saw that she had imprinted the Star of David into her palm.

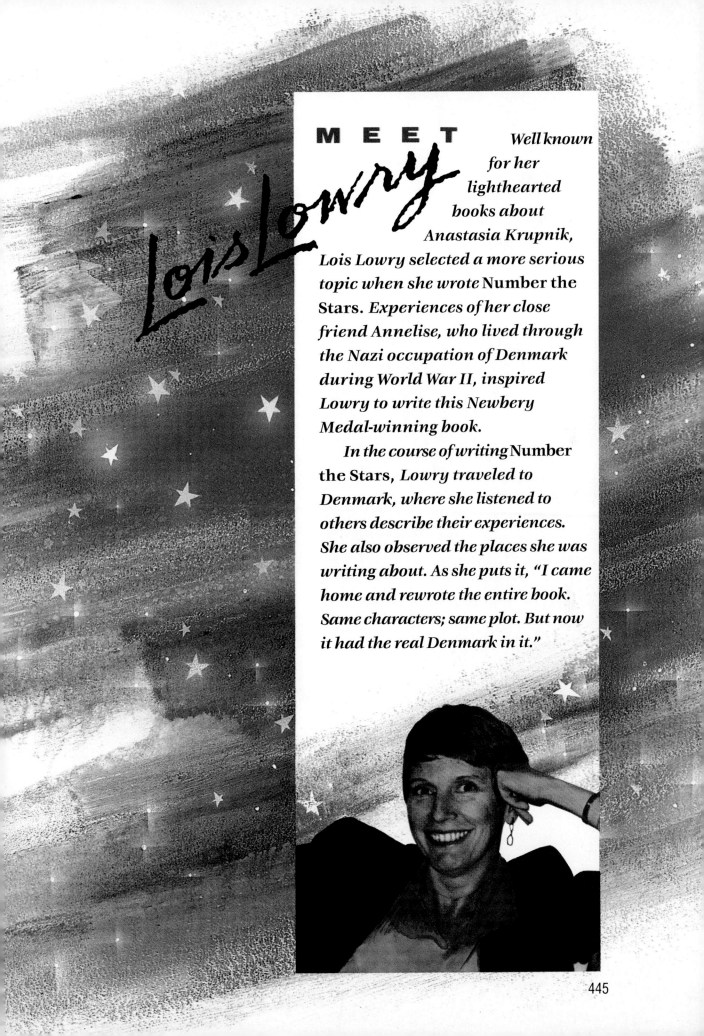

MEET Lois Lowry

Well known for her lighthearted books about Anastasia Krupnik, Lois Lowry selected a more serious topic when she wrote **Number the Stars.** Experiences of her close friend Annelise, who lived through the Nazi occupation of Denmark during World War II, inspired Lowry to write this Newbery Medal-winning book.

In the course of writing **Number the Stars,** *Lowry traveled to Denmark, where she listened to others describe their experiences. She also observed the places she was writing about. As she puts it, "I came home and rewrote the entire book. Same characters; same plot. But now it had the real Denmark in it."*

Those Brave Young Americans

In the selection from *Number the Stars*, Annemarie and her family, like many other Danish people, courageously stood up against the injustices of World War II. Most people are aware of the bravery that makes headlines in times of war or natural disaster. Yet acts of heroism in daily life often go unnoticed. Many people do not realize that young people, as well as adults, have often demonstrated great courage. In 1950, the United States government established the Young American Medal for Bravery to recognize courageous young people who have taken decisive action to save others in danger.

Angela Marie Campanoli

Lacey, Washington, 1988—The ocean off Hawaii can look inviting, but residents know when to stay out of the water. Two- or three-foot waves, a stiff breeze, and a strong riptide can signal potential danger. Eleven-year-old Angela Marie Campanoli was sunbathing at Polo Beach on just such a day in October 1988.

A family of three relaxed nearby. Without warning, the young son was in the water and beginning to panic as he fought the current. His parents rushed to help, but soon they, too, were in trouble.

As the father clung to the rocks and others rescued the boy, the current carried the mother farther and farther out to sea. Angela dived in, swam out to her, and then held the woman's head above water. With the aid of her brother, Angela stayed with the woman until help arrived.

Michael Browne

Dixon, New Mexico, 1980—Upon hearing that a climber, Susan Peoples, had been injured, Michael Browne decided to see if he could help. Living at the foot of a mountain range, Michael was already an expert climber at the age of thirteen. He knew it might take rescuers hours to reach Susan, so he grabbed a blanket and a flashlight and left by himself to search for her.

Michael managed to find Susan, who had fallen nearly forty feet onto a precarious ledge above the canyon floor. She was only partly conscious, having cut her arm badly and broken both ankles in her fall. Michael made his way to the ledge and covered her with the blanket. For more than two hours, through nightfall and a steady rain, he stayed with the injured woman, keeping her from losing hope or sliding off the edge. Even after rescuers arrived, he stayed to help take supplies and messages to her. Susan's life was saved thanks to Michael's concern, as well as his courage.

447

the Rescue

Running down the tracks one day,

thunder and lightning coming up on me,

and there a little girl crying

and walking,

looking at the sky.

Me scared to death of storms

crossing over:

You going home? Want me to walk with you?

And turning away from my house to walk her

through Beaver

to hers.

Lightning and thunder strong now.

So there's her mother on the porch, waving,

and she says bye to me then runs.

I turn around

and walk in the storm

slow and straight,

but inside,

a little girl crying.

—Cynthia Rylant

MEET
Lynn Hall

Lynn Hall's strongest childhood memory is of "trying to escape, not so much *from* something . . . but *to* something—to the country, to dogs and horses." After high school, she drifted from job to job. But one day she saw in a store window a children's book about horses. She read it and was amazed by how much the author did *not* know about horses. Believing that she could do better, Hall decided to take a big risk. She left her job to write children's books about animals.

That risk proved successful. Hall's books have won many awards, including the Boston Globe–Horn Book Award for *The Leaving*. Today she lives in the country and owns a "rare and wonderful" Paso Fino horse. (See photo below.)

Danza!

by LYNN HALL

For Paulo Camacho and his grandfather, Diego, raising fine Paso Fino horses on their Puerto Rican ranch is a family tradition. Paulo is especially proud of his own stallion, Danza. After a grueling ride one day, Paulo carelessly leaves the gate of Danza's pen unlatched. The thirsty, overheated horse escapes, drinks an unhealthy amount of water, and becomes seriously ill. Just when it becomes obvious that a way must be found to end Danza's suffering, Major Kessler appears. A deal is struck—he will take Danza, accompanied by Paulo, back to his Louisiana ranch and get medical care for the horse, and if Danza recovers, he will be lent to the major for one breeding season.

In Louisiana, months go by as Paulo painstakingly nurses Danza back to health. When Danza has nearly recovered, the major proposes that Danza, with Paulo riding him, be entered in the next season of horse shows. Danza and Paulo perform well in the shows but never win first prize. The major decides that Danza would win if he were ridden by a professional trainer. Against Paulo's wishes, he hires the trainer Jordan Welch to ride Danza in the upcoming Lake Charles Show.

The Lake Charles Charity Horse Show was a large and glittering affair. Although it was barely past noon there was a feeling of evening formality about the arena. Stewards wore formal hunt attire, and trophy presenters held up long-skirted gowns as they tiptoed through the tanbark.

For Paulo, seated in a ringside box with the major and the Felden family, it was a crazy day. There was Danza two buildings away in his stall, being readied for the Classic Fino class, and Paulo was forbidden even to see him.

"It would just upset him," the major explained when they arrived. "Jordan said he's had a hard enough time getting Danza's mind off of you. If that horse saw you now it would undo all the work Jordan's put in on him these last weeks."

Paulo had accepted the edict, but not gracefully.

Only one more class, now. A Saddlebred fine harness class. Four elegant high-headed horses circled the ring at a majestic trot, drawing behind them gleaming carts in which gowned and fancy-hatted women drove with high-held reins.

Paulo didn't see them.

Beside him, Marilyn Felden said,

"I bet you can hardly wait to see him, huh?"

Paulo made a tight little face, but said nothing.

"Boy, I'm sure glad my dad doesn't believe in hiring trainers. If he ever sent Nibs off someplace for some stranger to ride—"

Paulo turned on her. "What do you mean, he doesn't believe in trainers. He's the one who talked the major into hiring one. Well, one of the people anyway."

"Oh, that's different." Marilyn's round face grew unnaturally serious. "That's for people like him." She lowered her voice and slanted her eyes toward the major, who was talking in the other direction to Mrs. Felden. "People like the major are mainly in it for winning. In horses, I mean. Oh, they like their horses, maybe even love them, but not the same way we do, and you do, I think. If their horse can't win, they don't care about it anymore. Now me, and my family, we go to the shows mainly for fun. Our horses are our pets. I'd never sell Nibs, no matter what."

Paulo looked into that round, earnest face, and felt suddenly less alone.

The loudspeaker's music changed from Viennese to Spanish.

"Here they come," Paulo and Marilyn said together.

Danza was the first horse in the ring. Five others followed, but Paulo didn't see them. Three weeks without Danza, and Paulo was starved for the sight of him, the touch of him. His knees felt the curve of Danza's barrel between them; his hands lifted to the touch of Danza's mouth against the reins.

At first it was enough just to absorb the sight of that gleaming red body glinting gold in the highlights and fringed by a lengthening flow of black mane and tail. Black-booted legs, polished black hooves . . .

Paulo sat forward suddenly and stared at those legs, those hooves.

"He's not moving right," he said to the major.

Major Kessler, too, leaned forward and squinted as Danza danced by. "Looks all right to me. In fact, I like the way he's moving. Got more spirit than . . . before."

"Than when I was riding him?"

But the argument died as Paulo and the major turned their attention fully on Danza.

Paulo spoke only to himself now. He's picking his feet up too high. He's prancing like a darned Saddlebred or

something. That's not how a Paso is supposed to move. Don't these fools know that? Not a high prance. Quick snap at the pasterns, but keep the feet low to the ground. That's not right, what he's got Danza doing out there. What is he doing to my horse?

For a moment Paulo took his eyes away from Danza's feet and looked at the rest of the horse. Good weight, beautiful shine to his coat, but his ears were flattened, and every few steps Danza's tail made an angry wringing motion. As the horse came close again Paulo could see anger and . . . something else . . . in Danza's eyes. Pain? Was it pain?

The six stallions lined up, and the judge sent his message to the announcer.

"First place in Classic Fino, Stallions, is Danza, owned by

Diego Mendez, ridden by Jordan Welch. Second place—"

"Hooeee!" Major Kessler shouted, and banged Paulo's back. "Finally did it! He won his class. See, Paulo, it takes that little extra touch that only a professional can give a horse. I was right to send him to Welch. Now we have a real shot at the National Championship next week. Hooeee, we're on the right track now."

Paulo stood up. "I want to go see him."

"No." The major's voice was flat. "He'll be going back into the Championship class later on. And frankly, Paulo, Jordan doesn't want Danza to see you at all. Said it would just upset the horse, and with the National show next weekend, let's not take a chance. He's

the trainer, after all. I'm paying him for his expertise, and I intend to follow his advice."

Paulo stared down at the man. "You mean I can't see him at all? We drove all this way down here just to sit in the audience and—"

"Now, son . . ."

"I'm not your son," he flared, and ran from the box.

Paulo was out of the building and halfway to the barns when he heard Marilyn's voice. "Hey, wait up."

He stopped. A friend suddenly seemed just what he needed.

"What are you going to do?" Sweat trickled down her face from the running, and her eyes were warm with concern.

"See my horse."

She fell into step beside him.

But Jordan Welch met them in the aisle of the barn. Paulo asked politely, then tried to reason, then shouted in anger he could no longer hide. The man was adamant.

Paulo and Marilyn turned and went outside, but lingered at the edge of the door. When Paulo looked back down the aisle he saw Jordan Welch talking to a uniformed security guard, motioning to Danza's stall and to Paulo.

"Come on," Marilyn said, "let's go get something to eat. That guard isn't going to let you near Danza."

"But he's my horse."

"Yeah, but whose word do you think that guard would take, yours or old Welch's?"

Paulo caved in under her logic. He wasn't interested in food, but he followed Marilyn to the lunch stand to escape the tantalizing nearness of Danza. And to avoid being alone.

A thought, like a prick of pain, refused to be banished or ignored. The major. A firm word from the major and Paulo would be allowed to go to Danza. "Doesn't he know how bad I want to see my horse? Or aren't I important to him at all? I told him something was wrong with Danza, the way he was moving in that ring, but he didn't take my word for it. Or else he didn't care."

The lunchroom was a sprawling place with tables across one end where aproned women sold hot dogs and barbeques. Long tables filled most of the room. The main lunch rush was past, leaving empty paper cups and crumpled sandwich papers scattered over the tabletops. Paulo sat down sideways to a table, his feet on the next chair, his shoulders hunched against all his miseries, while Marilyn went for her food.

Two men stepped past him and sat behind Paulo at the next table. He glanced at them only long enough to catalog them, by their riding clothes, as Tennessee Walker people. Paulo had found mild amusement in the variety of show clothes these Americans wore. A distinct outfit for each kind of horse. Skinny, hipless girls in high black boots and pale breeches and velvet caps, those were hunters or hunt seat riders. Long-jacketed suits and little derby hats, Saddlebred people. For Walking Horses a similar outfit with subtle differences. For Quarter horses and Appaloosas, cowboy hats and fancy shirts and fringed suede chaps. And the Paso people in their dark Spanish-formal suits and ruffled shirts and flat-brimmed hats.

". . . Jordan Welch gone to Paso Finos now, I see."

The voice jerked at Paulo's attention. One of the men behind him. He sat rigid, listening.

"You're kidding," the other man said. "What's he want with a camel-shuffler?"

Paulo's eyes bulged with compressed anger.

"Got to make a living, I guess. He pretty well blew himself out of the water with the Walking Horse people, and I doubt he could get anything good in Saddlebreds now. Pasos might not be such a bad move for him, considering. Looked like a pretty decent horse he had. Won his class with him, I believe. I saw him coming out a while ago."

Marilyn approached, chattering. Paulo waved her silent, and motioned with his head toward the men, whose backs were toward Paulo.

One of them spoke, and Paulo strained to hear. "How'd you do last weekend? Were you at Mobile?"

Marilyn looked puzzled. She held her dripping chili dog aloft, waiting.

Abruptly Paulo swung around and tapped the nearer man on the arm. "Pardon me for interrupting. I heard you talking about Jordan Welch. What did he do to blow himself out of the water with Walking Horse people?" Paulo wasn't sure what the term meant, but his voice was as firm as if he did.

The men glanced at one another in a guarded way. "Why do you ask?"

"Because that camel-shuffler he's riding belongs to me. My grandfather. And I don't like the way he's treating him."

This time the exchanged glance between the men was one of doubt bordering on amusement. Paulo felt very young and very foreign and not at all like the owner of an expensive show horse.

The near man said, "If the horse belongs to you, then what's the problem? Fire Welch."

Suddenly it became vital for Paulo to know what these men knew about Welch. Armed with that information he could attack the major and convince him to get Danza away from that man. He was almost sure that the look he'd seen in Danza's eyes had been one of pain, and he could see that look clearly now. He scooted his chair around and hunched forward, his eyes burning.

"Look, it's true. Danza belongs to my grandfather, down in Puerto Rico, but he's always been my horse, to raise and train and ride. He got foundered and my grandfather couldn't take care of him good enough, so he loaned him to Major Kessler to bring up here where the vets are better. Major Kessler was just supposed to use him for one season of breeding and then send him back home, and me too. Only now he's started showing him and charging other people lots of money to breed their mares to him. And I wasn't winning enough with Danza, so he sent him away to Jordan Welch, and Danza was hurting. In the ring. I saw his eyes, and something was hurting him, but Mr. Welch won't let me in the barn so I can't see for myself."

This time when the men exchanged looks, there was acceptance of Paulo's story, and compassion.

The near man cleared his throat. "Well, we really don't know the facts of the situation. It's just stable gossip but, for what it's worth, maybe you have the right to hear it. Welch used to be a pretty successful trainer in Tennessee Walking Horses. Got a nice stable down around New Orleans, I think. Did a lot of winning, but he was in and out of trouble with the authorities all the time, for soring."

"Soring—" It all came clear in Paulo's mind. Danza's unusually high steps, the wringing tail, the look of pain in his eyes.

"Yes. Well, everybody does it, you understand. Only some people are more blatant about it than others. But what finally cooked it for Welch was, he sored a client's horse so badly that the horse was crippled for life. That happens from time to time, too, unfortunately, but in this case the owner was quite influential in the breed, and the horse was a special favorite of his. Just a young animal, lots of potential. The owner said Welch would never work in Walkers again, and I guess it wasn't an empty threat."

Crippled for life. Paulo sat back and let the horrible possibilities wash over him. A whole year of working and hoping and massaging, of caring for Danza when he was a blue-gray hairless pile of bones with no feet, of massaging wasted leg muscles until Paulo's own

muscles ached unbearably, rejoicing over that first rim of new hoof emerging from Danza's coronets— Was it all for this? The weeks and months of pampering those foundered feet so that no gravel, no concrete brought back the agony that Danza had borne longer than any innocent animal should have to bear anything . . . and now this stupid, criminal gringo was deliberately hurting those feet so the major could get his blue ribbon and Welch could make a living.

Marilyn ignored Paulo's sickened silence. She scooted her chair closer to the conversation and said, "But why do you people do that to your horses? How can you love horses and deliberately hurt them?"

The near man shook his head. "Believe me, honey, we don't like it. We do it because we have to. As long as everyone else is doing it, we have to or we simply won't be in the ribbons. I have hundreds of thousands of dollars wrapped up in my stock and my stable facilities, and I've got to be able to sell horses at substantial prices or I can't afford to stay in the business. And you have to have the show wins. And to win, your horse has got to do the big lick. It's as simple as that."

"But isn't it illegal or something?" Marilyn cried.

"Oh, yes. Certainly it's illegal. The Horse Protection Act passed in 1970, federal law. Didn't do a bit of good. Not enough money to enforce it. And when the inspectors find out how to detect one kind of soring, the trainers come up with another, more sophisticated. First it was oil of mustard. Caused terribly bloody blisters around a horse's coronets, under their boots. Bichloride of mercury was another one."

Marilyn's face flushed with emotion, but she said in an even voice, "Well, I'm sorry for your horses. And I'm just glad we don't have it in our breed."

Both men laughed, and one said, "Don't kid yourself, kid. Every breed has its secrets. Dilated eyes in Arabians, tranquilizers in Quarter horses, drug stimulants in Saddlebreds, and plenty more that I don't know about, I'm sure. It's in every breed at least to some degree— maybe just at the top levels of competition, but it's there."

Paulo muttered, "Americanos," and the near man turned on him. "It's in every country, too, kid. You don't need to be so holy. Down there you use yellow coral. Other things too, probably, but I've heard of that one."

He couldn't sit still any longer. Leaving Marilyn to end the conversation politely, he ran out of the building. Major Kessler was walking toward him.

Paulo dodged a hackney pony and cart, and ran to the major.

"Paulo, there you are. I was looking for you. Come on back to the box. The Fino Championship is after this next class. You don't want to miss that."

"I have to talk to you," Paulo panted. "We have to get Danza away from that man. He's hurting him."

"What? You don't know what you're talking about—"

A clot of laughing teenagers swarmed between them.

"Listen, major, I was just talking to these men in the lunchroom . . ."

The major took Paulo's arm and started him toward the show building. "This is no place to talk about it, and we don't want to miss Danza's class."

His voice was firm, almost as though he didn't want to hear what Paulo was going to say, Paulo thought.

Marilyn caught up with them, and the three of them climbed the steps to their box just as the Fino Championship class was entering the ring.

Paulo watched, in spite of his anguish. It was too late now to get Danza out of the class, anyway.

Six horses entered the ring, necks arched, long manes billowing, Danza and the second-place horse from the stallion class, then the first- and second-place winners from the gelding and mare classes. Again Danza moved with unnaturally high lifting of his feet, with the angry lashing of his tail.

"See," Paulo shook the major's elbow, "can't you see how he's moving?"

"He's moving like a winner, Paulo. Now, please keep your voice down." The major glanced toward Marilyn and her parents in the seats behind him and Paulo.

Paulo lowered his voice, but tried once again. "These men in the lunchroom, they know Mr. Welch, major. They were telling me he used to put things on Walking Horses' hooves to make them sore, so they'd win, and he made one horse permanently crippled and got into lots of trouble over it, and that's why he's trying to get into Paso Finos now. And I know he's doing it to Danza. You have to stop him."

"Doing what?" The major appeared to be only half-listening as he watched Danza, narrow-eyed.

"Putting mustard on his feet," Paulo shouted.

Several people turned to look at him, some grinning.

The major laughed openly.

Paulo grew red with fury, but lowered his voice again. "Some-thing like mustard. Something that burns their feet and makes awful blisters. That's why Danza is picking up his feet so high. It's hurting him. Please, major. Take him away from Mr. Welch."

The man laid a restraining hand on Paulo's knee. "Shhh. We'll talk about it later. I want to watch this."

The judge sent his message to the announcer, and the loudspeaker crackled. "Grand Champion, Fino Division, Danza, owned by—"

Paulo's heart sank.

As the major rose to leave the box, Paulo said, "Look at his feet yourself, if you don't believe me. Or make Mr. Welch let me see him. You're the one who hired him. He'll have to let you see Danza."

The major turned swiftly on Paulo and said in a low hard voice, "Now, you listen to me. I am paying Mr. Welch to use his expertise to get wins with Danza. You rode the horse all summer and never did better than second place. One time out, and Welch has won a Championship class with him. I am not going to insult the man by questioning his methods, and if he feels it would be bad for Danza for you to see him, then that's it. His word is final. As long as he can get results like this out of that horse, neither you nor I will interfere. Is that understood?"

"But he's hurting him," Paulo wailed.

The major was already down the steps and away to collect his rosette and trophy.

It was nearly midnight. Paulo lay on his bed in the motel room, staring at the television screen as though he were watching the movie. Except for the silvery light from the screen, the room was dark. It was a nice room, assembly line plush, a major motor hotel chain, with velvety wallpaper and pictures that looked like real art.

The major's bed, next to Paulo's, was still smoothly made. The major was out somewhere having dinner and drinks with Mr. Welch and some of the other Paso people. This time Paulo had not been invited, and he was glad, he told himself.

Restlessness grew in him, a need to do something. Finally he flung himself off the bed and pushed his feet into his loafers. He smacked the

on-off knob on the television, grabbed his room key, and fled down the long blue and green hallway and out the thick glass door at the end.

Outside, the highway stretched away toward the show grounds six, seven blocks away. Paulo started at an easy lope. As he ran he thought, How am I going to get in? The entrance will be guarded, for sure. And a Puerto Rican kid in old jeans and t-shirt, this time of the night, no way they're going to let me in. Over a fence, maybe, around at the back of the grounds. And if I can get in the barn, what then? Just see him? See his feet?

Just see him.

The ache in Paulo's chest had nothing to do with running.

The way in was easier than Paulo had expected, a side road, a gate that was padlocked but simple to climb over, and a barn still open and lighted at the far end where a knot of people were standing around a stall in the Saddlebred area, drinking and laughing.

Three aisles away in the row of Paso Fino stalls, the barn was dim and empty of people except for a young man in a sleeping bag in a vacant stall. A few horses shuffled and whickered at Paulo as he peered into stall after stall.

He heard Danza's soft snort from three stalls away. The dark shape of Danza's head appeared over the stall door, straining toward him.

"There's my boy," Paulo whispered. In his excitement he almost forgot to be quiet in opening the stall door.

"Danza."

Paulo wrapped his arms around the horse's neck and buried his face in the long, coarse strands of Danza's mane; the horse turned his head so far around that Paulo was enclosed in the bend of Danza's neck.

What have they been doing to you? Paulo wanted to ask. More strongly than ever before in his

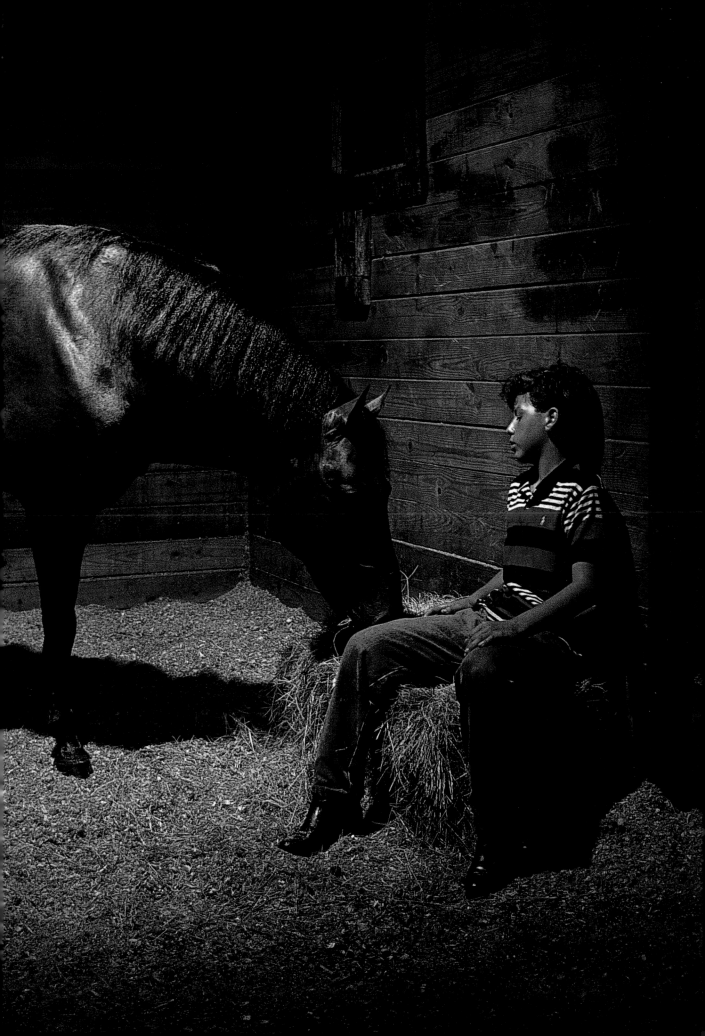

life, he wished for the ability to read Danza's thoughts, to communicate his own to the mind within that broad, flat skull.

The light within the stall was too dim to see details, but Paulo leaned against Danza's shoulder and ran his hand down the black-stockinged leg. "Give me your foot," he whispered.

Danza tensed, and stood firm. Never before had he refused to lift a foot, even during the painful months of his illness. Paulo's fingers

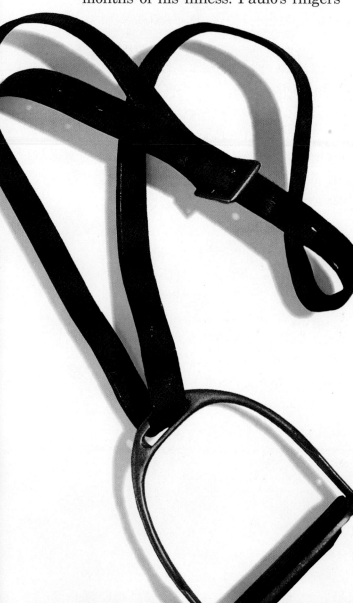

probed gently around the pastern, around the rim of the coronet. Heat. A puffy tenderness, like blisters. Danza snorted and shied away from Paulo's touch.

Paulo needed no bright lights to complete his examination.

For a long time he stood stroking Danza . . . thinking. Then, afraid of being seen, he sat down in a corner of the stall, elbows on his knees, hands dangling.

Think, think, think, he told himself. Got to get Danza away from that man. Got to do it now. First thing in the morning he's going to load him up and truck him back to his stable unless I stop him. How? Get him out of here. I could take him now. Probably nobody would stop me in the barn. But I couldn't get him through the gate. The guy at the gate would never believe he was my horse. They'd arrest me for horse-stealing.

And even if I could get him off the grounds, what would I do with him then? Can't ride him all the way to Puerto Rico. I don't know anybody here in Lake Charles. Nowhere to take him.

At the mental picture of himself kidnapping Danza, Paulo grew suddenly fierce.

Why should I have to sneak out of here like a thief with him? Danza is more mine than the major's. I have a right to protect him from being hurt. And after everything I went through to see that he has feet, I have a better right than anybody else to make sure nobody hurts him anymore. I hurt him in the first place by not being careful of that latch rope, but that's a whole lot different from putting acid or whatever on him and deliberately hurting him to get blue ribbons. He's my horse, and nobody does that to my horse.

After a while, with no real plan of action except to hold firm and demand justice, Paulo relaxed and dozed, his head back against the stall wall. Danza stood over him, his chin just above the boy's hair. For the first time in weeks, the little red stallion felt that his world was right.

"What in hell are you doing in there?" Welch shouted.

The morning sun was well up. Paulo had been awake for some time, waiting, rehearsing. He stood and brushed the wood shavings from his seat.

"I'm staying with my horse," he said. It didn't come out sounding as strong as he had meant it to.

"That's what you think. Listen, kid, what's your name, Paul, I told you I didn't want you upsetting Danza, and I meant it." He turned and shouted, "Watchman!"

"You mean you didn't want me to see his feet. You hurt him, and I'm not going to let you do it anymore. He belongs to my grandfather, and I am his agent in this country. You're fired."

Paulo almost smiled. That last part came out pretty good.

A uniformed watchman approached. Mr. Welch turned on him. "What kind of security do you people have in this place, anyway? This boy apparently got in here during the night. I want him out of here."

The guard moved to take Paulo's arm. Paulo stood his ground, but tightened the arm that lay across Danza's neck, as though to anchor himself.

He stood as straight as he could and said to the watchman, "This horse belongs to my family in Puerto Rico. Mr. Welch was just his trainer, but I fired him."

The watchman hesitated, looked at Mr. Welch. A few people

stopped in the aisle to watch and listen and glance curiously at one another.

"Is that right?" the watchman asked Mr. Welch.

The man looked suddenly defensive. "His grandfather is the official owner of the horse, yes, but I was hired by a Major Kessler who has the horse in this country on lease. He's the man who's paying me, and no little snot like this is going to stand there and tell me he's firing me."

Marilyn Felden's face appeared suddenly around the stall door.

Paulo said, "Marilyn! Go get the major. And your dad," he added as an afterthought. He felt cornered, overpowered by the authorities around him, and instinctively he wanted Mr. Felden's calm fair-mindedness.

Suddenly the major appeared. "Paulo, where on earth have you been all night? I was just about to—what's going on here?"

Paulo looked at him, and old emotions rose to clog his throat. This man, this good, kind, strong man who was the first to accord Paulo Camacho the dignity of respect—was he still there behind that familiar long freckled face? Was there any love? Was it all the hungry imaginings of his own need?

Dark eyes locked on pale ones. "Major, he has been blistering Danza's feet. I had to come and see for myself, and he has. Look. Come here and look." He picked up Danza's near hoof and touched the horny frog area. Danza jerked away.

The major looked, but from a distance. "Paulo, this is nothing to make a scene about. We'll talk about it later—"

"No." As Paulo spoke he felt the pain of betrayal. There was no time to probe it now, but it was there behind the urgency of the moment. "Danza is mine, and I'm taking him away from you. From both of you. I'm taking him home."

The crowd in the aisle was large by now. With a wash of relief Paulo saw Mr. Felden near the stall door. Paulo turned toward the crowd and raised his voice. "All you people out there. He's been soring my horse and I don't want him to. Can't somebody help?"

There was an uneasy silence, as though no one knew what action to take, what words to say.

Suddenly Mr. Felden said, "Paulo, if there's anything I can

do, if you need transportation or a place to keep Danza or anything like that, you can count on me."

The offer dazzled Paulo. The way out . . .

"What's the trouble here?" A new voice, a new face, an official from the show committee came through the crowd with the ease of authority.

The major said, "It's nothing, sir. We can handle it."

A woman in the crowd said, "The boy's made an accusation of soring, Mr. Kenney. I think you ought to look into it."

"Says it's his horse," another voice called.

And a lower mutter, "Jordan Welch. Isn't he the one that—"

"Some to-do about a Walking Horse, year or so ago, I remember that. At it again, looks like."

Mr. Kenney announced, "All right, folks, we'll take care of it. Now," in a lower tone, "Major Kessler, Mr. Welch, and you, young man, let's go over to the office where we can talk about this in private. We'll have the show vet examine the horse, and we'll take it from there."

In a small office behind the lunchroom they sat in a tense ring, Major Kessler, Jordan Welch, Mr. Felden—no one so far had objected to his presence, and Paulo was grateful to have him there—and Paulo himself. Mr. Kenney leaned back in his chair behind a cluttered desk, and drummed on the desk with his pen.

He heard them out, then looked up as the show veterinarian came in and handed him a paper. "Sored, all right, no question about that," the man said, and left.

Mr. Kenney sighed. "I'm not sure just what authority the show committee has in a situation like this. Ordinarily a complaint about soring comes from a competitor, not from the owner. Or, in this case, the owner's grandson." He glanced at Paulo, then at the major.

"Is there any dispute here about the ownership of the horse?"

Paulo shook his head. The major said, "I have only a verbal agreement with Mr. Mendez about the terms of the lease, as I already explained. It's up to Mr. Mendez to say when he wants the horse returned to Puerto Rico. There's no problem there."

Mr. Kenney looked at Jordan Welch. "Welch, we've been through this before with you. Whatever

disciplinary action the American Horse Show Association may want to take is up to them. Your horse will forfeit his wins at this show, of course, and if I may say so, it's a shame. I saw him in action; he's a fine animal and very probably would have won fairly if he'd been allowed to do so.

"Now, it's up to you people to work out your internal differences. If this young man wants to take the horse with him when he leaves here, and if he has the means of doing so, the show committee will allow that. Now, I'm needed over at the announcer's booth. You folks can stay and use the office if you'd like."

He nodded to them all, and left.

The room grew still and the atmosphere strained. Paulo ached to grab Danza and get out of here, away from Welch, and especially away from the major. He could hardly bear to look at the major for the flood of memories that threatened to smother him. The smiles, the words of praise, the major's arm dropped casually across his shoulder in a gesture that had the power to warm Paulo and expand him to man-size.

"How could you do it to Danza?" Paulo flared, startling even himself. "After all that horse went through, all the pain in his feet from the foundering. I worked so hard to get him better, and every day you came out to the stable to see how he was, just like you really cared about him. And now you hire this—this *asesino* to hurt Danza just so he wins better for you. Well, you aren't a good man, major. You aren't good enough to have my horse. Or my respect." Paulo finished on a note of triumph at the way his words sounded.

"Paulo, look, I didn't mean for it to turn out—" The major hesitated.

Mr. Welch stood up. "I don't have time to sit around in here all day. What's it going to be, major? Do I take the horse with me, or what?"

Major Kessler floundered. It occurred to Paulo that he and the major had driven down in the car. There was no way to transport Danza back to Paso Pines.

Mr. Felden cleared his throat. Paulo whirled to him. "Will you take me and Danza home with you? I'll call my grandfather and get the money to ship Danza home as quick as I can. Please. I don't want him to go back with Mr. Welch."

The major said, "Now, Paulie, there's no need for that. You come on home with me for now, and Jordan can take Danza back to his stable, just to board until we get this all settled. And don't forget the National next week. Danza is qualified and entered, and we want—"

"No." Paulo's voice cracked under the heat of his emotions.

Mr. Felden said, "We have room in our trailer, Paulo. You and Danza are welcome to come home with us for as long as necessary. For that matter, you could go to the National with us if you should decide to show him. We're only taking Nibs."

Paulo nodded. This kindness robbed him of his voice.

Mr. Felden stood up. "You know where our trailer is. You come along whenever you're ready. Major, I hope this won't cause undue hard feelings. I know I'm probably butting into something that isn't my concern. But, dammit, I've seen what this business of soring horses, drugging them, injuring them in all sorts

of ways—I've seen the harm it's done in other breeds, not only to the horses but to the people, to the spirit of the sport. I fell in love with Paso Finos because they are such fine creatures naturally. Naturally, major. When they collect themselves and move like poetry it's because they feel beautiful, not because they're in pain.

"I've got children at home, major, and thank God they are all animal lovers. My wife and I have taught them always to be thoughtful of their pets and to treat them with love. What kind of parents would we be if we began torturing our horses, or allowing our kids to do so, for any reason at all, but especially if we were doing it just to gain an unfair advantage in the show ring. I'll tell you something, major, I'd sell my horses first, and I love those nags of mine just about as much as I do my wife and kids. And if I can do one little thing, like helping Paulo out right now, to help stop the practice of soring before it gets started in our breed, then by God I'm going to do it."

He left, and Jordan Welch slipped out after him.

A Wrinkle in Time
by Madeleine L'Engle ◆ Dell, 1962

It was a dark and stormy night.

Shaka: King of the Zulus
by Diane Stanley and Peter Vennema ◆ Morrow, 1988

Once there was a little boy named Shaka, who would one day
grow up to be a legendary king.

a BOAT to nowHERE

by Maureen
Crane Wartski

illustrated by
Hui Han Liu

mai, her little brother Loc,

her grandfather, and Kien,

a fourteen-year-old orphan,

escaped from their Vietnamese

village when it was invaded.

They have been refused landing

in Thailand and attacked by

pirates. They have survived

storms at sea and an encounter

with other refugees who tried to

steal their boat. Their situation

grows even more desperate.

Two days out of Outcast Island, Thay Van Chi's cough returned.

"How stupid I was! Why did I throw those pills at Dr. Phan Tri!" Mai mourned.

"It was the only way to make him let go of the *Sea Breeze.* If the others had caught up to us, we'd never have escaped from Bác Thong," Kien comforted her.

But without the medicine, the old man sickened daily. Each day found him weaker, till he could no longer sail the *Sea Breeze,* even for a few minutes at a time.

By stingily dividing and rationing the few fish and coconuts they had brought with them, they managed to make the food last six days, but at the end of that time there was nothing left, not even a bone or a husk of coconut. Fortunately the monsoons had begun and there was plenty of rainwater. This became their only food.

Where was Malaysia? Kien asked himself over and over as he greedily scanned the horizon. The old man insisted that they were still traveling in the right direction, but could Thay Van Chi be relied upon anymore? Kien looked at the old teacher anxiously and saw with some surprise that the old man was watching him.

"You are sailing well, Kien," Thay Van Chi said in his weak whisper of a voice. "You will get the *Sea Breeze* to land. I know it."

"When that day comes you'll be right there with us, Uncle," Kien said, trying to make the Old One laugh. But Thay Van Chi closed his eyes and slid into a weak sleep. If only we hadn't had to leave Outcast Island, Kien thought bitterly. That miserable Bác Thong! Kien tried to get angry, angry enough to kill the pain and hunger and worry in him, but the anger didn't work. It only made things worse.

On the seventh day after leaving Outcast Island, Mai herself began to cough. The cough worsened rapidly, till she could hardly breathe for coughing. Loc was by now too weak and listless to care much, but Kien was terrified.

She needs help, he thought. She needs help, now! Otherwise she might . . .

He looked at Thay Van Chi and then at Mai. Help. Where could he find help? He desperately searched the horizon for anything that might give him hope, but there was nothing. No shadow, no sign—nothing.

On the eighth day a squall caught the *Sea Breeze,* spinning the boat around with strong winds and drenching everyone with rain. The next day, the ninth day, the sun came out—ferocious and merciless. Mai was so feverish she was delirious and lay talking nonsense in the bottom of the boat. The old man slept more and more, and Loc sat listlessly by Kien, drowsy from weakness.

Once Loc said, "Kien, do you remember the time I saw you in the forest and called you a Monster Man?"

Kien himself was so weak the thought brought tears to his eyes.

"Yes, little brother," he sighed. "I remember."

"You didn't like us very much, then, Kien. You and Mai were enemies back at the Village," Loc said. "You didn't have many friends."

"No," Kien agreed and hoped Loc would be silent, but the little boy went on.

"You did have a friend once. Remember? The one who gave you the watch. You gave Dao the watch to help us escape." Loc sighed and rested his head against Kien's knee. "It seems a long, long time ago . . ."

Yes, it seemed like a long time ago, Kien thought. He tried to remember how it had felt to be free, uncaring, bound to no one and to no loyalty, and he could not remember. He thought of the promise he had made to himself when Jim went away, the promise that never again would he be hurt by caring for anyone as he had cared for Jim. Then Mai began to cough, and all his other thoughts went away.

I have to get some food for her and the old man or they will die, Kien thought.

Without much hope, he dug around in the wooden sides of the boat until he found an old, rusty hook embedded in the wood. Then, tearing some strands from the blanket Mai had taken from Bác Thong's hut, he fashioned a rude fishline. He had no bait, none at all, and very little hope as he dropped the hook and line over the side of the boat, but the hook would not sink. He looked around the boat for something to weight his line, and then saw something small and bright and colorful protruding from the old man's shirt.

Kien reached for this and saw it was the bag of Vietnamese sand that Thay Van Chi had taken from the beach weeks ago. It was heavy enough to weight the fishing line, but . . .

"You can't use that, Kien!" Loc protested as Kien began to tie the bag of sand to the makeshift fishing line. "Grandfather won't like it!"

"He can't enjoy starving, either," Kien grunted. "Maybe sand from Vietnam will bring us good luck."

Perhaps it was the bright color of the bag that tempted the fish, or perhaps the sand did bring them luck. Within a half hour there was a fish! Kien could hardly believe it as he pulled the fish into the boat. He hastily returned the dripping bag of sand to Thay Van Chi, and then woke the old man and Mai. In silence the fish was divided four ways, and they ate it greedily, gulping bones, fins, and entrails.

"Courtesy of the 'sand of Vietnam,'" Kien said, and when he explained, even the old man smiled.

The "sand of Vietnam" plus the head of the first fish attracted two more fish that day, and the crew of the *Sea Breeze* ate them, too. Now, they felt a little stronger. But Mai's cough was worsening, and Thay Van Chi seemed to be sleeping more and more. Kien did not like it. He knew that people who were very sick often slipped into death in just that way.

Heaven, he prayed within himself, send us some help. We really need it now.

And on the afternoon of the tenth day a ship came.

At first they thought it was just a trick of light, a cloud sweeping low on the horizon. Then Loc, who had regained some of his strength since eating the fish, cried "Look, Kien! A ship!"

Kien looked up at once, and there it was, painted black and white, with a huge prow that cut through the water like a knife. It really was—

"A ship!" Kien screamed.

Mai sat up and looked around her dazedly.

"Wave your arms! Cry out!" she whimpered, and the old man gasped, "They *must* see us!"

Kien staggered up in the boat and waved his arms wildly. Loc got up and waved too.

"Here we are!" Loc croaked, and Kien shouted, "Come and save us!"

The ship seemed to swing nearer.

"It *sees* us!" Loc panted. "Grandfather, Mai, they *see* us!"

The ship was coming nearer still. Kien was filled with such excitement that he couldn't just stand there. With a shout he jumped into the water and began to swim toward the ship.

"I'm here! I'm here!" he gasped, as he made for the ship.

But he had forgotten how weak he was. The spurt of joy could not give him strength, and soon he felt weak all over. Now Kien could see men standing on the deck of the big ship. They were pointing toward him. Any moment now, Kien knew, they would stop.

The ship swept past him in a billowing wash of foaming water that nearly drowned him.

"Don't leave me!" Kien screamed. He began to swim after the ship, but he had no more strength. Water closed over his head. His lungs were bursting. Kicking, he forced himself back to the surface.

One of the men on the deck of the big ship was waving to Kien. He held something in his hand—a round, flat object with a large hole in the middle. A rope was attached to this object, and the man on the deck was making signs to Kien.

"Push your head and shoulders through this opening!" he seemed to say. Kien nodded weakly, and the man on the ship threw the object out into the sea.

It landed near Kien.

"Take hold of that and I'll save you!" the man seemed to be saying.

Desperately, Kien reached for the round object, which was bobbing around some yards away. He pushed himself through the hole in the center of the thing. The man on board nodded in a pleased way and made signs. "Now I am going to pull you on board. You are safe!"

"What about them?" Kien shouted. He jerked his head around, for by now they had passed the *Sea Breeze*. He could see Mai and Loc and the old man, who were all watching him in a bewildered way. "Save them, too!" Kien cried.

The men on the deck all shook their heads. The one who was beginning to haul Kien out of the water shook his head, too. He made a sign to Kien as if to say, "But we are going to save you."

Now Kien understood. The ship was not going to take Loc, Mai, or Thay Van Chi on board. Only he, Kien, would be saved, because he had swum after the boat, and the men on board did not want to see him drown. For a moment, he hung limply from the life saver, staring at the ship. Then he turned back to look at the *Sea Breeze*, already many yards behind him.

If I stay with this ship, Kien thought, I can live!

He wanted to live so much! He wanted to rest, to sleep. Not to worry about food or drink or storms. Mai was sick and the old man was dying. Loc would die soon. They won't blame me if I save myself. I am really not of their family. I don't belong to them.

"I am Kien!" he shouted out loud. "I care for no one! I belong to no one!"

He was being pulled up from the water, foot by foot.

"I want to live!" Kien sobbed. "Don't you understand?"

He turned to look back at the *Sea Breeze* and saw that they were watching him, as if they had heard his cry and understood. And as he looked, Mai waved at him.

Suddenly he saw them all clinging to the mast on the night of the great storm, singing together. He saw Mai feeding the old man that first coconut on Outcast Island, even before she ate anything herself. He felt the gentle touch of the old man's hand.

Without knowing what he did, Kien slid his arms out of the life saver. He felt the water close over his head and kicked himself to the surface. Dazedly he saw that the great ship was moving rapidly away, its deck crowded by watching, pointing men.

"Kien . . . Ki-en!"

The *Sea Breeze* was coming to get him, the old man at the tiller. Kien waited. There were a hundred questions bursting in his mind. Why? he asked himself. Why did I do that?

No one said anything as Kien pulled himself over the side and fell, exhausted, into the bottom of the *Sea Breeze*. As Kien felt again the familiar listing of the boat under him, Loc wailed, "But why didn't they stop for us?"

Mai began to cough.

"No one will stop," she whispered. "We are boat people." She looked hard at Kien. "Why didn't you go with them? They would have saved you."

Why? Kien asked himself again, and then he thought, This is the end. It has to be.

But there was no easy end. Pitifully, they continued to live. A fish caught shortly after the big ship passed them by kept them alive for a little while. And rain, falling almost continuously now, furnished them with water. Then there were no more fish, and only rainwater for food and drink. It distended their bellies and made them all so weak they could do nothing but drift and sleep.

Mai was worse, and Kien worried about her more than he worried about the old man. Mai, Kien felt, could still get well, but for the Old One it was only a matter of time. Then, one day, three days after their sighting of the big ship, Thay Van Chi woke from one of his long sleeps and appeared much stronger and very clear in his mind.

"Do you know our position?" he asked Kien.

Kien shook his head. "I've given up on a position," he admitted. "I don't know where we are. We could have sailed in a complete circle and I wouldn't know it." He stopped and looked hard at Thay Van Chi and added happily, "But you are better! Perhaps the crisis has passed and you can guide us again."

"It is said that before the end the lamp burns strongest," the old man said quietly. "It is so for me. I am dying, Kien."

"Don't talk like that!" Kien cried angrily. "What good does it do?"

"The truth must be faced," the old man said calmly. "I am sorry, for you will have to bear the burden, Kien. You are the oldest of this family."

"I am not—" Kien began.

But Thay Van Chi interrupted him to say, "You are also the strongest. You will survive the longest. It will be hardest for you."

"I don't want to listen to you," Kien said savagely, but the old man put his hand into his shirt and drew out the little colorful bag of Vietnamese sand.

"This is yours now," he said. "I give it to you."

"I don't want it. It has nothing to do with me. What good will it do me?"

"If you survive, you must keep my promise to return to Vietnam someday. It is our country, our beloved country, and though you may roam the earth, Kien, you must not forget it. You must someday return to Vietnam and say that Thay Van Chi kept his word."

Kien wanted to cry with frustration. The old man was looking at him. "You must carry out my dying wish," he said sternly.

"Old man," Kien said loudly, "I am not bound to you in any way. You are not my family. I belong to no one! I am here with you because all of us wished to escape from Guyen Thi Lam. Your dying wish does not concern me!"

"I have watched you change," Thay Van Chi said to Kien. "At first you were a beggar child who knew only how to survive through his wits, who would hurt and steal and lie to survive. Then that beggar child grew to care for the people of our Village. And when danger came to the Village, you gave up a precious keepsake to buy our safety." The old man closed his eyes, but his voice was strong. "I saw you risk your life to save Loc from the shark, and I have seen you weep when Mai coughs. Why would you have returned to us from that big ship, which would have saved you alone, if you did not care for any of us?"

Kien could say nothing. "I wish I had gone with them!" he finally cried, defiant. "I wish I had left you to die!"

"But you could not. Mai and Loc are your family, now," the old man said. Gently he added, "Kien,

none of us choose to be born into a family. Heaven wills that. Nor do we choose those we come to love."

Kien bowed his head and thought, It's true. After Jim, I never cared for anyone. I never wanted to care whether you lived or died, old man. I never meant this to happen.

"As my oldest grandson, you must promise to carry out my dying wish," the old man whispered. "Take care of Loc and Mai. You are the strongest."

Kien whispered back, "I will do what you ask."

The old man said nothing. Kien saw that the wise old eyes had become fixed and glazed. Thay Van Chi was dead.

As if the old teacher could still hear him, Kien went on, "I will carry out your promise someday. It is true. I have come to love you, my grandfather. I have come to love you all."

Only then did he begin to weep.

Several days after they buried Thay Van Chi, Mai, Loc, and Kien were rescued by the crew of the freighter Camelot. *When the crew found them, Mai and Loc were both very sick, and even Kien, the strongest, could barely speak and had to be carried to a bed. After being assured that Mai and Loc would be all right, Kien reaffirmed his promise to Thay Van Chi. He had, as the old grandfather had urged, taken care of Mai and Loc.*

Maureen Crane Wartski

Maureen Crane Wartski began her writing career at the age of fourteen, when she sold her first story. Today, with several books to her credit, Wartski acknowledges that a teacher helped her see the importance of writing about people and places that one is familiar with. Living in Bangkok, Thailand, from 1962 to 1966 and visiting Vietnam provided Wartski with the background she needed to write her book *A Boat to Nowhere.*

Wartski believes that the only way to write something of interest to young people is to get to know them and learn what they are interested in. She says, "Young readers react positively to issues that move them or capture their interest." Wartski's own experiences as a high school teacher and as a mother of two sons enabled her to write convincingly about the feelings of the young characters in *A Boat to Nowhere.*

TO STAY ON COURSE

If you were on a sea voyage like the characters in *A Boat to Nowhere*, how might you figure out where you were and where you were going?

Sailors of ancient times had no navigational equipment to guide them. They used several methods—some more reliable than others—to stay on course.

Lighthouse of Alexandria

The earliest navigators never ventured far from land, trying always to keep familiar landmarks in sight. One was the gigantic lighthouse of Alexandria, erected on the island of Pharos in the harbor of Alexandria, Egypt, in the third century B.C. It was visible for miles and stood for nearly 1,500 years. Light at the top of the tower was provided by a bonfire that burned continuously.

Clues from Nature

Observing nature could help a sailor navigate. The direction of certain wind currents, the flight of birds heading for home, or even the shape of waves could be important clues about a ship's position.

Star Guides

Eventually, sailors began to navigate by the stars. They noticed that some stars rose and set in the nighttime sky, as the sun did in daytime. By heading toward familiar stars each time, a

navigator could sail the ship in the same general direction.

Sailors in the Northern Hemisphere—the part of the earth north of the equator—also noticed one star that did not appear to move at all. This star, known as Polaris, or the North Star, was located almost directly above the earth's northern axis, off the North Pole. A sailor could always determine which direction was north by locating Polaris in the northern sky.

Of course, Polaris was not visible to sailors in the Southern Hemisphere, who relied on different stars to guide them.

Ursa Major, the Great Bear

The ancient mariners drew imaginary lines among the brightest stars and gave names to these shapes, or constellations. It helped them to remember where these bright stars could be found. Ursa Major, also known as the Great Bear, was a very important constellation. It contained the Big Dipper. A line drawn through two stars of the Big Dipper pointed directly to Polaris.

I GO FORTH TO MOVE

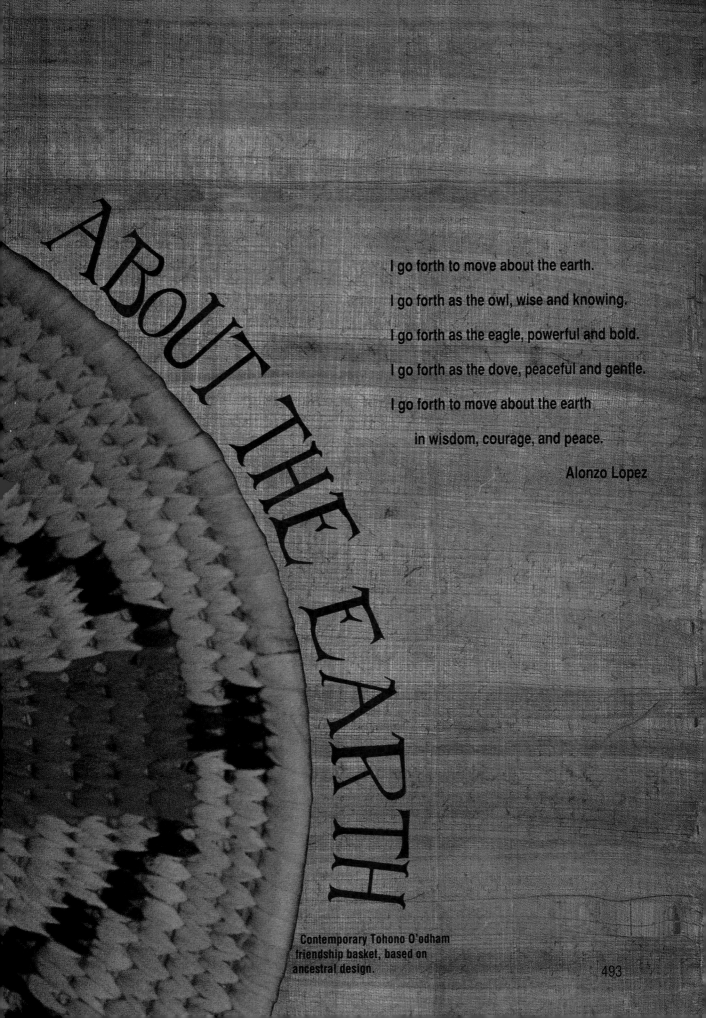

ABOUT THE EARTH

I go forth to move about the earth.

I go forth as the owl, wise and knowing.

I go forth as the eagle, powerful and bold.

I go forth as the dove, peaceful and gentle.

I go forth to move about the earth

in wisdom, courage, and peace.

Alonzo Lopez

Contemporary Tohono O'odham
friendship basket, based on
ancestral design.

IT IS 1942 AND THE WORLD IS AT WAR. ELEVEN-YEAR-OLD PHILLIP ENRIGHT AND HIS MOTHER HAVE LEFT THE ISLAND OF CURAÇAO, OFF THE COAST OF VENEZUELA, IN ORDER TO RETURN TO THEIR NATIVE UNITED STATES. BUT WHEN THEIR SHIP IS TORPEDOED, PHILLIP FINDS HIMSELF ALONE ON A RAFT WITH TIMOTHY, A WEST INDIAN. SOON, PHILLIP GOES BLIND FROM A HEAD INJURY HE RECEIVED IN THE SHIPWRECK. THE TWO ARE EVENTUALLY MAROONED ON A CAY—A SMALL ISLAND—IN THE CARIBBEAN. AT FIRST, PHILLIP IS DISTRUSTFUL OF TIMOTHY AND TREATS HIM DISDAINFULLY. GRADUALLY, HOWEVER, TIMOTHY'S KINDNESS WINS PHILLIP OVER, AND THEIR FRIENDSHIP GROWS.

THE CAY

BY THEODORE TAYLOR

ILLUSTRATED BY FLOYD COOPER

*O*ne very hot morning in July, we were down on north beach where Timothy had found a patch of calico scallops not too far offshore. It was the hottest day we'd ever had on the cay. So hot that each breath felt like fire. And for once, the trade wind was not blowing. Nothing on the cay seemed to be moving.

North beach was a very strange beach anyway. The sand on it felt coarser to my feet. Everything about it felt different, but that didn't really make sense since it was only about a mile from south beach.

Timothy explained, "D'nawth is alles d'bleak beach on any islan'," but he couldn't say why.

He had just brought some calico scallops ashore when we heard the rifle shot. He came quickly to my side, saying, "Dat b'trouble."

Trouble? I thought it meant someone had found the cay. That wasn't trouble. Excited, I asked, "Who's shooting?"

"D'sea," he said.

I laughed at him, "The sea can't shoot a rifle."

"A crack like d'rifle," he said, worry in his voice. "It can make d'shot all right, all right. It b'tell us a veree bad starm is comin', Phill-eep. A tempis'."

I couldn't quite believe that. However, there had been, distinctly, a crack like a rifle or pistol shot.

He said anxiously, "D'waves do it. Somewhar far off, out beyond d'Grenadines, or in dat pesky bight off Honduras, a hurrican' is spawnin', young bahss. I feel it. What we heeard was a wave passin' dis lil' hombug point."

I heard him sniffing the air as if he could smell the hurricane coming. Without the wind, there was a breathless

On north beach

silence around our cay. The sea, he told me, was smooth as green jelly. But already, the water was getting cloudy. There were no birds in sight. The sky, he said, had a yellowish cast to it.

"Come along, we 'ave much to do. D'calico scallop can wait dey own self till after d'tempis'."

We went up to our hill.

Now I knew why he had chosen the highest point of land on the cay for our hut. Even so, I thought, the waves might tumble over it.

The first thing Timothy did was to lash our water keg high on a palm trunk. Next he took the remaining rope that we had and tied it securely around the same sturdy tree. "In case d'tempis' reach dis high, lock your arms ovah d'rope an' hang on, Phill-eep."

I realized then why he had used our rope sparingly; why he had made my guideline down to east beach from vines instead of rope. Everyday, I learned of something new that Timothy had done so we could survive.

During the afternoon, he told me this was a freak storm, because most did not come until September or October. August, sometimes. Seldom in July. "But dis year, d'sea be angry wid all d'death upon it. D'wahr."

The storms bred, Timothy said, in the eastern North Atlantic, south of the Cape Verde Islands, in the fall, but sometimes, when they were freaks, and early, they bred much closer, in a triangle way off the northeast tip of South America. Once in a great while, in June or July, they sometimes made up not far from Providencia and San Andrés. Near us. The June ones were only pesky, but the July ones were dangerous.

"Dis be a western starm, I b'guessin'. Dey outrageous strong when dey come," he said.

Even Stew Cat was nervous. He was around my legs whenever I moved. I asked Timothy what we should do to protect him. He laughed. "Stew Cat b'go up d'palm on d'lee side iffen it b'gettin' too terrible. Don' worry 'bout Stew Cat."

Yet I could not help worrying. The thought of losing either of them was unbearable. If something bad happened on the cay, I wanted it to happen to all of us.

Nothing changed during the afternoon, although it seemed to get even hotter. Timothy spent a lot of time down at the raft, stripping off everything usable and carrying it back up the hill. He said we might never see it again, or else it might wash up the hill so that it would be impossible to launch.

Timothy was not purposely trying to frighten me about the violence of the storm; he was just being honest. He had good reason to be frightened himself.

"In '28, I be on d'*Hettie Redd* sout' o' Antigua when d'tempis' hit. D'wind was outrageous, an' d'ol' schooner break up like chips fallin' 'fore d'ax. I wash ashore from d'sea, so wild no mahn believe it. No odder mahn from d'*Hettie Redd* live 'ceptin' me."

I knew that wild sea from long ago was much on Timothy's mind all afternoon.

We had a huge meal late in the day, much bigger than usual, because Timothy said we might not be able to eat for several days. We had fish and coconut meat, and we each drank several cups of coconut milk. Timothy said that the fish might not return to the reef for at least a week. He'd noticed that they'd already gone to deep water.

After we ate, Timothy carefully cleaned his knife and put it into the tin box, which he lashed high on the same tree that held our water keg.

"We ready, Phill-eep," he said.

*A*t sunset, with the air heavy and hot, Timothy described the sky to me. He said it was flaming red and that there were thin veils of high clouds. It was so still over our cay that we could hear nothing but the rustling of the lizards.

Just before dark, Timothy said, "'Twon't be long now, Phill-eep."

We felt a light breeze that began to ripple the smooth sea. Timothy said he saw an arc of very black clouds to the west. They looked as though they were beginning to join the higher clouds.

I gathered Stew Cat close to me as we waited, feeling the warm breeze against my face. Now and then, there were gusts of wind that rattled the palm fronds, shaking the little hut.

It was well after dark when the first drops of rain spattered the hut, and with them, the wind turned cool. When it gusted, the rain hit the hut like handfuls of gravel.

Then the wind began to blow steadily, and Timothy went out of the hut to look up at the sky. He shouted, "Dey boilin' ovah now, Phill-eep. 'Tis hurrican', to be sure."

We could hear the surf beginning to crash as the wind drove waves before it, and Timothy ducked back inside to stand in the opening of the hut, his big body stretched so that he could hang onto the overhead frame, keeping the hut erect as long as possible.

I felt movement around my legs and feet. Things were slithering. I screamed to Timothy who shouted back, "B'nothin' but d'lil' lizzard, comin' high groun'."

Rain was now slashing into the hut, and the wind was reaching a steady howl. The crash of the surf sounded closer; I wondered if it was already beginning to push up toward our hill. The rain was icy, and I was wet, head to foot. I was shivering, but more from the thought of the sea rolling over us than from the sudden cold.

In a moment, there was a splintering sound, and Timothy dropped down beside me, covering my body with his. Our hut had blown away. He shouted, "Phill-eep, put your 'ead downg." I rolled over on my stomach, my cheek against the wet sand. Stew Cat burrowed down between us.

There was no sound now except the roar of the storm. Even the sound of the wind was being beaten down by the wildness of the sea. The rain was hitting my back like thousands of hard berries blown from air guns.

Once something solid hit us and then rolled on. "Sea grape," Timothy shouted. It was being torn up by the roots.

We stayed flat on the ground for almost two hours, taking the storm's punishment, barely able to breathe in the driving rain. Then Timothy shouted hoarsely, "To d'palm."

The sea was beginning to reach for our hilltop, climbing the forty feet with raging whitecaps. Timothy dragged me toward the palm. I held Stew Cat against my chest.

Standing with his back to the storm, Timothy put my arms through the loops of rope, and then roped himself, behind me, to the tree.

Soon, I felt water around my ankles. Then it washed to my knees. It would go back and then crash against us again. Timothy was taking the full blows of the storm, sheltering me with his body. When the water receded, it would tug at us, and Timothy's strength would fight against it. I could feel the steel in his arms as the water tried to suck us away.

Even in front of him, crushed against the trunk of the palm, I could feel the rain, which was now jabbing into me like the punches of a nail. It was not falling toward earth but being driven straight ahead by the wind.

Hurricane

We must have been against the palm for almost an hour when suddenly the wind died down and the rain became gentle. Timothy panted, "D'eye! We can relax a bit till d'odder side o' d'tempis' hit us."

I remembered that hurricanes, which are great circling storms, have a calm eye in the center.

"Are you all right?" I asked.

He replied hoarsely, "I b'damp, but all right."

Yet I heard him making small noises, as if it were painful to move, as we stood back from the palm trunk. We sat down on the ground beside it, still being pelted with rain, to wait for the eye to pass. Water several inches deep swirled around us, but was not tugging at us.

It was strange and eerie in the eye of the hurricane. I knew we were surrounded on all sides by violent winds, but the little cay was calm and quiet. I reached over for Timothy. He was cradling his head in his arms, still making those small noises, like a hurt animal.

In twenty or thirty minutes, the wind picked up sharply and Timothy said that we must stand against the palm again. Almost within seconds, the full fury of the storm hit the cay once more. Timothy pressed me tightly against the rough bark.

It was even worse this time, but I do not remember everything that happened. We had been there awhile when a wave that must have reached halfway up the palms crashed against us. The water went way over my head. I choked and struggled. Then another giant wave struck us. I lost consciousness then. Timothy did, too, I think.

When I came to, the wind had died down, coming at us only in gusts. The water was still washing around our ankles, but seemed to be going back into the sea now. Timothy was still behind me, but he felt cold and limp. He was sagging, his head down on my shoulder.

"Timothy, wake up," I said.

He did not answer.

Using my shoulders, I tried to shake him, but the massive body did not move. I stood very still to see if he was breathing. I could feel his stomach moving and I reached over my shoulder to his mouth. There was air coming out. I knew that he was not dead.

However, Stew Cat was gone.

I worked for a few minutes to release my arms from the loops of rope around the palm trunk, and then slid out from under Timothy's body. He slumped lifelessly against the palm. I felt along the ropes that bound his forearms to the trunk until I found the knots.

With his weight against them, it was hard to pull them loose, even though they were sailor's knots and had loops in them. The rope was soaked, which made it worse.

I must have worked for half an hour before I had him free from the trunk. He fell backwards into the wet sand, and lay there moaning. I knew there was very little I could do for him except to sit by him in the light rain, holding his hand. In my world of darkness, I had learned that holding a hand could be like medicine.

After a long while, he seemed to recover. His first words, painful and dragged out, were, "Phill-eep . . . you . . . all right . . . be true?"

"I'm okay, Timothy," I said.

He said weakly, "Terrible tempis'."

He must have rolled over on his stomach in the sand, because his hand left mine abruptly. Then he went to sleep, I guess.

I touched his back. It felt warm and sticky. I ran my hand lightly down it, suddenly realizing that I, too, was completely naked. The wind and sea had torn our tatters of clothes from us.

Timothy had been cut to ribbons by the wind, which drove the rain and tiny grains of sand before it. It had flayed his back and his legs until there were very few places that weren't cut. He was bleeding, but there was nothing I could do to stop it. I found his hard, horny hand again, wrapped mine around it, and lay down beside him.

I went to sleep too.

Sometime long after dawn, I awakened. The rain had stopped, and the wind had died down to its usual whisper. But I think the clouds were still covering the sky because I could not feel the sun.

I said, "Timothy," but he did not answer me. His hand was cold and stiff in mine.

Old Timothy, of Charlotte Amalie, was dead.

I stayed there beside him for a long time, very tired, thinking that he should have taken me with him wherever he had gone. I did not cry then. There are times when you are beyond tears.

I went back to sleep, and this time when I awakened, I heard a meow. Then I cried for a long time, holding Stew Cat tight. Aside from him, I was blind and alone on a forgotten cay.

*I*n the afternoon, I groped west along the hill. Thirty or forty feet from the last palm tree, I began to dig a grave for Timothy. I cleared palm fronds, chunks of sea grape, pieces of wood, dead fish, fan coral, and shells that the sea had thrown up. I marked out a space about seven feet long and four feet wide. Then I dug with my hands.

At first I was angry with Timothy. I said to Stew Cat, "Why did he leave us alone here?" Then as I dug, I had other thoughts.

With his great back to the storm, taking its full punishment, he had made it possible for me to live. When my grandfather died, my father had said, "Phillip, sometimes people die from just being very, very tired." I think that is what happened to Timothy.

I also think that had I been able to see, I might not have been able to accept it all. But strangely, the darkness separated me from everything. It was as if my blindness were protecting me from fear.

I buried Timothy, placing stones at the head of the grave to mark it. I didn't know what to say over the grave. I said, "Thank you, Timothy," and then turned my face to the sky. I said, "Take care of him, God, he was good to me."

There didn't seem to be anything else to say, so I just stood by his grave for a while. Then I felt my way back to the spot where our hut had been. I located wood and piled it around the base of the palm tree that held our water keg and the tin box. Both were to the lee side of the storm.

It took me a long time to get the keg and the tin box to the ground, but I found, on opening the bung, that the water was still sweet and that the matches, wrapped in cellophane inside the tin box, were dry. But the two small bars of chocolate that we had been saving for a "feast," were ruined. I had no taste for them, anyway.

Feeling it everywhere under my feet, I knew that the cay was littered with debris. I started cleaning the camp area, or what was left of it. I piled all the palm fronds, frayed by the wind, in one place; sticks of wet driftwood in another.

With Stew Cat constantly around—I stumbled over him several times—I worked until I felt it was nearing darkness. I'd found one lone coconut in a mass of sea grape and broken sticks. I opened it and ate the meat, offering to share with Stew Cat, who didn't seem interested.

alone

Then I made a bed of palm fronds and sprawled out on it, listening to the still angry sea as it tumbled around the damp cay and thinking: I must feed myself and Stew Cat; I must rebuild the hut and build another signal fire down on east beach; then I must spend each day listening for the sound of aircraft. I knew Timothy had already given up on any schooner entering the dangerous Devil's Mouth.

I was certain that the sea had washed away Timothy's markers atop the coral reef, and I was also sure that my guide vine-rope leading down to the beach had been snapped and tangled by the storm.

But now, for the first time, I fully understood why Timothy had so carefully trained me to move around the island, and the reef . . .

The reef, I thought.

How could I fish without any poles? They must have been washed away. Then I remembered Timothy saying that he would put them in a safe place. The trouble was he'd forgotten to tell me where.

I got up and began to run my hands over each palm trunk. On one of them I touched rope. I followed it around to the lee side with my fingers. And there they were! Not two or three, but at least a dozen, lashed together, each with a barbed hook and bolt sinker. They were one more part of the legacy Timothy had left me.

The sun came out strong in the morning. I could feel it on my face. It began to dry the island, and toward noon, I heard the first cry of a bird. They were returning.

By now, I had taught myself to tell time, very roughly, simply by turning my head toward the direct warmth of the sun. If the angle was almost overhead, I knew it was around noon. If it was low, then of course, it was early morning or late evening.

There was so much to do that I hardly knew where to start. Get a campfire going, pile new wood for a signal fire, make another rain catchment for the water keg, weave a mat of palm fibers to sleep on. Then make a shelter of some kind, fish the hole on the reef, inspect the palm trees to see if any coconuts were left—I didn't think any could be up there—and search the whole island to discover what the storm had deposited. It was enough work for weeks, and I said to Stew Cat, "I don't know how we'll get it all done." But something told me I must stay very busy and not think about myself.

I accomplished a lot in three days, even putting a new edge on Timothy's knife by honing it on coral. I jabbed it into the palm nearest my new shelter, so that I would always know where it was if I needed it. Without Timothy's eyes, I was finding that in my world, everything had to be very precise; an exact place for everything.

On the fifth day after the storm, I began to scour the island to find out what had been cast up. It was exciting, and I knew it would take days or weeks to accomplish. I had made another cane, and beginning with east beach, I felt my way back and forth, reaching down to touch everything that my cane struck; sometimes having to spend a long time trying to decide what it was that I held in my hands.

I found several large cans and used one of them to start the "time" can again, dropping five pebbles into it so that the reckoning would begin again from the night of the storm. I discovered an old broom, and a small wooden crate that would make a nice stool. I found a piece of canvas and tried to think of ways to make pants from it, but I had no needle or thread.

Other than that, I found many shells, some bodies of dead birds, pieces of cork, and chunks of sponge, but nothing I could really put to good use.

It was on the sixth day after the storm, when I was exploring on south beach, that I heard the birds. Stew Cat was with me, as usual, and he growled when they first screeched. Their cries were angry, and I guessed that seven or eight might be in the air.

I stood listening to them; wondering what they were. Then I felt a beat of wing past my face, and an angry cry as the bird dived at me. I lashed out at it with my cane, wondering why they were attacking me.

Another dived down, screaming at me, and his bill nipped the side of my head. For a moment, I was confused, not knowing whether to run for cover under sea grape, or what was left of it, or try to fight them off with my cane. There seemed to be a lot of birds.

Then one pecked my forehead sharply, near my eyes, and I felt blood run down my face. I started to walk back toward camp, but had taken no more than three or four steps when I tripped over a log. I fell into the sand, and at the same time, felt a sharp pain in the back of my head. I heard a raging screech as the bird soared up again. Then another bird dived at me.

I heard Stew Cat snarling and felt him leap up on my back, his claws digging into my flesh. There was another wild screech, and Stew Cat left my back, leaping into the air.

His snarls and the wounded screams of the bird filled the stillness over the cay. I could hear them battling in the sand. Then I heard the death caw of the bird.

I lay still a moment. Finally, I crawled to where Stew Cat had his victim. I touched him; his body was rigid and his hair was still on edge. He was growling, low and muted.

Then I touched the bird. It had sounded large, but it was actually rather small. I felt the beak; it was very sharp.

Slowly, Stew Cat began to relax.

The attack

Wondering what had caused the birds to attack me, I felt around in the sand. Soon, my hand touched a warm shell. I couldn't blame the birds very much. I'd accidentally walked into their new nesting ground.

They were fighting for survival, after the storm, just as I was. I left Stew Cat to his unexpected meal and made my way slowly back to camp.

Ten pebbles had gone into my "time" can when I decided to do something Timothy had told me never to do. I was tired of eating fish and sea-grape leaves, and I wanted to save the few green coconuts I'd managed to find on the ground. There were none left in the trees.

I wanted scallops or a langosta to roast over the fire. I didn't dare go out off north beach for scallops because of the sharks. But I thought there might be a langosta clinging to coral at the bottom of the fishing hole.

From what Timothy had told me, the sea entrance to the hole was too narrow for a large fish, a shark, to swim through. Barracuda, he'd said, could go through, but they were not usually dangerous. If there happened to be an octopus down there, it would have to be a very small one. The big ones were always in deep water. So he'd said it was safe for him to dive in the hole.

I sharpened a stick the way Timothy had done, but I knew that if I felt a langosta with my left hand, I would have to be very quick with my right hand, or he would use his tail to push away from me across the sand.

With Stew Cat, I went down to the reef and felt my way along it until I found the familiar edges of the hole. I told

Stew Cat, "If I'm not out in twenty minutes, you better jump in and get me."

The crazy cat rubbed along my leg and purred.

Holding the sharpened stick in my right hand, I slipped into the warm water, treading for a moment, waiting to see if anything came up. Then I ducked my head underwater, swam down a few feet, and came up again. I was certain that nothing was in the hole aside from the usual small fish I yanked out each morning.

After a few minutes, I had my courage up and dived to the bottom, holding the sharp stick in my left hand now, and using my right hand to feel the coral and rocks. Coming up now and then for air, I slowly felt my way around the bottom of the small pool, touching sea fans that waved back and forth, feeling the organ-pipe coral and the bigger chunks of brain coral.

Several times I was startled when seaweed or sea fans would brush against my face and swam quickly to the surface. It must have taken me nearly thirty minutes to decide that I could hunt langosta in the hole.

This time, I dived in earnest. I went straight down, touched the bottom, and then took a few strokes toward the coral sides of the pool. Timothy had said that langosta were always on the bottom, usually over against the rocks and coral. To my amazement, I touched one on the first sweep and drove the sharp stick into him, swimming quickly to the surface.

Panting, I shouted to Stew Cat, "Lobster tonight!"

I swam to the edge, pushed the langosta off the stick, caught my breath again, and dived.

I dived many times without again touching the hard shell that meant langosta. I began sticking my hands deeper into the shelves and over the ledges near the bottom.

I rested a few minutes, then decided I'd make one more dive. I was happy with the lobster that was now on the reef, but it was quite small, barely a meal for Stew Cat and myself.

I dived again, and this time found what seemed to be an opening into a deep hole. Or at least, the hole went far back. There has to be a big lobster in there, I thought. Up I came again, filled my lungs, and dived immediately.

I ran my hand back into the hole, and something grabbed it.

Terrified, I put my feet against the rocks to pull away. The pain was severe. Whatever had my wrist had the strength of Timothy's arms. I jerked hard and whatever it was came out with my arm, its tail smashing against my chest. I kicked and rose to the surface, the thing still on my wrist, its teeth sunk in deep.

I'm sure I screamed as I broke water, flailing toward the edge of the hole. Then the thing let loose, and I made it up over the side and out of the hole.

Pain shooting up my entire arm, I lay panting on the edge of the pool and gingerly began to feel my wrist. It was bleeding, but not badly. But the teeth had sunk in deep.

It wasn't a fish, because the body felt long and narrow. Some time later, I made an informed guess that it had been a large moray eel. Whatever it was, I never got back into the hole again.

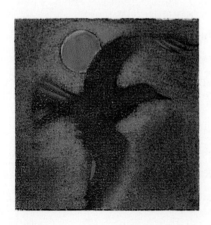

There was no day or night that passed when I didn't listen for sounds from the sky. Both my sense of touch and my sense of hearing were beginning to make up for my lack of sight. I separated the sounds and each became different.

I grew to know the different cries of the birds that flew by the cay, even

The dive

though I had no idea what any of them were. I made up my own names for them according to the sound of their cries. Only the occasional bleat of the gull gave me a picture of that bird, for I had heard and seen them many times around the sea wall in Willemstad.

I knew how the breeze sounded when it crossed the sea grape. It fluttered the small leaves. When it went through the palm fronds the storm hadn't ripped away, it made a flapping noise.

I knew the rustle of the lizards. Some were still on the island after the storm. I could only guess they'd somehow climbed high into the palms. Otherwise, how could they have lived with water lapping over the entire cay?

I even knew when Stew Cat was approaching me. His soft paws on a dried leaf made only a tiny crackle, but I heard it.

One midmorning in early August, I was on the hill, near the camp, when I heard the far-off drone of an airplane. It was up-wind from me, but the sound was very clear. I reached down to feel Stew Cat. He had heard it too. His body was tense; his head pointed toward the sound.

I dropped to my knees by the fire, feeling around the edges until I grasped the end of a stick. I drew it back. Timothy had taught me to lay the fire sticks like a wheel, so that the fire burned slowly in the center, but always had a few unburned ends on the outside. I tended the fire a half dozen times each day.

I spit on the stick until I heard a sizzle. Then I knew there was enough fire or charring on it to light off the base of dried palm fronds beneath the signal fire.

I listened again for the drone. Yes, it was still there. Closer now.

I ran down the hill straight to the signal fire, felt around the palm fronds, and then pushed the stick over them. I blew on it until I heard the crackle of flames. In a few minutes the

signal fire was roaring, and I ran to south beach where
I would be able to hear the aircraft without hearing the
crackling fire.

Standing on south beach, I listened. The plane *was* coming closer!

I yelled toward the sky, "Here! Down here!"

I decided to run back to east beach to stand near the fire
and the new arrangement of rocks that spelled out "Help."

Thinking any moment the plane would dive and I would
hear the roar of its engines across the cay at low altitude, I
stood with Stew Cat a few feet from the sloshing surf. I waited
and waited, but there was no thundering sound from the sky.
I could hear nothing but the crackling of the fire, the washing sound of the surf.

I ran back to south beach, where I stood very still and
listened.

The plane had gone!

Slowly, I returned to east beach and sat down in sea-grape
shade. I put my head down on my arms and sobbed, feeling
no shame for what I was doing.

There seemed to be no hope of ever leaving the cay, yet I
knew I could not always live this way. One day I would become ill or another storm would rage against the island. I
could never survive alone.

There had been many bad and lonely days and nights,
but none as bad as this.

Stew Cat came up, purring, rubbing along my legs. I held
him a long time, wondering why the aircraft had not come
down when the pilots saw the smoke.

At last I thought, perhaps they didn't see the smoke. I
knew it was going up into the sky, but was it white smoke
that might be lost in the blue-white sky, or was it dark and
oily smoke that would make a smudge against the blueness?
There was no way to tell.

signal fire

If only there were some oily boards! The kind that drifted around the waters of the Schottegat. But I knew that the wood floating up on the beach consisted mostly of branches or stumps that had been in the water for weeks or months. There was nothing in them to make dark smoke.

I began to think of all the things on the island. Green palm fronds might send off dark smoke, but until they were dried, they were too tough to tear off the trees. The vines on north beach might make dark smoke, but the leaves on them were very small.

The sea grape! I snapped some off, feeling it between my fingers. Yes, there was oil in it. I got up and went over to the fire, tossing a piece in. In a moment, I heard it popping the way hot grease pops when it is dropped into water.

I knew how to do it now.

The smoke would rise from the cay in a fat, black column to lead the planes up the Devil's Mouth. If I heard another aircraft, I'd start a fire and then throw bundles of sea grape into it until I was certain a strong signal was going up from the island.

Timothy hadn't thought about black smoke, I was sure. That was it!

Feeling better now, I walked back up the hill to gather the few palm fronds that were left for a new fire base.

I woke up at dawn on the morning of August 20, 1942, to hear thunder and wondered when the first drops of rain would spatter on the roof of the shelter. I heard Stew Cat, down near my feet, let off a low growl.

I said, "It's only thunder, Stew Cat. We need the water."

But as I continued to listen, it did not seem to be thunder. It was a heavy sound, hard and sharp, not rolling. More like an explosion or a series of explosions. It felt as if the cay were shaking. I got up from the mat, moving out from under the shelter.

The air did not feel like rain. It was dry and there was no heavy heat.

"They're explosions, Stew," I said. "Very near us."

Maybe destroyers, I thought. I could not hear any aircraft engines. Maybe destroyers fighting it out with enemy submarines. And those heavy, hard, sharp sounds could be the depth charges that my father said were used by the Navy to sink U-boats.

This time, I didn't bother to take a piece of firewood down to east beach. I dug into the tin box for the cellophane wrapped package of big wooden matches. Four were left. I ran down the hill.

At the signal fire, I searched around for a rock. Finding one, I knelt down by the fire and struck a match against it. Nothing happened. I felt the head of the match. The sulphur had rubbed off. I struck another. It made a small popping noise and then went out.

I had two more matches left, and for a moment, I didn't know whether to use them or run back up the hill to the campfire.

I stopped to listen, feeling sweat trickle down my face. The explosions were still thundering across the sea.

Then I heard the drone of an aircraft. I took a deep breath and struck the next to last match. I heard it flare and ran my left hand over the top of it. There was heat. It was burning.

I reached deep into the fire pile, holding the match there until it began to burn the tips of my fingers. The fire caught and in a moment was roaring.

I ran across the beach to begin pulling sea grape down. I carried the first bundle to the fire and threw it in. Soon, I could smell it burning. It began to pop and crackle as the flames got to the natural oils in the branches.

By the time I had carried ten or fifteen bundles of sea grape to the fire, tumbling them in, I was sure that a column of black smoke was rising into the sky over the cay.

Suddenly, a deafening roar swept overhead. I knew it was an aircraft crossing the cay not much higher than the palms. I could feel the wind from it.

Forgetting for a moment, I yelled, "Timothy, they've come."

The aircraft seemed to be making a sharp turn. It roared across the cay again, seeming even lower this time because the rush of wind from it was hot. I could smell exhaust fumes.

I yelled, "Down here, down here," and waved my arms.

The plane made another tight circle, coming back almost directly over me. Its engine was screaming.

I shouted at Stew Cat, "We'll be rescued!" But I think that he'd gone to hide in the sea grape.

This time, however, the aircraft did not circle back. It did not make another low pass over the island. I heard the sound going away. Soon, it had vanished completely. Then I realized that the explosions had stopped too.

A familiar silence settled over the cay.

All the strength went out of my body. It was the first real chance of rescue, and maybe there would not be another. The pilot had flown away, perhaps thinking I was just another native fisherman waving at an aircraft. I knew that the color of my skin was very dark now.

Worse, I knew that the smoke might have blotted out the lines of rocks that spelled help.

Feeling very ill, I climbed the slope again, throwing myself down on the mat in the hut. I didn't cry. There was no use in doing that.

I wanted to die.

After a while, I looked over toward Timothy's grave. I said, "Why didn't you take us with you?"

It was about noon when I heard the bell.

It sounded like bells I'd heard in St. Anna Bay and in the Schottegat. Small boats and tugs use them to tell the engineer to go slow or fast or put the engines in reverse.

For a moment, I thought I was dreaming.

Then I heard the bell again. And with it, the slow chugging of an engine. And voices! They were coming from east beach.

I ran down there. Yes, a small boat had come into the Devil's Mouth and was approaching our cay.

I yelled, "I'm here! I'm here!"

There was a shout from across the water. A man's voice. "We see you!"

I stood there on east beach, Stew Cat by my feet, looking in the direction of the sounds. I heard the bell again; then the engine went into reverse, the propeller thrashing. Someone yelled, "Jump, Scotty, the water's shallow."

The voice was American, I was certain.

The engine was now idling, and someone was coming toward me. I could hear him padding across the sand. I said, "Hello."

There was no answer from the man. I suppose he was just staring at me.

Then he yelled to someone on the boat, "My Lord, it's a naked boy. And a cat!"

The person on the boat yelled, "Anyone else?"

The rescue

I called out, "No, just us."

I began to move toward the man on the beach.

He gasped. "Are you blind?"

I said, "Yes, sir."

In a funny voice, he asked, "Are you all right?"

"I'm fine now. You're here," I said.

He said, "Here, boy, I'll help you."

I said, "If you'll carry Stew Cat, you can just lead me to the boat."

After I had climbed aboard, I remembered Timothy's knife stuck in the palm tree. It was the only thing I wanted off the cay. The sailor who had carried Stew Cat went up the hill to get it while the other sailor asked me questions. When the first sailor came back from the hill, he said, "You wouldn't believe what's up there." I guess he was talking about our hut and the rain catchment. He should have seen the ones Timothy built.

I don't remember everything that happened in the next few hours but very soon I was helped up the gangway of a destroyer. On deck I was asked so many questions all at once that one man barked, "Stop badgering him. Give him food, medical care, and get him into a bunk."

A voice answered meekly, "Yes, sir, Cap'n."

Down in sick bay, the captain asked, "What's your name, son?"

"Phillip Enright. My father lives in Willemstad. He works for Royal Dutch Shell," I answered.

The captain told someone to get a priority radio message off to the naval commander at Willemstad and then asked, "How did you get on that little island?"

"Timothy and I drifted on to it after the *Hato* was sunk."

"Where's Timothy?" he asked.

I told the captain about Timothy and what had happened to us. I'm not sure the captain believed any of it, because he said quietly, "Son, get some sleep. The *Hato* was sunk way back in April."

I said, "Yes, sir, that's right," and then a doctor came in to check me over.

That night, after the ship had been in communication with Willemstad, the captain visited me again to tell me that his destroyer had been hunting a German submarine when the plane had spotted my black smoke and radioed back to the ship.

There was still disbelief in his voice when he said he'd checked all the charts and publications on the bridge; our cay was so small that the charts wouldn't even dignify it with a name. But Timothy had been right. It was tucked back up in the Devil's Mouth.

The next morning, we docked at the naval base in Cristóbal, Panama, and I was rushed to a hospital, although I really didn't think it was necessary. I was strong and healthy, the doctor on the destroyer had said.

My mother and father flew over from Willemstad in a special plane. It was minutes before they could say anything. They just held me, and I knew my mother was crying. She kept saying, "Phillip, I'm sorry, I'm so sorry."

The Navy had notified them that I was blind, so that it would not be a shock. And I knew I looked different. They'd brought a barber in to cut my hair, which had grown quite long.

We talked for a long time, Stew Cat on my bed, and I tried to tell them all about Timothy and the cay. But it was very difficult. They listened, of course, but I had the feeling that neither of them really understood what had happened on our cay.

Four months later, in a hospital in New York, after many X rays and tests, I had the first of three operations. The piece of timber that had hit me the night the *Hato* went down had damaged some nerves. But after the third operation, when the bandages came off, I could see again. I would always have to wear glasses, but I could see. That was the important thing.

In early April, I returned to Willemstad with my mother, and we took up life where it had been left off the previous April. After I'd been officially reported lost at sea, she'd gone back to Curaçao to be with my father. She had changed in many ways. She had no thoughts of leaving the islands now.

I saw Henrik van Boven occasionally, but it wasn't the same as when we'd played the Dutch or the British. He seemed very young. So I spent a lot of time along St. Anna Bay, and at the Ruyterkade market talking to the black people. I liked the sound of their voices. Some of them had known old Timothy from Charlotte Amalie. I felt close to them.

At war's end, we moved away from Scharloo and Curaçao. My father's work was finished.

Since then, I've spent many hours looking at charts of the Caribbean. I've found Roncador, Rosalind, Quito Sueño, and Serranilla Banks; I've found Beacon Cay and North Cay, and the islands of Providencia and San Andrés. I've also found the Devil's Mouth.

Someday, I'll charter a schooner out of Panama and explore the Devil's Mouth. I hope to find the lonely little island where Timothy is buried.

Maybe I won't know it by sight, but when I go ashore and close my eyes, I'll know this was our own cay. I'll walk along east beach and out to the reef. I'll go up the hill to the row of palm trees and stand by his grave.

I'll say, "Dis b'dat outrageous cay, eh, Timothy?"

MEET THEODORE TAYLOR

Theodore Taylor says of *The Cay*, "After . . . hearing Dr. Martin Luther King singing spirituals in the lobby of a hotel, I decided to go ahead with the long-brewing story. . . . Three weeks later *The Cay* was completed."

Taylor's interest in writing began at an early age. When he was thirteen, he worked as a cub reporter for the Portsmouth, Virginia, *Evening Star.* Later, experiences in the Naval Reserve gave him the chance to explore firsthand the area of the Caribbean where *The Cay* is set.

The Cay has won many literary awards, including the Lewis Carroll Shelf Award. The book was made into a television movie starring James Earl Jones.

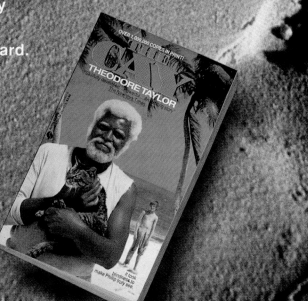

Photograph of march for civil rights (Selma to Montgomery, Alabama) by *Look* photographer James H. Karales, March 1965

from
I Am a Man
Ode to Martin Luther King, Jr.

"Keep to the march. Keep to the song.
"Keep on resisting where there is wrong.

"Fight to be equal, fight to be free,
"but only fight non-violently."

"I have a dream," said the man with no gun,
"of equality for everyone,
"of an end to war and poverty.

"The poor are a mighty family.
"Brothers and sisters, join with me."

EVE MERRIAM

INFORMATION ILLUSTRATED

Your guide to a world of information— with examples related to the themes you are exploring!

CONTENTS

ADVERTISEMENTS

DISASTERS
Some Notable Shipwrecks Since 1850
(Figures indicate estimated lives lost; as of mid-1990)

1854, Mar.-City of Glasgow; British steamer missing in North Atlantic; 480.

1854, Sept. 27-Arctic; U.S. (Collins Line) steamer sunk in collision with French steamer Vesta near Cape Race; 285-351.

1856, Jan. 23-Pacific; U.S. (Collins Line) steamer missing in North Atlantic; 186-286.

1858, Sept. 23-Austria; German steamer destroyed by fire in North Atlantic; 471.

1863, Apr. 27-Anglo-Saxon; British steamer wrecked at Cape Race; 238.

1865, Apr. 27-Sultana; a Mississippi River steamer blew up near Memphis, Tenn; 1,450.

1869, Oct. 27-Stonewall; steamer burned on Mississippi River below Cairo, Ill; 200.

1870, Jan. 25-City of Boston; British (Inman Line) steamer vanished between New York and Liverpool; 177.

1870, Oct. 19-Cambria; British steamer wrecked off northern Ireland; 196.

1872, Nov. 7-Mary Celeste; U.S. half-brig sailed from New York for Genoa; found abandoned in Atlantic 4 weeks later in mystery of sea; crew never heard from; loss of life unknown.

1873, Jan. 22-Northfleet; British steamer foundered off Dungeness, England; 300.

1873, Apr. 1-Atlantic; British (White Star) steamer wrecked off Nova Scotia; 585.

1873, Nov. 23-Ville du Havre; French steamer, sunk after collision with British sailing ship Loch Earn; 226.

1875, May 7-Schiller; German steamer wrecked off Scilly Isles; 312.

1875, Nov. 4-Pacific; U.S. steamer sunk after collision off Cape Flattery; 236.

1878, Sept. 3-Princess Alice; British steamer sank after collision in Thames River; 700.

1878, Dec. 18-Byzantin; French steamer sank after Dardanelles collision; 210.

1881, May 24-Victoria; steamer capsized in Thames River, Canada; 200.

1883, Jan. 19-Cimbria; German steamer sunk in collision with British steamer Sultan in North Sea; 389.

1887, Nov. 15-Wah Yeung; British steamer burned at sea; 400.

1890, Feb. 17-Duburg; British steamer wrecked, China Sea; 400.

1890, Sept. 19-Ertogrul; Turkish frigate foundered off Japan; 540.

1891, Mar. 17-Utopia; British steamer sank in collision with British ironclad Anson off Gibraltar; 562.

1895, Jan. 30-Elbe; German steamer sank in collision with British steamer Craithie in North Sea; 332.

1895, Mar. 11-Reina Regenta; Spanish cruiser foundered near Gibraltar; 400.

1898, Feb. 15-Maine; U.S. battleship blown up in Havana Harbor; 260.

1898, July 4-La Bourgogne; French steamer sunk in collision with British sailing ship Cromartyshire off Nova Scotia; 549.

1898, Nov. 26-Portland; U.S. steamer wrecked off Cape Cod; 157.

1904, June 15-General Slocum; excursion steamer burned in East River, New York City; 1,030.

1904, June 28-Norge; Danish steamer wrecked on Rockall Island, Scotland; 620.

1906, Aug. 4-Sirio; Italian steamer wrecked off Cape Palos, Spain; 350.

1908, Mar. 23-Matsu Maru; Japanese steamer sank in collision near Hakodate, Japan; 300.

1909, Aug. 1-Waratah; British steamer, Sydney to London, vanished; 300.

1910, Feb 9-General Chanzy; French steamer wrecked off Minorca, Spain; 200.

1911, Sept. 25-Liberté; French battleship exploded at Toulon; 285.

1912, Mar. 5-Principe de Asturias; Spanish steamer wrecked off Spain; 500.

1912, Apr. 14-15-Titanic; British (White Star) steamer hit iceberg in North Atlantic; 1,503.

1912, Sept. 28-Kichemaru; Japanese steamer sank off Japanese coast; 1,000.

1914, May 29-Empress of Ireland; British (Canadian Pacific) steamer sunk in collision with Norwegian collier in St. Lawrence River; 1,014.

1915, May 7-Lusitania; British (Cunard Line) steamer torpedoed and sunk by German submarine off Ireland; 1,198.

1915, July 24-Eastland; excursion steamer capsized in Chicago River; 812.

1916, Feb. 26-Provence; French cruiser sank in Mediterranean; 3,100.

1916, Mar. 3-Principe de Asturias; Spanish steamer wrecked near Santos, Brazil; 558.

1916, Aug. 29-Hsin Yu; Chinese steamer sank off Chinese coast; 1,000.

1917, Dec. 6-Mont Blanc, Imo; French ammunition ship and Belgian steamer collided in Halifax Harbor; 1,600.

1918, Apr. 25-Kiang-Kwan; Chinese steamer sank in collision off Hankow; 500.

1918, July 12-Kawachi; Japanese battleship blew up in Tokayama Bay; 500.

1918, Oct. 25-Princess Sophia; Canadian steamer sank off Alaskan coast; 398.

1919, Jan. 17-Chaonia; French steamer lost in Straits of Messina, Italy; 460.

1919, Sept. 9-Valbanera; Spanish steamer lost off Florida coast; 500.

1921, Mar. 18-Hong Kong; steamer wrecked in South China Sea; 1,000.

1922, Aug. 26-Niitaka; Japanese cruiser sank in storm off Kamchatka, USSR; 300.

1927, Oct. 25-Principessa Mafalda; Italian steamer blew up, sank off Porto Seguro, Brazil; 314.

1928, Nov. 12-Vestris; British steamer sank in gale off Virginia; 113.

1934, Sept. 8-Morro Castle; U.S. steamer, Havana to New York, burned off Asbury Park, N.J.; 134.

1939, May 23-Squalus; U.S. submarine sank off Portsmouth, N.H.; 26.

1939, June 1-Thetis; British submarine, sank in Liverpool Bay; 99.

1942, Feb. 18-Truxtun and **Pollux;** U.S destroyer and cargo ship ran aground, sank off Newfoundland; 204.

1942, Oct. 2-Curaçao; British cruiser sank after collision with liner Queen Mary; 338.

1944, Dec. 17-18; 3 U.S. Third Fleet destroyers sank during typhoon in Philippine Sea; 790.

1947, Jan. 19-Himera; Greek steamer hit a mine off Athens; 392.

1947, Apr. 16-Grandcamp; French freighter exploded in Texas City, Tex., Harbor, starting fires; 510.

ATLAS

THE SOLAR SYSTEM

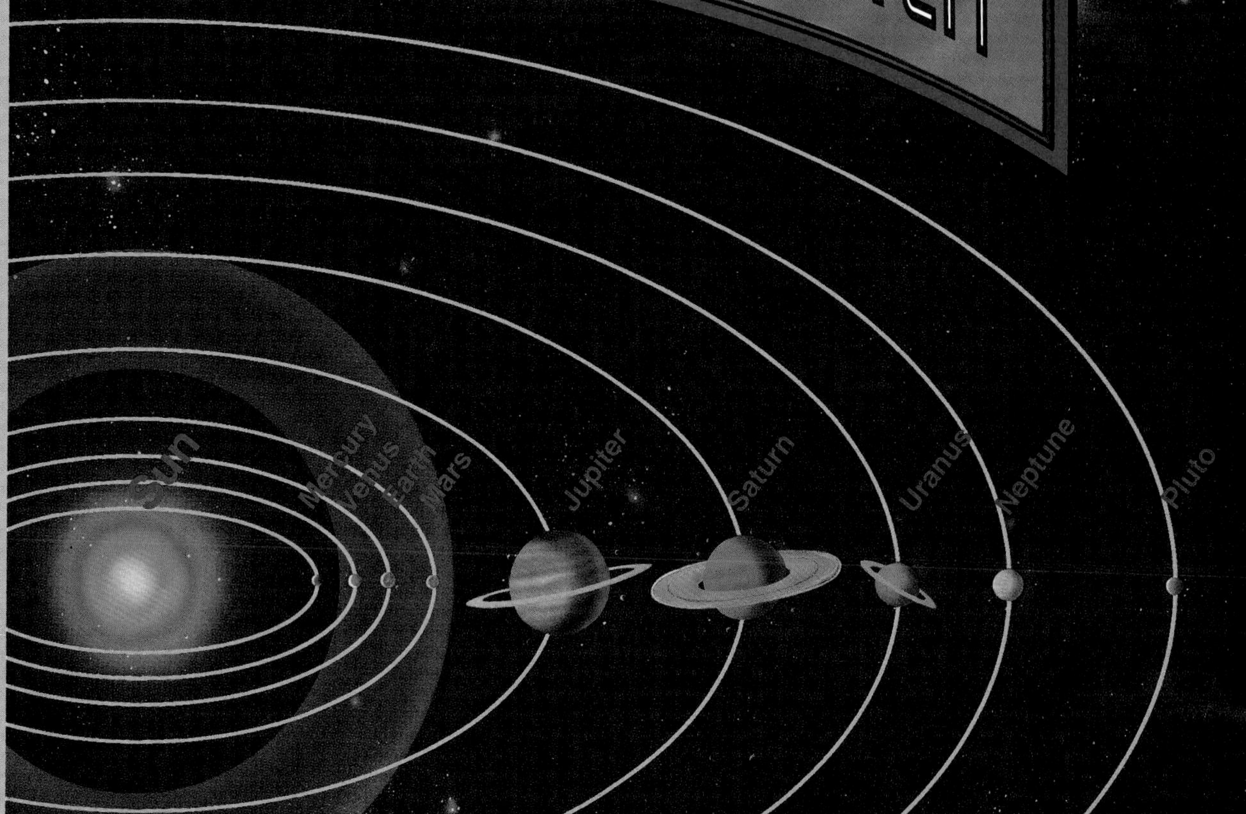

Sun
Mercury
Venus
Earth
Mars
Jupiter
Saturn
Uranus
Neptune
Pluto

The major planets of the solar system are shown in their relative orbital positions. Sizes and distances are not to scale. The shaded ring indicates the **ecosphere** — the area around the sun where, other conditions being suitable, temperatures are neither too hot nor too cold for life to exist.

ATLAS

THE OCEAN FLOOR
NORTH ATLANTIC

From Goode's World Atlas © 1991 by Rand McNally R. L. 91-S-221

535

For Further Reading

Baker, J. "Casting a Long Shadow." *Newsweek* January 2, 1989: 32.

Gessel, P. "Tasting Bitter Failure." *Macleans* April 6, 1987: 21-22

Jacobson, Daniel. *The Hunters.* New York: Franklin Watts, 1974.

Levenson, Dorothy. *Homesteaders and Indians.* (A First Book.) New York: Franklin Watts, 1971.

Lewin, R. "Speaking in Many Tongues." *Science* November 27, 1987: 1232.

Linderman, Frank B. *Plenty-Coups, Chief of the Crows.* New York: John Day, 1972.

Ruhlen, M. "Voices from the Past." *Natural History* March 1987: 6+.

Standing Bear, Luther. *My People the Sioux.* Lincoln, Nebr.: University of Nebraska Press, 1975.

Williams, T. "On the Reservation." *National Review* May 8, 1987: 28-30.

Yellow Robe, Rosebud. *An Album of the American Indian.* New York: Franklin Watts, 1969.

CARD CATALOG
AND LIBRARY CLASSIFICATION SYSTEMS

000 – 099	Generalities
100 – 199	Philosophy
200 – 299	Religion
300 – 399	Social Sciences
400 – 499	Language
500 – 599	Pure Sciences
600 – 699	Technology (Applied Sciences)
700 – 799	The Arts
800 – 899	Literature and Rhetoric
900 – 999	General Geography, History, and Related Disciplines

DEWEY DECIMAL CLASSIFICATION SYSTEM (DDC)

LIBRARY OF CONGRESS CLASSIFICATION SYSTEM (LC)

A	General Works
B	Philosophy – Religion
C	History – Auxiliary Sciences
D	History and Topography (except America)
E F	American History
G	Geography, Anthropology, Folklore, Manners and Customs, Recreation
H	Social Sciences
J	Political Sciences
K	Law of the United States
L	Education
M	Music and Books on Music
N	Fine Arts
P	Language and Literature
Q	Science
R	Medicine
S	Agriculture – Plant and Animal Industry
T	Technology
U	Military Science
V	Naval Science
Z	Bibliography and Library Science

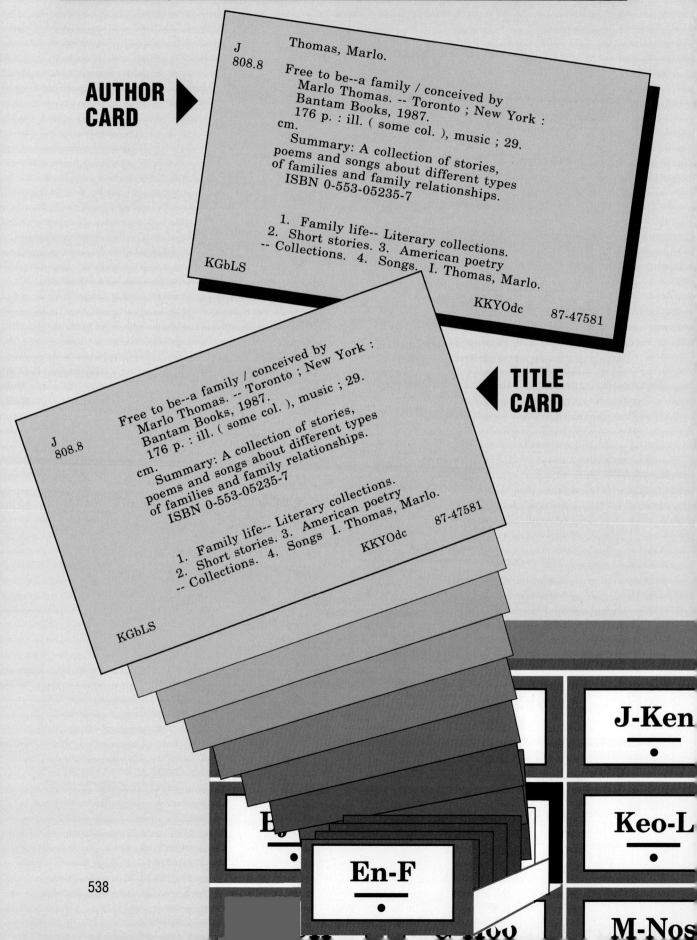

AUTHOR CARD ▶

J
808.8   Thomas, Marlo.

Free to be--a family / conceived by
Marlo Thomas. -- Toronto ; New York :
Bantam Books, 1987.
176 p. : ill. (some col.), music ; 29.
cm.

Summary: A collection of stories,
poems and songs about different types
of families and family relationships.
ISBN 0-553-05235-7

1. Family life-- Literary collections.
2. Short stories. 3. American poetry
-- Collections. 4. Songs. I. Thomas, Marlo.

KGbLS

KKYOdc   87-47581

◀ **TITLE CARD**

Free to be--a family / conceived by
Marlo Thomas. -- Toronto ; New York :
Bantam Books, 1987.
176 p. : ill. (some col.), music ; 29.
cm.

J
808.8   Summary: A collection of stories,
poems and songs about different types
of families and family relationships.
ISBN 0-553-05235-7

1. Family life-- Literary collections.
2. Short stories. 3. American poetry
-- Collections. 4. Songs I. Thomas, Marlo.

KKYOdc   87-47581

KGbLS

J-Ken
•

Keo-L
•

En-F
•

M-Nos

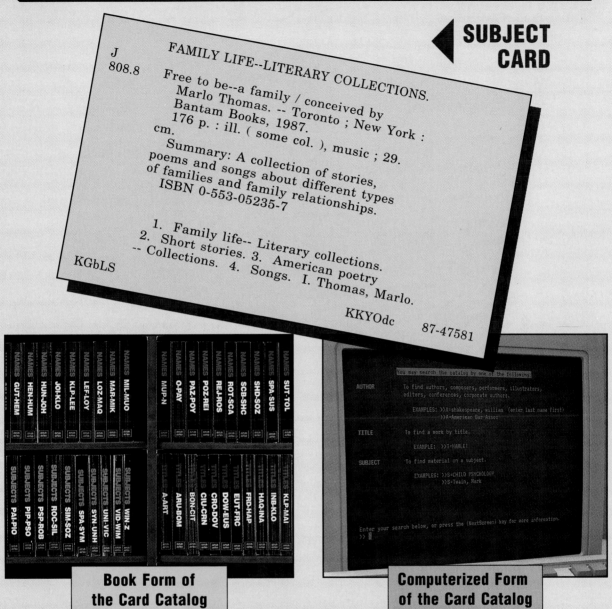

SUBJECT CARD

J
808.8

FAMILY LIFE--LITERARY COLLECTIONS.

Free to be--a family / conceived by
Marlo Thomas. -- Toronto ; New York :
Bantam Books, 1987.
176 p. : ill. (some col.), music ; 29.
cm.

Summary: A collection of stories,
poems and songs about different types
of families and family relationships.
ISBN 0-553-05235-7

1. Family life-- Literary collections.
2. Short stories. 3. American poetry
-- Collections. 4. Songs. I. Thomas, Marlo.

KGbLS

KKYOdc   87-47581

**Book Form of
the Card Catalog**

**Computerized Form
of the Card Catalog**

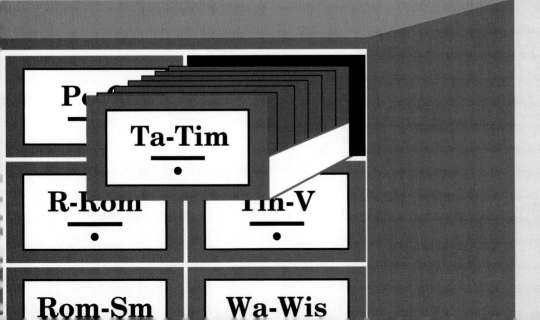

CARTOONS

ARRIVALS

FLIGHT	FROM	TIME DEPARTS	TIME ARRIVES	ODDS
62	CHICAGO	8:04	10:20	3-1
104	DETROIT	8:30	10:50	5-3
205	PHILADELPHIA	10:05	11:30	9-5
96	PITTSBURGH	11:17	12:40	4-1
329	HOUSTON	12:04	2:15	15-1
51	LOS ANGELES	12:40	4:05	26-1
126	DALLAS	1:15	4:30	18-1
31	BOSTON	3:20	5:15	3-2
241	DENVER	4:30	7:30	12-5
180	ST PAUL	7:40	9:25	10-1

"*I can see why they made February the shortest month of the year.*"

CARTOONS

"I don't have TIME to clear off the table! They want us bus boys there by FIVE!"

"Everyone be home by two o'clock!"

541

SOME FAMOUS PYRAMIDS

NAME	LOCATION	ORIGINAL HEIGHT (approx.) in meters	WHEN BUILT (approx.)	REMARKS
Step Pyramid	Saqqara, Egypt	60	middle 2700s B.C.	earliest pyramid—built for the pharaoh Zoser
Meidum Pyramid	Meidum, Egypt	80	early 2700s B.C.	original structure added to twice—not certain for which pharaoh it was built
Bent Pyramid	Dahshur, Egypt	101	late 2600s B.C. (before Red Pyramid)	built at two different angles—built for the pharaoh Snofru
Red Pyramid	Dahshur, Egypt	100	late 2600s B.C. (after Bent Pyramid)	named for its distinctive color—built for the pharaoh Snofru
Great Pyramid, or Pyramid of Khufu (Cheops)	Giza, Egypt	150	middle 2600s B.C.	largest pyramid—built for the pharaoh Khufu (Cheops)
Pyramid of Khafre (Chefren)	Giza, Egypt	140	early 2600s B.C.	built for the pharaoh Khafre (Chephren)
Pyramid of Menkaure (Mycerinus)	Giza, Egypt	70	late 2500s B.C.	built for the pharaoh Menkaure (Mycerinus)
Pyramid of the Sun	Teotihuacán, Mexico	70	between 1 and 100 B.C.	built as a temple that may have been devoted to the worship of the sun

CHARTS AND TABLES

THE PLANETS

PLANET	RANK IN SIZE	DIAMETER AT EQUATOR (km)	AVERAGE DISTANCE FROM SUN (millions of km)	PERIOD OF ROTATION		PERIOD OF REVOLUTION	
				earth days	earth hours	earth years	earth days
Mercury	8	4,878	58	58.6			88
Venus	6	12,104	108	243			225
Earth	5	12,756	150	1		1	
Mars	7	6,794	228		24.6	1.9	
Jupiter	1	142,800	778		9.8	11.9	
Saturn	2	120,000	1,427		10.2	29.5	
Uranus	3	52,000	2,870		16-28	84	
Neptune	4	48,400	4,497		18-20	164.8	
Pluto	9	3,000	5,899	6.3		247.7	

DIAGRAMS

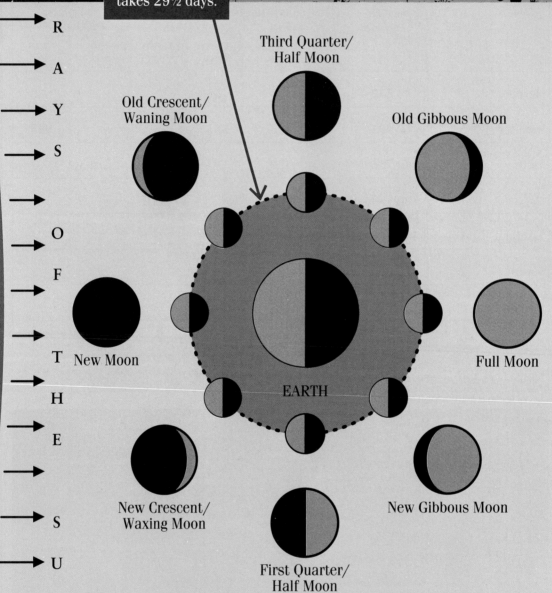

Moon's Orbit
A complete orbit takes 29½ days.

RAYS OF THE SUN

Third Quarter/
Half Moon

Old Crescent/
Waning Moon

Old Gibbous Moon

New Moon

EARTH

Full Moon

New Crescent/
Waxing Moon

New Gibbous Moon

First Quarter/
Half Moon

THE PHASES OF THE MOON

A WEIGHT–DRIVEN CLOCK

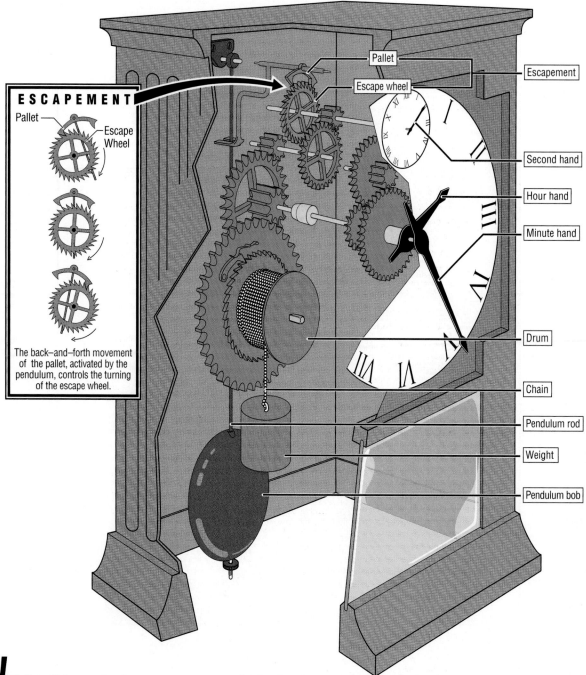

ESCAPEMENT

Pallet

Escape Wheel

The back–and–forth movement of the pallet, activated by the pendulum, controls the turning of the escape wheel.

Pallet

Escapement

Escape wheel

Second hand

Hour hand

Minute hand

Drum

Chain

Pendulum rod

Weight

Pendulum bob

Weight–driven clocks are powered by the energy of a slowly descending weight. The weight is attached to a chain or cord wound around a drum. As the weight falls, it pulls the line and turns the drum. The turning drum drives the hands of the clock by means of a system of gears, which also drives a device called an escapement. The escapement consists of a small toothed wheel—the escape wheel—and a curved metal device—the pallet. As the escape wheel turns, its teeth catch the ends of the pallet and cause it to rock back and forth.

The pallet is connected to a pendulum that swings as the pallet rocks. The rate of rocking—and the rate at which the hands of the clock turn—can be adjusted by raising or lowering the bob, or weight, at the end of the pendulum.

DICTIONARY

Main Entry and Syllable Division

Usage Label

Pronunciation

Adjective Forms

Idioms

Part of Speech

Inflected Forms

Illustrative Sentence

Etymology

Illustrative Phrase

Guide Words

Variant Spelling

Definition

Compound

Homographs

Illustration

Cross-reference

Run-on Entries

Pronunciation Key

litter / livid

lit·ter (lit′ər) *n.* **1.** bits or scraps of paper or other rubbish scattered about carelessly; mess: *Broken bottles and other litter filled the empty lot.* **2.** young animals born at one time: *a litter of kittens.* **3.** loose straw, hay, or similar material used as bedding for animals. **4.** any absorbent, granular material used to soak up urine and moisture from feces, usually placed in a box or pan to be used by household pets, especially cats, for defecation and urination: *cat litter.* **5.** a vehicle made up of a couch usually enclosed by curtains and carried by people on their shoulders or by animals: *Four attendants carried the ruler's litter in the procession.* **6.** a stretcher for carrying a sick or injured person. —*v.t.* **1.** to make disordered or untidy by scattering bits of rubbish about carelessly: *to litter a street with trash.* **2.** to provide (animals) with litter for bedding. —*v.i.* **1.** to scatter bits of rubbish about carelessly: *Don't litter; it's against the law.* **2.** to give birth to young.

litter *(def. 5)*

lit·ter·bug (lit′ər bug′) *n. Informal.* a person who litters public places.

lit·tle (lit′əl) *adj.*, **less** or **less·er**, or **lit·tler**, **least** or **lit·tlest.** **1.** small in size: *A pebble is a little stone.* **2.** short in time or distance; brief: *a little while, a little walk.* **3.** small in amount or degree; not much: *Add a little water to the mixture.* **4.** small in importance or interest; trivial: *a little problem.* **5.** small in nature, mind, or spirit; mean; narrow: *a nasty, little mind.* —*adv.*, **less, least.** to a small extent; not much; slightly: *That poet is little known outside this country.* —*n.* **1.** a small amount: *I ate only a little.* **2.** a short time or distance: *Step back a little.* —lit′tle·ness, *n.*

·**little by little.** by slow degrees; gradually.
·**to make little of.** to treat as unimportant.
·**to think little of.** to have a low opinion of; consider to be unimportant or worthless.

li·tur·gi·cal (li tûr′ji kəl) *adj.* **1.** of or relating to liturgies. **2.** used in a liturgy. Also, **li·tur·gic** (li tûr′jik). —li·tur′gi·cal·ly, *adv.*

lit·ur·gy (lit′ər jē) *n., pl.* **lit·ur·gies.** in various churches, the set form of public worship.

liv·a·ble (liv′ə bəl) *also*, **live·a·ble.** *adj.* **1.** fit to live in; habitable: *The old house was not livable.* **2.** worth living; endurable: *to feel that life would not be livable as a slave.*

live¹ (liv) *v.*, **lived, liv·ing.** —*v.i.* **1.** to be alive; have life: *to have lived before the turn of the century.* **2.** to continue to exist; remain alive: *The large turtle lived for one hundred years.* **3.** to support oneself: *That family lives on a small income.* **4.** to feed; subsist: *Some birds live on bugs and worms.* **5.** to make one's home; dwell: *We live on the east side of town.* **6.** to pass or spend one's life: *to live happily.* **7.** to get the fullest enjoyment from life: *They really began to live when they moved to the country.* —*v.t.* **1.** to pass or spend (one's life): *to live a life of luxury.* **2.** to practice or express in one's life: *to live a lie.* [From the Old English words *libban* and *lifian*, both meaning "to live, be alive".]

·**to live down.** to live in such a way that (a past mistake, such as a crime) is forgotten or forgiven.
·**to live up to.** to abide by or fulfill: *to live up to one's end of the bargain.*
·**to live with.** to bear with; endure: *to live with one's mistakes.*

live² (līv) *adj.* **1.** having life; living: *The hunter brought back a live elephant.* **2.** filled with life; energetic; lively: *a live personality.* **3.** of present interest or importance; current: *a live topic.* **4.** burning: *a live coal.* **5.** containing an explosive charge: *live ammunition.* **6.** carrying electrical current. **7.** seen or presented while actually happening, as on the stage or on radio or television: *a live performance, a live broadcast.* [Short for *alive.*]

live·a·ble (līv′ə bəl) another spelling of **livable.**

live·li·hood (līv′lē hud′) *n.* the means of staying alive or supporting life: *Their livelihood is fishing. They earn a livelihood by farming.*

live·long (liv′lông′) *adj.* whole; entire: *to work the livelong day.*

live·ly (līv′lē) *adj.*, **live·li·er, live·li·est.** **1.** full of life, energy, or movement; vigorous; active: *a lively walk.* **2.** gay; cheerful: *a lively tune.* **3.** stimulating; exciting: *a lively debate.* **4.** inventive or creative: *a lively imagination.* **5.** striking; vivid: *lively colors.* **6.** springing back quickly: *a lively tennis ball.* —*adv.* in a lively manner; energetically; vigorously: *to step lively.* —live′li·ness, *n.*

liv·en (lī′vən) *v.t.* to make more cheerful, active, or exciting: *Their arrival livened the party.* —*v.i.* (usually with *up*) to become more cheerful; brighten: *to liven up after taking a shower.*

live oak (līv) an evergreen oak tree native to the southeastern United States.

liv·er¹ (liv′ər) *n.* **1.** a large, reddish brown glandular organ that produces bile, stores carbohydrates, filters poisons from the blood, and performs various other body functions. **2.** the liver of certain animals, used as food. [From the Old English word *lifer* meaning this organ.]

liver¹ *(def. 1)*

liv·er² (liv′ər) *n.* a person who lives in a certain manner: *an easy liver.* [*Live¹* + *-er¹.*]

liv·er·ied (liv′ə rēd) *adj.* dressed in livery: *liveried servants.*

liv·er·leaf (liv′ər lēf′) *n.* hepatica.

liv·er·wort (liv′ər wûrt′) *n.* any of various plants similar to mosses but mostly lacking stems and leaves. They are found throughout the world, growing mostly in damp, shady areas.

liv·er·wurst (liv′ər wûrst′) *n.* a sausage made mostly of liver, especially pork liver.

liv·er·y (liv′ə rē) *n., pl.* **liv·er·ies.** **1.** a uniform provided for servants: *a bellhop in livery.* **2.** any distinctive dress or uniform worn by members of a group or profession. **3.** the stabling and feeding of horses for pay. **4.** see livery stable.

livery stable, a stable where horses are cared for and let for hire, with or without vehicles.

lives (līvz) the plural of **life.**

live·stock (līv′stok′) *n.* domestic animals, such as cattle, horses, sheep, or pigs.

live wire (līv) **1.** a wire carrying an electrical current. **2.** *Informal.* an energetic, alert person.

liv·id (liv′id) *adj.* **1.** having a pale, usually bluish color: *a face livid with rage.* **2.** furious; enraged. **3.** having a grayish blue color from a bruise. —liv′id·ly, *adv.* —liv′id·ness, *n.*

at; āpe; fär; câre; end; mē; it; īce; pierce; hot; ōld; sông, fôrk; oil; out; up; ūse; rüle; pull; tûrn; chin; sing; shop; thin; this; hw in white; zh in treasure. The symbol ə stands for the unstressed vowel sound heard in about, taken, pencil, lemon, and circus.

559

DICTIONARY OF THE ENGLISH LANGUAGE

546

RUSSELL

RUSSELL, WILLIAM *(b. Glasgow, Scotland, 1798; d. Lancaster, Mass., 1873)*, educator. Emigrated to Georgia, 1817–18; taught at and conducted schools in many towns along the eastern seaboard. As principal of the New England Normal Institute, 1853–55, he made it an important center of Pestalozzianism in the United States. First editor of the *American Journal of Education* (1826), he was the author of a number of textbooks.

RUSSELL, WILLIAM EUSTIS *(b. Cambridge, Mass., 1857; d. St. Adelaide, Quebec, Canada, 1896)*, lawyer, politician. Democratic governor of Massachusetts, 1891–94.

RUSSELL, WILLIAM HENRY *(b. Nicholas Co., Ky., 1802; d. Washington, D.C., 1873)*, lawyer, Kentucky legislator, California pioneer. An associate of John C. Fremont in the early government of California, Russell later practiced law there. A large, expansive, bombastic man, he bore the nickname of "Owl" Russell.

RUSSELL, WILLIAM H___N *(___ ___ 18___)* was a ___ of Princeton Univers___ and Queen's College; the latter institution changed its name to Rutgers in his honor.

RUTH, GEORGE HERMAN (BABE) *(b. Baltimore, MD., 1895; d. New York, NY., 1948)*, baseball player. Legally committed to St. Mary's Industrial Home for Boys, Baltimore, at age seven, he became the school's star baseball player. In 1914 Ruth joined the Baltimore club of the International League, but because of a financial squeeze, he was sold the same year to the major-league Boston Red Sox. With a brilliant overall record for 1914, his major-league career was launched. Over the next four years, as a regular Red Sox pitcher, Ruth helped Boston win three American League pennants and three World Series titles. Overall, his six years as a Boston pitcher showed eighty-nine victories and forty-six losses, a pace which, if continued, would surely have ranked him as one of baseball's greatest pitchers.

But Ruth's versatility ended his pitching. His exceptional abilities as a hitter prompted Boston manager Ed Barrow in 1918 to place him full-time in the outfield, where he played thereafter. In 1918 he batted .300 and hit eleven homers; a year later he astounded the baseball world by clubbing a record twenty-nine

RUTLEDGE

homers on a .322 batting average. In 1919 Ruth was sold to the New York Yankees. He was the dominant figure in American baseball from 1920 to 1935, leading the Yankees to seven league pennants and five World Series championships. In 1925, he was hospitalized and underwent surgery for an intestinal abscess. After engaging a trainer to help him lose weight, he effected a comeback and over the seasons of 1926–1928 led the Yankees to three straight pennants. In 1927, after hitting his all-time seasonal high of sixty homers, Ruth toured the Far West.

In a fifteen-year career as a Yankee, Ruth set many records. His overall performance was the more remarkable since he had spent a quarter of his big-league career as a pitcher. In 1935 the Yankees released him to the Boston Braves; disillusioned, Ruth quit in midseason. In 1936 he was elected a charter member of the Baseball Hall of Fame. Two years later he accepted a coaching offer from the Brooklyn Dodgers, but resigned before the end of the season. In 1948, shortly before his death, he saw himself portrayed in a Hollywood film, *The Babe Ruth Story.*

RUTHERFORD, JOSEPH FRANKLIN *(b. near Boonville* the time of Henry A. Rowland. Rutherford took a ___ in establishing the department of geodesy and practical astronomy at Columbia, 1881.

RUTLEDGE, EDWARD *(b. Charleston, S.C., 1749; d. Charleston, 1800)*, lawyer, statesman. Brother of John Rutledge. Member of the First Continental Congress, 1774, and of the Second Continental Congress, 1775–76, he seconded the opinions of his brother. At first opposing independence, he influenced the South Carolina delegation to vote for it and was a signer of the Declaration. Returning home in November 1776 to serve in the defense of the state, he was taken prisoner at the fall of Charleston but was exchanged in time to take his seat in the legislature in January 1782. Although he drew up the bill proposing confiscation of Loyalist property, he was influential in moderating its effect. An active member of the legislature, 1782–98, he was a stiffly conservative Federalist. Elected governor, 1798, he served until his death.

RUTLEDGE, JOHN *(b. Charleston, S.C., 1739; d. 1800)*, statesman, jurist. Brother of Edward Rutledge. After study-

BIOGRAPHICAL DICTIONARY

DIRECTIONS

DONNING EQUIPMENT FOR SCUBA DIVING

In general, you will don your equipment in this order: wet suit, boots, BCD (Buoyancy Control Device), scuba unit, weight belt, mask and snorkel, fins. Always work with a buddy.

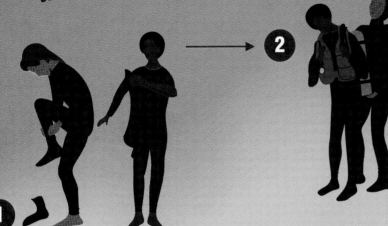

BCD and Scuba Unit – If you are using a front-mounted BCD, put this on next. Then have your buddy help you attach the scuba unit. If you are using a jacket- or back-mounted BCD, put it on simultaneously with the scuba unit (illustrated). Prepare and adjust harness and shoulder straps before putting on jacket and scuba unit. Connect all quick releases. Have your buddy hold the integrated unit while you slip into it. Fasten waist belt.

1 If a wet suit is to be worn: Put the wet suit on first. Put on boots. If you are not using a wet suit: Put on boots. It is recommended that you wear a T-shirt or sweatshirt to prevent chafing from tank and BCD straps.

4 **Weight belt –** Put on the weight belt and make sure it is free and clear of all other equipment. Be sure you wear the weight belt so that it can be released by the right hand (buckle on left-hand side). Adjust weights.

3 Bend forward to check balance of scuba unit. Have your buddy help you make necessary adjustments.

5 **Mask and Snorkel –** Prepare mask to prevent condensation. Position mask over face with one hand while using other hand to pull strap over back of head. Adjust mask and snorkel.

6 **Fins –** Fins are the last piece of equipment to don. Put these on at water's edge. To make it easier to put fins on, wet boots first. You may need the help of your buddy to steady yourself as you put fins on.

7 **Inspection –** Have your buddy help you inspect your equipment for position and functioning before you enter water.

548

ENCYCLOPEDIA

guide words

entry word

plane. *See under* GEOMETRY.

planet (plan′ət), a massive spherical body that revolves around a star and shines by reflected light. The solar system has nine planets. More than 50,000 rocky fragments encircle the sun, mainly between the orbits of Mars and Jupiter. These are the asteroids, also known as planetoids or minor planets. The asteroids are thought to have formed, along with the sun and the larger planets of the solar system, from swirling clouds of dust and gas about 4.6 billion years ago. A few of the closest stars are believed to have planets, but such planets are too far away and hence too faint to be directly observed. However, according to modern theories on planet formation, planetary systems should be common throughout the universe. A useful book is *The Planetary System* by David Morrison and Tobias Owen (Addison-Wesley, 1988). *See also* ASTEROID; SOLAR SYSTEM: *Planet Formation; and articles on the individual planets.* *Lloyd Motz

cross reference

plane table. *See under* SURVEYING.

planetarium (plan′ə tãr′i əm), an optical instrument that displays the positions and motions of heavenly bodies by projecting their images on the inside of a hemispherical dome. The term "planetarium" is also used for the building that houses the instrument.

A planetarium can project the images of as many as 9,000 or more stars, although in the actual heavens only about 2,500 or 3,000 are visible to the naked eye in each hemisphere. In addition, the moon, the sun, and the planets Mercury, Venus, Mars, Jupiter, and Saturn can be represented. Other aspects of the heavens, such as the Milky Way, comets, meteors, and nebulas, can also be projected by a modern planetarium. Even the paths of artificial satellites can be shown. For purposes of instruction, reference lines for celestial-coordinate systems, figures representing the various constellations as visualized by different peoples, and an arrow to serve as a pointer are often provided.

A planetarium dome is made to appear as similar as possible to the night sky by lighting effects and by placing the outline of a city skyline or the like around the edge of the hemisphere, where the horizon would be seen around a real sky. Other realistic effects include the dimming of stars as they approach the horizon.

The instrument itself is usually a large dumbbell-like apparatus mounted on a framework that allows it to be turned in various directions. Often more than 150 projection units are used to project the images of the heavenly bodies. The images of fixed stars are formed through tiny holes etched into the metal plate. Projection lights of various intensities make it possible to focus sharp images of the stars on the dome. (The images are brighter than the stars they represent.) The sun, of course, is not represented with its actual brilliance, and thus it is possible to show its motion against the background of fixed stars.

Electric motors rotate the planetarium about various axes to show the appearance of the heavens during the course of a single day or over the course of a

year. Another rotation shows the heavens from any latitude, from the North Pole to the South Pole. One motion of the planetarium imitates the precession of the equinoxes, the wobble of the earth's axis that occurs over a cycle of about 25,800 years. All of these motions are accomplished by a combination of various motors in a matter of minutes. Thus, it is possible to form an image of the sky as it would appear at any time, past, present, or future, from any latitude.

The first projection-type planetarium was designed and produced in 1923 by Carl Zeiss Optical Works of Germany. It was demonstrated on October 21 of that year in Munich, Germany. This original model showed only the heavens as visible from Munich, at 48° north latitude. It was redesigned shortly afterward to show the sky from any latitude.

The first planetarium to be installed in the United States was the Adler Planetarium, in Chicago. Nearly a dozen U.S. cities now have large planetariums, and many others have smaller ones. *Lloyd Motz

author

A planetarium projects the images of stars and planets on the inside of a spherical dome.

planetary gear (plan′ə ter′i), or epicyclic gear, a special type of gear train that is used in the automatic transmissions of many automobiles.

Four main moving parts make up the basic form of the planetary gear. The sun gear is at the center and meshes with the planet gears, which are placed around it but which do not mesh with one another. The planet gears are free to turn on the planet gear mounting. They mesh with the internal gear, which surrounds the rest of the mechanism.

The gear train transmits power when one of the principal parts is prevented from turning or when two of them are locked together. For example, it might be supposed that the planetary gear is part of

pronunciation

FORMS AND APPLICATIONS

CAMP MAPAWA
Eagle Ridge, Colorado

RESERVATION FORM

Camp Mapawa offers 12 one-week sessions of exciting camping experience for young people from ages 8 to 16. Located in the magnificent Colorado Rockies, Camp Mapawa is licensed by Certified Camps of America and provides experienced leaders in all fields of outdoor life.

To apply, complete the form below.

PLEASE PRINT

Name <u>Morton   Amanda   L.</u> AGE <u>12</u> PHONE (**000**) <u>555-7294</u>
        last   first   middle   years

ADDRESS <u>84 Locust Street   Modena   Maine 00000</u>
           number and street   city   state   zip

Please check the sessions you wish to attend. Rates are $250 per week.

❑ June 13 - June 20	❑ July 11 - July 18	❑ August 8 - August 15
❑ June 20 - June 27	☒ July 18 - July 25	❑ August 15 - August 22
❑ June 27 - July 4	☒ July 25 - August 1	❑ August 22 - August 29
❑ July 4 - July 11	❑ August 1 - August 8	❑ August 29 - September 5

Camp Mapawa offers special activities at additional charges.
Check the ones in which you wish to participate.

☒ Horseback Riding   ☒ Sailing   ☒ Orienteering
   ($75.00 per week)   ($50.00 per week)   ($25.00 per week)

A medical certificate completed and signed by a doctor must accompany this application.
☒ Medical certificate enclosed.

number of sessions			amount
2	x $250		$ 500.00

special activity	number of weeks	dates	
Horseback Riding	2	July 18-August 1	150.00
Sailing	1	July 18-July 25	50.00
Orienteering	1	July 25-August 1	25.00
		Total	$ 725.00

PAYMENT must accompany this application.
❑ Check or money order
☒ Credit card (see below)
❑ Mastercard   ☒ American Express   ❑ Visa

CARD NUMBER <u>0000-0000-000-0000</u> EXPIRATION DATE <u>5/95</u>

SIGNATURE OF CARD HOLDER <u>John Morton</u> DATE <u>5/23/93</u>

GRAPHS

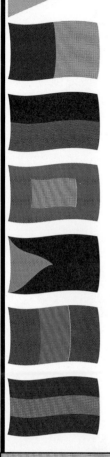

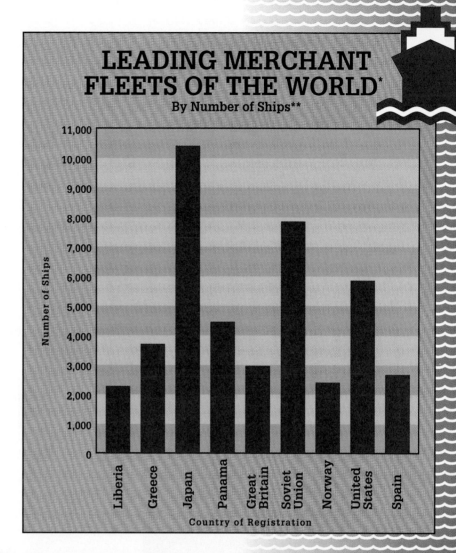

LEADING MERCHANT FLEETS OF THE WORLD*
By Number of Ships**

Number of Ships (y-axis): 0, 1,000, 2,000, 3,000, 4,000, 5,000, 6,000, 7,000, 8,000, 9,000, 10,000, 11,000

Country of Registration (x-axis): Liberia, Greece, Japan, Panama, Great Britain, Soviet Union, Norway, United States, Spain

BAR
GRAPHS

LEADING MERCHANT FLEETS OF THE WORLD*
By Tonnage**

Country of Registration (y-axis): Liberia, Greece, Japan, Panama, Great Britain, Soviet Union, Norway, United States

Millions of tons (x-axis): 0, 10, 20, 30, 40, 50, 60, 70, 80

* According to country of registration (late 1980s)
** Including ships of 100 tons or more (late 1980s)

551

INDIAN RESERVATIONS
PERCENT BY STATE

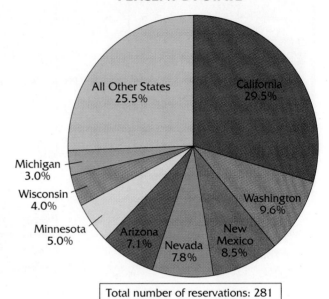

California 29.5%

All Other States 25.5%

Michigan 3.0%

Wisconsin 4.0%

Minnesota 5.0%

Arizona 7.1%

Nevada 7.8%

New Mexico 8.5%

Washington 9.6%

Total number of reservations: 281

RESERVATION LANDS
PERCENT BY STATE

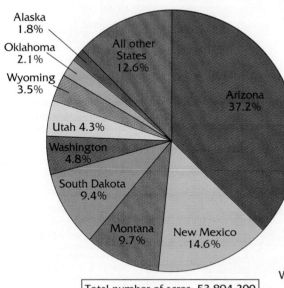

Alaska 1.8%

Oklahoma 2.1%

Wyoming 3.5%

Utah 4.3%

Washington 4.8%

South Dakota 9.4%

Montana 9.7%

All other States 12.6%

Arizona 37.2%

New Mexico 14.6%

Total number of acres: 53,894,200

CIRCLE GRAPHS

INDIAN RESERVATION POPULATION
PERCENT BY STATE

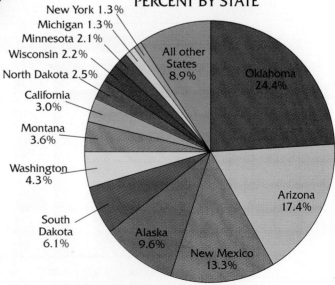

New York 1.3%

Michigan 1.3%

Minnesota 2.1%

Wisconsin 2.2%

North Dakota 2.5%

California 3.0%

Montana 3.6%

Washington 4.3%

South Dakota 6.1%

Alaska 9.6%

New Mexico 13.3%

All other States 8.9%

Oklahoma 24.4%

Arizona 17.4%

Indian population living on reservation lands: 949,075
(Total Indian population: 1,700,000)

552

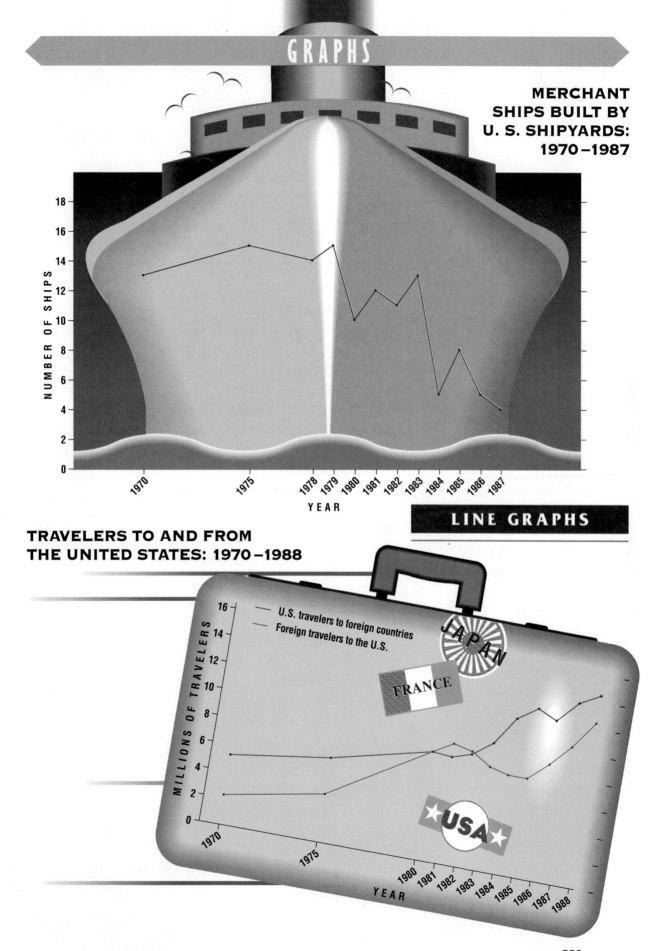

GRAPHS

MERCHANT SHIPS BUILT BY U. S. SHIPYARDS: 1970–1987

LINE GRAPHS

TRAVELERS TO AND FROM THE UNITED STATES: 1970–1988

— U.S. travelers to foreign countries
— Foreign travelers to the U.S.

553

MAPS

UNITED STATES
THE SOUTHEAST

OH
PA
MD
NJ
DE
IN
Ohio River
WEST VIRGINIA
VIRGINIA
Chesapeake Bay
MO
IL
KENTUCKY
ALLEGHENY MOUNTAINS
APPALACHIAN MOUNTAINS
Potomac
Cape Hatteras
PLATEAU
NORTH CAROLINA
▲ Mt. Mitchell 6,684 ft. (2,037m)
35°N
75°W
OZARK
TENNESSEE
CUMBERLAND PLATEAU
BLUE RIDGE MTS.
Great Smoky Mts.
ARKANSAS
SOUTH CAROLINA
TX
MISSISSIPPI
ALABAMA
GEORGIA
PIEDMONT
COASTAL PLAIN
ATLANTIC OCEAN
LOUISIANA
Red River
C O A S T A L   P L A I N
30°N
Lake Pontchartrain
90°W
FLORIDA
Cape Canaveral
80°W
Gulf of Mexico
Lake Okeechobee
25°N
85°W

THE SOUTHEAST: Elevation

.... Fall Line
▲ Mountain peak

Elevations
Feet   Meters

Above 1,500—Above 500
700—   —200
0—   —0

N

0   100   200   300 Miles
0 100 200 300 400 Kilometers

67°W   66°W
ATLANTIC OCEAN
PUERTO RICO
Caribbean Sea
18°N

0   25   50 Miles
0 25 50 75 Kilometers

QUEEN OF THE CARIBBEAN
Deck Plans

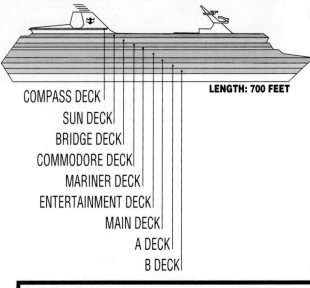

LENGTH: 700 FEET

COMPASS DECK
SUN DECK
BRIDGE DECK
COMMODORE DECK
MARINER DECK
ENTERTAINMENT DECK
MAIN DECK
A DECK
B DECK

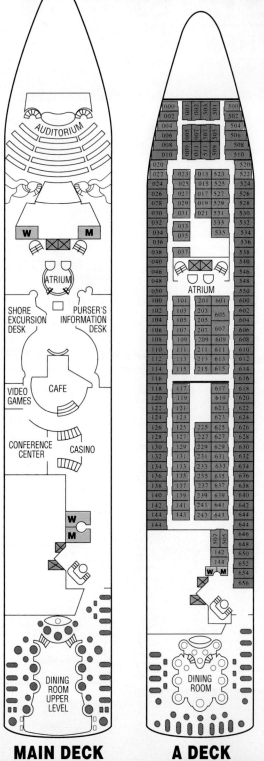

MAIN DECK

- AUDITORIUM
- W   M
- ATRIUM
- SHORE EXCURSION DESK
- PURSER'S INFORMATION DESK
- VIDEO GAMES
- CAFE
- CONFERENCE CENTER
- CASINO
- W M
- DINING ROOM UPPER LEVEL

A DECK

- ATRIUM
- DINING ROOM
- W M

CABIN CATEGORIES

A Deck – standard outside stateroom, two lower beds

A Deck – smaller outside stateroom, two lower beds, or inside stateroom, two lower beds

A Deck – inside stateroom, two lower beds

Stateroom Numbers Shown

⊠	Elevator
W	Women's Restroom
M	Men's Restroom
☰	Stairs
◖❚◗	Dining Room Tables

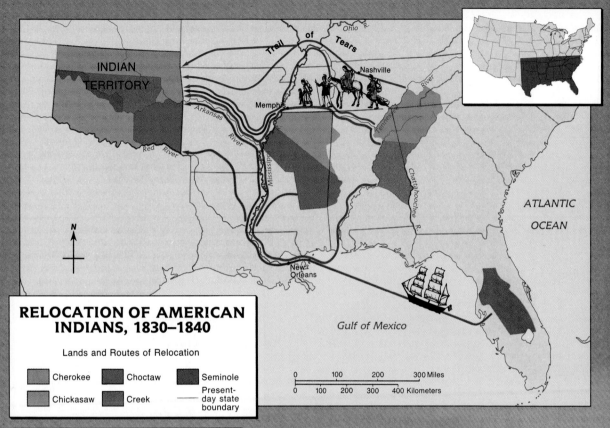

RELOCATION OF AMERICAN INDIANS, 1830–1840

Lands and Routes of Relocation

- Cherokee
- Chickasaw
- Choctaw
- Creek
- Seminole
- Present-day state boundary

INDIAN TERRITORY

Trail of Tears

Ohio R.
Nashville
Memphis
Arkansas River
Red River
Mississippi
Tennessee River
Chattahoochee R.
New Orleans
ATLANTIC OCEAN
Gulf of Mexico

| 0 | 100 | 200 | 300 Miles |
| 0 | 100 | 200 | 300 | 400 Kilometers |

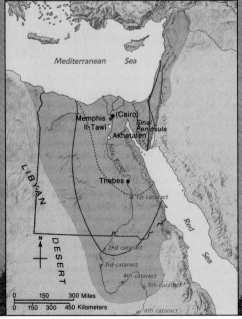

Mediterranean Sea
LIBYAN DESERT
Memphis
It-Tawi
(Cairo)
Akhetaten
Sinai Peninsula
Thebes
Nile River
1st cataract
2nd cataract
3rd cataract
4th cataract
5th cataract
6th cataract
Red Sea

| 0 | 150 | 300 Miles |
| 0 | 150 | 300 | 450 Kilometers |

GROWTH OF ANCIENT EGYPT

- New Kingdom
- Middle Kingdom boundary
- Old Kingdom boundary
- ∥ Cataract
- Boundary of modern Egypt
- ○ New Kingdom capital
- ● New Kingdom and Middle Kingdom capital
- ○ Middle Kingdom capital
- ● Old Kingdom capital
- ● Capital of modern Egypt

557

Lifestyles
Moms Going Home
More and more career mothers put careers on hold to stay at home with kids.
Page 4

Teenagers
C U R F E W ?
Center City has no curfew for youths. Parents and kids speak out.
Page 8

Sports
NFL Season
Latest scores, highlights of games.
Page 11

Weather
High / Low
86   62
Partly sunny today, E winds 5 mph, 10 percent chance of rain.
Page 15

Center City Times

Monday, September 6, 1993   Center City, Idaho   2 Sections   22 pages   Delivered 25¢   Newsstand 35¢

Children Found After Two-Day Search

by PAUL METZ
Times Reporter

Today may be Labor Day, but for one local family it feels more like Christmas Day.

After an intense two-day search through the Wilderness Mountain Wildlife Refuge, Mark and Becky Liff were found safe and sound late last night.

The two children had been missing since Friday night, after being separated from their family at a picnic area in the state park. The two were found by Wallace Higgins, a local pharmacist. Higgins was the unofficial leader of a search team that included local townspeople, state park rangers, the local national guard, and city police rescue

Mark and Becky Liff with Wallace Higgins, the Center City pharmacist who led local residents in assisting the rescue effort.

LABOR DAY WEEKEND – SAFE SO FAR HERE

BY JILL HENDRON
Times Reporter

So far across the nation, Labor Day weekend has taken its predictable toll in accidents. But it's been a safe holiday in Center City.

While many families took advantage of this late summer holiday for excursions to nearby parks, lakes, and mountains, others stayed at home to take part in some of the activities planned and sponsored by local service clubs.

The "Sportorama" sponsored by the local sports

State Lottery Experiments with Vending Machines

Capital City (AP)—The State lottery has begun to add vending machines to its marketing schemes. The lottery commission has been experimenting for several months with machines that automatically dispense tickets. So far, the results are promising.

The lottery commission placed machines in three Capital City businesses in June, July, and August. It has also installed four machines at the state fairgrounds. Sales Director Jordan Garcia said officials wanted to determine whether machines would increase ticket sales. Merchants who have tried the machines

M O N D A Y
AND THE WEEK AHEAD

Bus Fares – Starting tomorrow, it will cost more to ride the Center City buses. Fares increase from 50 cents to 75 cents for adults, and from 30 cents to 50 cents for children. Fares for the elderly and handicapped will remain at 25 cents. For the time being, shuttle service will continue to be free.

Radio – The state's first statewide public affairs radio series—"Status of the State"—will debut at 7:00 p.m. today on KZCX-FM/90.3.

Holiday – Today is Labor Day. Government agencies, business offices, schools, and other institutions will be closed, and there will be no mail service. Most malls will be open for business.

Sports – The fall high school sports season begins Friday night when Center City High meets East Linville High at 7:00 p.m. on the Center City Field. The Cross Country Invitational will take place Saturday, beginning at 10:00 a.m. at Center City Track.

Chili Feed and Contest – The tenth annual Chili Festival will be held Saturday at the Savemore Stores parking lot, Carter and 10th Streets, beginning at 10 a.m. The event features food, entertainment, a chili-eating contest, and a street dance. Admission is free until 6 p.m., when a $5 cover will be charged for the dance.

Local Youth Wins Grand Championship in Lamb Division

Capital City (UPI)—Sara Renton of Center City walked off as Grand Champion in the Lamb Division at the State Fair on Saturday. Her market lamb was rated as the best in the field of about 500 by show judge Larry Major.

It was the biggest prize ever won by Sara, the daughter of Kathleen and Thomas Renton. Sara's lamb had earlier won grand champion at the Center County Fair. "It was great winning at the county fair," said Sara, "but I really didn't expect to come in very well at the State Fair."

Sara, who is a senior at Center City High, has three more years of eligibility in 4-H. "I had planned to go out seriously for volleyball this

year," she commented, "but now I'm going to have to think about it. I'm not so sure I shouldn't spend more time with 4-H projects, including raising more lambs."

Judge Major said that Sara's lamb had a lot of "eye appeal." "Of course," he said, "the bottom line is meat production." The lamb was purchased by Creighton Industries of Center City.

Sara has been a member of the Happy Valley 4-H Club for eight years. During that time she has shown lambs, calves, and turkeys. She has seven grand championship ribbons from county fair judges.

For Home Delivery
CALL 555-3232

STATE FAIR

Winners, Page 10

Newspaper – Front Page

520 Houses for Rent

1 bedroom, $225 + utilities and deposit. 121 West Grange. 555-3020

1036 Oak Drive. Older home, 2 bedrooms, no pets. $360. 555-9021

1516 Eastridge. Remodeled 3-bedroom home with garage, garden. $450 + deposit. No pets. 555-3612

1617 Wadsworth. 3 bedrooms, garage. Available Oct. 1. $425 + utilities. Call after 6 p.m. 555-9172

1742 Pearl. 2 bedroom brick home with sauna, garage, garden. $600 + utilities. Cats or dogs only. 555-6345

1192 South Norwood. Stone, 3 bedroom, garage, basement. 555-3950

4-bedroom split-level home in Waverly subdivision. 1-year lease only. $650. Available Oct. 1. Call 555-3765 days/555-3865 nights.

CLASSIFIED ADS

Mother, daughter learning together
Opportunities knock at Emily Griffith

By J. Sebastian Sinisi
Denver Post Staff Writer

The students have changed since Emily Griffith got the Denver Board of Education to approve her radical idea for a vocational school 75 years ago, but the goals haven't.

Mother and daughter Lolita and Antoinette Ortiz are among the latest of 1.5 million people to pursue Griffith's—and their own—version of the American dream at the school.

Flexible hours

Both are taking advantage of its flexible hours and free instruction to return to the classroom long after traditional students have graduated and entered the workplace.

Having worked a dozen years as a computer assembler in California's Silicon Valley, Lolita, a mother of five whose husband retired from the U.S. Navy, is taking cosmetology courses at Griffith. She wants to open her own beauty shop and eventually work as a cosmetologist on a cruise ship.

Despite her years of experience in computer assembly—demanding work that offers no margin for error—Ortiz found she couldn't earn nearly as much in Colorado as she did in California.

"No future for me"

"There was no future for me in electronics anyway," she said last week. "I want to accomplish something and to be somebody. And, for me, this school is the best thing that happened. The teachers are very helpful and I know that, after I get my license, I'm going to do well and that I do have a future." Ortiz heard about the school from 21-year-old Antoinette, who dropped out of a San José high school seven years ago because she was involved with drugs.

Tired of dead-end jobs after she moved to Denver three years ago, Antoinette earned a high school diploma through Griffith's "second chance" program. After 18 months in class, she graduated last June with an "A" average.

The diploma was a start, but not enough for Antoinette, who has an 8-month-old son at
Please see GRIFFITH on 6B

FEATURE STORY

Our View
YES to "Sweat Equity"

For far too long, the lack of affordable housing has plagued the San Pedro metropolitan area. The problem has persisted through the administrations of leaders of both political parties. We've seen a great deal of frustration and finger-pointing, but very little leadership.

That's why last week's session of the city council was a breath of fresh air. Finally, two of our representatives came forth on the issue, not with political slogans, but with good ideas.

Councilpersons José Alvarez and Mildred Cohen startled those assembled in the council chamber with their call for a revamping of the city's housing program. The proposal was startling in many ways. One, it was the first serious proposal to deal with the issue to be introduced in years. Second,

Alvarez is a Republican and Cohen is a Democrat. The two reached across the political divide to work together on this issue.

So just what is sweat equity? In a nutshell, it allows people in need of housing to take over abandoned buildings owned by the city. The new residents do not pay for the property, instead their equity is in the form of "sweat." In return for long-term leases, they must improve and rehabilitate the property.

The proposal is, of course, much more complicated than this brief description indicates. The proposal of Councilpersons Alvarez and Cohen needs to be fleshed out and its details examined. But it's a good start, one that the Tribune heartily endorses.

EDITORIAL

Thanks, Stranger

To the editor:
I would like to thank a nice man. Last Saturday my car stalled out in the middle of Franklin Boulevard. I couldn't get it started again. Traffic whizzed by, and horns blared, but nobody stopped to help. Finally, out of nowhere a young man with a pickup truck appeared. Before I knew it, he had the battery cables hooked up and the car started. He just as quickly packed up his gear and left, and wouldn't give me his name or take a reward. I would just like to say thank you, stranger.

—Joe Pirelli, Midvale

Get on the Ball

To the editor:
I have lived near the corner of Maple and Broadway for the last five years. Because of the opening of the Riverhead Shopping Mall, traffic has increased in the area tremendously. Because of all this traffic, we need traffic lights, especially at Maple and Broadway. Will the Traffic Safety Department wait until an accident happens before they get the message?

—Maggie Ortiz, Maplewood

Lifelong Learning
To the editor:

LETTERS TO THE EDITOR

Newspaper

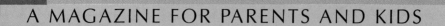

A MAGAZINE FOR PARENTS AND KIDS

FAMILY
T·I·E·S

Volume 20, Number 6   June 1993

DOCUMENTING YOUR
FAMILY HISTORY

Magazine – Cover Page

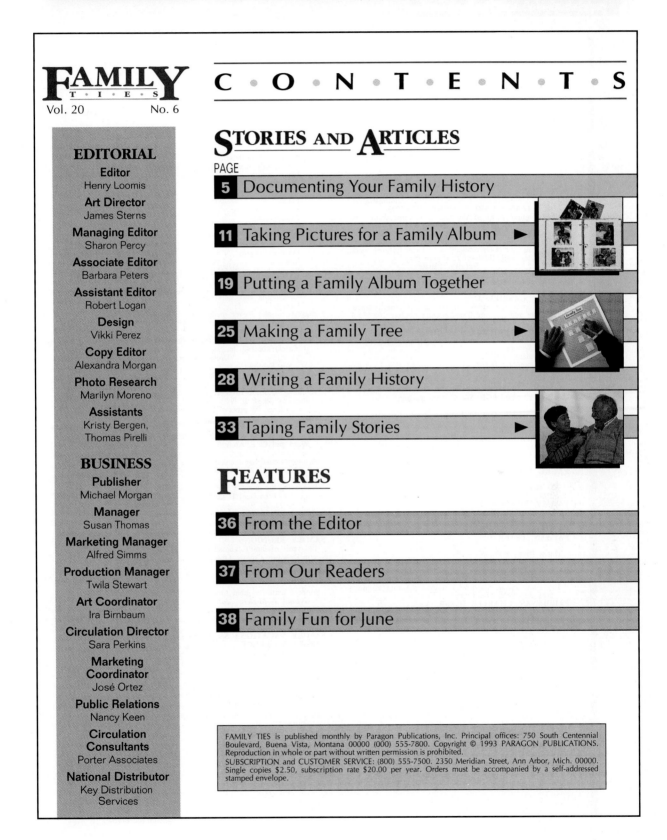

FAMILY TIES

Vol. 20   No. 6

EDITORIAL

Editor
Henry Loomis

Art Director
James Sterns

Managing Editor
Sharon Percy

Associate Editor
Barbara Peters

Assistant Editor
Robert Logan

Design
Vikki Perez

Copy Editor
Alexandra Morgan

Photo Research
Marilyn Moreno

Assistants
Kristy Bergen,
Thomas Pirelli

BUSINESS

Publisher
Michael Morgan

Manager
Susan Thomas

Marketing Manager
Alfred Simms

Production Manager
Twila Stewart

Art Coordinator
Ira Birnbaum

Circulation Director
Sara Perkins

Marketing Coordinator
José Ortez

Public Relations
Nancy Keen

Circulation Consultants
Porter Associates

National Distributor
Key Distribution Services

C·O·N·T·E·N·T·S

STORIES AND ARTICLES

FEATURES

FAMILY TIES is published monthly by Paragon Publications, Inc. Principal offices: 750 South Centennial Boulevard, Buena Vista, Montana 00000 (000) 555-7800. Copyright © 1993 PARAGON PUBLICATIONS. Reproduction in whole or part without written permission is prohibited.
SUBSCRIPTION and CUSTOMER SERVICE: (800) 555-7500. 2350 Meridian Street, Ann Arbor, Mich. 00000. Single copies $2.50, subscription rate $20.00 per year. Orders must be accompanied by a self-addressed stamped envelope.

Magazine – Contents Page

EYE MOVEMENTS *See* Eye—Movements
EYEGLASSES
　　　See also
　　　Sunglasses
EYES *See* Eye

F

F-16 AIRPLANES *See* Airplanes, Military
F-22 AIRPLANES *See* Stealth aircraft
FAA *See* United States. Federal Aviation Administration
FABRE, JEAN HENRI CASIMIR, 1823-1915
　　The conjugal meal of the mantis [excerpt from The insect world of J. Henri Fabre]; tr. by Alexander Teixeira. il *Harper's* 283:32-3 Jl '91
FACE
　　Faceprints [computer recognition of facial features; work of Peter Tal] *Discover* 12:16+ Je '91
　　　　　　Surgery, Plastic
　　See Surgery, Plastic
FACIAL CREAMS *See* Cosmetics
FACIAL MASKS *See* Cosmetics
FACKRE, GABRIEL J.
　　Reorientation and retrieval in systematic theology [adaptation of address] bibl *The Christian Century* 108:653-6 Je 26-Jl 3 '91
FACSIMILE TRANSMISSION *See* Fax machines
FACTORIES
　　　See also
　　　Airplane factories
　　　Automobile factories
　　　　　　Location
　　See Location in business and industry
FACTORY AND TRADE WASTE *See* Trade waste
FACULTY, COLLEGE *See* College teachers
FADS
　　From coonskin caps to Farrah's locks, TV has been America's no. 1 fad factory. G. A. Rosen. il *TV Guide* 39:18-20+ Jl 27-Ag 2 '91
FAGAN, PAUL J., AND OTHERS
　　The chemical nature of buckminsterfullerene (C_{60}) and the characterization of a platinum derivative. bibl f il *Science* 252:1160-1 My 24 '91
FAGET, MAXIME A.
　　　　　　about
　　100 stars of space. L. David. il por *Ad Astra* 3:36 Jl/Ag '91
FAHMY, MOHAMED NABIL
　　Obey the U.N. Charter. il *The Bulletin of the Atomic Scientists* 47:30-1 Je '91
FAILURES, BUSINESS *See* Business failures
FAIMAN, PETER
　　　　　　about
　　Dutch [film] Reviews
　　　People Weekly il 36:12-13 Jl 29 '91. R. Novak
FAIR, CURTIS
　　　　　　about
　　Teen ump ejects coach who returns shooting at him. pors *Jet* 80:50 Jl 15 '91
FAIRBANKS, CHARLES H., JR.
　　Russian roulette. il *Policy Review* 57:2-13 Summ '91
FAIRFAX (JOHN) LIMITED *See* John Fairfax Limited
FAIRS
　　　See also
　　　Book fairs
　　　　　　New York (State)
　　Big [B. Silverstein utilizes Big Chair to take novelty photographs at New York City street fairs] *The New Yorker* 67:22-3 Jl 22 '91
FAITH
　　The illusion of disillusionment [excerpt from address, April 1991] C. Lasch. il *Harper's* 283:19-22 Jl '91
FAITH CURE
　　　See also
　　　Miracles
　　A miracle of faith [C. Leland seeks a sign from the Virgin Mary in Medjugorje, Yugoslavia; cover story] T. Junod. il pors *Life* 14:28-36 Jl '91
　　Pray for peace [relaxation response theories of H. Benson] C. Perlmutter. il *Prevention (Emmaus, Pa.)* 43:42-5 Je '91
FAITH HEALING *See* Faith cure
FALCON (GAME)
　　Iraq attack: a first look at Falcon 3.0 [computer game] R. G. Sheffield. il *Compute* 13:108-10+ Je '91
FALK, RICHARD A.
　　[Patriotism] *The Nation* 253:86-8 Jl 15-22 '91

FALSE ARREST *See* Miscarriage of justice
FALSEHOOD *See* Lying
FAME
　　　See also
　　　Black celebrities
　　　Celebrities
FAMILY
　　　See also
　　　Aged—Family relationships
　　　Alzheimer's disease patients—Family relationships
　　　Black family
　　　Children
　　　Divorce
　　　Fathers
　　　Foster home care
　　　Grandparents
　　　Husbands
　　　Marriage
　　　Marriage counseling
　　　Married couples
　　　Mothers
　　　Parent-child relationship
　　　Parents
　　　Siblings
　　　Stepparents and stepchildren
　　　Uncles
　　Biggest mistake I ever made [need to make more time for family] H. S. Kushner. *Reader's Digest* 139:69-71 Jl '91
　　The importance of family togetherness. R. S. Shanok. il *Parents* 66:147 Je '91
　　　　　　United States
　　See Family
FAMILY BUSINESS *See* Family corporations
FAMILY CORPORATIONS
　　Avoiding "business divorce" court. S. Nelton. il *Nation's Business* 79:34 Jl '91
　　Have patience for process [family businesses] J. L. Ward and C. E. Aronoff. il *Nation's Business* 79:34-5 Jl '91
　　How to enhance communication [family firms] J. L. Ward and C. E. Aronoff. il *Nation's Business* 79:65-6 Je '91
　　A tougher challenge for family firms [managing diversity] S. Nelton. il *Nation's Business* 79:65 Je '91
FAMILY DAY CARE
　　Improving the quantity and quality of child care [Atlanta and San Francisco] T. Lurie. il *USA Today (Periodical)* 120:68-71 Jl '91
FAMILY FINANCE *See* Finance, Personal
FAMILY INCOME *See* Income
FAMILY RESORTS *See* Resorts
FAMILY REUNIONS
　　100 years of family [annual reunion of Thurston family in Delaware County, Ohio] L. A. Naylor. il map *Better Homes and Gardens* 69:69-70+ Jl '91
　　All in the family. C. Weston. il *Redbook* 177:96-7+ Jl '91
　　Modern maturity: great American family reunion [special section] il *Modern Maturity* 34:51+ Je/Jl '91
FAMILY SUPPORT GROUPS
　　Help for busy parents. B. Weissbourd. il *Parents* 66:141 Je '91
FAMILY VACATIONS *See* Vacations
FAMILY VIOLENCE
　　　See also
　　　Child abuse
FAMOUS MEN AND WOMEN *See* Celebrities
FANDRAY, DAYTON
　　Free advice from retired execs. il *New Choices for the Best Years* 31:72-3 Je '91
FANTASY COMPUTER GAMES *See* Computer games
FAO *See* Food and Agriculture Organization of the United Nations
FARABUNDO MARTI NATIONAL LIBERATION FRONT
　　Profiles (II) [R. G. Weakland, Archbishop of Milwaukee, at the NCCB meeting and in El Salvador] P. Wilkes. *The New Yorker* 67:46-60+ Jl 22 '91
FARES, AIRLINE *See* Airlines—Fares
FARM BUILDINGS
　　　See also
　　　Barns and stables
FARM CREDIT *See* Agricultural credit
FARM EQUIPMENT INDUSTRY *See* Agricultural equipment industry

SCHEDULES

Boston...New Haven...New York...Philadelphia...Washington

Train Name →					Night Owl	Metroliner Service	Metroliner Service	Carolinian	Express Metroliner Service	Metroliner Service
Train Number →					67	201	101	79	203	103
Days of Operation →					Daily	ExSaSu	ExSaSu	Daily	ExSaSu	ExSaSu
Train Service →					🛏 ⊗	Ⓡ ✪ ⊗ ☎	Ⓡ ✪ ⊗ ☎	⊗	Ⓡ ✪ ⊗ ☎	Ⓡ ✪ ⊗ ☎
	Mile	**Symbol**								
(Amtrak)										
Boston, MA–South Sta.　(ET)	0	♿	Dp	⊞	10 10P					
Boston, MA–Back Bay Sta.	1	♿		⊞Ⓡ	10 19P					
Route 128, MA	11				10 31P					
Providence, RI	44	♿		⊞	11 06P					
Kingston, RI (Newport)	71				11 30P					
Westerly, RI	87				11 45P					
Mystic, CT (Mystic Seaport)	96									
New London, CT	106	♿		⊞	12 08A					
Old Saybrook, CT	124				12 28A					
New Haven, CT	160	♿	Ar	⊞	1 08A					
			Dp	⊞	1 23A					
(Metro-North)										
Bridgeport, CT	173									
Stamford, CT	196	♿		⊞	2 13A					
New Rochelle, NY	212									
(Amtrak)										
New York, NY–Penn. Sta.	231		Ar	⊞	3 02A					
			Dp	⊞	3 45A		6 00A	6 20A	6 50A	7 00A
Newark, NJ (World Tr. Ctr. via PATH)	242	♿		⊞	4 02A	Ⓡ 6 13A	Ⓡ 6 34A			
Metropark, NJ	256	♿			4 21A	Ⓡ 6 26A		6 49A	Ⓡ 7 13A	Ⓡ 7 13A
New Brunswick, NJ	264						6 57A			Ⓡ 7 26A
Princeton Jct., NJ (Princeton)	280	♿					6 42A	7 11A		
Trenton, NJ	289	♿		⊞	4 48A		6 51A	7 20A		
North Philadelphia, PA	318							7 54A		
Philadelphia, PA–30th St. Sta.	322	♿		⊞	5 41A	6 50A	7 20A	8 14A	Nonstop Express	8 12A
Wilmington, DE	348	♿		⊞	6 06A	7 12A	7 42A	8 38A		8 33A
Newark, DE	360									
Aberdeen, MD	386					6 35A				
Baltimore, MD–Penn. Sta.	416	♿		⊞	7 10A	7 56A	8 25A	9 22A	8 53A	9 17A
BWI Airport Rail Sta., MD	427	♿			7 21A			9 34A		
New Carrollton, MD	448	♿			7 43A	D 8 24A		9 53A		
Washington, DC　(ET)	457	♿	Ar	⊞	7 55A	8 35A	9 03A	10 06A	9 25A	9 55A

Services On Board Northeast Corridor Trains
Services on board each train are noted with symbols and can be found in the "Train Service" area above.

Ⓡ　All reserved train. Reservations required.
✪　Club Service
⊗　Sandwiches, snack and beverage service.
⊞　Checked Baggage Service.
☎　Railfone public telephone service available on food service cars, Club cars and some coaches.

Services On Board The Night Owl/Executive Sleeper

Sleeping Cars – Reservations required. Roomettes and bedrooms. Complimentary continental breakfast, coffee, tea and juice, served 6:30 AM to arrival.
Boston–Washington – Sleeper available for occupancy at 9:30 PM at Boston South Station.
New York–Washington – Train 867–Sleeper available for occupancy in New York at 9:30 pm.
Cafe Car – Sandwiches, snacks and beverages.

Other Symbols and Reference Marks

A　Time symbol for A.M.
P　Time Symbol for P.M.
ET　Eastern Time
D　Stops only to discharge passengers.
R　Stops only to receive passengers.

🛏 Sleeping car service — Reservations required. Roomettes and bedrooms. First class service includes complimentary meals.
♿ The station and/or platform area is accessible to disabled and elderly passengers. Please call 1-800-USA-RAIL to make special arrangements when boarding/detraining assistance is required.

RAILROAD TIMETABLE

Emergencies

WHERE TO CALL

All Emergencies

911

 Fire
Incendio
555-1555

 Ambulance
Ambulancia
555-2211

 Police/Sheriff
Policía/Cherife
555-1512

 Poison control
Control antitóxico
555-1123
TDD***555-9565

The following numbers are for TDD*** users in areas where 911 is not available.

ALL EMERGENCIES	555-3131
FIRE	555-1535
POLICE	555-4077
AMBULANCE	555-9111
SHERIFF	555-8111

***TDD — Non-verbal Telecommunications Device for the Deaf

EMERGENCY NUMBERS

34 BAKER – BARNUM

Baker Alfred 771 Glade	555-5541
Baker Carol 206 E 8	555-2325
Baker Darrell 1221 Court Pl	555-6879
Baker Marcia 1713 Sunset	555-2920
Baker Roger 205 W 3	555-4450
BAKER SURPLUS STORES	
1580 Lenora Dr	**555-9000**
Baker Vera 512 Walker	555-2232
Balderson Jerome 400 W 7	555-3832
Baldwin A S 1861 College	555-7066
Baldwin Gayle 2007 Broadway	555-2453
Baldwin Keith 2007 Broadway	555-7854
Bales Fred 124 W 17	555-2806
Ball Alma 501 Howard	555-2017

BANBURY BALLOON SHOP	
214 N Quincy	**555-2920**
Bandell Lynette 517 Mission	555-4384
Bandt Charles 713 Court Pl	555-4841
Bane Nina 513 Sunset	555-2544
Bannister Karen 512 College	555-2405
Banzet Cecil & Viki 420 E 6	555-3683
Baptist Church Walker & 3	555-3048
Barber Charles 315 Howard	555-3197
BARBER DOUGLAS MD	
1225 Main	**555-2655**
Residence 801 College	555-3621
Barclay William 705 Grant	555-3978
Barnes Dennis 304 E 4	555-6169
Barnes Lila 540 Maple	555-5123

WHITE PAGES

A Aircraft   57

Aircraft Schools

ABC Aviation School	
Century Airport	555-9866
AIR FAIR FLYING CLUB	
County Airport	**555-5633**

ALOFT PILOT CENTER

Learn to fly with Us
Integrated Flight Training System

12830 Tower Rd **555-9150**

CLOUD NINE

Glider Rentals and Instruction

City Airport **555-6880**

EAGLE AVIATION
County Airport **555-8888**

Falcon Flights
Century Airport 555-2828

YELLOW PAGES

THESAURUS

Guide Words

Entry Word

Synonyms

Antonym

gigantic • goal

gigantic colossal, huge, giant, vast, immense, enormous, mammoth tiny

giggle laugh, chuckle, snicker

give present, hand over, provide, supply take

glacier iceberg

glad happy, pleased, cheerful, delighted, joyful, satisfied unhappy

glamorous beautiful, attractive, stunning, gorgeous, dazzling unattractive

glance look, glimpse

glare stare, scowl

glaring bright, shining, glowing, flashing, dazzling, blinding dim

gleaming bright, shining, glowing, beaming, sparkling dim

gli

BASIC THESAURUS, DICTIONARY FORM

Guide Words

motivation 441 **mouth**

Entry Word

Synonyms

Usage

Part of Speech

Antonyms

Cross-reference

arouse, impel, provoke, inspirit, hearten, influence, prompt, persuade, goad.

ant. discourage, deter, dissuade, dishearten.

motivation *n.* MOTIVE.

motive *n.* reason, cause, inducement, motivation, provocation, stimulus, spur, rationale, grounds, purpose, incentive, aim.

motley *adj.* assorted, varied, various, miscellaneous, mixed, divers, diverse, multifarious, manifold, variegated, differing, multiple, hetero-

mount[1] *v.* 1 ascend, rise, climb, go up, scale, clamber, shinny. 2 increase, grow, soar, escalate, pile up, accrue, accumulate, heighten, enlarge, amplify, gain, swell, multiply. —*n.* MOUNTING.

ant. *v.* 1 descend, go down. 2 decrease, lessen, lower, fall, diminish, decline, plunge.

mount[2] *n.* MOUNTAIN.

mountain *n.* 1 mount, eminence, height, alp, elevation, highland, peak, tor, cliff, butte, range. 2 mass

pile, abundance, accumulation, ocean, ton, slew, overflow, pile-up.

ant. valley, hollow, dale, glen.

mountainous *adj.* alpine, hilly, elevated, craggy, rocky, steep, high.

ant. flat, low, level, unbroken.

mountebank *n.* charlatan, quack, fraud, cheat, rascal, swindler, humbug, faker, bluffer, liar, phony (*Slang*), con man (*Slang*), grifter (*Slang*).

mounting *n.* frame, mount, support, backing, setting, framework, background, set, base, pedestal

self-effacing, resolved, withdrawn, inconspicuous, unobtrusive, unnoticed, dull, colorless, vapid.

ant. bold, brazen, self-assertive, noisy, jazzy.

mouth *n.* 1 maw, gullet, muzzle, lips, jaws, trap (Slang), kisser (Slang), yap (Slang). 2 opening, entrance, access, ingress, orifice, hole, aperture, inlet, top, vent, spout, gateway, entry, avenue, approach, adit. —*v.* declaim, speechify, orate, echo, repeat, spout, harangue, mince, rant, imitate, duplicate, mimic, reiterate.

STANDARD THESAURUS, DICTIONARY FORM

TIME LINES

Gnomon – before 1500 B.C.
Sundial – around 1500 B.C.

Clepsydra (water clock) – around 1400 B.C.

DEVELOPMENTS IN TIME-KEEPING DEVICES

Sundial

Hemicycle sundial – 300 B.C.

B.C.

A.D.

Pendulum clock

Sandglass

Digital clock

Mechanical clock (with weights, wheels, gears) – late 1200s

Sandglass (hourglass) – 1400s
Spring-driven clock – 2nd half 1400s
Portable clock (watch) – early 1500s

Pendulum clock – 1650

Chronometer (ship's clock) – 1750
Self-winding clock, alarm clock, wristwatch – late 1700s

Electric clock – 1840

Quartz crystal watch – 1920s
Electronic watch – 1960s

Digital clock, watch – 1970s

GLOS

This glossary can help you to pronounce and find out the meanings of words in this book that you may not know.

The words are listed in alphabetical order. Guide words tell you the first and last words on the page.

Each word is divided into syllables. The way to pronounce each word is given next. You can understand the pronunciation respelling by using the key to the right. A shorter key appears at the bottom of every other page.

When a word has more than one syllable, a dark accent mark (´) shows which syllable is stressed. In some words, a light accent mark (´) shows which syllable has a less heavy stress.

Information about the history, or etymology, of selected words is presented in brackets following the definition.

The following abbreviations are used in this glossary: *n.* noun, *v.* verb, *v.t.* transitive verb, *v.i.* intransitive verb, *adj.* adjective, *adv.* adverb, *prep.* preposition, *pl.* plural.

The entries in the glossary are based on entries in *The Macmillan/McGraw-Hill School Dictionary 2.*

a	at, bad	d	dear, soda, bad
ā	ape, pain, day, break	f	five, defend, leaf, off, cough, elephant
ä	father, car, heart		
âr	care, pair, bear, their, where	g	game, ago, fog, egg
e	end, pet, said, heaven, friend	h	hat, ahead
ē	equal, me, feet, team, piece, key	hw	white, whether, which
i	it, big, English, hymn	j	joke, enjoy, gem, page, edge
ī	ice, fine, lie, my	k	kite, bakery, seek, tack, cat
îr	ear, deer, here, pierce	l	lid, sailor, feel, ball, allow
o	odd, hot, watch	m	man, family, dream
ō	old, oat, toe, low	n	not, final, pan, knife
ô	coffee, all, taught, law, fought	ng	long, singer, pink
ôr	order, fork, horse, story, pour	p	pail, repair, soap, happy
oi	oil, toy	r	ride, parent, wear, more, marry
ou	out, now	s	sit, aside, pets, cent, pass
u	up, mud, love, double	sh	shoe, washer, fish, mission, nation
ū	use, mule, cue, feud, few	t	tag, pretend, fat, button, dressed
ü	rule, true, food	th	thin, panther, both
u̇	put, wood, should	t͟h	this, mother, smooth
ûr	burn, hurry, term, bird, word, courage	v	very, favor, wave
		w	wet, weather, reward
ə	about, taken, pencil, lemon, circus	y	yes, onion
b	bat, above, job	z	zoo, lazy, jazz, rose, dogs, houses
ch	chin, such, match	zh	vision, treasure, seizure

A

ac•a•dem•ic (ak´ə dem´ĭk) *adj.* **1.** relating to liberal or general education, especially to studies that prepare a student for college. **2.** of or relating to an academy, school, or college.

ad•a•mant (ad´ə mənt, ad´ə mant´) *adj.* not changing position at all; totally unyielding. [From the Old French word *adamant,* meaning "hardest metal," going back to the Greek word *adamas,* with the same meaning, from *a-,* "not," and *daman,* "to subdue."]

adz (adz) *also,* **adze.** *n.* a tool resembling an ax, used for trimming and shaping timber.

al•a•bas•ter (al´ə bas´tər) *n.* a smooth, whitish stone used especially in sculpture.

alabaster

a•miss (ə mis´) *adj.* not as it should be; out of order; wrong.

an•no Dom•i•ni (an´ō dom´ə nī´, dom´ə nē´)

An•ti•gua (an tē´gə, an tē´gwə)

a•se•si•no (ä´sā sē´nō) Spanish for "assassin" or "murderer."

a•sy•lum (ə sī´ləm) *n.* **1.** a place that provides care for helpless people, such as orphans or the insane. **2.** shelter or protection, such as that sought by a fugitive. Some countries grant political asylum to political fugitives from other countries.

ax•is (ak´sis) *n., pl.* **ax•es** (ak´sēz). a real or imaginary straight line around which an object or body, such as the earth, rotates or seems to rotate.

B

Ba•bel (bā´bəl, bab´əl) *n.* **1.** in the Old Testament, another name for the city of Babylon, in which a tower was begun by the descendants of Noah in order to reach heaven. God kept them from finishing the tower by changing their language into many different languages so that they could not understand each other. **2.** *also,* **babel.** a confused mixture of many voices or languages.

Bac Thong (bä tông)

ba•o•bab (bā´ō bab´) *n.* a tree found mostly in tropical Africa, having a broad trunk, thick, spreading branches, and a fruit resembling a gourd.

bar•bar•ic (bär bar´ik) *adj.* **1.** unciv-ilized or savage. **2.** crude or wild in style or manner.

bar mitz•vah (bär mits´və) **1.** a cere-mony held for a Jewish boy when he becomes thirteen, marking his assumption of religious responsibili-ties. [From the Hebrew phrase *bar mitzvah*, meaning "son of the com-mandment," from the words *bar*, "son" + *mitzvah*, "law, command-ment."]

blight (blīt) *n.* **1.** something that dam-ages, ruins, or destroys. **2.** any of several diseases that wither or kill plants.

bol•lard (bol´ərd) *n.* a strong, short, thick metal support on a ship and on a dock to which ropes are attached for securing the ship to the dock.

bom•bard (bom bärd´) *v.t.* **1.** to keep on attacking vigorously. **2.** to attack with artillery or bombs.

bon•jour (bōn zhür´) French for "good morning" or "good day."

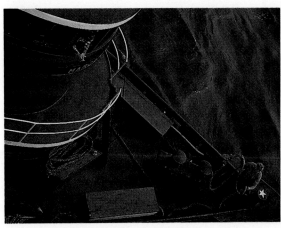
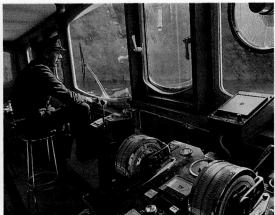

bridge[1]

bat•tle•ment (bat´əl mənt) *n.* **1.** a low wall formerly built along the top of a fort or tower, having a series of open-ings through which soldiers could shoot at the enemy. **2.** a similar wall built for decoration.

bel•lig•er•ent (bə lij´ər ənt) *adj.* eager or willing to fight; hostile.

ber•serk (bər sûrk´, bər zûrk´) *adv.* into a wild or violent rage. —*adj.* in a wild or violent rage. [From the Old Norse word *berserkr*, meaning "a frenzied Scandinavian warrior clothed in bearskin," from *ber*, "bear" + *serkr*, "coat." According to legend, when the warrior was in a berserk state, he was invulnerable.]

bla•tant (blā´tənt) *adj.* impossible to overlook; conspicuous; very obvious.

bridge[1] (brij) *n.* **1.** a raised structure on a deck of a ship, from which the ship is navigated and steered. **2.a.** any structure built over a river, railroad track, highway, or other obstacle or gap to allow passage for people or vehicles. **b.** something that provides a connection between two places, processes, eras, or the like. [From the Old English word *brycg*, meaning "bridge."]

at; āpe; fär; câre; end; mē; it; īce; pîerce; hot; ōld; sông; fôrk; oil; out; up; ūse; rüle; pull; tûrn; chin; sing; shop; thin; this; hw in white; zh in treasure. The symbol ə stands for the unstressed vowel sound in about, taken, pencil, lemon, and circus.

bridge² (brij) *n.* a card game played by four players in teams of two. [From the earlier word *biritch,* meaning this game, of uncertain origin.]

Bud•dha (bŭd´ə, bü´də)

bung (bung) *n.* a stopper for closing the hole in a barrel or cask.

bush (bŭsh) *n.* **1.** wild, uncultivated, or unsettled land covered with shrubby growth. **2.** a woody plant smaller than a tree and having many stems that branch at or near the ground; shrub.

ca•fé (ka fā´) *also,* **ca•fe.** *n.* **1.** café. French and Spanish for "coffee." **2.** a coffeehouse or restaurant.

Cai•ro (kī´rō) the capital of Egypt, in the northeastern part of the country. It is the largest city in Africa.

cal•lig•ra•phy (kə lig´rə fē) *n.* **1.** beautiful or elegant handwriting. **2.** handwriting; penmanship.

can•o•py (kan´ə pē) *n.* an overhanging shelter or covering.

Cape Verde Islands (kāp vûrd ī´ləndz)

cap•stan (kap´stən) *n.* a device with an upright spindle that is turned by hand or by motor to wind up a rope or cable, as in hoisting an anchor.

cat•e•chism (kat´ĭ kiz´əm) *n.* **1.** a small book or manual in which the principles of a religion are set forth in the form of questions and answers. **2.** a similar book or manual about any subject.

cay (kā, kē) *n.* a small island of sand or coral.

chasm (kaz´əm) *n.* **1.** a deep, yawning crack or gap in the earth's surface; gorge. **2.** a great difference of feelings, beliefs, opinions, or the like.

Chi•chén It•zá (chē´chən ēt´sə, chē-chen´ ēt sä´)

cir•cuit (sûr´kit) *n.* **1.** a regular journey from one place to another, as by a judge or preacher. **2.** the district traveled through in such a journey, especially the district assigned to a judge for holding court. **3.** the act of going around; a circular course; revolution.

clock•wise (klok´wīz´) *adv., adj.* in the direction in which the hands of a clock move.

canopy

col (käl) *n.* **1.** a pass in a mountain range. **2.** a saddle-shaped depression in the crest of a ridge.

com•mon e•ra (kom´ən îr´ə, er´ə) *n.* the period of time since the birth of Christ; technically, the period of time from the year A.D. 1 to the present.

con•fi•den•tial•ly (kon´fi den´shə lē) *adv.* in a secret or private way.

con•quis•ta•dor (kon kēs´tə dôr´, kon-kwis´tə dôr´) *n., pl.* **con•quis•ta•dors** or **con•quis•ta•do•res** (kon kēs´tə-dôr´ās, kon kēs´tə dôr´ēz). a Spanish conqueror in Mexico and Peru during the sixteenth century. [From the Spanish word *conquistador,* from *conquistar,* meaning "to conquer," going back to the Latin word *conquirere,* "to seek for, collect," from the prefix *com-,* "with, together" + *quaerere,* "to ask, seek."]

conquistador

con•tempt (kən tempt´) *n.* a feeling that a person or thing is low, mean, or worthless; scorn; disdain.

Co•pen•ha•gen (kō´pən hā´gən) the capital of Denmark.

Co•per•ni•cus, Nicolaus (kə pûr´ni-kəs, nik´ə lā´əs)

cor•o•nar•y (kôr´ə ner´ē, kor´ə ner´ē) *n. Slang.* heart attack. —*adj.* of or relating to either of two arteries that branch from the aorta and supply blood to the muscular tissue of the heart.

cor•o•net (kôr´ə net´, kor´ə net´) *n.* **1.** the lower part of a horse's foot just above the hoof, where the hoof terminates in skin. **2.** a small crown worn by a noble.

cre•vasse (kri vas´) *n.* a deep crack or crevice, especially in a glacier.

Cris•tó•bal (kris tō´bäl)

Cu•ra•çao (kyür´ə sō´, kür´ə sou´)

D

Dane (dān) *n.* a person who was born in or is a citizen of Denmark.

de•ceased (di sēst´) *n.* **the deceased.** dead person or persons.

de•feat•ist (di fē´tist) *adj.* characteristic of a person who expects defeat or who accepts it too readily or too soon.

de•fect (*v.,* di fekt´; *n.,* dē´fekt, di-fekt´) *v.i.* to desert a group, country, or cause, especially to go to another that is opposed to it. —*n.* an imperfection, flaw, or weakness; fault; blemish.

at; āpe; fär; câre; end; mē; it; īce; pîerce; hot; ōld; sông; fôrk; oil; out; up; ūse; rüle; pull; tûrn; chin; sing; shop; thin; this; hw in white; zh in treasure. The symbol ə stands for the unstressed vowel sound in about, taken, pencil, lemon, and circus.

del•uge (del´ūj, del´ūzh) *n.* **1.** a heavy rain; downpour. **2.** a great flood.

Den•mark (den´märk) a country in northern Europe, between the North and Baltic seas. Capital, Copenhagen.

des•o•late (des´ə lit) *adj.* **1.** lacking inhabitants; deserted. **2.** left alone; without companionship; lonely. **3.** laid waste; devastated. **4.** miserable; cheerless; dreary.

Die•go (dyā´gō)

Din•e (din ā´)

din•gy (din´jē) *adj.* having a dirty, dull, or dreary appearance; not bright and fresh.

dis•ar•ray (dis´ə rā´) *n.* a condition of disorder or confusion; lack of orderly arrangement.

dis•own (dis ōn´) *v.t.* to refuse to recognize as one's own; deny responsibility for or connection with; reject.

dis•re•pute (dis´ri pūt´) *n.* lack or loss of reputation or regard; ill repute; discredit; disfavor.

dis•tend (di stend´) *v.t.* to enlarge by pressure from within; stretch out; swell; expand.

di•vine (di vīn´) *v.t.* **1.** to guess. **2.** to foretell (the future or the unknown) by interpreting signs or omens or by magic. —*adj.* **1.** of or relating to God or a god. **2.** excellent or extremely talented. **3.** *Informal.* extremely delightful.

dou•ble-dutch (dub´əl duch´) *n.* a form of the game of jump rope in which two persons holding the respective ends of two long jump ropes swing them at the same time, usually in an inward direction, so that the ropes are going in opposite directions for one or two others to jump over.

double-dutch

drudg•er•y (druj´ə rē) *n.* wearying, boring, or menial labor.

du•bi•ous (dü´bē əs, dū´bē əs) *adj.* **1.** feeling or showing doubt or uncertainty; hesitant; skeptical. **2.** of questionable character; suspect. **3.** causing doubt; not clear.

Du•ha•mel, Henri-Louis (dü´ä mel´, än rē´ lwē)

dy•nas•ty (dī´nə stē) *n.* **1.** a line of rulers who belong to the same family. **2.** the period of time during which a dynasty rules.

east•ern sea•board (ēs´tərn sē´bôrd´) *n.* land near or bordering on the Atlantic Ocean; eastern coast.

eaves•drop•ping (ēvz´drop´ing) *n.* the act of listening to the private conversation of others without their knowing it.

eb•on•y (eb´ə nē) *n.* a hard, black wood, used especially for piano keys, knife handles, and cabinets.

ebony

e•clipse (i klips´) *n.* a partial or total darkening or hiding of the sun, the moon, or a planet. In a solar eclipse, the moon passes between the sun and the earth. In a lunar eclipse, the earth moves between the sun and the moon.

eclipse

el che•que (el chā´kā) Spanish for "the check."

El•is•cue (el´is kū)

E•me•ke (e me´ke)

en•trails (en´trālz, en´trəlz) *pl. n.* the inner part of a human being or animal, especially the intestines.

e•on (ē´ən, ē´on) *also,* **ae•on.** *n.* a very long, indefinite period of time.

ep•i•dem•ic (ep´i dem´ik) *n.* **1.** the rapid spread or sudden, widespread appearance of anything. **2.** the rapid spread or sudden, widespread appearance of disease among many people at the same time.

ep•och (ep´ək, ep´ok, ē´pok) *n.* a period of time marked by some extraordinary characteristic, development, or course of events.

at; āpe; fär; câre; end; mē; it; īce; pîerce; hot; ōld; sông; fôrk; oil; out; up; ūse; rüle; pùll; tûrn; **ch**in; sin**g**; **sh**op; **th**in; **th**is; **hw** in **wh**ite; **zh** in treasure. The symbol ə stands for the unstressed vowel sound in **a**bout, tak**e**n, penc**i**l, lem**o**n, and circ**u**s.

575

e•ra (îr´ə, er´ə) *n.* **1.** a period of time measured from or beginning with a particular event. **2.** a period of time marked by certain events, conditions, ideas, persons, or things.

E•ron•ni (e ron´nē)

e•se (ā´sā) Spanish for "that" or "that one."

E•thi•o•pi•a (ē´thē ō´pē ə)

Eu•phra•tes (ū frā´tēz)

ex•pert•ise (ek´spər tēz´) *n.* special skill or knowledge.

fa•cil•i•ty (fə sil´i tē) *n.* **1.** *often,* **facilities.** something, as a building or piece of equipment, that provides a convenience or serves a particular purpose. **2.** ease of doing; freedom from difficulty. **3.** skill or ability; aptitude.

fen (fen) *n.* a marshy lowland; swamp; bog.

fer•tile (fûr´təl) *adj.* **1.** producing or able to produce crops or vegetation abundantly. **2.** able to produce young, eggs, seeds, pollen, or the like.

fine-comb (fīn´kōm´) *v.t.* to search thoroughly for subtle and small details or clues.

fore•most (fôr´mōst´) *adj.* first in position, rank, or importance.

for•feit (fôr´fit) *v.t.* to lose as a penalty for some fault, mistake, or misdeed.

foun•der[1] (foun´dər) *v.i.* **1.** to fill with water and sink. **2.** to fall down. **3.** to fail completely. **4.** to stumble and become lame and disabled. —*v.t.* to cause to founder. [From the Old French word *fondrer,* meaning "to sink," from the word *fond,* "bottom," from the Latin word *fundus,* "bottom, base."]

foun•der[2] (foun´dər) *n.* a person who founds, starts, or sets up something.

frac•tious (frak´shəs) *adj.* **1.** bad-tempered or quarrelsome; cranky. **2.** difficult to control; unruly.

frig•id (frij´id) *adj.* **1.** very cold. **2.** lacking warmth of feeling or enthusiasm; unfriendly or indifferent.

fen

fry bread (frī bred) *n.* a round, deep-fried unleavened bread traditionally made by many Native American tribes.

fur•tive•ly (fûr´tiv lē) *adv.* in a manner characterized by shiftiness, stealth, slyness, or secrecy.

G

ga•ble (gā´bəl) *n.* **1.** the section of an outside wall surface, usually triangular, between the sides of a sloped roof. **2.** any architectural feature having the form of a gable, as over a door or window.

geld•ing (gel´ding) *n.* a castrated animal, especially a castrated horse.

ge•o•graph•ic pole (jē´ə graf´ik pōl) *n.* either end of a planet's axis; on earth, the North Pole or South Pole.

gim•let (gim´ lit) *n.* a tool used to create holes. A gimlet has a wooden handle that fits into the palm of the hand and a spiraling shaft with a sharp, pointed tip.

Gi•o•van•ni, Nikki (jē´ō vä´nē, nik´ē) (1943–) a well-known female African-American poet.

glow•er (glou´ər) *v.i.* to look at angrily or threateningly; scowl. —*n.* an angry or threatening stare.

Greek Or•tho•dox (grēk ôr´thə doks´) *adj.* belonging or relating to the branch of the Eastern Orthodox Church that constitutes the national church of Greece.

Gre•go•ri•an (gri gôr´ē ən)

Gren•a•dines (gren´ə dēnz´)

grin•go (gring´gō) *n.* in Latin America, a foreigner, usually a North American. It is usually an insulting term.

Guyen Thi Lam (win tē läm)

H

Ham•mu•ra•bi (hä´mủ rä´bē)

hap•py beads (hap´ē bēdz) *n.* multicolored beads worn by the so-called flower children of the 1960s as a way of expressing a commitment to a world of love and joy.

happy beads

at; āpe; fär; câre; end; mē; it; īce; pîerce; hot; ōld; sông; fôrk; oil; out; up; ūse; rüle; pủll; tûrn; chin; sing; shop; thin; this; hw in white; zh in treasure. The symbol ə stands for the unstressed vowel sound in about, taken, pencil, lemon, and circus.

He•brew (hē´brü) *n.* **1.** a member of one of the Jewish tribes of ancient times; Israelite. **2.** a Semitic language originally spoken by the ancient Jews. It is the religious language of Judaism. A modern form of Hebrew is the official language of Israel. —*adj.* another word for **Hebraic,** of or relating to the Hebrews, their language, or their culture.

heir (âr) *n.* a person who inherits or is entitled to inherit money, property, or the like after the death of the owner.

hin•der (hin´dər) *v.t.* to delay or make difficult the movement or progress of; hold back. [From the Old English word *hindrian,* meaning "to obstruct, keep back."]

Ho•hen•lin•den (hō´ən lin´dən)

I

ill at ease (il ət ēz) *adj.* nervous and uncomfortable.

il•leg•i•ble (i lej´ə bəl) *adj.* difficult or impossible to read; not legible.

il•le•git•i•mate (il´i jit´ə mit) *adj.* **1.** born to parents who are not married to each other. **2.** not authorized; not lawful.

im•pe•ri•ous (im pîr´ē əs) *adj.* **1.** haughty or arrogant; domineering; overbearing. **2.** necessary; urgent.

im•pro•vised (im´prə vīzd´) *adj.* **1.** made from whatever materials are on hand. **2.** made up and performed without preparation or previous thought.

in•cul•cate (in kul´kāt) *v.t.* to fix firmly in the mind or memory by repeated teaching or example.

in•dulge (in dulj´) *v.t.* to yield to the whims or wishes of; give in to.

in•fer•no (in fûr´nō) *n.* **1.** any place resembling hell, especially in being hot or fiery. **2.** hell. **3.** a large, intense, or particularly destructive fire. [From the Italian word *inferno,* meaning "hell," going back to the Latin word *infernus,* "lying beneath" or "of the underworld."]

in•gen•ious (in jēn´yəs) *adj.* **1.** made with or showing cleverness, originality, or imagination. **2.** having creative ability; imaginative; inventive.

in•ter•cept (in´tər sept´) *v.t.* **1.** to seize or stop on the way. **2.** to stop the course or progress of; check. **3.** *Mathematics.* to mark off or bound some part of a line, plane, or surface.

intercept

i•ron•ic (ī ron´ik) *adj.* of, relating to, or characterized by an event or outcome of events opposite to what was, or might naturally have been, expected.

J

Jed•e•di•ah (jed ə dī´ə)

joint cus•to•dy (joint kus´tə dē) *n.* caretaking or guardianship of a child shared equally by parents after a divorce or during a separation.

joy•stick (joi´stik´) *n.* the flight control lever of an aircraft or other vehicle.

Ju•da•ism (jü´dē iz´əm, jü´dā iz´əm, jü´də iz´əm) *n.* the religion of the Jews, based chiefly on a belief in one God and the teachings of the Old Testament and the Talmud, a collection of Jewish law.

K

Kien (kin)

kin•dred (kin´drid) *adj.* **1.** like; similar. **2.** related by history or origin; having common ancestors.

L

lan•gos•ta (läng gōs´tə) *n.* a type of spiny lobster, a kind of shellfish. [From the Old French *langosta*, from the Latin variant *locusta*, meaning "lobster."]

langosta

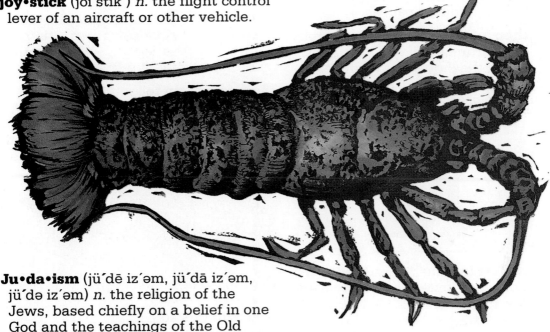

le ba•teau (lə bä tō´) French for "the boat."

Le ba•teau est sur l'eau. (lə bä tō´ ä sûr lō) French for "The boat is on the water."

at; āpe; fär; câre; end; mē; it; īce; pîerce; hot; ōld; sông; fôrk; oil; out; up; ūse; rüle; púll; tûrn; chin; sing; shop; thin; this; hw in white; zh in treasure. The symbol ə stands for the unstressed vowel sound in about, taken, pencil, lemon, and circus.

lee (lē) *adj.* sheltered from the wind. —*n.* **1.** a shelter or protection. **2.** the side or part, especially of a ship, sheltered or turned away from the wind.

Leth•ar•gar•i•ans (leth´ər jâr´ē ənz)

loam (lōm) *n.* soil that is a mixture of clay, sand, and silt, often containing decaying leaves and plants.

Loc (lô)

loi•ter (loi´tər) *v.t.* to waste (time); dawdle. —*v.i.* **1.** to linger idly or aimlessly about a place. **2.** to move slowly or with frequent pauses.

Lu•ther•an (lü´thər ən) *adj.* of or relating to Martin Luther, his doctrines, or one of the Protestant churches named after him. —*n.* a member of a Lutheran church.

M

ma•chet•e (mə shet´ē, mə chet´ē) *n.* a broad, heavy knife used as a tool and weapon.

machete

Macht (makt)

mag•ne•tic pole (mag net´ik pōl) *n.* either of two points on a planet's surface that are the poles of the magnetic field, and toward which a compass needle points.

Mai (mī)

maize (māz) *n.* a grain that grows in rows on the large ears of a tall, coarse grass, used for food. Also, **corn.**

maize

Mai•zon (mā sō´)

Ma•lay•sia (mə lā´zhə) a country in southeastern Asia.

ma•roon¹ (mə rün´) *n.* a dark brownish-red color. —*adj.* having the color maroon. [From the French word *marron,* meaning "a kind of chestnut."]

ma•roon² (mə rün´) *v.t.* **1.** to put ashore and leave on a desolate island or coast. **2.** to leave helpless and alone. [From the Spanish word *cimarrón,* meaning "wild." The word *cimarrón* later came to mean "runaway slave," especially one who escaped to an island or some other remote place.]

mar•tyr (mär´tər) *n.* **1.** a person who willingly suffers greatly or sacrifices much. **2.** a person who suffers death rather than give up his or her religious faith.

mon•soon (mon sün´) *n.* a seasonal wind of the Indian Ocean and southern Asia, which blows from the southwest toward the land in summer and from the northeast toward the ocean in winter.

monsoon

Med•i•ter•ra•ne•an Sea (med´i tə-rā´nē ən sē)

mel•o•dra•ma (mel´ə drä´ mə, mel´ə-dram´ə) *n.* a dramatic performance or play characterized by exaggerated emotions, sensational or overly sentimental incidents, and usually a happy ending.

Men•dez, Paulo (men´dez, pou´lō)

Mes•o•po•ta•mi•a (mes´ə pə tā´mē ə)

Mo•bile (mō bēl´, mō´bēl) a port city in southwestern Alabama.

Mon•go (mong´gō)

mus•lin (muz´lin) *n.* any of a large group of cotton fabrics, varying from lightweight, sheer materials used for such items as blouses to heavyweight materials used for sheets and pillowcases.

at; āpe; fär; câre; end; mē; it; īce; pîerce; hot; ōld; sông; fôrk; oil; out; up; ūse; rüle; pull; tûrn; chin; sing; shop; thin; this; hw in white; zh in treasure. The symbol ə stands for the unstressed vowel sound in about, taken, pencil, lemon, and circus.

N

Na•po•le•on (nə pō´lē ən)

Na•zi (nät´sē, nat´sē) *n.* **1.** a member or follower of the fascist political party that controlled Germany under the leadership of Adolf Hitler from 1933 to 1945. **2.** a person holding views similar to those of the Nazis.

N•du•mu (ən dü´mü)

New Or•le•ans (nü ôr´lē ənz, ôr´lənz, ôr lēnz´) a city in southeastern Louisiana, a port on the Mississippi River.

New Orleans

niche (nich) *n.* **1.** a decorative, usually arch-shaped recess or hollow in a wall, often used as a setting for statues or other ornaments, such as vases or glassware. **2.** a place, position, or situation for which a person is especially suited.

Ni•zam (ni zäm´)

no•mad•ic (nō mad´ik) *adj.* of or relating to nomads, a group or tribe that has no permanent home; wandering.

No•va Sco•tia (nō´və skō´shə) a province of Canada, in the southeastern part of the country.

nov•el•ty (nov´əl tē) *n.* **1.** the quality of being new; newness. **2.** something that is new or unusual, such as a thing or an event. **3. novelties.** small, inexpensive, manufactured articles, such as ornaments or toys.

O

oc•cu•pa•tion (ok´yə pā´shən) *n.* **1.** the act or process of seizing and maintaining control of enemy territory by military force. **2.** the work that a person does to earn a living; profession; trade.

o•men (ō´mən) *n.* a sign or event that is supposed to foretell good or bad luck.

ot•to•man (ot´ə mən) *n.* a low, box-like, padded seat or footstool.

o•ver•wrought (ō´vər rôt´) *adj.* **1.** worked up to a state of excessive excitement or nervousness. **2.** too elaborate or fancy; overdone.

P

pa-hay-o•kee (pä´ā ō´kē) a Seminole term for the Florida Everglades.

pains•tak•ing•ly (pānz´tā´king lē) *adv.* in a manner characterized by close, careful work or attention.

Pan•a•ma (pan´ə mä´)

pa•pas (pä´päs) Spanish for "potatoes."

pa•py•rus (pə pī´rəs) *n., pl.* **pa•py•ri** (pə pī´rī, pə pī´rē). **1.** a writing material made from the stems of a plant (see *def. 2*), used by the ancient Egyptians and other peoples. **2.** a plant found growing in swamps and along rivers in northern Africa and southern Europe, having dark green, hollow stalks.

papyrus

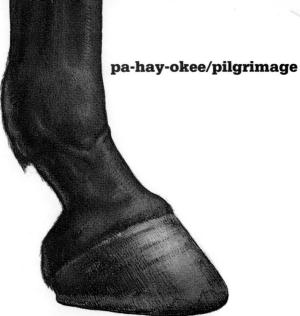
pastern

pas•tern (pas´tərn) *n.* the part of a horse's foot just above the hoof.

per•se•cute (pûr´si kūt´) *v.t.* **1.** to subject continually to cruel, harmful, or unjust treatment. **2.** to harass, vex, or annoy constantly.

Per•sian Gulf (pûr´zhən gulf) a shallow body of water between Iran and Arabia.

pert (pûrt) *adj.* **1.** showing disrespect in speech or behavior; saucy; impudent. **2.** spirited; lively. **3.** trim and smart-looking.

pe•tang (pə tang´) Yankton Sioux for "otter."

Phan Tri (fän trē)

phar•aoh (fâr´ō) *n.* a king of ancient Egypt.

Phoe•nix (fē´niks) the capital and largest city of Arizona, in the south-central part of the state.

pil•grim•age (pil´grə mij) *n.* **1.** any long journey. **2.** a journey to a sacred or revered place.

---

at; āpe; fär; câre; end; mē; it; īce; pîerce; hot; ōld; sông; fôrk; oil; out; up; ūse; rüle; pu̇ll; tûrn; chin; sing; shop; thin; <u>th</u>is; hw in white; zh in treasure. The symbol ə stands for the unstressed vowel sound in about, taken, pencil, lemon, and circus.

pinion¹

pin•ion¹ (pin´yən) *n.* a bird's wing, especially the outermost segment. —*v.t.* to prevent (a bird) from flying by clipping or binding the pinions. [From the Old French word *pignon,* meaning "a bird's wing," going back to the Latin word *penna,* "feather."]

pin•ion² (pin´yən) *n.* a small wheel with cogs that lock into the cogs of a larger wheel or rack. [From the French word *pignon,* with the same meaning, from the Old French word *peigne,* "a comb," from the Latin word *pecten,* "a comb, rake."]

pocked (pokt) *adj.* marked with holes or cavities.

po•rous (pôr´əs) *adj.* having or full of very small openings.

port•side (pôrt´sīd´) *adj.* of, relating to, or located on the left side of a boat or ship. Also, **larboard.**

po•tent (pō´tənt) *adj.* having force, effectiveness, strength, or power.

pre•par•a•to•ry school (pri par´ə-tôr´ē skül, prep´ər ə tôr´ē) *n.* a school, especially one that is private, that prepares students for college. Also, **prep school.**

Prince Ed•ward Is•land (prins ed´-wərd i´lənd) the smallest province of Canada, consisting of an island in the Gulf of St. Lawrence.

pri•or•i•ty (prī ôr´i tē, prī or´i tē) *n.* **1.** the condition of coming before another or others, as in order of importance. **2.** the right to have superior or special treatment. **3.** a matter deserving or receiving special emphasis or attention.

pro•cras•ti•nat•ing (prō kras´tə nā´-ting) *n.* putting off doing something until a future time, especially when this is done as a habit.

prone (prōn) *adj.* **1.** lying with the face or front downward. **2.** naturally inclined; disposed.

Pro•vi•den•cia (prō´vē den´syä)

prov•i•den•tial (prov´i den´shəl) *adj.* coming about as if through divine guidance: fortunate.

punc•tu•al (pungk´chü əl) *adj.* arriving at the correct time; on time; prompt.

qualm (kwäm) *n.* **1.** a twinge of conscience. **2.** a sudden feeling of uneasiness or doubt; misgiving.

Qui•to Sue•ño (kē´tō swā´nyō)

quiz•zi•cal•ly (kwiz´i kə lē, kwiz´i klē) *adv.* in a manner characterized by questioning, uncertainty, or puzzlement.

Ra•dosh (rā´dosh)

ram•bling (ram´bling) *adj.* **1.** spread out irregularly or unsystematically. **2.** roaming aimlessly. **3.** wandering from one subject to another.

ra•za-style (rä´sä stīl´) *adv.* in a way characteristic of Hispanic Americans.

res•in (rez´in) *n.* any of various yellow or brown sticky substances that come from certain trees, such as pine and balsam.

re•tort (ri tôrt´) *v.i.* to make a reply, especially in a quick, witty, or sharp manner. —*n.* a quick, witty, or sharp reply. [From the Latin word *retortus*, past participle of *retorquēre*, meaning "to twist back, return," from the Latin prefix *re-*, "back, again" + *torquēre*, "to twist."]

Rosetta Stone

Ro•set•ta Stone (rō zet´ə stōn) *n.* a basalt stone found near Rosetta, Egypt, in 1799. The writing on the stone was of three kinds (Greek, Egyptian hieroglyphics, and demotic, a simpler and more popular form of Egyptian writing) and therefore became the key to decoding Egyptian hieroglyphics.

Ruy•ter Kade (rī´tər kād)

---

at; āpe; fär; câre; end; mē; it; īce; pîerce; hot; ōld; sông; fôrk; oil; out; up; ūse; rüle; pull; tûrn; chin; sing; shop; thin; this; hw in white; zh in treasure. The symbol ə stands for the unstressed vowel sound in about, taken, pencil, lemon, and circus.

S

Sab•bath (sab´əth) *n.* the day of the week for rest and religious worship. Sunday is the Sabbath for most Christians; Saturday is the Sabbath for Jews and members of certain Christian churches; Friday is the Sabbath for Muslims.

sa•lu•do de va•to (sä lü´thō dä bä´tō) Spanish for "a kind of greeting."

San An•drés (sän än dres´)

Sat•urn (sat´ərn) the second largest planet of the solar system and sixth in order of distance from the sun.

Schar•loo (skär´lü)

Schot•te•gat (sko´tē got´)

sea grape (sē grāp) *n.* a tropical tree whose clusters of edible purple berries resemble grape clusters, or the berry of this tree.

Sem•i•nole (sem´ə nōl´) *n., pl.* **Sem•i•nole** or **Sem•i•noles.** a member of a group of Native Americans, originally living in Florida and now mostly in Oklahoma.

Se•rra•ni•lla Banks (se´rä nē´yä bangks)

shard (shärd) *n.* a fragment of some brittle material, as of glass or pottery.

sheep•dog moons (shēp´dôg´ münz) *n.* natural satellites discovered near Saturn and possibly Uranus by the *Voyager 2* probe. These particular moons are near rings surrounding those planets and, by their gravity, may play a role in keeping the rings in formation around the planets.

sheer[1] (shîr) *adj.* **1.** utter; downright. **2.** straight up or straight down; steep. **3.** very thin and fine; nearly transparent. [From the Middle English word *shire,* meaning "bright, fair" or "pure," from the Old English word *scir,* "clear, bright."]

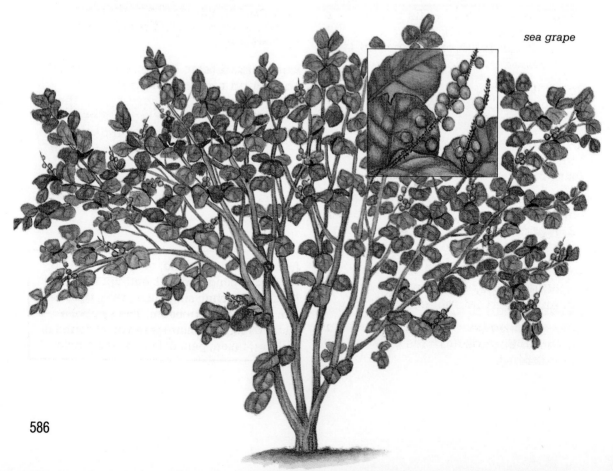

sea grape

sheer²

sheer² (shîr) *v.i.* to turn from a course; swerve. [Probably from the Middle English word *sheren,* meaning "to cut, divide" or "to swerve," from the Old English word *sceran,* "to cut, shear."]

shrew•ish (shrü´ish) *adj.* bad-tempered.

so•phis•ti•cat•ed (sə fis´ti kā´tid) *adj.* **1.** developed to a highly complex level. **2.** having worldly knowledge and experience; not naive.

spot•ty (spot´ē) *adj.* **1.** not regular or consistent. **2.** marked or covered with spots; spotted.

star•board (stär´bərd) *adj.* of, relating to, or on the right side of a boat or ship.

Star of Da•vid (stär əv dā´vid) *n.* a six-pointed star, a symbol of Judaism and of the nation of Israel.

stim•u•lant (stim´yə lənt) *n.* **1.** a drug, drink, or other substance that speeds up the activity of the mind or body. **2.** anything that moves to action.

stin•gi•ness (stin´jē nəs) *n.* reluctance or unwillingness to give or share something.

stok•er (stō´kər) *n.* a person who tends and supplies fuel to a furnace or boiler, as on a steamship or locomotive.

stren•u•ous (stren´ū əs) *adj.* **1.** requiring or characterized by great effort or exertion. **2.** very active or energetic; vigorous.

sub•stance (sub´stəns) *n.* **1.** high quality; value. **2.** that which a thing consists of; matter; material. **3.** material or matter of a particular kind. **4.** the real or essential thing or part, especially of something written or spoken.

sub•tle (sut´əl) *adj.* having a faint, delicate quality, so as to be nearly impossible to perceive.

Su•mer (sü´mər)

su•per•flu•ous (sủ pûr´flü əs) *adj.* **1.** more than is needed or wanted. **2.** needless; unnecessary.

su•per•struc•ture (sü´pər struk´chər) *n.* **1.** the part of a ship, especially a warship, above the main deck. **2.** the part of a building above the foundation.

swad•dled (swo´dəld) *adj.* wrapped or bound with bandages.

swank•y (swang´kē) *adj. Slang.* having much elegance; stylish; posh. Also, **swank** (swangk).

syn•a•gogue (sin´ə gog´, sin´ə gôg´) *n.* a building used for religious instruction and worship by Jews.

---

at; āpe; fär; câre; end; mē; it; īce; pîerce; hot; ōld; sông; fôrk; oil; out; up; ūse; rüle; pủll; tûrn; chin; sing; shop; thin; this; hw in white; zh in treasure. The symbol ə stands for the unstressed vowel sound in about, taken, pencil, lemon, and circus.

T

tan•bark (tan´bärk) *n.* a kind of shredded bark that is traditionally used to cover the floor of circus tents, racetracks, and other places where animals walk.

tan•ta•lize (tan´tə līz´) *v.t.* to tease or torment by tempting with something that is out of reach. [From *Tantalus,* a character in Greek mythology who was punished in Hades by being immersed in water that moved away as he bent down to drink it and by being surrounded with delicious fruit that rose beyond his grasp as he reached up to eat it.]

tat•too¹ (ta tü´) *v.t.* to mark permanently with colored figures or designs, usually by pricking with a pointed instrument that has been dipped in pigment. [From the Polynesian word *tatau,* "a tattoo."]

tat•too² (ta tü´) *n.* **1.** a military signal, as on a bugle, given at night to call soldiers or sailors to return to their quarters. **2.** a rapid, continuous beating or tapping. [From the Dutch word *taptoe,* with the same meaning.]

tel•e•mo•tor (tel´ə mō´tər) *n.* a device by which the movement of the wheel on a ship's bridge operates the steering gear at the stern.

ter•mi•nal (tûr´mə nəl) *n.* **1.** a station at either end of a railroad, bus, air, or other transportation line. **2.** a part at the end of something. —*adj.* **1.** ending in death. **2.** at, forming, or coming at the end or boundary of something.

Thai (tī) *adj.* of or relating to Thailand, its people, their language, or their culture. —*n.* **1.** a person who was born in or is a citizen of Thailand. **2.** the official language of Thailand.

Thai•land (tī´land´) a country in southeastern Asia. Formerly, **Siam.**

Thay Van Chi (tī vän chē)

thresh•old (thresh´ōld) *n.* **1.** a piece of wood, stone, or metal that forms the bottom of a door frame. **2.** a point of entering or beginning.

Ti•gris (tī´gris)

Tiv•o•li Gar•dens (tiv´ə lē gär´dənz) an amusement park in the heart of Copenhagen, Denmark.

Tivoli Gardens

token

U

U-boat (ū´bōt´) *n.* a German submarine, especially one used in World War I or II.

un•eth•i•cal (un eth´i kəl) *adj.* not according to accepted standards of conduct, especially the standards or codes of a profession.

U•ra•nus (yùr´ə nəs, yù rā´nəs)

V

val•iant (val´yənt) *adj.* brave; courageous.

van Bo•ven, Henrik (von bō´ven)

veer (vîr) *v.i.* to change in direction or course; shift; turn.

Ven•e•zue•la (ven´ə zwā´lə, ven´ə zwē´lə) a country in northern South America, on the Caribbean Sea.

ven•i•son (ven´ə sən, ven´ə zən) *n.* the flesh of a deer, used as food.

ver•bal (vûr´bəl) *adj.* expressed in speech; oral; not written.

to•ken (tō´kən) *n.* **1.** a piece of metal resembling a coin, used as a substitute for money, as in paying for transportation fares. **2.** something that serves to indicate or represent some fact, event, object, or feeling; sign; symbol.

tract[1] (trakt) *n.* **1.** a stretch or expanse of land; area; region. **2.** a group of parts or organs in the body that together have a particular function. [From the Latin word *tractus,* meaning "a drawing out."]

tract[2] (trakt) *n.* a booklet or pamphlet, especially one on a religious or political subject. [From the Latin word *tractatus,* "a handling, treatment."]

trea•son (trē´zən) *n.* the betrayal of one's country, especially by giving aid to the enemy in wartime.

Très bien. Par•lez-vous fran•çais? (trä byan pär´lā vü frän sā´) French for "Very good. Do you speak French?"

truce (trüs) *n.* a temporary halt to fighting by mutual agreement, often in order to reach a final settlement.

at; āpe; fär; câre; end; mē; it; īce; pîerce; hot; ōld; sông; fôrk; oil; out; up; ūse; rüle; pùll; tûrn; chin; sing; shop; thin; **th**is; **hw** in **wh**ite; **zh** in treasure. The symbol ə stands for the unstressed vowel sound in about, taken, pencil, lemon, and circus.

vi•cin•i•ty (və sin´i tē) *n.* the area near or surrounding a particular place; neighborhood.

Vi•et•nam (vē´et näm´, vē´et nam´) *also,* **Vi•et Nam.** a country in southeastern Asia, divided from 1954 to 1975 into North Vietnam and South Vietnam.

vim (vim) *n.* energy, strength, or enthusiasm.

vin•di•cate (vin´di kāt´) *v.t.* **1.** to clear (someone) of suspicion or charges of wrongdoing. **2.** to maintain or defend (a right or claim) against opposition. **3.** to justify.

vi•tal (vī´təl) *adj.* **1.** of greatest importance; essential. **2.** of, relating to, or characteristic of life. **3.** necessary to or supporting life. [From the Old French word *vital,* meaning "having or supporting life," from the Latin word *vitalis,* "of life," from the word *vita,* "life."]

wane (wān) *v.i.* **1.** to draw to a close. **2.** to become less or smaller, as in size, brightness, or strength.

West In•di•an (west in´dē ən) *adj.* of or relating to the West Indies, a large group of islands extending from Florida to the northern coast of South America.

whick•er (hwik´ər, wik´ər) *v.i.* (of a horse) to neigh gently.

whim (hwim, wim) *n.* a sudden or unexpected notion or fanciful idea.

Will•em•stad (vil´əm stät´) capital of the Netherlands Antilles on the island of Curaçao.

wrest (rest) *v.t.* to pull, twist, or take away by force or violence.

Yu•ca•tán (ū´kə tan´, ū´kə tän´) a peninsula in southeastern Mexico and northeastern Central America, between the Gulf of Mexico and the Caribbean Sea. It was the center of Mayan civilization.

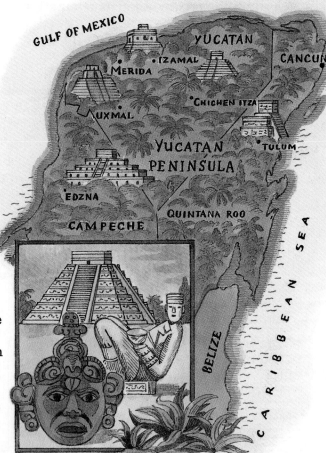

"The World Is Not A Pleasant Place To Be" from MY HOUSE by Nikki Giovanni. Copyright © 1972 by Nikki Giovanni. Reprinted by permission of William Morrow and Company, Inc./Publishers, New York.

"The Year" from THE SONG IN MY HEAD by Felice Holman. Copyright © 1985 by Felice Holman. Reprinted by permission of Charles Scribner's Sons, an imprint of Macmillan Publishing Company.

"Your Three Minutes Are Up" from IF THIS IS LOVE, I'LL TAKE SPAGHETTI by Ellen Conford. Reprinted with permission of Four Winds Press, an imprint of Macmillan Publishing Company.

"Your World" by Georgia Douglas Johnson appeared originally in HOLD FAST TO DREAMS selected by Arna Bontemps. Extensive research has failed to locate the author and/or copyright holder of this work.

INFORMATION ILLUSTRATED

Almanac: Excerpt from THE WORLD ALMANAC & BOOK OF FACTS, 1991 Edition, copyright Pharos Books 1990, New York, NY 10166. Reprinted by permission of The World Almanac and Book of Facts.

Atlas: Map of the North Atlantic Ocean floor from GOODE'S WORLD ATLAS, 16th edition, copyright © 1991 by Rand McNally R. L. 91-S-221. Cartoons: From THE NEW YORKER ALBUM OF DRAWINGS, 1925-1975, Viking Penguin, 1975. Copyright © 1970 (Gerberg); 1971 (Drucker); 1972 (Price) by the New Yorker Magazine, Inc. Reprinted by permission of The New Yorker Magazine, Inc. From JUST WAIT TILL YOU HAVE CHILDREN OF YOUR OWN! by Erma Bombeck and Bil Keane, Fawcett Crest, 1971. Reprinted by permission of Bil Keane and Aaron M. Priest Literary Agency, Inc., agent for Erma Bombeck. From THE NEW YORKER BOOK OF CAT CARTOONS, copyright © 1990 by Alfred A. Knopf, Inc. Reprinted by permission of Alfred A. Knopf, Inc. From THOMPSON IS IN TROUBLE, CHARLIE BROWN by Charles M. Schulz, Holt, Rinehart and Winston, 1973. Reprinted by permission of United Features Syndicate, Inc.

Dictionary: Except from MACMILLAN DICTIONARY 2, copyright © 1991 by Macmillan/McGraw-Hill School Publishing Company. Reprinted by permission of Macmillan/McGraw-Hill School Publishing Company. Excerpt from CONCISE DICTIONARY OF AMERICAN BIOGRAPHY, 2nd edition, Charles Scribner's Sons, 1977. Reprinted by permission of the American Council of Learned Societies.

Directions: Excerpt from FIRST AID: A RANDOM HOUSE PERSONAL MEDICAL HANDBOOK, by Paula Dranov, Random House, 1990. Copyright © 1990 by Paula Dranov. Reprinted by permission of Barbara Lowenstein Agency.

Encyclopedia: Excerpt from "planet" and "planetarium" by Lloyd Motz and "planetary gear" by J. J. Jaklitsch, Jr., from MERIT STUDENT ENCYCLOPEDIA, vol. 4. Copyright © 1991 by Macmillan Educational Company. Reprinted by permission of the publisher.

Maps: "The Southeast: Elevation" from WORLD ATLAS FOR INTERMEDIATE STUDENTS, copyright © 1991 by Macmillan/McGraw-Hill School Publishing Company. "Relocation of American Indians, 1830-1840" from U.S. AND ITS NEIGHBORS, copyright © 1991 by Macmillan/McGraw-Hill School Publishing Company. "The Growth of Ancient Egypt" from THE WORLD PAST AND PRESENT, copyright © 1991 by Macmillan/McGraw-Hill School Publishing Company. The preceding selections were reprinted by permission of Macmillan/McGraw-Hill School Publishing Company.

Newspapers and Magazines: "Mother, daughter learning together: Opportunities knock at Emily Griffith" by J. Sebastian Sinisi, from The Denver Post, Sept. 16, 1991. Reprinted by permission.

Reader's Guide: Excerpt from the READER'S GUIDE TO PERIODICAL LITERATURE, vol. 91, no. 9, Sept. 10, 1991. Copyright © 1991 by The H. W. Wilson Company. Material reprinted with permission of the publisher.

Schedules: From AMTRAK Northeast Timetable. Reprinted by permission of AMTRAK/National Railroad Passenger Corp.

Thesaurus: Excerpt from A FIRST THESAURUS by Harriet Wittels and Joan Greisman, copyright © 1985 by Harriet Wittels and Joan Greisman. Used by permission. Excerpt from ROGET'S THESAURUS IN DICTIONARY FORM, edited by Norman Lewis. Copyright © 1978 by G. P. Putnam's Sons. Reprinted by permission of The Putnam Berkley Group, Inc.

COVER DESIGN: WYD Design
COVER ILLUSTRATION: Joe Fleming

DESIGN CREDITS

Sheldon Cotler + Associates Editional Group, Units 2 & 4
Designframe Incorporated, 58-59, 138-139, 208-209, 292-293, 368-369, 474-475
Notovitz Design Inc., Information Illustrated
Curriculum Concepts, Inc., Glossary

ILLUSTRATION CREDITS

Unit 1: Joe Burleson, 16-19; Lori Osiecki, 40-41; Marty Gunsaullus, 70-71. **Unit 2:** Mick Wiggins, 92-95; Steve Stankiewicz (tech art), 99, 111; John Batchelor, 116-117; SC & A, 156-157; Christopher Aw, 170-171; SC & A bkgd., 272, 273, 276, 277, 280, 281, 284, 285, 288, 289. **Unit 3:** Eric Joy-

ner, 172-175; Nicholas Wilton, 208-209; Scott Macneil, 223; Michael Shumate, 224-225. **Unit 4:** Nancy Stahl, 246-249; Leonard Everett Fisher, 270-289; Bill Mayer, 292-293; Bob Pepper, 297, 299, 307, 308, 403; Kelly Maddox, 298. **Unit 5:** Bert Monroy, 326-329; Scott Macneil, 349; José Ortega, 386-387. **Unit 6:** David Montiel, 420-423; Marc Yankus, 490-491. **Information Illustrated:** Anatoly Chernishov, 532, 567; Jon Wieman, 534, 543; Lori Weber, 536; JAK Graphics, 542; Clarence Feng, 545; Lino Saffioti, 547; Eliot Bergman, 548, 553; Kazu, 557; Lorraine Williams, 562; Chris Reed, 563. **Glossary:** Neverne Covington, 579; Jean Stephens, 580; Alex Bloch, 583A, 586B; James Needham, 583, 584; Wendy Smith Griswold 586; Rodica Prato, 590.

PHOTOGRAPHY CREDITS

All photographs are by the Macmillan/McGraw-Hill School Division (MMSD) except as noted below.

Table of Contents: 7:l. Lee Boltin; t. r. NASA. 11:b.l. Jerry Sarapochiello/Bruce Coleman. **Unit 1:** 37: Hilary Sio. 39: © The Estate of Keith Haring, 1993. 57: b. r. Sonlight Images for MMSD. 58-59: Geoff Spear. 60: Jayne Scheer. 70: Scott Harvey for MMSD. 71: b.l. Ken Karp for MMSD; m.r. Andy Alonso for MMSD. 72-73: Steve Niedorf/The Image Bank. 74, 77, 78, 81: Paul Conklin. 84: Michael Freeman/Bruce Coleman. 85: t. Adam Woolfit/Woodfin Camp; b. Lois Moulton/f/Stop Pictures. 89: b. Sonlight Images for MMSD; t. Jennifer Ashabranner. 91: Marlborough Gallery, Inc. **Unit 2:** 101: Ken Marschall/Madison Press Books Toronto. 106: The Illustrated London News Picture Library. 107: The Mariner's Museum, Newport News, VA. 108-113: Ken Marschall/Madison Press Books Toronto. 115: Terri Corbett. 116-117: Institute of Nautical Archaeology/Donald A. Frey. 118: Richard Chesnut for MMSD; t. Jean Craighead George. 136-137: Charles Krebs/The Stock Market. 138-139: John Rizzo. 140: t.l. Julius Fekete/The Stock Market; t.r. Robert Frerck/Odyssey Productions; m. Brian Brake/Photo Researchers. 140-141: Comstock. 142: t. Egyptian Expedition of the Metropolitan Museum of Art, Rogers Fund, 1930 (30.4.144); 142-153: borders by Rapho Div/Brian Brake/Photo Researchers; b. Courtesy of the Egyptian Museum, Cairo. 144: Luis Villota/The Stock Market. 148-149: Griffith Institute, Ashmolean Museum. 150-151: b. Griffith Institute, Ashmolean Museum. 151: l. Lee Boltin. 153: t. The Granger Collection; m.l. Charles Yerkow; b. Richard Chesnut for MMSD; b.r. Robert Frerch/Odyssey Productions. 154: Photofest. 155: t. Time Magazine; b. Silkeborg Museum, Denmark. 156-157: The Granger Collection. 158-167: NASA, color enhanced by publisher. 168: Yerkes Observatory. 169: b.l. Richard Chesnut for MMSD; b.r. NASA, color enhanced by publisher. 189. Mrs. Jay Williams. **Unit 3:** 206-207: Shooting Back/Gamma-Liaison. 222-223: Clyde H. Smith/Peter Arnold. 243: t. Pat Cummings; b. Scott Harvey for MMSD. 244-245: Larry R. Ditto/Tom Stack & Associates. **Unit 4:** 267: Copyright Harcourt Brace Jovanovich. 269: t.l. Ultratec; t.r. Stockphotos, Inc.; b.l. Culver Pictures; b.r. Motorola. 289: t.l. Richard Chesnut for MMSD. 290-291: Ted Streshinsky/The Stock Market. 294-295, 296-309: headlines, Jerry Sarapochiello/Bruce Coleman. 296: r. Kalish/Dimaggio/The Stock Market. 297: t.l. Comstock; r. Gabe Palmer/The Stock Market; r. inset Richard Chesnut for MMSD. 298: The Bettmann Archive. 298: Jerry Sarapochiello/Bruce Coleman. 299: t.l., m.l., b.l. Jane Burton/Bruce Coleman; r. The Bettmann Archive. 300: t.r. Photofest; t.r. inset Obremski/The Image Bank. 301: Tom O'Brien/Tony Stone Worldwide/Chicago Ltd. 303: Art Resource. 304: Richard Chesnut for MMSD; t. Benn Mitchell/The Image Bank; m. Cara Moore/The Image Bank; b. Alice K. Taylor/Photo Researchers; b.r. The Bettmann Archive. 305: m. Peter Garfield/The Stock Market; t.l. Richard Hutchings/PhotoEdit; t. G & M David De Lossy/The Image Bank; m.r. Mary Kate Denny/PhotoEdit; b.l. Stephen Marks/Stockphotos, Inc.; b.r. Caroline Brown/Fran Heyl Associates. 308: b. The Bettmann Archive. 309: Richard Chestnut for MMSD. 310: t. Jose Fuste Raga/The Stock Market; b. John V.A.F. Neal/Photo Researchers, Inc. 311: The Time Museum, Rockford, Ill. 312-313: Comstock. 314: John Martin. **Unit 5:** 328: t.l. Courtesy of Pan American Phoenix, NYC; t.r. Courtesy of Time Will Tell, NYC.; m.r. Scott Harvey for MMSD; m.l. Isayo Kiyonaga Yoshida, Courtesy of National Park Service/MetaForm, Inc.; (boat); Al Satterwhite/The Image Bank; (car). Mahaux/The Image Bank. 329: l., m.r., b.l. Scott Harvey for MMSD; m.l. Courtesy of Dr. Muriel Petioni/MetaForm, Inc.; b.r. National Baseball Library, Cooperstown, NY. 347: Jerry Spinelli. 365: b.l., b.m. Sonlight Images for MMSD; b.r. Joanne Ryder. 366-367: A. Clevenger/Westlight. 366: Reproduccion Autorizada por El Instituto Nacional de Bellas Artes y Literatura. 368-369: Lynn Sugarman. 370: t. C. Marc Weinstein; b. Sonlight Images for MMSD. 417: t. E. Stuart McDonald Estate and L.M. Montgomery Collection. Archival and Special Collections, University of Guelph Library. 418-419: Marianne De Nagy, Courtesy Tibor De Nagy Gallery. **Unit 6:** 445: Amanda Smith. 446: Dean Beasom Studio for MMSD. 447: U.S. Department of Justice. 448-449: Scott Harvey for MMSD. 450: b.l. Donna J. Menken. 451: r. Steve Dunwell/The Image Bank. 455-463: Scott Harvey for MMSD. 466-470: Scott Harvey for MMSD. 474-475: Glen Wexler. 489: Maximillian M. Wartski. 492-493: William Harris for MMSD. 527: Bruce Wodder/The Image Bank; l. Theodore Taylor. 528-529: © James H. Karales. 539: Scott Harvey for MMSD. 549 t.r. Allstock; m.r. John Neubaver/Photo Edit. 550: Stock Imagery. 554: t.r. Superstock/Four by Five; m.r. John Kelly/The Image Bank; b.r. Larry Gatz/The Image Bank. 555: Will McIntyre/Photo Researchers. 556: Uniphoto. 560: t. Comstock; b.r. Culver Pictures. 561: t. Scott Harvey for MMSD; m., b. Ken Karp for MMSD. 564: Superstock. **Glossary:** 568: t.r. The Stock Market; b.l. Lee Boltin Picture Library. 569: Michal Heron for MMSD. 570: Lee Boltin Picture Library. 571: m.r. Bruce Coleman, Inc.; m.l. Uniphoto. 572: Tom Stack & Associates. 573: Culver Pictures. 574: InfoEdit. 575: b.l. The Stock Market; t.r. Photo Researchers. 576: The Stock Market. 577: Michal Heron for MMSD. 578: David Madison. 580: TSW. 581: Photo Researchers. 582: Leo de Wys. 585: Art Resource. 587: First Light. 588: The Stock Market. 589: Michal Heron for MMSD. End papers: West Light.

Danza! location photography in Florida was made possible for MMSD through the courtesy of Charlton and Rita Smith of Ameripaso Farms; the horse Contratista ("Danza") was made available through the courtesy of Andres Mejia, El Juncal Farm.